· The School Book ·

ALSO BY MARY SUSAN MILLER

Childstress!

Bringing Learning Home

The Scarsdale Nutritionist's Diet Program for Teens (with Judy Corlin)

The Scarsdale Nutritionist's Weight Loss Cookbook (with Judy Corlin)

SAS Exercises in the Chair

Straight Talk to Parents (with Samm Baker)

The Teachers' Roundtable on Sex Education

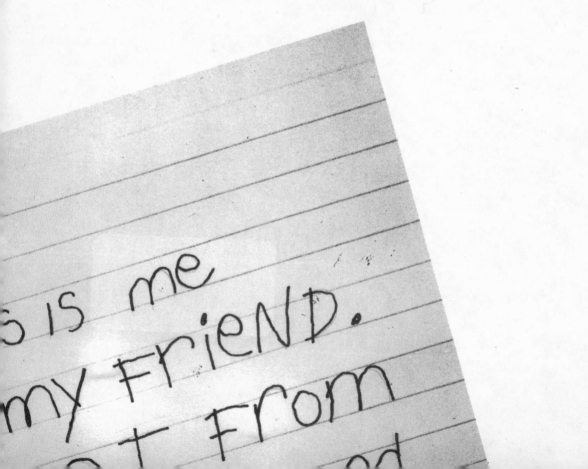

· The School Book ·

*Everything Parents Must Know About
Their Child's Education From Preschool
Through Eighth Grade*

Mary Susan Miller, Ph.D.

ST. MARTIN'S PRESS
NEW YORK

Design by Judith A. Stagnitto

Library of Congress Cataloging-in-Publication Data

Miller. Mary Susan.
   The school book : everything parents should know about their
child's education, from preschool through eight grade /
Mary Susan Miller.
     p.   cm.
   ISBN 0-312-05578-1   ISBN 0-312-05508-0 (pbk)
    1. Education—United States—Parent participation. 2. Home and
school—United States.   I. Title
LC225.3.M55 1991
370.19'31—dc20   90-49811
                                                          CIP

First Edition: August 1991

10 9 8 7 6 5 4 3 2 1

For
Ed
Chris, Eric, Amy
Abby, Darcy, Alexa, Noah, Lulu
and their children in tomorrow's world

Contents

CONTENTS

What if my child is not ready for kindergarten? • How can I prepare my child for kindergarten?

What if my child is afraid of school? • What if my child begins wetting himself in kindergarten? • What if my child has temper tantrums in school? • What if my child hits other children? • What if my child is different in school than he is at home? • What if kindergarten is exhausting my child? • How academic should the kindergarten program be?

How can an elementary school meet the needs of my child? • What kinds of elementary schools best meet these needs?

Does my child have to go to kindergarten? • When is my child ready for first grade? • What if the teacher wants to hold my child back? • If my child is already reading, should I have her skip first grade? • Should I get my child switched if her friends are in a different class? • When should my child start getting homework? • We're moving; is entering a new school going to pose problems? • How can I tell if my child is placed in the wrong grade?

What should I look for in a good junior high? • What kinds of junior high schools will meet these needs?

How is junior high school different from elementary school? • What if my child can't handle independence? • What should my child do about all the elective courses? • How many extracurricular activities should my child take on? • How can I be sure my child makes the right friends?

at school? • How can I stop my child from shutting herself off from me by watching television when I'm home?

after a conference? • How telling is a preschool evaluation? • How should I react when my child earns gold stars? • What should I do if the teacher praises my child too much?

What kinds of marks do schools use at these levels? • What can I do to help my child keep marks in perspective? • How do I handle report cards? • Should I give any kind of reward or punishment for marks? • What if the school and I differ about marks? • What do I do about a poor student who can't do better? • What do I do about a child who fails and doesn't care? • What do I do when my child pushes too hard for good marks?

What different kinds of tests does my child take? • How can I help my child when tests are coming up?

How much playtime should a preschool have? • Will preschool eliminate a child's speech problem? • What do I do if my child is out of step with her classmates? • How does a preschooler learn socialization?

What should elementary school curriculum cover? • What can I do if the curriculum is too easy for my child? • What can I do if the curriculum is too difficult for my child? • How important is sex education in elementary school?

What is a basic junior high school curriculum? • What is all this talk of year-round schools? • Is tracking good or bad? • How do I get outside help for my child? • What if sex, drugs, or guidance classes upset my child?

Homework is for learning. • Homework is for responsibility.

CONTENTS

CONTENTS

Acknowledgments

I am deeply grateful
   to Victoria Pryor for her trust . . .
   to Hope Dellon for her care . . .
   and to the parents, students, and
teachers I know for the contributions they
have made to this book and to my life.

CHAPTER 1

Parent Power

· Mothers and Fathers as Parents ·

"I'm only a mother."

A young woman I know, mother of an infant and a two-year-old, was at a cocktail party. As a small group of people found themselves drawn together, one of the women attempted to throw out a connecting line by asking the man on her right, "What do you do?"

"I'm a lawyer," he replied, "and you?"

"I sell advertising."

"Interesting. What kind of advertising?" Everyone listened as she explained.

The group continued the Q&A session, which revealed a pediatrician, a graduate student, and a magazine editor, all of whom elicited oohs, ahs, and further questions. Finally the group turned to my friend, who later admitted that with her head half buried in her shoulders, she had answered in a small voice, "I'm only a mother."

The ensuing dead silence might have been a repeat of many such gatherings, many such questions, and many such embarrassed answers, but this time it was different because a man in the group reached over to shake her hand. "Congratulations," he said. "In my line of work, we need mothers."

"What do you do?" several people asked at once.

"I'm a former child."

Although my friend never saw the man again and doesn't even know his name, she says she will never forget the sensitivity he showed to her feelings and his awareness of the need to give motherhood what she calls a "facelift." "Only a mother"—those apologetic words minimize a job that determines the shape of the world as forcefully as any job in history. Can you imagine Isaac Newton describing his work by saying "I only sit under apple trees," or Benjamin Franklin by stating "I only fly kites"? Gravity and electricity changed the way we understand the world, but being a mother changes the world itself.

The strong impact mothers have is hardly news. St. Augustine announced their importance over sixteen hundred years ago as he looked around at the pagan world of barbarism surrounding him. Remembering the gentle teachings that his Christian mother whispered to him as a child, he longed for the kinder world she enabled him to visualize. "Give me other mothers," he cried out, "and I'll give you another world!"

Although a look at the world today suggests that few have heeded St. Augustine's plea, the message rings as true as ever: A mother shapes the character of her child, and her child shapes the character of the future.

In this century Hans Selye, after devoting a lifetime to research on stress and coping, echoed St. Augustine. Shortly before his death I asked him, "Can you isolate any single factor that determines what a person becomes?"

Without hesitation he replied, "His mother."

"What about fathers?"

Fatherhood has always given birth to pride along with babies. Who has heard a father explain apologetically, "I'm only a father?" Not those men handing out cigars at the office, not those house-husbands we see glorified on TV sitcoms, not even those businessmen who alternate child-care shifts with their wives. Fathers feel proud of their role and of the child care it demands. "Can you believe it?" my professor son exclaimed, his face aglow with success. "I'm the one who gives the baby baths!" There is no need, therefore, to elevate the status of fatherhood; it has been high as the sky since God created Adam.

Fathers have a special role to play in their child's development, different from that of mothers. Feminists who, in their ardent struggle, confuse equality of the sexes with sameness cheat both mothers and fathers of the unique relationship each has with a child. An infant bonds with his mother—in the womb and at her breast—finding security in her arms and a reflection of himself in her eyes. From his mother comes trust in the internal world. However, growth demands reaching out, and it is his father who serves as a guide to the larger world—his father who was nonexistent for nine dark months, whose breast filled no hunger, whose arms are harder, whose skin is rougher, who smells and sounds different. From his father comes trust in an external world.

Joseph Chiltern Pearce, author of *The Magical Child* and a father himself, claims that a child has only one true relationship in his life— with his mother—and that everyone else is merely a relation. As devotedly as I admire Pearce, I can't agree with him. It is true that the mother-child relationship strongly affects children's feelings about themselves, but it is also true that the father-child relationship affects children's feelings about the larger environment with which they will have to cope throughout their lives. Both make them the person they are. Fortunately, today more than ever before in history, parents are beginning to recognize the equal importance of their different roles in the development of their child.

· 3 ·

· Mothers and Fathers as Teachers ·

"What do I know about teaching?"

Recently I asked a random sample of parents what they thought was the most important factor in the way a child performs in school. The majority answered, "The child's IQ." A good many others named race or socioeconomic status, and some said the school's geographic location or teacher-student ratio. Not one identified what a 1988 University of Chicago study discovered: that it is *parents* that make the big difference in a child's school achievement.

What comes as a shock is not the study's revelation, but the fact that it surprised anyone. Parents have been a child's teachers since the first little cave baby learned to stay away from fire. As a mother of a five-year-old said to me, "I don't know why Terri has to go to kindergarten. She's already learned what's important—how to act out stories and cuddle the cat, how to tie her shoes, how to sing to the baby, and how to get along with an impossible person like me!"

Who taught Terri all that? Her mother and father, of course, master teachers as most parents are. Let's not forget what educational statisticians tell us: Children learn proportionately more in their first year of life than they learn throughout their entire twelve years of school. No wonder: They have a mother-teacher to create self-confidence and a father-teacher (or as new life-styles evolve, a father-figure–teacher) to instill trust in the lessons of the world.

The lessons parents teach at home are not only the first children learn, but often the longest lasting as well. Few children or adults remember the dates of the Civil War or the succession of American Presidents, facts their teachers drummed into them; yet most hold fast to the feelings and opinions assimilated when they were very young. For instance, children who learn aggression at home in any of its varied forms turn out to be aggressive adults, while children who learn caring and nonviolence grow up to be the world's peacemakers.

Similarly, studies show that adults who can laugh and play are those who learned to laugh and play with their parents. Adult readers read with their parents, and adults who love learned to love with their parents. The impact of first teachers resounds within each of us, determining the way we relate to ourselves and to the world around us. Above all, it determines the kind of first teachers we ourselves become to our children.

· 4 ·

"We leave school to the professionals."

When I was a principal, I had a conference with a couple I had invited to my office to discuss their third-grade daughter's refusal to do her homework.

"Have you tried to discover why she won't do her work?" I asked.

"Oh, we know," her father replied. "She gets a sheet of math problems, which she has already done in school, and the teacher gives her an assignment with the same kind of problems and tells her to do them again."

"She says she is bored with them," the mother explained.

Horrified, I asked whether they had spoken to the teacher.

"Oh, no," the father answered. "We leave school to the professionals."

"*You* are the professionals," I all but shouted. I spent the next half hour convincing them that they knew their daughter far better than the teacher did and were obligated to share their knowledge. Timidly they agreed and, I might add, solved the problem in short order.

Until the last decade or so, most parents and educators felt the way those parents did. Parents felt unqualified to "interfere" with the learning that took place at school, and educators staunchly reinforced their feeling, thereby maintaining absolute control. However, as changing life-styles shifted children's needs, educators realized that they were failing. They had new challenges to meet: to help children make decisions in the face of new stimuli, to teach them to solve problems with new technology, to guide them in decision making, and to rebuild foundations as the traditional structure of the home fell apart. Suddenly education had to offer more than English and math in a classroom; suddenly teachers saw that learning takes place everywhere; suddenly schools sought new resources. Teachers needed help, and suddenly they enlisted parents.

Although long in coming, the parent role in education is now firmly established. "We can't do the job alone," educators admit, reaching out for help to the twenty-four-hour-a-day teachers, the parents of the children whom they see only from nine until three. After a series of studies the National Parent-Teacher Association published convincing evidence of educational parent power. They found that...

· Students learn more when their parents are involved.
· Involvement gives parents greater clout.
· Parents approve more of schools in which they are involved.
· Parents share accountability for their child's learning when they are involved.

As a result of this new awareness of their essential role, millions of mothers who previously entered the education process only through the kitchen with a trayful of cookies and fathers who entered only through the tax rolls are not only welcomed, not only invited, but actively urged to unite parent and teacher professionalism. The result: children who learn.

"What can I do to get involved?"

You are part of your child's school performance whether you intend to be or not. When you are interested and actively participate, you place a value on education that makes your child care more and work harder. In the same way, if you express little interest and take no active part, you make it clear that education has a low priority in your value system.

You send a message of "Why bother?" Your children hear you and in response *don't* bother.

Your attitude makes a difference:

- Be interested.
- Consider school important to the whole family.
- Take it seriously.

Your involvement also makes a difference. As the University of Chicago found, children of actively involved parents are usually better students than those with parents who do not get involved. Therefore, give your child a chance by sharing the school experience with her:

- Attend school functions.
- Get to know the teachers.
- Volunteer your help where possible.
- Support the schoolwork she is doing at home.

Attitude and involvement, however, are only the groundwork for the vast education framework that you can help plan and build. As a parent you have power tools that you can use to demolish what no longer works in your child's school, to alter and reconstruct in order to meet your child's needs, and to build strong supports under your child's learning. If you leave teaching to the teachers, you deny yourself the status you have earned as a parent-professional. A closer look at how learning takes place may help you understand.

Learning is not a closed circuit between a teacher and your child:

TEACHER ⟶ CHILD

Your child does not pick up learning from her teacher as if it were a voice on a telephone wire. If she did, she would become as compartmentalized as the switchboard itself, a series of unrelated wires connecting and disconnecting throughout the day.

On the contrary, education is an equilateral triangle with your child, her teacher, and you hooked up on a three-way call.

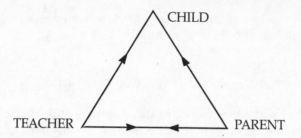

What a child receives turns into learning only when it takes on meaning through experience. For instance, a child may learn by rote that two plus two equals four, but not until she actually puts two fingers or two apples or two dolls alongside another two has she learned addition. She may read *Romeo and Juliet* when she's twelve, but not until she falls in love later on will she know what it is really about.

As parents provide most of a child's experiences, they are in the best position to make learning gel. When she is little, they help her understand pain when she cuts her finger, grief when her dog dies, wonder when the leaves turn gold, disappointment when a friend lets her down, success and failure and joy and hope. As she gets older, when school opens the magic box of numbers and letters and words, parents turn the magic into the everyday experiences of puzzles and shopping trips, stories and dinner talk. In that way they become co-teachers with the school.

In a similar way a teacher turns what your child receives at home into learning at school. I saw an example of this recently with my grandson Noah, who loves not only movies but movie reviews and wants to be a movie critic when he grows up. For his ninth birthday his mother bought him a copy of Roger Ebert's movie reviews from the Chicago *Sun-Times*, which he studies avidly. Aware of Noah's passion, his teacher arranged for him to write a movie review for each edition of the class newspaper. At one point of the triangle, Noah's mother supported an interest; at another point of the triangle, the teacher activated the interest; at the third point of the triangle, Noah had a learning experience.

You, the teacher, and your child are all vital parts of the teaching triangle, members of a team that can spare no player. Successful education depends on the interaction of all three as much as baseball's immortal double plays depended on the interaction of Tinkers and Evers and Chance. If any one of the teaching triangle reneges on their responsibility, learning suffers. For instance, if Noah's mother had not reinforced his interest at home or if his teacher had not provided him an opportunity to put his interest to use in school, or if Noah himself had not been willing to do the extra work involved, he wouldn't have learned all he has about critical thinking and writing.

"One lone parent—what difference can I make?"

Looking at the American education system with its huge bureaucracy, its endless problems, and its ever-growing needs, a parent is bound to feel like the little girl from Indiana whom I took to Jones Beach for her first view of the ocean. "Well, what do you think?" I asked.

After studying it for a few minutes, she observed, "It's big."

Education is big. A parent feels that she, one ever-so-small mother, cannot possibly challenge it any more than she could challenge the Atlantic. Yet just as individuals have dared sail the ocean alone in tiny boats, so parents have changed the shape of education. Schools are big but, unlike the ocean, they are not immutable.

Each year hundreds of parents across the country find their children trapped in school situations that make them decide "I'm going to do something about this." And they do—parents no different from you. Consider the parent . . .

· 8 ·

- · Whose child fell behind the class in math. Her mother insisted that the school find an older student to tutor her during a free period until she caught up.
- · Whose child's class study of Africa seemed sterile and boring. Both parents encouraged the teacher to organize an Africa Day of crafts, food, and customs in which the whole community participated.
- · Who felt his children in a small rural school were missing what children in urban areas had. The father got the school board to raise money for computers and to send teachers to workshops to learn to use them.
- · Whose child was lost in a class of thirty-two. The mother enlisted parents to volunteer as class aides to give more individual attention, and a relieved teacher welcomed them.
- · Whose child reported every day that the teacher hated him. She brought the child and the teacher together to talk through their mutual hostility.
- · Whose overweight child's classmates taunted her. She got the guidance counselor to conduct discussions on individual differences and prejudice, and the teasing abated.

This handful of parents set about rectifying situations that made their children's education less than it should have been by solving small problems that arise daily in most schools. Problems roll in endlessly. One by one these parents—and parents all over the country—plunged in to make things better.

Parent power does not stop just with solving day-to-day problems that surround children in school. It extends to the vast education system itself. Today parents bring about school changes that both they and the school would have thought impossible ten or fifteen years ago. As a home repairs advertisement said, "We do a hard job quickly; the impossible takes a little longer."

Parents like you find they can tackle seemingly impossible situations when they see their children stuck in poor schools. Let's look at a few examples.

• When California was pressured into increasing teachers' salaries by 16 percent, schools had to cut back curriculum offerings and eliminate reading, art, and music faculty in order to pay. Determined not to let the schools water down their children's education, parents forced the state to cut back the salary increase.

• When parents of children in a rural midwestern school realized that their children's scores on standardized tests fell far below national averages, they decided to do some investigating. Finding that the principal had hired many unqualified teachers, they demanded that all newly hired teachers be certified and that currently employed teachers without certification enroll in qualifying courses. Today all the teachers in the school are certified, and reading scores have shot up.

• When a rigid and noninnovative temporary principal was about to receive a permanent appointment, parents of children in a New York elementary school united to block the appointment and succeeded in putting in a principal more in tune with their progressive philosophy.

• In Missouri parents believed that children should be introduced to job and professional opportunities in junior high school. The principal disagreed, shoring up his opinion with the argument that he had no money for career education. Parents solved the problem by finding community volunteers to run the program.

• Parents in several schools I know found their children stuck with poor teachers, whom the principal retained because they were tenured and he saw no way to fire them. Parents put so much pressure on the district superintendents that the teachers were removed from the classroom and transferred to the administrative staff.

• Parents whose children attended a much-loved one-room school in Utah that included kindergarten through sixth grade found it slated for closing in a new consolidation plan. Arming themselves with solid arguments, parents fought hard and succeeded in keeping their school.

· Parents of children in a midwestern junior high school overcame the arguments of the kitchen staff and their own children and succeeded in abolishing both junk foods and snack machines.

· A group of parents in a wealthy New York suburb was locked into a traditional, achievement-oriented school system that met the demands of the highly competitive majority. Feeling that their children would benefit from a more low-key, individualized approach, they petitioned the superintendent. After strong arguments and many meetings over a few years, they were able to establish an alternative program within the traditional school system in their district.

· In Tennessee a group of Moral-Majority parents brought about massive school book banning on the grounds that the books taught lessons their religion opposed. Another group of parents, determined that their children not be deprived of opportunities to evaluate other viewpoints, took the issue to the state legislature, which banned the book banning.

· 10 ·

These are just a few of the many substantial results of parent power throughout the country, bringing about changes that affect not only a child's daily learning but the shape of the school as well. Educators today openly acknowledge the right of parents to be involved and the benefits that classrooms and schools derive from their involvement. In many states they go even further and include parents at the highest level of educational planning, a level previously reserved for legislators and top administrators.

A clear example is New York City, where schools for decades were controlled by a central district office from which orders were issued to all schools in the district. Some years ago, as various ethnic groups moved in to specific areas of the city, districts became heterogeneous. With the population of one school vastly different from that of another, the needs of children in each school were vastly different too. Although it became obvious that orders issuing from a central office no longer applied, administrators were loath to relinquish their power. Parents struggled for several years to have a voice in running the schools their children attended, valiantly fighting the huge education establishment. Eventually they forced the system to abolish central control and install local boards with decision-making power on curriculum, hiring, and spending (in compliance with broad state requirements). When a new school chancellor took office in 1989, his vow to New York parents was not only to retain community control, but to give parents, along with teachers, an even stronger voice on the boards that run their children's schools.

New York is just one of many states that have recognized that while administrators may know educational skills, parents know their children. At the highest level, together they put the parent-teacher part of the education triangle to work in a variety of ways.

· Parents in California have gained control of educational policy in their local schools and have taken over allocation of a discretionary school improvement fund.

· Parents in Florida and South Carolina have formed an advisory board that is carefully heeded in matters of long-range educational planning, assessing student achievement, and evaluating the school.

· A group of parents from Washington, D.C., has formed a lobbying group to pressure Congress into passing voucher and tuition tax credit bills.

· Chicago parents, in conjunction with business leaders, have forced the elimination of a thousand administrative jobs in the educational bureaucracy and have won the majority of control for their local schools. Parents, not administrators, decided how to allocate the money they saved.

The human spirit will not dwell forever under domination. From America's own early history to modern Czechoslovakia, the lesson is clear: *sic semper tyrannis*. While the assertion of individual rights may take hundreds of years and much bloodshed, people power wins in the end.

For too many years the education establishment played the tyrant to the nation's parents, spending *their* money, hiring teachers and determining curriculum for *their* children, keeping *their* voices silent. For too many years parents submitted, even in the face of disillusionment and failure, because education was the job of professionals.

Finally, parents began to fight back, and parent rumbles gradually turned into a parent movement that rocked the system, causing chinks and crevices that the parents themselves stepped in to repair. Parent power toppled the education establishment and replaced it with a partnership. The strength of that partnership has been acknowledged at the highest levels of government. In appointing members of the National Commission on Excellence in Education, President Reagan selected Annette V. Kirk, a parent of four schoolchildren, to speak for the first time with an official voice for education in the United States.

All parents have the official voice of Annette Kirk. They have the power to speak; what they need is the confidence to use it. By the end of this book, I hope parents will call out in a powerful voice to classrooms and administrative offices throughout this country so that every school, from the tiny one-room schoolhouse to the massive urban institution, will have to hear. Only then will all children learn as they are capable of learning, grow as they are worthy of growing, and live as they are intended to live.

· The Ultimate Path to Power: Home Schooling ·

Parents sometimes find themselves faced with an untenable situation: The local public schools are terrible, and the private schools are too expensive. What is the solution?

"Move" is what many parents say. Some find the kind of school they want no farther away than the next district, while thousands form a migration from big cities to the suburbs. Still others take even greater leaps, and disregarding the emotional and financial expense, quit jobs, leave homes, and uproot family and friendships in order to resettle in distant areas where they feel their children will get a good education.

Another group of parents, however, stands firm: If the schools cannot provide the education they want, they determine to do it themselves. From parents like these, the home schooling movement took shape under John Holt in the liberated sixties and grew to include about 15,000 children in the seventies, over 260,000 in the eighties, and nobody knows yet how many in the nineties.

Because the home was education's point of origin centuries ago, home schooling does not resound with a revolutionary ring. Yet the furor it created, while not causing any bloodshed, has led to lawsuits and jail sentences for parents who openly defied the law. Those who became closet home-schoolers, educating their children under cover, found themselves spied upon and ostracized like Kentucky moonshiners.

Parents who opt for home schooling are within their legal rights and have carried their cause to the country's highest courts after being thwarted within their states. As early as 1897 the Supreme Court decided in their favor; later decisions came in 1925, 1969, and as recently as 1972. Through the years individual cases of home schooling have come under attack in court state by state, and battle by battle parents have fought back. By 1986 parent power had won the war, and every state now allows parents to provide some kind of home schooling for their children—although often, not without a fight.

A number of questions arise when parents consider the possibility of home schooling:

"Should we take our children out of school and educate them ourselves at home?"

Not unless you can find no other solution. Is there any way you can improve the school situation for your child? Can you supplement the school weakness at home? Can you move to a better school? Think more than twice before deciding on home schooling.

"Are there any requirements for educating children at home?"

Get in touch with the state Department of Education in your state capital. They regulate all home schooling in diverse ways. For instance, at latest count, Connecticut, Florida, Georgia, Kentucky, Nebraska, New Mexico, New York, North Carolina, Oregon, South Dakota, Tennessee, Virginia, Washington, and West Virginia all require state testing for parents interested in home schooling. Some with more stringent regulations, such as Iowa, Michigan, and North Dakota, when last surveyed, demand that parents be certified teachers. Find out what your particular state requires.

"How would I go about home schooling?"

Go see the person in charge of home schooling in your state Department of Education. Some states will help you design a program of home education; others, like Washington, will actually send teachers to your home to help develop curriculum, check on your child's progress, and keep in close touch to assure that you are doing an adequate job.

If your state does not give you advice and specific aids, you can get help from the following:

SANTA FE COMMUNITY SCHOOL
P.O. Box 2241
Santa Fe, NM 87501

THE CALVERT SCHOOL
Tuscany Road
Baltimore, MD 21210
(301) 243-6030

THE CHRISTIAN LIBERTY ACADEMY
Arlington Heights, IL 60008
(312) 259-8736

· 13 ·

THE CLONLARA SCHOOL
1289 Jewett
Ann Arbor, MI 48104
(313) 769-4511

HEARTHSIDE SCHOOL
2 Smith Street
Farmingdale, NJ 07727

THE SMITHSONIAN FAMILY LEARNING PROJECT
P.O. Box 28
Edgewater, MD 21037

In addition, read a few books on the way children learn before undertaking home schooling. In my opinion, among the best are these three by John Holt:

How Children Learn (Dell, 1983)

How Children Fail (Delacorte, 1982)

Instead of Education (E. P. Dutton, 1976)

Also, *Home Schools: An Alternative* by Cheryl Gorder (Blue Bird Pub., Columbus, OH, 1985) gives you a first-hand account, along with resources of a home-schooling family. *Home School: Taking The First Step* by Borg Hendrickson (Mountain Meadow Press, 1989) is the most comprehensive of the books I know.

"Will my children suffer if I educate them at home?"

Very few measurements have been taken to evaluate the effectiveness of home schooling, but educators have unearthed a few facts.

- Home-schooled students have been admitted to prestigious universities, such as Harvard, and to scores of other colleges and universities.
- They have won national academic prizes.
- Alaska and Washington and the city of Los Angeles have conducted studies that find home-schooled children averaging higher scores on standardized tests than children in traditional schools.

On the other hand, many educators point out the disadvantages of home schooling.

· Few parents are qualified in a broad enough range of subjects to replace a school faculty.
· Parents may be too emotionally involved with their children to be effective teachers.
· Children educated at home miss out on the learning experiences of relationships with peers and nonfamily adults.

Parents have the power to choose the paths along which their children will travel. How they make those choices is the subject of the next chapter.

CHAPTER 2

Paths of Power: Where to Go When There's a Problem at School

You have come home after a day at work. Your second grader circles you, retelling his day's activities. "...and we learned how Abraham Lincoln told his father the truth when he chopped down the cherry tree," he announces excitedly.

"That's a wonderful story," you answer, "but wasn't it George Washington?"

With total confidence he assures you, "Oh, no. My teacher says it was Abraham Lincoln."

What do you do now? Remember, you are the first teacher, and whatever you say is part of your lesson plan.

You can make your point bluntly and announce, "Well, your teacher is wrong. It was George Washington." That sledgehammer approach will hit your child over the head with the realization that Mom or Dad is pitted against the school and that his teacher is obviously dumb.

On the other hand, you can take a nonconfrontational way out and yield with "I guess I'm wrong. Maybe it was Abraham Lincoln." You know he will learn the truth eventually, and as the story is only a myth, what difference does it make? The difference is that you teach your child that teachers know everything and parents are dumb. That's worse than the former lesson.

Then too, you can stand your ground with a defensive tone: "That's impossible. You weren't listening and heard it wrong." In this scenario you teach the worst lesson of all: that your child is the dumb one.

All of those lessons set the stage for problems your child will have in future schooling due to lack of trust in the school, in his parents, or, worst of all, in himself. Let's check out a possible fourth response.

"We really have a disagreement here, you and I, don't we?" you can begin. Then you and your child can put your heads together in search of a resolution. "How do you think we can settle it?" Together you can investigate possibilities: Will your child ask the teacher tomorrow? Will he check with an older sibling? Will he look it up in the *Book of Knowledge*? Whatever course he decides to take will set him straight on the cherry tree tale and will in the process teach him far more important lessons:

· 17 ·

- · He will learn that Mom and Dad and the teacher are all on the same side.
- · He will learn that contradictions can be sorted out by rechecking facts.
- · He will learn that no one is dumb because of a mistake.
- · He will learn that he is good enough, smart enough, and mature enough to solve a problem—the best lesson of all.

Unfortunately though, most problems children bring home from school are more difficult to clean up. You can't do it over dinner; you actually have to go to school and face someone. Where do you turn first?

· Climbing the Bureaucratic Ladder ·

Start with the teacher.

As most of a child's tears and worries begin in the classroom, most of them can be solved with the teacher. Expect to find yourself seeking solutions to problems such as "I hate my teacher," "My teacher hates me," "Everyone says my hair is stupid," and "I forgot my homework." Chapter 12 deals with teacher-child problems and the different ways to handle them in great detail. However, as your child may have a problem right now before you have a chance to flip through to that chapter, here are a few general guidelines.

- When your child brings home a complaint, don't rush into school immediately. Discuss it with her and wait to see what happens. Maybe it has arisen from a particularly bad day and will go away of its own accord. In other words, don't create a mountain every time your child brings home a molehill.
- If the complaint persists, however, and appears to have a real basis, talk to the teacher. (Chapter 12 has suggestions on what to say.)
- Make every effort to include your child in the conference.
- Keep calm when confronting the teacher. A set jaw, glaring eyes, and roaring voice are certain to put him on the defensive and block the solution you are seeking.

If you get nowhere, try the principal.

The principal of a school has to be available to parents. If she is not—and I have seen some who do their best to avoid parents—don't take no for an answer. Insist. You have the right and, lest you forget, the power.

Don't go running to the principal with every grievance. Save your sprint for two circumstances under which you should see the principal.

First, if you have talked with the teacher and met a brick wall—she's either unwilling or unable to correct an unhappy classroom situation—take your complaint to the principal. Remember, however, that one of the main roles of the principal is to support her faculty. If she took action with every parental accusation, half of the faculty would leave and the other half would be too undermined to teach. Therefore, even if you are angry after getting nowhere with your child's teacher, present the problem to the principal in a resolution-seeking rather than in an attacking manner.

Do not growl, "Mr. Allen has no understanding of children. He hates Johnny for no reason at all and says it is all his fault." If you do, the principal will have no recourse other than defense.

"Come now," she will have to say. "Perhaps other teachers are having trouble with Johnny too. I know Mr. Allen makes every effort..." You will be back at the starting gate and have gotten nowhere in solving Johnny's problem.

Try a positive approach instead: "Mr. Allen and Johnny don't seem to be getting along. I thought perhaps you could help them straighten things out."

"Have you spoken to Mr. Allen about it?" she will ask.

"Yes, but he can't seem to reach Johnny any more than Johnny can reach him. I think they need you to mediate."

Because you have brought a genuine concern to the principal's attention and enlisted her help in addressing it, instead of rising to defend the teacher, she can safely say "I'll see what I can do."

If the cause lies with the teacher—maybe he really does pick on Johnny—the principal should, and probably will, request that Mr. Allen alter his attitude and be grateful that you enabled him to prevent future similar problems. If the cause lies with Johnny—maybe he misbehaves more often than his classmates, giving the teacher reason to "pick on" him—the principal will probably ask you, Mr. Allen, and Johnny to meet and find out why. In either case, Mr. Allen won't "pick on" Johnny any more, at least temporarily until either the teacher vents his dislike or Johnny fails to control his behavior again. At that time, you may have to reenact the scenario.

Second, if the problem you have identified is not one your child faces with a teacher but one arising from a broader issue relating to the school as a whole, you should also see the principal. You may want to suggest a long-term change over which the teacher has no control. Although even the principal may not be able to effect such a change, she is in a position to guide you and offer support as you pursue your aim. But if you bypass the principal by going over her head, thereby making her resentful, she is also in a position to block your progress.

A principal may react in one of several ways when confronted by a dissatisfied parent who has a suggestion for change. Let us assume that you want to introduce French in the elementary school instead of having children wait until junior high. You present your case, to which the principal may reply in one of a number of ways.

· Proud of "her" school as it is, she may be defensive and say, "Small children have enough worries without a foreign language." ·

· On the other hand, she may have investigated the possibility herself and offer a valid reason for excluding French from the curriculum: "We simply haven't the budget."

· If you are lucky, she may respond to your idea enthusiastically and, seeing you as a possible ally, admit, "I've been trying to get French into the elementary school for years."

· The most probable instant reaction is apt to be a noncommittal "Hmm. That's an interesting idea."

In any case, the next move is yours. You thank her affably and mention casually "I think I'll talk to the superintendent about the possibility."

Find out who the superintendent is.

The superintendent (usually a man, but sometimes a woman) is the chief administrator of the public school district and can be found in the district education office, the address and phone number of which you can obtain from your principal's secretary. The superintendent and his staff support the broad educational philosophy of the state and city, assure that requirements are met, and determine the allocation of state and local funds—important duties that have little to do with French in kindergarten. More creatively, however, they initiate programs and oversee all aspects of public high schools, junior highs, elementary schools, and preschools in the district.

Because the superintendent usually hires and always works closely with the principal of each school, the positive relationship you establish with the principal will earn you Brownie points with the superintendent. I know a very bright mother whose aggressiveness had so turned off the principal that he had forwarded the label "troublemaker" to the district office, and the superintendent wouldn't even see her.

The superintendent's office is usually a bustle of day-late deadlines with people, papers, and phone calls coming and going in all directions. Therefore, do not be disappointed if you are turned over to the assistant superintendent instead. He can become a valuable ally, so treat him with respect. The secret of success in catching the interest of the superintendent or of an assistant is one the Boy Scouts discovered eighty years ago: Be prepared. Here's why.

You begin by telling the superintendent, "I think we should start French in the early grades instead of waiting until junior high school."

No matter how firm your voice, he is bound to ask "Why?" How are you going to answer?

Maybe: "Well, I think it would be better for the children."

Perhaps: "My daughter likes it."

Or: "I had French in first grade."

Even: "A lot of parents want it."

With answers like those you will get no more than a polite smile and a quick dismissal. End of idea. "*C'est fini*," which your child will never get to say in elementary school.

If you want results, even just the superintendent's attention, you will have to do better than that; you will need convincing facts to support your proposal. Therefore, go in like the professional you are. Prepare your case ahead of time.

· 21 ·

- · See whether other elementary schools in the district offer French.
- · If none does, contact the state Education Department. Someone in that office can tell you which schools, if any, in the state introduce early French.
- · If you still come up with a blank, don't give up. Get in touch with the National Association of Foreign Language Teachers, which will help you locate elementary schools in other states that offer French. Most public libraries have catalogs containing the addresses and phone numbers of all national associations; ask the reference librarian for help if you need it.
- · After finding a school that has elementary French, talk to the principal, in person if the school is nearby, by phone if it is not. Ask her at what grade she begins French; what advantages she finds; what disadvantages, if any; what the cost of the program is. Ask her how long the program has been in existence. Do the children like it? The teachers? The parents? Does she?

When you have gathered your information, talk to other parents in your school. How do they feel about initiating the program you have in mind? If you feel one or two of them would lend support, you might suggest they see the superintendent with you.

When the superintendent looks at you after you present your proposal and asks "Why?" you will be ready with answers:

· "Because young children look on French as a game and never develop the fear with which older children often face it."
· "Because by getting used to the sounds of French early, they develop better accents later on."
· "Because schools find that parents and children and teachers too are happy with the program."
· "Because the additional cost to a school averages only [whatever you have discovered] dollars."

In the face of such carefully researched and intelligent arguments, the superintendent is bound to take your suggestion seriously. However, he may still respond negatively: "You present a strong case, but there is no way we can consider your proposition at this time. We have other priorities. Sorry." If this happens, you might as well dismiss him with a pleasant "Thank you" and go in a different direction.

Even if the superintendent shows interest in your idea, don't expect immediate action. He will not shout "Good idea. We'll do it!" because bureaucracies don't work that way. Even the most enthusiastic superintendent will probably respond cautiously, having banged his head against many stone walls in past efforts to bring new ideas to life. Probably the best you can expect is "I like the idea. We'll give it some thought."

If the superintendent shows any real interest, though, don't let him off the hook. Call him in several weeks to see where matters stand. Your call will serve as a reminder and will also offer you a chance to suggest that you and some other interested parents speak to him at greater length.

The superintendent's office works slowly, and although you do not want to become a pest, you should call every month or so until you see progress or at least feel continued interest. A group of parents concerned that their suburban school was not adequately challenging bright students persisted in their efforts with the district superintendent for two years. They were rewarded when the superintendent instituted a daily two-hour enrichment program in one of the schools to which bright students from all elementary schools in the district were bused.

Although success, obviously, is possible, you may not achieve it in the district office. If the superintendent out-and-out rejects your proposal, thank him for his time and set your sights elsewhere.

Contact the Board of Education.

If you have ever come face to face with the Board of Education, you have realized that, as Pogo described the enemy, they are *us*—citizens from the community interested, but not necessarily trained, in educational practices. They are usually elected rather than appointed and are responsible for the educational philosophy and the financial resources that support the schools.

You can always talk with members of the board. They represent you in the school system and best serve that system when they keep an ear open to their constituents. Therefore, if you fail with the superintendent, do not hesitate to take a step higher up the ladder.

You can approach the Board of Education a couple of ways.

First, if you know a member of the board, take advantage of the connection and ask for an appointment; personal contact makes it easier. You might, like a man I know, ask a friend who knows a board member to introduce you and make a contact that way. When you set up an appointment, make your proposal exactly as you did to the superintendent, presenting the facts and expert opinions you have gathered.

If the board member likes your idea, she may offer to bring it up at the next board meeting for further investigation. If she disagrees with you and rejects the idea outright, you may still be able to persuade her to ask for the opinion of the rest of the board. If she is a conscientious board member, aware of widespread opinions on the board, she may go out of her way to be helpful.

However, if you have no personal connection, I suggest that you—either individually or with a small group of other parents—write a letter to the Board of Education, outlining your proposal. Give your reasons and the supportive arguments you have developed from your research. If the board is even mildly interested, you may be invited in for further discussion. If it is not, you will probably receive a "Thanks anyway" note, and that is that.

Only public schools fall under the jurisdiction of the Superintendent of Schools and the Board of Education. Parents of children in private or parochial schools must take their problems elsewhere. Their course, like that of all parents, begins at the desk of the teacher and the principal but diverges if they receive no satisfaction there.

If you have a child in a private school, whether independent or religiously affiliated, you should turn to the Board of Trustees, which is the sole body responsible for the operation of the school.

If you have a child in a Catholic school, you may climb a ladder of hierarchy, as public school parents do. You should first see the local priest who serves as district superintendent. Above him is the Vicar of Education, a bishop in charge of the Office of Education of the archdiocese. In any other schools governed by an overall religious organization, you follow a similar procedure.

· The End of the Line? ·

Although the ladder reaches higher than the local Board of Education and you can continue to climb farther in your effort to bring about change, don't expect great success. There is a lot going on up there.

· 24 ·

The step above the Board of Education is the state commissioner, sometimes called superintendent, of education. His office, located in the state capital, heads up the state Education Department of which he (and in a few states, she) is the boss. His department determines basic requirements for all schools, conducts statewide tests for evaluation, budgets the state's share in school funding, and makes sure that every school complies with state and federal laws.

With these weighty matters on his mind and on his desk, the commissioner is not able to concern himself with a proposal to introduce French in your child's elementary school. Chances are he will not see you, but he may assign a staff member to hear your cause. If by some great luck the commissioner himself has been urging schools to adopt a similar program, it is just possible—not probable, mind you, but possible—that he will pick up the phone and call your school superintendent. "Jim," he might say, "I've got a parent here as eager as I am to see French started earlier. Why not set up a pilot program and see how it works?"

Don't count on such a fantasy scenario, but contact the commissioner if you are determined. You might make greater headway, however, if you broaden your commitment and approach the commissioner not as a mother with a plea for her child's school but as an education-minded citizen with a proposal to improve the state's foreign language education.

If you fail to sell your idea at this level, there is little chance of success higher up. You don't have to surrender altogether, though; put the idea on hold and try again in a few years. Perhaps administrators with new attitudes and educational theories will have replaced the old ones, and will be more receptive to your ideas. Meanwhile you and your child can make French a learning experience at home. Even if you finally succeed, your child may already be in high school before anyone else's child sings "Frère Jacques" in first grade. The wheels of education turn slowly and frequently get stuck in the mud along the way.

Legislators' say in education

Both houses of the state have education committees which write bills that affect schools within the state mainly through budgeting. These bills greatly determine what programs can be carried out. When the legislature cuts school funding, districts have to decide which programs to eliminate; and you can be sure that elementary French, were it already in the school, would be one of the first to go. In the past art, music, gym, and reading have been dropped as "fluff" courses in an effort to stretch the budget.

· 25 ·

Therefore, even if the legislative committee accepted your proposal, wrote a bill, debated, and voted on it, the budget would be the determining factor in whether or not the proposal was implemented. You have every right to contact your state senator or assemblyman with an educational proposal. However, realize that with weightier matters at hand, he has every right to reject it.

The top person in education

The U.S. Secretary of Education, appointed by the President, presides over a bureaucracy housed in two monolithic buildings in Washington, D.C. There a budget of over $20 billion is allocated and spent. Civil rights, school crime, and drugs in the playground belong here, but not the introduction of French in kindergarten.

Still, parents can use the U.S. Department of Education to great advantage. Any time you want information or statistics on any aspect of education—state, national, and to some degree, international—you can secure them by writing to:

UNITED STATES DEPARTMENT OF EDUCATION
Office of Educational Research & Improvement
Washington, D.C. 20208-56410

In reply you will receive a cordial letter, an envelope of countless printed materials, and suggestions of other resources to contact. While the federal education administration may not take up your cause, it will certainly provide materials to support it.

Guidance counselors

It is difficult to discuss guidance counselors in general because they—and their responsibilities—vary greatly among schools. Most of them, particularly in public junior high and high schools, devote a good part of their time to course selection and tracking in college- and non-college-bound programs. With large student loads to handle, these counselors can give far less attention to personal guidance than many students need and than they themselves would like.

· 26 ·

Although few public elementary schools at this time have guidance counselors on staff, schools are slowly providing funds to acquire them as the need increases. Working with individuals and with small groups, counselors help children articulate their stress, develop insights, and learn skills with which to cope with their innumerable problems.

Most private schools have guidance counselors who are an integral part of the program of instruction. They hold regular group meetings, work individually with children who are having problems, meet with parents, and even conduct teacher-parent workshops.

While most guidance counselors cannot help you introduce French in kindergarten, they may prove to be an even more helpful resource. Counselors can help you and your child overcome more immediate hurdles that block her joy and learning: trouble with a teacher, rejection by peers, behavior problems, shyness, academic weakness, depression, and so on.

You should turn to your school guidance counselor as a source of help in two particular circumstances.

First, if your child's teacher or principal offers no solution to a problem, the guidance counselor may. For instance, Norah, who is in seventh grade, suddenly developed such a negative attitude toward school that she got headaches and fevers, even vomited frequently in the morning. The doctor found no physical cause, and all the girl herself could say was "I hate school."

After speaking with three of her daughter's teachers, Norah's mother still was no closer to pinpointing the cause of the problem, so she decided to present the problem to the guidance counselor. He had two private sessions with the girl and spoke with her teachers. What he learned was that as a school party approached, groups of girls gathered at every free period to discuss whom they were going with, what they would wear, whom they would sit with, and so on. Norah, considered less "cool" than many of her classmates, was excluded and felt miserable. Not even her homeroom teacher had noticed until the counselor began probing, but once alerted, the teacher called a meeting at which all the girls together discussed the party.

In this instance the guidance counselor enabled Norah to see that it was up to her to reach out for friendships instead of waiting for everyone else to reach out to her. At lunch one day sometime later, Norah was able to take the initiative and ask, "May I join you guys?" End of that problem.

The second time to turn to your guidance counselor is when a child's problem is of such a personal nature that you do not want it divulged to the teacher or principal. For instance, parents I know who suspected their son of smoking marijuana received much-needed emotional and practical assistance from a school guidance counselor. The counselor discovered through talks with the boy that he was smoking marijuana with another classmate on weekends. She counseled the parents to confront the boys, and, when they felt uneasy about it, set up a meeting for the boys and their parents in her office. Although understanding of the boys' curiosity to experiment, she was tough in her insistence that experimentation time was over and there could be no more drugs. Strengthened by the counselor's lead, the parents handled the problem from then on themselves at home. The parents had no more trouble with their son and drugs, and word of the problem remained confined to the counselor's office, the parents' memory, and the lesson their son learned.

When counselors are faced with problems that appear to have a less obvious origin and possible serious consequences, they will want more information than they can secure by talking with the child or his parents and teachers. Do not think the world has come to an end if a counselor suggests that your child undergo a neurological or psychological examination. These are purely diagnostic, providing data that enable the counselor and/or another professional to better meet your child's needs. These problems and procedures will be discussed more fully in Chapter 19.

The media

A wonderfully creative principal told me in despair, "It's as difficult to get a positive story about a school into the newspaper as it is to keep a negative story out!" He had tried for years to get the local newspaper to do a story on his innovative programs—fourth graders who had pen pals in a home for the aged, third graders with an art show at the local bank, a schoolwide civic committee that sent suggestions to the mayor. No success. The newspaper seemed determined to keep his school a community secret . . . until trouble came along. One day a teenage dropout entered the school and stole a teacher's pocketbook from her desk; the next day the newspaper featured a story.

Depressing as the media attitude is, it can sometimes work to your advantage. While local television, radio, and newspapers may avoid publicizing the good programs and events that please you in your child's school, they may, like you, want to uncover issues that need to be improved.

The media is always on the lookout for a cause. Therefore, if you can approach them, not as a bitter mom or dad with a grudge against the school but as a concerned citizen aware of a problem, you have a chance of gaining an ally. If you can win over journalists with the same combination of fervor and facts that you used on the superintendent, your voice will sound through a bullhorn. I am not sure the media will share your commitment to introducing French in elementary school, but they may very well take up causes that have greater impact on the community. It is worth a try.

The PTA's clout

The PTA has so much clout that I discuss it separately in detail in Chapter 11. Just as a union can exert greater power than any single worker, so the PTA can make demands more forcefully than you as one individual parent.

CHAPTER 3

The New Family

· New Parents ·

Years ago mothers stayed home, fathers went to work, and teachers taught their children. Life may not have been as satisfying or effective as it is today, but it certainly was a great deal simpler because people with clearly defined roles felt secure in their niches. Because people conformed to established patterns, the problems they created tended to be similar, and the solutions almost as predetermined as if painting by number. Who is at home to make Polly do her homework? Color me Mother. Who disciplines Peter for sassing the teacher? Color me Father. Who discusses their progress over dinner? Color me the Family.

Today, however, very few families seem to fit the traditional model. Consider these facts:

- Over 75 percent of today's mothers work outside the home, over half going back to work when their youngest child is under a year old.
- Millions of children live in single-parent homes; the exact numbers are almost impossible to determine because the situation changes so frequently.
- Millions of children live with a mother and stepfather,

seeing their father and often a stepmother on regular visits. The Census Bureau estimates that there are almost 4.5 million stepfamilies in the United States today with close to 9 million children under the age of seventeen. In fact, every day sees the birth of about thirteen hundred new stepfamilies, a figure that by the twenty-first century may outnumber that of traditional families.

· Increasingly, the courts are ordering joint custody, thus putting children into family structures that were unheard of a decade or two ago.

· Millions of children share their mother with a live-in boyfriend, or their father with a live-in girlfriend.

· Some children even share their mother with a live-in girlfriend, or their father with a live-in boyfriend.

· Anywhere from 2.5 to 7 million children between the ages of five and thirteen (statistics vary) return to an empty house after school each day.

· Almost one-fifth of the total number of schoolchildren speak a foreign language at home. The 654 students in a Virginia elementary school a few years ago spoke twenty languages—not quite from A to Z, but from Amharic and Arabic to Vietnamese.

With these statistics glaring at us, we can no longer color the solutions to problems Mother, Father, or Family, for it is unclear who each of them is. While the channels from home to school remain the same today as they used to be, changes in the home structure may block a parent's use of those channels, or at best make them difficult to use. Special problems make traditional methods of parent-school interaction outmoded for the new family.

· New Problems ·

"When will schools adapt to the needs of working parents?"

Three out of four parents never see their children's teachers, some because they are not interested, but most because they work and cannot fit a school visit into their work schedule. Take heart, though: Schools are beginning to recognize that a high percentage of mothers and fathers not only are at their office all day but may be away at other offices for weeks at a time. Still, questions with which parents continually barrage me are proof that schools are slow to break with tradition.

"How can I talk with my child's teachers when the school is closed by the time I get home?"

Some schools solve the problem by setting up early-morning, late-afternoon, or evening appointments for working parents, with child care available. They also encourage what used to be forbidden: evening phone conversations with teachers. If your school has not yet faced this problem, explain it to the principal. Ask the principal to check the number of single-parent families in the school and point out that their children are being deprived. You may convince him to reschedule teacher availability. If you do not convince him, set up a time during the day when you can speak with your child's teacher on the phone, and do not hesitate to communicate via child-delivered notes.

"How can I take part in class activities when they take place during the day?"

When a class activity is planned, take the initiative to ask the teacher how you can participate at home: for example, bake for the class party, make costumes for the play, deliver posters at night, handle a booth at the Saturday fair. If a weekend trip or an evening party is planned, offer to be a chaperone. The close contact you keep with your child's school activities not only reinforces the importance of school, but keeps open channels of communication between you and the teacher.

"How can I drive my child to a weekly after-school activity when I am still at work?"

Obviously you can't. You can, however, arrange with the parent of another child involved in the same activity to do the driving. If you return from work in time, you can chauffeur both children home. If you are unable to do this, you can still reciprocate if the parent needs help with her child on an evening or on Saturday or Sunday. If there seems to be no way to return the parent's kindness, why not invite the other child to join you and your child in special treats—a movie, picnic, trip to the zoo, and so on—or give the parent an occasional small gift to say "Thank you."

"What if my child is alone at home after school?"

With over half of American mothers in the work force, your child joins millions of others who return from school to a home far different from the TV scene of Mrs. Cleaver with kisses at the door and fresh-from-the-oven cookies on the kitchen table. Schools are beginning to realize that some working parents can't find or afford adequate after-school care and are keeping their own doors open until five or six o'clock. As pressure from parents has been the driving force in initiating after-school activity programs, here is a way to put your parent power to work if your school has not already made accommodations.

You are probably no different from the working mothers who in a recent survey said that their chief concern was finding good child care, while their second was guilt in being unable to find it. However, new studies reveal findings that may lessen both your concern and your guilt: Unsupervised or so-called latch-key children, when properly prepared, become more confident and responsible than their supervised counterparts. In response to the large numbers of children alone at home after school, some principals and superintendents have sent home safety guidelines.

- Lock doors and windows, avoid the stove, be familiar with a quick escape plan, have emergency numbers near the phone.
- Telephone one of your parents upon returning home from school.
- Spend the afternoon in something more productive than watching TV; get your homework done in order to have free time with your parents in the evening and then read, listen to music, play a game, or work on a hobby.

"Does the school think I'm the only single parent in the world?"

Single parents raise the same questions that working parents do, because in most cases they also go to work. They have, however, some questions uniquely their own.

"How can I keep my child from feeling uncomfortable at having only one parent in a school system built around moms and dads?"

Fortunately, schools are waking up to the fact that a large percentage of their students live with only one parent and, with growing sensitivity to their feelings, have introduced changes. For instance, they have turned the traditional father-daughter and father-son dinners into parent-son or -daughter dinners. They no longer send home notices addressed "To the parents of Jimmy" or "To Alice's mother and father," but rather "To *a* parent of Jimmy" or "To Alice's mother *or* father."

If your school principal has not initiated this practice, it is high time he did. Go see him. Explain that a child with one parent is made to feel like a freak when the school's basic assumption is the two-parent family. Furthermore, urge him to set up a teacher workshop at which a professional counselor can explain the diverse shapes of families today and point out the hurt that teachers inadvertently cause by their ignorance. In one school a sixth-grade teacher discussing the role of families in socializing children added, in deference to her students with single parents, "Of course, children like you without families have ways of being socialized too."

Most of the children whom she isolated in this manner just sat there hurting; but one little boy jumped from his chair. "I have a family," he said, "My mom and me. We socialtize, or whatever you call it, each other."

Teachers like that mean no harm but desperately need help so they will *do* no harm.

"What school rights does a noncustodial parent have?"

In most states the courts have made clear that the noncustodial parent should receive all school notices, including his child's report cards, may set up conferences with his child's teachers, and may attend school functions to which parents are invited. The noncustodial parent may not, however, attend a function that requires a special invitation unless either his child or the school extends one to him—such as the parent-daughter or -son dinner.

Single parents who wish further information may locate a single-parent center in their area or may contact the New York center for names and addresses of local groups:

THE SINGLE PARENT RESOURCE CENTER
1165 Broadway, Room 504
New York, NY 10001
(212) 213-0047

"When is a stepparent a parent?"

While scores of interfamilial problems arise in the stepparent-child relationship, the school problem centers largely around one question:

"Who attends school functions?"

Should a child invite his father or his stepfather, his mother or his stepmother, to school affairs such as the parent-daughter (or -son) dinner? Only one person can answer that—the child himself. What the other adults are in a position to do, and *must* do in the child's best interest, is accept and support the decision he makes without resentment or malice.

Who should talk to the teacher when troubles are afoot—the child's mother and stepfather or the child's mother and natural father? Or the natural father and stepmother? The answer here is more complex. The custodial parent, usually the mother, should certainly be one of the parents at the conference, as she is the one entrusted with supervision of the child's schoolwork. Whether the stepfather or natural father accompanies her depends on which one is more involved. If the natural father attends school functions, confers with the teachers, checks report cards, and is genuinely interested in the child's progress, he is probably the one to answer the teacher's call. If, however, his relationship develops into more of a father-child weekly play day, perhaps the stepfather is in a better position to deal with whatever problem has arisen. While the child should have a say, the mother may be able to make a more objective decision.

CHAPTER 4

Choosing a School

· Checking Your Options ·

In the private school I attended as a child, half of my graduating classmates had entered in kindergarten and attended classes in the same building every school day for thirteen years. I myself had been in the school since fourth grade. Today that kind of continuity is rare, even in rural areas where children are able to attend a central unified school for the full thirteen years.

The division of education into elementary, junior high, and high schools accounts in part for the fact that the average American child receives schooling in at least three separate schools. Social change is responsible as well. As more mothers entered the work force and needed preschool care, nursery schools sprouted up; and as families became more transient, relocations put their children in an average of six or seven schools by the time they graduated.

Even politics played a role. In former times, the keystone of education used to be the neighborhood where children lived, went to school, and played together, where parents knew each other and even teachers were apt to live in houses next door. The 1954 school desegregation ruling by the Supreme Court changed all that with the introduction of busing, which added still another new school for children to get used to.

Like moving to a new community, moving to a new school can be traumatic for a child. She leaves familiar surroundings, routines, faces, and friendships to enter uncharted territory. Even twelve-year-olds, having reigned with increasing lordship in the elementary school, enter junior high with qualms not unlike those of five-year-olds on their first day in kindergarten or three- and four-year-olds as they leave home for nursery school.

It is important, therefore, for house-hunting parents—and for couples intending to become parents—to check out the school their child will attend, not just this year but in future years.

"I feel as if I'm in a cafeteria with too much food on the counter," a parent told me, trying to explain the difficulty she felt in deciding where her son should go to high school. Her husband was pushing for the prep school he had attended, but the boy wanted to go to the public high school with his friends. She herself favored the Catholic school, which she heard was good, but friends told her that some of the private schools in the area were really better. "It's so much simpler to just sit down and be served a blue-plate special," she said with a sigh. "What should I do?"

Neither I nor anyone else can tell her what to do; her decision must be personally and uniquely that of her family. Guidance and information I can offer, but she must make the final choice with her family, just as you must, whether your child is starting out in nursery school or finishing junior high.

Let me add a word of reassurance, though. I have both attended and taught in private schools, where I have seen caring and challenge combined in the rich, loving teaching from which children grow in heart and mind. I have also both attended and taught in public schools and interviewed teachers for the National Teacher of the Year program for the past twenty years. I have seen firsthand the very best in public school education in areas as diverse as Valdosta, Georgia; Escondido, California; Perry, Oklahoma; Montrose, Colorado; and Hanover, New Hampshire; and one of the best, to my great joy, at the edge of a ghetto in New York City.

The cafeteria is filled with choices. The selection is up to you.

· Looking at Independent Schools ·

Independent schools are controlled by a board of trustees and are not subject to rules set down or standards set up by any outside body, not the Board of Education or the district superintendent, not even the state legislature. In short, each independent school may be whatever it wants. It merely has to meet the state's basic requirements in areas such as curriculum, safety, and attendance, which assure parents that their children are in safe hands.

"Why is there so much vacation?"

Parents of private schoolers may wonder why their child has much more vacation than his friends in public school. Does this mean he is getting less education?

The answer is no. Although the state education commission determines the number of days children in both public and private schools must attend, it demands fewer for the latter. Private schools, having in general smaller classes and more personal attention, intensify teaching and learning. While a public school may need 185 days to do the job, a private school may need only 170.

Please note, however, that both public and private schools are beginning to add days to the school year, and there is a strong movement to shorten summer vacations. What the future holds, no one knows, but it is a safe bet that private schools will continue to close earlier in June and have longer Christmas, midwinter, and spring vacations than public schools—with no academic ill effects.

"Are private school teachers as good as public school teachers, even though they're not certified?"

They may be better or they may be worse, because state certification cannot assure good teaching any more than the lack of it does. While certification aims to regulate the base of information and technical skill that a teacher must have before taking over a classroom, there is no way in which it can regulate a teacher's broader knowledge of a subject, understanding of children, enthusiasm, caring, creativity, sense of humor, curiosity, and the hundred other qualities that make a good teacher. Those are not certifiable.

Certification serves public schools by making sure that children are kept safe from teachers who do not meet minimum standards. Most private schools forgo a certification requirement, preferring to select teachers on the basis of the professional standards and personal qualities that best fit into the school philosophy.

Certification is no badge of excellence. Good teaching is not identified like a brain, a heart, and courage by the Wizard of Oz, but by the children who sit in a classroom. I have seen both certified public school and noncertified private school teachers electrify their classrooms.

"What kind of private school should I choose for my child?"

This is an enormous question that reminds me of a homework assignment my granddaughter Darcy brought home one day from third grade. "I have to interview you, and I can only make up five questions," she explained, settling herself down with pencil and a pad on which she had already written her questions: 1. "How old are you?" 2. "Are you married?" 3. "How many children do you have?" 4. "What do you think about life and death?" We didn't get to number five till the next morning as she hurried out the door: "What is your favorite kind of ice cream?" Fortunately I could shout out "butter pecan" before she reached the bus stop.

The variety among private schools is almost as broad and endless as thoughts on life and death, and your choice of one has to be just as personal. The following are some of the major types of private schools along with a few guidelines to help you select the right match for your family. You have to do the soul-searching.

Profit or nonprofit schools?

A few private schools operate like businesses, with the aim of making money for the owners. Although this does not preclude their providing a good education, it does mean that any income that exceeds expenses may go into the owners' bank account rather than into improvements for the school.

Most private schools are not run for profit. In fact, as most operate at a loss, parents and often grandparents are expected to contribute to the annual giving program, which is actually budgeted along with tuition. Large schools, such as Exeter and Andover, have income from sizable endowments to fall back on, but smaller schools work pretty much hand to mouth. As salaries, costs, and requests for tuition aid rise, it becomes more and more difficult for the hand of income to reach the mouth of expenses.

How to choose? Personally, I opt for the nonprofit school. Although it may end up costing you more, I feel more confident of the quality of education.

Boarding or day?

Boarding schools are a tradition in many families, with sons and daughters packing their bags and heading for the campus where class pictures of their mom or dad and even their grandparents hang on the walls. While most boarding schools start in seventh grade and continue through twelfth, some accept children as early as third and fourth, and others extend to the first two years of college.

Many parents see boarding school as the best way for their child to assert independence; and although this may be true, I have heard of too many tears in a lonely room at night when a child's independence was not yet ready to be asserted. To other parents, boarding school offers a haven for children whose homes fail to meet their needs. I think specifically of Tyler, smothering under the hostility of an autocratic father whom he could never please, withdrawing from his friends, failing in his studies, a sad and angry boy headed for trouble. At the urging of his mother, Tyler left for a New Jersey boarding school at the end of seventh grade. There he found understanding where there had been anger, fun where there had been resentment, calm where there had been turbulence. Boarding school helped him rebuild a life; it may even have saved it.

Many children have parents whose work or preference involves continual travel. Often those children are better off under the stable guidance of a boarding school.

Day schools have their own set of advantages. Many educators feel that growing up amid the problems and pains of family life equip a child to cope with adult life better than avoiding them during adolescence in the ivory tower of boarding school. In addition, day schools provide a greater opportunity for parents to involve themselves in their child's schooling, which educators point out as a distinct advantage.

Nevertheless, in a day school a child has more outside temptations and dangers to avoid than in the controlled boarding school setting. For example, although drugs and liquor do get sneaked into dormitories, they are far less available to boarding school students than to students in day schools who can easily buy them in stores and on street corners.

How to choose? There is no single answer, but the common denominator of all answers is that the child as well as you must make the decision. Weigh the advantages and disadvantages of each kind of school as they apply to your child and to your entire family. Before deciding for or against either a boarding or day school, ask yourself this important question: "Can this child grow better—and that means learn not only academically, but socially and emotionally as well—at home, as imperfect as it may be, or in a boarding school's controlled environment?

The decision for a day school is not valid if it is rooted in "I can't bear to part with him."

The decision for a boarding school is not valid if it is rooted in "I did it; so he has to," or "I can't stand him here another day."

The only valid answer must be rooted in the belief "We all think this will better serve his needs."

Coed or single sex?

Sending girls to all-girls schools and boys to all-boys schools used to be par for the course. Parents and educators believed that little boys and girls hated each other too much to learn together and that big boys and girls distracted each other too much. In addition, they felt that the needs of boys and girls differed so sharply that they could grow and learn more productively in programs designed specifically for them.

Today, however, single-sex schools are a dying breed, and the reason for the trend toward coeducation is not always educational. Many single-sex schools that merged or became coed during the last twenty years, even bastions of masculinity such as Choate and of femininity such as Rosemary Hall, took the step because they had discovered that educating boys and girls together prepared them better for life. Other schools went coed for more pragmatic reasons. Hearing the feminist message, girls began to demand an equal share of the male world, with the result that the single-sex schools whose coffers they had previously filled could no longer stay in business unless they merged or opened their doors to boys. So successful were their campaigns for boys that many of the boys schools found themselves in similar financial trouble and had to admit girls.

A few schools stood their ground. Today, while coed schools abound, parents may have to search to find the single-sex school they want.

How to choose? Coeducation in elementary school enables children to interact at a time when they are coming to terms with their own sexuality and learning about the male and female sex roles played out around them. I am all for it. A little later sex may become too overwhelming for some junior high children to take in stride, in which case they may fare better without close daily distractions from the opposite sex. I know a seventh-grade boy, Robbie, whom the girls drove to near madness with nightly phone calls, party invitations, and notes passed to and about him in class until he invented reasons to miss school; he flourished after his parents transferred him to a boys school.

The sex avalanche was equally distressing to the parents of Jill in the sixth grade, whose marks fell during a heavy preoccupation with boyfriends and breakups. "I'm sick and tired of all this," her father scolded one evening after an hour-long phone conversation about who was going with whom and why he won't speak to her . . . or vice versa. "Put down the phone and do your homework."

"I *am* doing my homework," Jill answered with the self-righteous conviction familiar to parents of eleven-year-olds.

"What kind of homework is that dumb conversation?" the frustrated father shouted.

With total calm, Jill smiled the smile reserved for parents and other idiots. "Sex education."

If you have a Jill or Robbie in your home, weigh the coed and single-sex advantages and disadvantages and see which wins.

Coed schools

Advantages: Your children probably want it, and it gives them the chance to work their way through sexuality while they are still young and somewhat protected.

Disadvantages: Their marks may suffer, and the family will be in an uproar. Also, you may have to buck the tide of precocious "dating" and "going steady" like a salmon going upstream.

Single-sex schools

Advantages: Your children will be able to concentrate on school, and you will have more peace.

Disadvantages: They will be resentful and may have to go through a sexual storm later on anyway.

It will take a lot of dialogue between you and your children to make that decision. Jill and her parents agreed that she could remain in her present coed school if she put her schoolwork on at least an equal basis with boys and limit phone calls to ten minutes; Robbie and his parents opted for an all-boys school, where he found relative calm. Both families were happier.

Religious or nondenominational?

Religious schools have a long tradition in the United States, stemming from the days when both state and church schools (all Protestant at the time) taught religion and received state aid. Sectarianism, however, led to conflict when the government made it clear that state schools could not teach any specific Protestant denomination. As a result, Protestants formed their own Sunday schools and church-related day schools to ensure indoctrination of their children into their own denomination. The establishment of Catholic and Hebrew schools followed soon after, growing enormously after the influx of immigrants from European countries.

Congress has striven over the years to protect the religious and nonreligious rights of American children through the separation of church and state set forth in the Constitution. In 1963, it enacted the ultimate ban from public schools of prayer, study of the Bible, and even silent meditation.

As a result, private Catholic, Protestant, and Hebrew schools flourish throughout the country. As the law demands that they adhere to state requirements, they offer a basic academic program, which they may enrich as they choose. In addition, they offer the religious instruction prohibited in public schools.

There are more Catholic parochial schools today than any other kind of religious school, and they are relatively inexpensive. Run by the diocese for children of the local parish (although they will accept non-Catholics when space is available), their goal is to prepare children for a Catholic high school and Catholic life, with a strong emphasis on morality and church teaching. In addition, individual Catholic orders also run private Catholic schools that, unlike parochial schools, are single sex and as costly as other private schools in the community.

As the quality of education varies greatly among Catholic schools, parents should investigate thoroughly rather than assume that because they are church-related, they are good. In parochial schools, look for these problem areas, which tend to appear as diocesan funds diminish: oversize classes, excessive regimentation, a lack of opportunity for the teachers' professional growth, below-level reading and math scores. Private Catholic schools are usually of a high quality, especially those run by the Jesuits and Sacred Heart orders. In such schools you may expect to find education similar to that of any other good traditional private school.

Hebrew schools make heavy demands of children. Their hours are long because they include a full academic program in the morning and a program of Hebrew studies in the afternoon and on Sunday. Talmud

Torah, Lubavitch, and orthodox are more rigid than reform, Solomon Schecter, and conservative schools. All meet state requirements; most educate the sexes separately; and all share the aim of preparing boys for their Bar Mitzvah and girls for their Bas Mitzvah. Orthodox schools have the additional aim of preparing boys to become rabbis and girls to assume their role as Jewish women.

Parents who want further information should contact their rabbi.

Protestant schools are developed and run by religious groups, but in most cases, unlike Catholic and Hebrew schools, they do not focus on the religious teachings of that group. For example, Episcopal and Quaker schools, which conduct morning prayers and meeting respectively, still build their educational programs along the broad lines of other independent, nonreligious schools. Like them also, Protestant schools vary widely from traditional to open, competitive to more relaxed; and in selecting one, parents go through the same investigative procedure.

One kind of Protestant school, the fundamentalist, mushroomed after the 1963 Supreme Court decision ruling prayer in schools unconstitutional. While many parents fought—and still fight—the decision through demonstrations and efforts to ban books, others, realizing few successes, abandoned their legal hopes and formed their own schools to teach what they wanted. Curriculum in these schools is heavy on creationism, morality, and prayer, light on personal decision-making skills, and totally nonexistent on sex education, evolution, and discussion of other religious viewpoints.

I consider fundamentalist schools detrimental to children's growth. By withholding exposure to diverse viewpoints, they prevent the development of personal values and deprive children of decision-making skills. They narrow the mind instead of broadening it—as education should—and build in the long run a solid wall of bigotry.

How to choose? If you want to assure your child of a strong foundation in Catholicism or Judaism, a religious school is a good choice. Before deciding, however, make sure the school is teaching religious concepts that you and your family can accept. Catholic parents of a child in a nondenominational school where I was principal transferred her to a parochial school for the religious training she would receive. What they did not know was that the school denied evolution, which they themselves placed alongside the biblical explanation of creation. Unable to reach an agreement with the school, and unwilling to send double messages to their daughter, they transferred her back to my school and left her religious education to Sunday school and communion classes.

Protestant schools make no promises of a strong religious foundation because most of them, although under the direction of a religious group, offer nondenominational education. Like most private schools, however, they place a heavy emphasis on the teaching of values.

If you are concerned about lax discipline and behavior problems in the school your child currently attends, chances are you will find a Catholic or Hebrew school more rigidly supervised. Discipline in Protestant schools differs little from that in similar non-church-related schools.

Traditional, open, or Montessori?

The terms "traditional" and "open" are tossed about with as much abandon by educators as the terms "liberal" and "conservative" are by politicians. Supporters of open schools hurl such epithets at their opponents as unimaginative, dull, unchallenging, and rote; supporters of traditional schools use accusations such as chaotic, nonacademic, aimless, nonachieving. Both are wrong. There are good traditional schools and good open schools; their differences rest not in their degree of excellence, but in their basic philosophy.

The chief difference is one of approach: Traditional schools provide teachers to teach children; open schools provide learning experiences from which children learn. In traditional schools children turn to their teachers for answers; in open schools they discover answers themselves. In traditional schools teachers find ways of motivating children to learn; in open schools children learn by motivating themselves.

Specifically, traditional classrooms are focused on the teacher, who gives instructions that students follow; who conveys information on which students take notes; who teaches skills that students practice; who assigns lessons that students complete; who designs achievement tests that students take.

Open classrooms, on the other hand, are focused on the needs and level of understanding of each individual child, who finds stimulation in objects grouped by subject around the room; whose curiosity leads him to probe the subject; who turns to the teacher as a resource; who evaluates his own progress by completing units of work he and the teacher have planned.

Although educators have polarized traditional and open classrooms, the truth is that most of them borrow techniques from each other. A good traditional teacher individualizes segments of work according to the students' interests and abilities, and a good open teacher reaches a point where she takes the reins and says, "Come on, Billy, get to work on your math." What may surprise you is that open classrooms are as structured as traditional classrooms in their own way, with the room strategically set up and each child's progress carefully followed and recorded. In the sixties when open education surged into the United States on a tidal wave from England, few teachers knew that and as a result open classrooms became open chaos.

American education used to be highly traditional, following the European system from which it grew, until the early twentieth century when the discoveries of Sigmund Freud and John Dewey brought about a reassessment: Freud made us aware of a child's psychological needs, and Dewey explained how schools could meet them. From then on education theory has ridden a seesaw of ups and downs between traditional and open, reflecting the nation's attitudes and politics, with a lot of name-calling from both sides. Today, just as the fashion industry has finally given legitimacy to both maxi-and miniskirts, leaving the choice up to the individual, so has education come to an agreement. While there is at the moment a conservative swing to traditional schools, open schools exist throughout the country with equal status.

Montessori schools, created by Maria Montessori near the turn of the century, share the philosophy of self-motivation with open schools and the emphasis on planned structure with traditional schools. Yet in practice they differ widely from both. Open schools use individual children's interests and activities as the source of learning, with children gravitating to centers in a mosaic mix that piques their curiosity. Montessori schools, on the other hand, use what Dr. Montessori called "a prepared environment" as the source of learning—"attractive, scientifically developed, sequenced and interrelated materials that allow the child to explore relationships by a process of manipulation and discovery," as the Greenwich, Connecticut, Whitby School brochure explains. Children progress at their own pace, and while teachers guide the children in the use of the materials, unlike teachers in traditional schools, they do not tell them precisely how or what to learn. By and large, children discover for themselves.

It may be difficult for a parent to distinguish a Montessori from an open school. You may notice more small groups working with a teacher in the former and more individual work in the latter, but in both you will see informal interaction between students and teachers, tables rather than desks, corners with cushions, computers, and a kaleidoscope of materials and children's work. In order to get a better understanding, ask the teacher to explain what is going on.

How to choose? The choice of traditional, open, or Montessori education depends on your child's needs. While your own personal attitude will play a part, your child is separate from you, an individual in his own right; therefore the question for you to ask is "Will a traditional, an open, or a Montessori approach best help him grow and learn?"

· 45 ·

A suburban family who recently asked me this question serves as a good case history in seeking an answer. Molly Ward, let's call her, has two children, Kim, eleven, and Teddy, eight, both in the public school in their suburban town since kindergarten and both top students in their class. Molly, however, feels that the school is unchallenging and the teachers for the most part uncreative. Some of them, she hears, play favorites and actually hurt children emotionally. She has decided to remove her children and is looking for private schools.

Kim is quiet, serious, and extremely shy, with little confidence in her many intellectual and creative abilities. She is most comfortable when she knows she is in control of a situation, "like cleaning out her bureau drawers or alphabetizing the books on her shelf," her mother explains. Teddy appears to be the exact opposite—outgoing, mentally quick, passionate about baseball, and always ready to make a joke. Both children are earnest about their studies and do A work.

In the public school, which made little effort to meet their individual needs, Kim was lost in the crowd, and Teddy was bored with worksheets. The children needed a different school—not only different from the one they were currently in, but different from each other. Molly looked around for six months until she found what she thought was right for each child. Teddy can go on the bus, but Molly has to drive Kim an extra half hour on her way to work every morning. "We'll just have to suffer a little," she says, "because I know it's a good school for Kim."

She's right. In smaller classes with teachers sensitive to her shyness, Kim has begun to blossom. In the school's traditional approach, she has the demanding directed study in which she finds security: home assignments, long-term projects, tests; she knows what she is supposed to do, and she does it. As Kim grows in self-confidence, Molly sees her extending herself as she never dared before—joining the glee club, trying out for a play, baking cookies for a class fund-raiser. "We found a wonderful school," Molly says, adding, "and Kim found a wonderful girl!"

When Molly visits Teddy's school, she laughs at the difference. Thirty-three children in grades 3, 4, and 5 share a big room with three teachers, "although I can't ever find the teachers," she adds, "because they are in little groups all over with the kids." The room is filled with computers, scientific equipment, books, art supplies, puzzles, and scales in centers where children work alone or in twos. Every week Teddy must complete a work plan designed by him and a teacher. Although he has no home assignments, he must read and is currently researching France, which he has chosen in the class study of the world.

Both children are extremely happy in their new schools. Kim has just finished an integrated unit on Africa and is learning a tribal dance.

On weekends Teddy actually misses school because he has to leave the weather station he set up.

Montessori schools have just as many success stories to tell as the traditional and open schools Molly found. Because Montessori learning builds sequentially year by year from nursery school through the middle years (not all schools offer the complete program), a child who enters midway is apt to undergo a longer period of adjustment than he would when transferring to another kind of school. Children learn to function under the new approach at different rates according to their individual curiosity and self-motivation.

More academic or less academic?

Just as private schools differ in their educational philosophies, so they differ in their goals. Some offer a demanding academic preparation for top colleges and universities; others aim for less prestigious and two-year colleges. What parents must realize is that both kinds of schools—and both kinds of colleges—are of equal worth for the simple reason that the children who attend them are of equal worth.

The academically oriented school offers advanced courses even at elementary and middle school levels, demands higher levels of achievement, and may offer fewer "soft" subjects such as art, music, photography, drama, and so on. Many top academic schools have strong extracurricular athletics, however.

Less academically oriented schools provide a basic academic program that the school is able to strengthen or ease according to the individual needs of students by placing them in different levels of English, math, science, history, and foreign language. Arts programs are usually strong in these schools.

How to choose? The choice here is obvious: Send your academic children to one kind of school and your nonacademic ones to the other. Let them both be achievers. Success leads to confidence; confidence leads to learning, and a child does not have to be headed to Smith or Yale to attain it. Hans Selye, my stress guru, told me, "The trouble with children is that their parents don't realize some of them are turtles, not racehorses!"

"The trouble is," I added, "that our world doesn't appreciate turtles." And we both sighed in sorrow.

Military schools

Like the armed services themselves, military schools, which used to be strictly male, are now largely coed, a change that has tempered their steely image. Although most military schools begin at the junior high level, some accept children as early as fifth grade.

· 47 ·

In military schools, students wear uniforms, earn rank, and parade; along with regular academic subjects, they study military history and procedures. Discipline is strictly enforced, with demanding rules and inevitable punishment for infractions. I used to put military schools into the same category as West Point's infamous Beast Barracks and the marines' basic training, but after talking to a wise and gentle man who taught at a military school for some years, I erased my preconception. "Some kids love it; some hate it," he told me. "It all depends on why they're there."

How to choose? If you have a child who is rebelling against authority at home and at school, don't send him to a military school for the cure. If he can't accept the less stringent demands of civilian life, he probably won't undergo a miraculous transformation under military demands. While the military school may keep him under control through fear, it may only dig his anger into a deeper pit, to erupt at a later date. Help him work through his rebelliousness before he represses it in a military school uniform.

If, on the other hand, your child likes regimentation and flourishes when obeying and giving orders, a military school may be the right place for him. He will enjoy the competition for rank and have opportunities to develop qualities of leadership. At the opposite extreme, if he is careless and sloppy in his work habits, the discipline of a military school will enforce order and neatness.

The surest argument for military school applies to the boy or girl who hopes to gain admission to one of the armed services colleges—West Point, Annapolis, the Virginia Military Institute, or the Air Force Academy. Military schools are designed with these colleges in mind; children who attend will be assured proper preparation and probably an edge on admissions as well.

Although I personally am not a great proponent of military schools, believing that children can acquire the same qualities and learn the same lessons under less authoritarian conditions, I know boys and girls who have attended them enthusiastically, graduated successfully, and gone on to a variety of colleges.

Whites-only schools

After the civil rights movement won the long, hard fight to desegregate schools, a new kind of school sprang up throughout the southern states. As any American living in the years following the 1954 Supreme Court ruling remembers, resistance broke out in rage and violence. With the passing of time, however, most local communities acquiesced, and black and white children—especially in elementary schools—found they could learn together peacefully. Not all parents agreed: Large numbers of them, still refusing to send their children to desegregated schools, did what the fundamentalists did—opened their own schools. Although not accredited and receiving no government aid, all-white schools still exist today in many southern communities.

How to choose? I feel that all-white schools reinforce prejudices that our nation is slowly and painstakingly striving to eliminate. Children, as the song says, "have to be taught to hate," and the schools that sprang up from the sole purpose of keeping white children away from black children teach that lesson. Children are not color blind, as some people say. They recognize their differences: I have seen black and white kindergartners feeling each other's skin and hair, studying the contrast in their fingers as they hold hands. What children don't do is judge each other's differences with labels of good and bad, better and worse.

To be fair to your child and to the future of the United States, don't send her to a whites-only school.

If you are considering private schools and need further information, you can check your local library for either of these books: *The Handbook of Private Schools* (P. Sargent, Boston, 1990) and *The Bunting and Lyon Blue Book: Private Independent Schools* (Wallingford, CT, 1990). In addition, you can contact

· 49 ·

NATIONAL ASSOCIATION OF INDEPENDENT SCHOOLS
18 Tremont Street
Boston, MA 02108
(617) 542-1988

"How do I apply to a private school?"

If you ask this question of parents in a big city, such as New York, where admissions are highly competitive, they will answer, as one father did, "It is terrible. The only worse experience we ever had was being called to the IRS to review our tax return."

On the other hand, if you ask parents in less competitive areas of the country, you will hear something like "It's easy. Just fill out the form, take your kid for an interview, and you're in."

Whether the procedure is horrendous or painless, the steps you take are pretty much the same:

1. Fill out the admission form that the school sends you. In most cases you have to include a nominal fee, anywhere from ten to twenty-five dollars.
2. The new school will set up an interview for you and your child, at which you will meet either the school head or the director of the division to which your child is seeking admission.
3. Alert the principal of the school your child is currently attending because the new school will write asking for your child's record. This includes marks and scores on national tests, but not notes on any personal or behavior problems she may have had.
4. If everything has gone well so far, an appointment will be made for your child to take standardized tests to determine her levels of achievement in verbal and numerical skills and, in some cases, thinking and creative skills as well. The teacher's observation of the child in the classroom, plus a one-on-one evaluation of her skills, usually takes the place of formal tests for kindergartners and first graders.
5. Now you wait, and this is the hard part. Some schools boast of accepting only one of every twenty applicants; some actually tell you, "We can only accept two new students in her grade this year." The competitive pressure is so strong in some areas that parents use bribes and any pull they have in order to have their child beat out someone else's. Don't attempt it.
6. When the school is ready, you will receive a letter that may accept your child with pleasure, reject her with regret, or place her on a waiting list with withheld emotion.

I urge you, where possible, to apply to more than one school so that your child may have a better chance on the odds. I also urge you to be realistic in the schools to which you apply: Don't try to get your child into a top academic school if she isn't a top academic student. She has a better chance of acceptance in a school whose program is less demanding, and she will certainly be happier and more successful there.

Personally I would steer clear of highly competitive schools for most children; I don't think the value system under which they operate sets a good example for children. There *are* things more important than high marks. And there are many smaller, excellent schools that you will find less stressful to apply to . . . and to attend.

· Looking at Public Schools ·

"I feel trapped in an urban school."

There was a time when everybody's children attended the same city schools, but not so today. The country's big cities have become polarized between a small number of wealthy people, whose children attend private schools, and a majority of poor people, whose children attend public schools. This is too bad because it deprives children of knowing others from diverse national, racial, and socioeconomic groups that could expand their horizons.

Urban schools are contending with such serious problems relating to drugs and crime that the quality of their education gets less attention—and less money—than it deserves. Ernest Boyer, president of the Carnegie Foundation for the Advancement of Education, has called urban schools "a national disgrace." Despite this bleak picture—and it is far bleaker in high and junior high schools than in elementary schools—there are some good urban public schools. I know; I have visited them.

What to do? If your child attends an inadequate city school, you have three ways to go. First, fight for changes. You will be in for a long, hard battle with no insurance for success, but it's worth a try. Reread Chapter 2 for suggestions. Second, admit the school is an immovable mountain and fill in the weak spots yourself. Turn the three Rs into fun and games at home and use the whole city as a center of art and learning. Third, give up and get your child into another school. Move to another district or town or turn to a private school; all but parochial schools (which take non-Catholics when they have space) are expensive, but you may qualify for tuition aid. If all else fails, talk to the school superintendent about transferring your child to a better school, either within the district or in another district. Magnet schools, which draw students from an entire city to their particular area of specialization, and the voucher system, which lets you spend your education dollars in any school of your choice, will eliminate the difficulty of switching schools. As these innovations appear, parents and children may never have to feel trapped again.

"I'm in a suburban rat race."

The vast middle class, both blue and white collar, uses suburban school systems. Either unwilling or unable to send their children to

· 51 ·

private schools in the city, they have fled to communities in which the top priority is a good school. Putting great pressure on the school for high national test scores, lots of homework, and high marks, parents sometimes turn their schools into what children perceive as a pressure cooker. Because children learn best in a more relaxed atmosphere, parents defeat their original purpose.

What to do? Follow the advice of a Glencoe, Illinois, child whose father got angry after a look at a C in math on her report card. "Cool it, Dad," she said. "Think how much I learned in order to get that C."

Most suburban schools give a child a strong basic education, and many offer enrichment programs as well. Support the school in its efforts, but support your child too. The greatest help you can give is to let your child know how wonderful she is—with As or with Cs. Even if Fs come along, *she* remains wonderful; it's the schoolwork that poses a problem. Keep your child's stress at a minimum: Cool it.

· 52 ·

"We're losing our rural school!"

As small farms across the country close down, along with their support services, the population of rural areas is declining. Fewer children attend the scattered rural schools whose bells used to resound through the countryside. Education systems have met the growing cost per child by consolidating schools—closing small ones and busing children to central large ones. So widespread is this change that the 150,000 school districts the United States had at the beginning of the twentieth century have dwindled to only 15,000 today, with the greatest consolidation having taken place within the past thirty years.

What to do? It is difficult for parents to buck the tide of consolidation, although some have succeeded. Through sheer determination parents kept a one-room schoolhouse I visited in Utah and an elementary school in Massachusetts alive and well: They demonstrated and countered the district's arguments with numbers and finally won.

If you are unable to hang on to your rural school, all is not lost. The central school your child will now attend has use of funds from the schools that closed. This means more and better teachers, a broader curriculum, richer arts classes, and reinstatement of special programs such as reading.

If you fear that the loss of your rural school will destroy your child's sense of community, work with other parents to preserve it: Strengthen

Scouts and 4-H and church youth group activities. Also, include class-mates from the new school so that your child will learn to experience community in the broader, more diverse terms that our shrinking world imposes.

· 53 ·

CHAPTER 5

Getting Started in Preschool

· The Needs of Preschool Children ·

Although American educators acknowledged the value of early learning as long ago as the seventeenth century, they thought of it in terms of training rather than growth. In 1669, Increase Mather wrote the first comprehensive child-care guide, in which he instructed parents how to make their children obedient, moral, and dutiful; qualities "as will afterwards make them useful in their places."

John Dewey, at the turn of the century, and Jean Piaget, somewhat later, developed the first real research on early learning, which was shelved by many educators and parents because it threatened the foundations upon which American schools had been built. These pioneers demonstrated that a sequentially developing process of experimentation and discovery provided sounder and more lasting learning than the repetition and memorization most schools used.

It was not until the 1960s that early learning really came into its own, with the revelation that the most concentrated learning of a lifetime takes place within a child's first four years. In fact, basic intelligence grows as much in a child's first four years as it will in the next thirteen.

With this discovery, the United States jumped on the early learning bandwagon: television produced *Sesame Street* and *Mister Rogers*; educational toys flooded the market; more states began offering kindergarten; and preschools sprouted up everywhere. While at the turn of the century there were only 31,000 children in kindergarten, today there are over 2.5 million.

When I discuss preschools, I include nursery school with three- and four-year-olds and kindergarten with five-year-olds. (Some states offer kindergartens for four-year-olds as well.)

"What are the special needs of preschoolers?"

The needs of preschool children, ages three to six, are not so different from those of other school children, but are often far more intense:

· They need, above all, emotional security. Progressing from the womb of the mother to the womb of the family, preschoolers are now stepping out into a strange new environment called the world. They enter it alone. No matter how kind and loving their teachers may turn out to be, preschoolers enter a classroom where they are no longer the one special person they have been to Mommy and Daddy. Furthermore, with nothing familiar—not the teachers, not the other children, not the playthings, not the routine—life can be terrifying. Suddenly they find more expected of them: They have to wipe up spilled juice and put on their own coats and share toys they want to play with. In the unsettling new world of preschool, children need to be reassured all day that life can still be trusted and enjoyed.

· Preschoolers need other children. From them they learn how to play and love and get angry and cry and laugh. With them they learn cooperation and learn the lessons of life. And as their classmates respond to them, preschool children begin to develop their own image.

· They need space. In order to develop large-muscle skills, they need room for running, rolling, climbing, riding tricycles, swinging, and sliding.

· They need words. In order to develop language skills, they need to talk and be talked to, to read, to sing, and to listen to songs.

· They need to make sense of the world—to look at pictures and draw their own pictures to interpret it; to try out different roles by playing house or Superman or store; to develop a sense of community

· 55 ·

by visiting the firehouse and post office and park and by sharing in the community of their class.

· They need to use their hands in order to develop small-muscle coordination—to learn to tie their shoes and zip zippers, to get buttons buttoned and laces through holes, to use crayons and scissors, to play games on their fingers, and to build with blocks.

· They need to develop cognitive skills—to learn colors and shapes and sizes of things; to ask questions and discover answers and remember; to put puzzles together; and as they grow older, to learn what letters and numbers mean and how they fit together.

· Above all, they need to begin to know who they are—to draw themselves and see themselves grow; to feel good about hanging up their smocks and putting toys away by themselves; to feel important enough to show and tell what matters to them; to realize they can survive a fall or a push or a mean word from a friend.

What preschool children *need not* learn—and should not be pushed to learn—is how to read. Longitudinal studies that follow children from preschool through the lower elementary grades show no correlation between early reading and reading competence in grades 1 and 2. If parents would recognize this truth, they could support their children's reading development in constructive ways and put less pressure on both their children and themselves. Children who are read to, who see other family members reading, who come to know reading as fun— these children will read when they are ready. If pushed by their parents, they may not get ready.

Educational fads, which come and go, convince parents from time to time that if their child cannot read by age four or five, they have failed as parents and must bear the shame. This is totally false. The wisest child experts, from John Dewey to Erik Erikson and Joseph Chiltern Pearce, argue that pushing a young child into reading not only offers no advantage, but may actually impede a child's learning later on. My own experience confirms this, and yet I have too often failed to convince parents. I recall a beautiful, bright little girl who, alone in nursery school, could pick out words in the books we read. Her parents boasted of the nightly reading drills they gave her, berating me for not instructing the whole class in reading. By kindergarten, when a few other children had begun to read, that child had stopped; and in first grade, when most of the class had learned, she refused even to open a book.

The moral to the story is this: Don't push a child to read in preschool. If a child's natural curiosity leads him into early reading, give him books and play word games with him. Otherwise, the best way to get your child to read is to read to him and to support his readiness in all other areas of his development. And one more point: Let him see you with your nose in a book too.

"How can I tell if the school meets my child's needs?"

While there is no quick and easy test you can give the school, there are signs for which you should be on the lookout:

· I think the best indication of a good school is the children within it. Is your child happy? Does he like going to school in the morning? Does he like his teachers? Has he made friends? If you answer yes, the school must be doing something right.

· Another indication is the physical plant. Is the classroom large enough for the children to move around freely, sprawl, play games in a circle, jump on mats? Are there also provisions for quiet time alone—cushions in a corner, a raised platform, a little tent? Is there an outdoor area where children can run, play action games, and make noise, uninhibited by others? A good preschool provides both kinds of space.

· The equipment the school has is equally important. Indoors a child needs a wide variety of well-constructed playthings to stimulate activity—books, puzzles, building equipment, art and science supplies, and so on. (You will not find the usual store or dollhouse corner in Montessori schools, though, because they eschew the make-believe of buying and selling for the real experience, and they reject toy stoves and dishes in favor of real cooking, pouring, and eating.)

· If the school is meeting your child's needs, you will see signs of learning in all areas of her growth. Not only will she acquire more skills, but she will use them. You can't stop a child from learning in a conducive environment any more than you could stop her from breathing where there is oxygen. Her drawing and speech and singing will take on shape; the play with friends, which used to be side by side, will become real interaction; she will become more coordinated; she will express pride in her achievements.

· If your child talks too much, asks too many questions, gets into too many things, and is always too busy to listen, you may be driven crazy, but you can probably relax about her school. Curiosity and excitement about life are good indications that the school and you are doing your job.

· The ultimate indication of a school's success is how your child feels about herself. If the school is doing what it should, she will feel unthreatened by the challenges it presents. You will see her more able to cope with stress at home and more willing to risk failure in new undertakings.

A good school, no matter what philosophy it embraces, will encourage and support your child's growth, evidences of which you will see extended into your home. The differences between traditional and open schools rarely appear at the nursery-school level, where children in both kinds more or less go their own way. By kindergarten, however, differences may become evident. Traditional classes structure the day more rigidly into time slots, while open classrooms run on a more flexible schedule. Also, traditional kindergartens focus on teaching children numbers and letters through drill and homework assignments, while open kindergartens, through exposure to books and word and number games, let children lead themselves into the world of math and reading. Montessori schools follow their own program throughout.

The difference between a good and bad preschool is not what it teaches a child but, far more important, whether it sets the child on the path to learn for the rest of her life. Security, self-confidence, mental stimulation, creativity—these are the lessons of a good preschool.

I think the most significant indication of a school's worth came from a four-year-old, whose grandfather asked, "What do you like best in your school?" She considered the question for a moment. Then, tilting her brown curly head to the side, she answered, "Me."

· 58 ·

· Starting Nursery School ·

"Do I have to send my child to nursery school?"

There is no hard-and-fast rule that says children must go to nursery school; for years they grew into relatively happy adults without it. Yet times have changed, and nursery school today offers what many homes cannot provide. One is an ever-present nurturer. With mothers spending less time at home and nannies often inadequately trained and apt to come and go, nursery school provides consistent and trained caregivers. Another advantage is a group of friends with whom children develop social awareness and skills. A third is an environment planned to stimulate growth in the diverse areas of a child's makeup. A fourth is the self-confidence nursery school fosters in children as they learn survival in a world away from home.

"What's the best age to start nursery school?"

A child is ready for nursery school—and I am not including day care for infants and toddlers—when she can leave her parents without feeling abandoned. She may shed a few tears at the door for a week or so when her mother or father kisses her good-bye, but if she is able to stop in a few minutes and get involved in play, she is still ready for nursery school.

At four most children are ready; at three many of them are. Often the school insists that they no longer wet their pants and be able to handle the toilet, although occasional accidents are expected. (Children who have frequent accidents may be required to wear diapers until they develop better control.) They should be able to speak well enough to communicate their needs.

It is not always easy to tell whether a child is ready without a trial period in which the teacher can observe and report back. At three a little boy I know was eager to go to nursery school to emulate his sister in first grade. Yet every morning he entered the room with his hands covering his eyes, having to be led around as if he were blind. Because he took part in singing and storytelling, and even uncovered his eyes to paint or build blocks and to play in the yard, the teacher felt certain he was handling school satisfactorily. Still, his mother had doubts. Not until he was seven years old did this child explain why he covered his eyes every morning: "I didn't want to look at the teacher. She was ugly."

· 59 ·

"How can I get my child ready for nursery school?"

What children need most in preparation for nursery school is self-confidence—to know they can overcome fear of a new situation, to know they will be all right for a while without Mother or Dad, to know they can make friends. Self-confidence comes to children from years of being loved enough to believe they are wonderful. It comes from the encouragement parents give when children dare to try what is new—be it walking or using a spoon or pulling on socks—from parental support when they fail, and from their own pride when they succeed.

With self-confidence as the keystone, you can ease your child's adjustment to nursery school in many specific ways:

· Get her used to staying with grandmother or a baby-sitter for a few hours at a time so she will know that when absent, her parents will return.

· Let her get used to playing at a friend's house so that an unfamiliar adult in an unfamiliar place will be less frightening. I heard an older sister reassure her brother on his first day of nursery school by telling him "It's just the same as being at Patti's birthday party with a different mom."

· Take her to visit the nursery school, perhaps spend a morning there, so that she can familiarize herself with the teacher and the surroundings.

· Assure her that her blanket (or whatever transitional object she may have) will go to nursery school too. Without it she might be comfortless. Cassie had two stuffed animals as her constant companions: Bootie, a small bear, and Dodo, a monstrous Brontosaurus. In deference to the teacher, Cassie's parents explained that only Bootie could go to school, and, though not completely sold on the idea, Cassie waved good-bye to her mother the first day clutching the bear tightly in her arms. When her mother picked her up, with Bootie still in tow, she asked, "Did you feel lonesome?" "No," the little girl answered, patting her bear, "but Bootie did. He wants Dodo to be with him." What did the mother do? She let Cassie take both animals until she felt secure enough to let them keep each other company at home.

· Arrange with the parents of another child entering nursery school to have your two children spend a little time together before school starts; in this way each will see a familiar face on the first day and feel less alone. That familiar face may be as consoling to your child as it was to a child I know who, seeing her mother turn to leave on the first day, began to cling, her lip trembling. As she was about to burst into tears, she suddenly spotted the little girl with whom her mother had arranged an introductory playtime the previous week. Her face brightened as she looked up and asked, "Will my teacher let me play dolls with my new best friend?"

· If your child wants to, ask the teacher whether she may take a special toy to share with the other children in school. It will bring a touch of home to school with her and at the same time make her feel important. Don't force the idea, though, because some children at this age still want to keep their toys to themselves and some teachers don't want to put them to the test. Noah's teacher allowed him to bring in my miniature dachshund one morning. The teacher told me that he sounded like a college professor when he explained to the greatly impressed class, "Dachshund means badger hound in Chinese"!

· Show an interest in whatever your child does in school. Chapter 10, which deals with the problems of communicating, recognizes that it isn't always easy to get children to talk about school. "What did you do in school today?" may elicit no more information than "I ate snacks," or "I played." Sometimes even "I'm not telling" or "Nothing" is all you get. Your question may be too broad; try a more specific one like "What was the most fun thing you did?" or "Did the teacher tell a story today?" and then follow up from there. Don't push or nag for an answer, though; if your child is reluctant to talk, respect her feelings and suggest, "Maybe you'll share it with me later on." Often stories pour out at bedtime. What matters most is that you let her know you are interested in her life without being intrusive.

· Always have her in school on time so she will have the security of being part of the group. I have seen children develop actual school phobia because they had to break into the already-formed morning circle like an intruder every day. It is equally important that you arrange to have your child picked up on time when school is over. I recall too many sad little eyes watching for a familiar face at the door of an empty room with only the teacher left, working at her desk.

"What should I do if my child cries every morning?"

As discussed, a crying child may not be ready for nursery school. If this is his first time away from you, he may simply need greater maturity to gain confidence that he can handle life on his own for a few hours. Maturity comes with the passing of time; so keep the child home for a while and then try nursery school again. Talk to the teacher; you and she together can fairly accurately judge when your child is ready.

· 61 ·

There are other reasons for tears, however. A common one is the fear that the parents may disappear while the child is at school. Even a child with two working parents who has adjusted to staying home with a sitter may be tremulous in the environment of nursery school. The best way to solve this problem is by spending about fifteen minutes or so in the classroom for the first few days or a week; after that, let your child know that you will wait outside. The child may ask to see you at first, then, satisfied, return to the class. After a week or so, he will probably be adequately confident of your permanence to join with the class group as school begins.

Tears may also arise from a situation created at home. For instance, Mother may be in the hospital, Grandmother may have died, or a new baby may be occupying Mother and Dad's attentions. In cases like these, children feel abandoned because their parents, who used to focus all their attention on them, now allocate a share of it elsewhere. The solution lies in reassuring your child of your continued love and of her continued importance to them: Let her draw a picture for Mother if she is in the hospital and help prepare the house for her return home; let her attend Grandmother's funeral, take flowers to her grave, or comfort Grandfather; let her hold the new baby and draw a picture for his wall. When Noah was born, Darcy, then three, used to pull up her shirt and nurse her doll alongside her mother, who was nursing the baby. It was her way of becoming part of the new baby scene.

Some feel that a child cannot adjust to her changed role in the family when a new baby arrives unless she is dislodged from the old one first. I have seen parents send the older child to the grandparents' or a classmate's home for a short time; I even know a child whose aunt and uncle took him on a trip to Disney World when his mother had a baby. This may work, but personally, I think a child is better off making the adjustment right from the start as an integral part of the family. In fact, I think it is a good idea to keep a child home from nursery school for a few days after a new baby steals the spotlight, so that she can be included in what her parents do in caring for the baby, instead of feeling set apart.

· 62 ·

"What should nursery school teach my child?"

Concerned parents always ask me what nursery school should teach their child. My answer shocks them: "Nothing."

Nursery school is for learning, not for teaching. A good nursery school sets the stage and lets the players improvise their development under a minimum of authority. They learn by painting and building and listening to stories; they learn by interacting with friends and teachers; they learn by running and falling and getting up to run again; they learn by passing graham crackers and throwing away paper cups. Each "lesson" they learn lays one more brick on the road extending through a lifetime. If they learn in joyous fun, they will continue learning forever; but if they learn under pressure and fear, they will lock themselves up and only go through the motions.

Moral: Let little children be little children until they are big. Play is the most important work they can do!

· Starting Kindergarten ·

Although still a preschool grade, kindergarten is considered important enough to be offered to five-year-olds in all fifty states. While only 68 percent of the states provide kindergarten for four-year-olds, more are joining the list every year.

"How can I tell when my child is ready for kindergarten?"

A child is ready for kindergarten when he is mature enough to handle the new experiences and stresses it presents. A happy and successful experience in nursery school is the best predictor of an easy adjustment to kindergarten. A child who has not attended nursery school may also be secure and mature enough to enter kindergarten with few qualms and fit right into the program without problems.

If you are uncertain of your child's readiness for kindergarten, ask yourself the following questions, using the proportion of yes-and-no answers as a guide:

- · Can he function away from you?
- · Does he get along with other children?
- · Can he go to the toilet alone?
- · Can he listen quietly for short periods of time?
- · Can he follow simple directions?
- · Can he communicate orally?
- · Can he engage in physical activities satisfactorily?
- · Does he have a large enough a degree of both small- and large-motor coordination (use of crayons and tricycles)?

Louise Bates Ames and Frances Ilg of the Gesell Institute of Child Development describe more specific signs of kindergarten readiness in their book *Your Five Year Old* (Delacorte, 1979):

- · Your child should know three or four colors.
- · He should be able to draw a square.
- · He should be able to identify a cross, a square, a circle.
- · He should be able to repeat four numbers the first time he tries.
- · He should know his left from his right hand.

- He should be able to draw with some sense of order.
- He should know materials like wood, metal, leather, etc.

Kindergarten teachers know what specific skills they expect children to have when they come to class in September; you and your child's nursery school teacher have seen most of them develop over the course of the previous year. If you are concerned, ask the kindergarten teacher; she will probably calm your fears. One teacher had a stock answer for anxious parents who admitted hesitantly, "I haven't worked with my child on his numbers and letters yet."

"Congratulations!" she would exclaim. Handing them a gold star, she'd add, "You've earned this."

In addition, most teachers sit down and talk with small groups of prospective kindergartners in the late summer before school opens. This early get-together makes children feel more at ease about entering kindergarten and, at the same time, enables the teacher to evaluate each child's readiness. Because the teacher, unlike you, is able to view your child in relation to the group as a whole, she is in a good position to know whether he is ready. If a child cries and clings to his mother, constantly interrupts or bothers other children, she will express concern.

Children don't look at the session as a test and usually enjoy it. After finishing with an enthusiastic young teacher who played with him for close to an hour, putting puzzles together, building with blocks, drawing pictures, one child asked his mother, "Why did we play a long time? I'm not in school."

"It's to find out about being ready for school," she explained.

Nodding his head wisely, the little boy passed judgment: "I think she's ready."

"What if my child is not ready for kindergarten?"

If you feel your child is not ready, you would be wise to consult the kindergarten teacher, because your expectations for the child may be too high or your evaluation of him too low. Let the teacher talk with your child, as she does with the other children, and give you her opinion. If she says he is ready after her evaluation of the child and of your doubts, I suggest going along with her evaluation.

When a kindergarten teacher feels that your child is not ready for kindergarten, try to keep your pride uninvolved and realize she is not saying he is not smart enough. It is not a matter of intelligence but of maturity. Children mature at different rates, and when educators designate five as the age for kindergarten, they are considering averages. Some children are adequately mature at four, others not until six.

If your child is not ready for kindergarten, let him wait. Another year of nursery school will probably help him achieve the needed maturity. If he returns to the same nursery school, he may benefit from being one of the oldest; if he enters a different one, he may see it as a step forward and feel better. You and his teacher are in the best position to make this decision.

What is important is not pushing a child into kindergarten before he is able to handle it. If you do, he will become aware of his inadequacies in relation to the other children and develop a sense of failure that makes him either stop trying to keep up or act out aggressively. With such a destructive start, his future in school looks bleak.

"How can I prepare my child for kindergarten?"

While a positive nursery school experience may serve as good preparation for kindergarten, it does not always succeed. Small nursery schools, where five or six children meet in someone's home, may create so protected an atmosphere that some children still find the transition difficult. Even children who have been in larger nursery schools with fifteen or twenty classmates may find the transition to the different conditions in kindergarten somewhat frightening.

- · The classroom is large and probably part of a larger school building.
- · There are many more children to deal with.
- · The teacher gives less personal attention.
- · There is more noise.
- · The day may be longer.
- · There are more rules to follow.
- · The child has to meet higher expectations.

Specific preparation for kindergarten includes all of the steps suggested under "How can I get my child ready for nursery school?" with the following additions:

· If your child is to ride a school bus, familiarize him with the procedure beforehand—let him watch older children board the bus in the morning and leave it in the afternoon. Many school districts arrange a school bus ride for children who will be entering kindergarten; if your district does not, you might suggest it. If possible, have your child sit on the bus with an older sibling or a friend for the first week or so.

· If your child is used to a nap after lunch and is assigned to half-day kindergarten in the afternoon, ease him into a new nap habit before school starts. Otherwise he may become cranky and develop a dislike for kindergarten. Full-day kindergarten programs, which more and more schools now have, build nap time into the regular after-lunch activities.

· Work toward having your child dress himself, even put on his own shoes and socks, before he enters kindergarten. This accomplishment will make him feel independent and will also let him take care of himself in school—although the teacher's plea for children who can tie their own shoes may have been answered by Velcro! My son Eric was determined to assert his independence with no interference from me and wore his shoes on the wrong feet for the first week of school. On Friday when he came home from school, he handed me a note from his teacher:

> Dear Mrs. Miller,
>   I admire your restraint in letting Eric dress himself for school every morning. A lot of the boys don't tuck in their shirts or zip up their pants, and that is fine. But would you mind if I put his shoes on the right feet? I am worried about possible damage to his feet in the future.
>
>   Regards,
>   Mary Lewis

Eric is now in his thirties. I may claim partial credit for his self-reliance, but surely he owes his healthy feet to Miss Lewis.

· Let your child play on the school's outdoor equipment before school starts so he will look forward to fun. Don't overdo it, though, as little Joey's mother must have, for he reported with shock and indignation at the end of his first day, "She made us come inside."

· Take a special trip with him to buy pencils, an eraser and a pencil case, perhaps a lunch box if he needs it. Let the selections be his. You will get used to packing sandwiches in Batman or Barbie.

· Talk to your child often about kindergarten. Let him know that it is a grown-up step about which the whole family is extremely proud.

· Special Concerns for Kindergarteners ·

"What if my child is afraid of school?"

Two kinds of fear are common in kindergarten. One develops from insecurity in leaving home and can usually be overcome after you spend a few days in school with the child—fifteen minutes or so in the classroom and later waiting nearby. In addition, letting her take a picture of you or some small item, such as your scarf, may relieve fear of separation.

The second kind is less fear of school than fear of something specific in school. For instance, the teacher may yell at the class, or one of the other children may have hit your child or teased her, or she may have wet her pants and feel ashamed. As newspaper headlines have pointed out, there is even a possibility she may have been abused in school. The following suggestions should help ease her fear:

· Talk to your child about it. Discover the source of her fear. Even if she is reluctant to tell you, keep trying gently. "What are you afraid of?" will probably not elicit an answer. "I know that lots of things can seem scary at school. Will you tell me about some of them" is apt to bring forth an outpouring.
· No matter how trivial the source of your child's fear may seem to you, to her it is big and real. Acknowledge it as such.
· Talk to her teacher about her fear. If it stems from the actions of another child or from the teacher herself, she may be able to change them, thus ending the fearful situation. If it stems from embarrassment over something the child did, the teacher can offer her support and comfort.
· Take her into school for a few days.
· If there are any physical marks on the child, have her checked by a doctor.
· If the fear continues, ask for a conference with the school's psychologist, and see what she suggests.
· Do not let the child give in to the fear and stay home. If you do, the fear will not miraculously disappear, but may instead become a far more serious phobia.

· 67 ·

"What if my child begins wetting himself in kindergarten?"

The onset of wetting accidents indicates a heavy stress load, which your child is coping with by reverting to calmer baby days. If the stress is coming from school—too much pressure, too much independence, people or situations that are frightening, feelings of inadequacy, and so on—a talk with the teacher should bring relief. If the stress stems from home—new baby, divorce, absent parents, and so on—you should discuss it with the child and set up new patterns of action at home, if necessary. In either case, never make fun of a child for wetting his pants; treat it as matter-of-factly as a runny nose and look for the cause. If wetting continues, you may want professional advice.

"What if my child has temper tantrums in school?"

A child who throws temper tantrums in school has probably found them to be successful at home. Give yourself an honest appraisal here, and if you are guilty, stop giving in to the tantrums. Even though it is difficult, begin walking away from them instead. A mother told me that her son chose the most awkward times to throw a tantrum—"when I'm on the phone or have company"—and that she gave in to it to avoid embarrassment.

"He's a smart little boy to catch you when you're most vulnerable," I pointed out. "Why not just carry him to his room, tell him to stay until he can control himself, then close the door and return to your guests?" If your child has temper tantrums, you might try following the same advice. It worked in a short time for her.

Temper tantrums in school indicate that your child is frustrated at being unable to cope with something that is going on there. Suggest a three-way conference so that you, your child, and the teacher can get at the root of it. Together you may be able to alleviate the situation; if not, you can suggest other ways for her to act when she is frustrated.

I sat in on a conference with a little girl who banged her head on the wall whenever she could not have what she wanted. "She does it at home too," her mother said, sighing helplessly.

"Why do you bang the wall?" the teacher asked.

"I'm mad."

"Mad at the wall?"

"No."

"What are you mad at?"

"You," the child answered. "You're bossy."

"I guess it looks that way when I tell you what to do," the teacher said. Then, clapping her hands together, she suggested, "Let's see if we can find something that would make the mad go away . . . and I don't mean banging on me!" The little girl giggled. Then she, her teacher, and her mother had a brainstorming session, tossing out alternative outlets for the child's anger. The teacher had to remind her in class frequently, but that year the little girl painted a lot of pictures in bold, black strokes, played loud music on the piano low notes, and ran fast around the beech tree in the yard. I can't say she never had another temper tantrum, but they were fewer and farther between.

"What if my child hits other children?"

Like temper tantrums, aggressive behavior may highlight a child's immaturity and unawareness of other options he has in a situation that displeases him. A talk with him and his teacher may solve your problem. Make it clear that hitting and kicking are not acceptable and that your child will have to find some other way to express his anger. If you and the teacher suggest other ways he can let off steam, he may even add a few of his own.

On the other hand, aggressive behavior, especially in boys, may stem from subtle reinforcement at home, a practice parents may not even be aware of. A father who boasts that his six-year-old "can beat up that second-grade kid down the street," or the brother who teaches him how to land an uppercut conveys the message that aggressiveness wins acceptance. As a child's chief aim is to be considered okay, check to see whether your family is sending subtle messages that acting tough wins a pat on the back.

At its most serious, aggressive behavior may be a manifestation of repressed hurt and anger, which you or, if necessary, a professional must bring to the surface and discuss. A beautiful little second grader, whom I'll call Cary, was sent to my office for counseling one day after getting into a fight with a classmate. He sat trembling in rage on the couch next to me, his fists clenched. "I could beat you up," he said with a snarl.

"I'm sure you could," I said.

"I could punch you hard."

"Yes, you could hurt me, and I'd probably cry. I hope you don't want to because I like you so much."

The little boy remained quiet, looking down. Tears began to run down his still baby-soft cheeks. Sniffling, he said, "I could punch you right now, you know."

"I know," I whispered softly, pulling him into my arms, where he lay until his body relaxed and his fists opened into chubby hands.

I called his mother after he returned to class. She explained that his father, from whom she was divorced, had promised to spend Sunday with him. Cary had waited all afternoon. He wouldn't eat dinner, wouldn't go to bed, finally fell asleep by the front door. In the morning, saying nothing, he left for school as usual, but his little body could not contain the big hurt, and Cary lashed out.

"It's not the first time his father has let him down," Cary's mother told me.

"And it's not the first fight," I acknowledged. "Let's talk together and get some help."

If your child fights with other children, try to look at his home situation realistically. Is something going on to build hurt and resentment—a new baby who gets all the attention? Overly harsh discipline? Not enough time with Mom and Dad? Too high expectations? Sibling jealousy? There are a hundred other possibilities that, unknown to you, may cause pain which festers into resentment and anger and finally finds release in violence.

If your child continues aggressive behavior in school and you cannot identify or change its cause, turn to a professional for guidance.

· 70 ·

"What if my child is different in school than he is at home?"

I remember a mother at a conference who was convinced the teacher had her confused with some other child's mother when she said, "Your son seems to be behaving a little bit better this past month, but he still upsets the class."

"No." The woman smiled confidently. "I'm Bobby Jackson's mother."

"Yes, I know," the teacher answered.

Very often angels at home toss off their halos in the classroom.

On the other hand, the scene is just as often played this way:

"I don't know what to do about Timmy. He drives us all crazy at home," says the mother.

"Why, I can't understand that," the teacher replies, beaming. "He is such an angel at school."

"Are you sure you mean Timmy Butler?"

If children become Jekylls and Hydes upon entering kindergarten, there are a number of possible explanations.

The school angel may act up at home because he is allowed to and behave cooperatively at school because he is expected to. If so, the cure is simple: Establish greater expectations and guidelines for meeting those expectations at home.

It is also possible, however, that a child lets off steam at home after keeping the lid on it all day in school because home is where he is loved no matter how he acts. When Danny's mother asked him why he acted so ugly when he came home from school every day, he explained, "I don't want my teacher to see."

"Why not? You don't seem to care that I see," said his mother.

"Yeah, but she wouldn't like me," he answered.

As an adult, you are under pressure yourself much of the time—at work or on social occasions—when you have to behave because you don't want someone "to see." You know how it feels. Let your child know that you understand why he acts up when he comes home. Say something like "I know it's hard to do all the things you're supposed to in school, and I know you need to let off steam when you come home. We love you even when you're grumpy, but we can't have fun together when you act like that."

At the same time, you have to let your child know that, no matter how he feels, he has no right to tyrannize the family. "You can't keep doing that," you will have to explain, "because no one has a right to hurt the rest of us. You wouldn't want us to do it to you."

Help your child find other ways to release the tensions of school. Some children need a rough-and-tumble outdoor game; others relax better when the parent or caretaker reads them a story; Noah and Darcy used singing and dancing as a way to let off after-school steam; and I know a child who calms down in a warm bubble bath. Sometimes after interacting with so many children in school all day, just playing alone may be the best way for a child to stabilize.

On the other hand, the home angel who acts up in school may be under such severe threats of discipline at home that he is afraid to misbehave and, therefore, releases his steam where his parents cannot see—at school. In this case parents should reevaluate their disciplinary procedures with a view to making changes. A child who grows up thinking his parents love him only when he is "good" is headed for a great deal of trouble.

"What if kindergarten is exhausting my child?"

If a child returns from kindergarten too exhausted to eat or do much more than fuss, if you are certain she is getting enough sleep, the problem may be too demanding a program. Arrange with the teacher and principal to let her begin the year by staying through only half of the day. As she adjusts to it, she can remain longer until she is able to handle the full program. If extreme fatigue continues, take her to the doctor for a checkup.

If your child is overexhausted by kindergarten, if she begins wetting or throwing temper tantrums or hitting other children, and if these symptoms persist, perhaps she is not mature enough for kindergarten yet. Talk to her teacher and principal about letting her wait another year.

"How academic should the kindergarten program be?"

· 72 ·

The purpose of kindergarten is readiness—to get children ready to begin learning the basic skills with which they will be challenged in first grade. In other words, academics happen in first grade; readiness to undertake them happens in kindergarten.

Therefore, in answer to the questions I have been asked a hundred times by parents:

· No, I don't think a child should be taught to read in kindergarten. If he picks up reading by himself, fine, but don't push it.

· No, I don't think a child should have homework in kindergarten. His work at home should be playing and listening to stories and putting napkins on the dinner table and going to the market with his parents.

CHAPTER 6

Getting Started in Elementary School

· The Needs of Elementary-Age Children ·

The child from six to twelve is very different from the preschool child: Whereas the latter is ruled from within as she struggles to understand the larger world, the former is ruled from the outside. She wants rules and order and competition through which she can find her place. She wants outside stimulation to motivate her interests. She wants responsibilities in order to assert her independence. Psychologists have named these years, give or take a year or two on either side, the latency period because the inner drives of younger years quiet down for a rest before resurfacing in the rigors of puberty and adolescence.

"How can an elementary school meet the needs of my child?"

- It must have space—both physical and emotional—in which this independence-seeking child can feel like an individual and not just part of a mass.
- It must have some degree of individualized instruction so that the child may grow in his unique way, not as an image of the whole class as the teacher sees it.
- It must create an environment that stimulates children into self-teaching—science to explore, animals to care for, books about real people—so children will become lifelong learners.
- It must give children real-life problems to solve and decisions to make so they may begin to develop their individual conscience and morality.
- At the same time, it must set down clearly defined guidelines, for only within them can children this age find the freedom they need to grow.
- Above all, it must provide a new set of role models for children as their worldview expands beyond Mother, Father, and family to include teachers and principal and classmates.

"What kinds of elementary schools best meet these needs?"

At this level, I consider coeducational schools more constructive for most children than single-sex schools because they more accurately reflect the real world into which children are fitting themselves as boys and girls.

Preoccupation with sex does not set in until sixth grade or so. The sexual problem of the elementary grades is quite the opposite: Boys and girls stay as far away from each other as possible. I remember three girls who swept into my office like the Furies when a teacher assigned a boy to their table in the hope of settling him down. They were in no mood for charitable deeds!

When I asked Noah in third grade who were his friends in the new class, he said with a sweep of his arm, "Every one of them." Then, lest I should misunderstand, he added quickly, "Except the girls, of course." Of course.

I strongly favor day schools over boarding schools for elementary school children except in cases where the home is incorrigibly destructive. The normal family can provide more love and security and far more personal involvement than even the most caring school. A large part of growing up evolves from learning to survive the pains and frustrations that arise in family relationships and that become bonding cement. Children whose parents lend support in weathering these frustrations grow stronger in trust and self-esteem.

I think nonreligious schools tend to provide a more panoramic background against which to guide children into forming their own beliefs than do religion-oriented schools. However, the religious training in church-related schools offers strong guidelines for religious and personal behavior and reinforces at least early adherence to a faith, which parents may hold as a high priority.

Many parents send their children to a religious school as an alternative to a public school they feel is inadequate. Some church-related schools, especially Catholic parochial schools, are considerably less expensive than regular private schools and usually have a more disciplined environment than public schools. Because they provide a similar traditional basic education, parents turn to them, particularly in large urban areas.

When it comes to school philosophy, I must confess a bias. I favor open and Montessori over traditional schools at the elementary level because their environment affords greater opportunity for children to test their independence, their conscience, and their sense of responsibility. In addition, they give children an opportunity to work on individualized programs that assure them of progressive levels of success. A child in a traditional school, which aims at grade level rather than individual goals, is more apt to see himself when not successful as an all-round failure.

Before selecting a Montessori school, I suggest that parents learn something about the philosophy upon which the program is built. You can talk to a Montessori teacher or read one of many books on the subject. *Montessori, a Modern Approach* by Paula Lillard (Schocken Books, 1988) explains the method fully and understandably.

One aspect of Montessori schools that I consider particularly beneficial for this age group is the lack of competitiveness. Children do not receive marks, and a great deal of the work is done in teams so that children can understand the strength of cooperation when they enter the too-competitive adult world.

In selecting an open school, parents must ascertain that they are getting open learning, not open chaos. The teacher in a good open school knows precisely what each child is working on, what level of achievement he has attained, and what he has to do. At every plateau she introduces him to another opportunity to climb. Although the child discovers learning himself, the teacher makes sure the adventure is in reach.

To be fair, I must point out that many educators disagree with me. They think traditional schools demand more learning and prepare students far better for the real world of hard work, mental discipline, and competition. The choice is yours.

There is no way to advise you whether to choose an independent or a public elementary school. I have seen the best in each of them, and I have seen the worst. The best advice is to check carefully before deciding: The child who receives a good elementary school education will have a much easier and happier time in all future schools.

· Concerns in Starting Elementary School ·

"Does my child have to go to kindergarten?"

Kindergarten is a fairly recent addition to American education. In the past parents kept children at home until they were old enough to enter first grade. When educational studies began to reveal the advantages of kindergarten in preparing children for first grade, kindergartens for five-year-olds sprang up and are now offered in all fifty states.

Some educators today believe that because children mature more quickly than they used to, they should enter kindergarten at four instead of five and then first grade at five instead of six. In this way, they contend, children would graduate from high school a year earlier and avoid the social problems that arise from teenage boredom. I disagree; I am firmly convinced that six is none too old for a child to shoulder the stressful responsibility of school.

Six-year-olds, I think, are well prepared for first grade when they spend a year in a good kindergarten. Parents can do part of the job at home, but the introduction to school and class rules and social interaction that kindergarten offers make adjustment to first grade quicker and easier for children.

"When is my child ready for first grade?"

There is a great deal of talk these days about readiness. When Adam's parents received his end-of-year report card from kindergarten, they read aloud with pride, "Adam is ready for first grade."

"I'm ready too," his three-year-old sister chimed in.

"You are not," Adam assured her firmly.

"Are too," she insisted. "I got pencils."

Obviously it takes a great deal more than pencils to be ready for first grade. Yes answers to the following questions will give you an indication.

- Has your child the emotional maturity to express her feelings in positive rather than negative ways?
- Has she the social maturity to work and play with groups of other children?
- Has she large-motor skills to handle her body with ease and pleasure?
- Has she small-motor skills for writing and reading and working arithmetic, for artwork and for dressing herself?
- Has she conceptual understanding in order to follow directions and comprehend what she reads and listens to?
- Has she oral language in order to communicate basic needs and feel some control of her life?
- Can she take responsibility for her possessions and for herself?
- Does she know letters and numbers by sound and sight and understand their use?
- Above all, does she feel good about herself—capable of success in work and in friendships?

When you and her kindergarten teacher can answer yes to most of these questions, your child is probably ready for first grade. In their book *Your Six Year Old*, Louise Bates Ames and Frances Ilg (Dell, 1981) give a more specific checklist for parents who question their child's readiness for first grade. A high percentage of yes answers should ease your mind. If you get too many nos, talk to your child's kindergarten teacher.

1. Does the kindergarten teacher consider her ready?
2. Will she be six before school starts?
3. Does she seem as mature to you as her classmates?
4. Do you see signs of six year old rebelliousness creeping into the easy amiability of the fives?
5. Can she copy a triangle, a rectangle with divided lines crossing the center and a circle counterclockwise, starting at the top?

6. Does she hold a pencil well?
7. Can she print her first name?
8. Can she recognize capital and lower case letters separately?
9. Can she count to thirty?
10. Can she write numbers to twenty?
11. Does she know her right from left hand?
12. Does she know how old she is and in what month she was born?
13. Can she stand on one foot for the count of eight?
14. Can she throw a ball overhand?
15. Can she tie her shoelaces? (Or does she have Velcro?)
16. Can she repeat four numbers in a row the first time?
17. Can she add and subtract within twenty?

"What if the teacher wants to hold my child back?"

Not every child is ready for first grade at the end of the kindergarten year. Some are simply too immature to go on, and parents have to realize that "immature" is not a dirty word. As a principal I know said to a parent who was furious at being told her son should wait a year, "If you can't be immature in kindergarten, when on earth can you?"

Although you may see signs of maturity at home that the teacher is unaware of, you must remember that the teacher sees your child in relation to his peers. If he can't ride a tricycle or cut paper or draw a figure at their level, then he would be entering first grade with a handicap that could block his learning for the next twelve years. Some teachers, in the face of parental argument, resort to objective tests as a way to evaluate children, but most find their own observation equally accurate and far more humane.

A teacher does not easily or quickly make the decision to hold a child back. It is difficult, and there are convincing arguments on both sides.

Educators who favor holding children back if they have not reached a certain level after kindergarten use these arguments.

· Children who start first grade behind their classmates struggle all through school.
· A child at the top of the age level in school is a better student than one at the bottom.
· Kindergarten-age children are too young to feel a stigma at being held back.
· If a child is given a different kindergarten teacher, she will have the experience of a new grade.

- The kindergarten teacher should ask the child herself whether she feels she should go ahead, because she knows when she is unable to keep up with her classmates.
- When children are pushed into grades beyond their ability, they tend to develop behavior problems.
- Children who cannot keep up with classwork often develop a sense of failure in other areas of their life and give up trying.
- Early intervention has proven more successful in warding off children's problems than later treatment has in curing them. Therefore, a child has a better chance of avoiding trouble if she gets off to good start by repeating kindergarten.
- The biggest block to holding children back is not the child, but the parents, whose egos hate to admit their child "couldn't make the grade."

On the other hand, educators who oppose holding back kindergarten children even when they seem unready for first grade argue as follows.

- Because children mature at different rates, a child who is behind in kindergarten may suddenly catch up in first grade or even second.
- Teachers should ask the child. If, in spite of difficulties, she wants to go on with her classmates, let her.
- There is no reason to believe a second year of kindergarten would be any more profitable than the first.
- The stress of being singled out as less able than her classmates may so wound a child's self-esteem that she will remain a poor achiever throughout school.
- The child will suffer so much at leaving her classmates that she will never be able to view school in a positive light.
- Many schools hold children back not to help the children but in order to raise the schools' reading scores; a low achiever in first grade lowers the average.

Both sides have voices of authority to support their arguments.

Dr. Ames of the Gesell Institute of Human Development has always counseled parents this way: "We maintain that even if it is traumatic to keep them back, it's better to traumatize them once and get it over with than to face problems every day for the next twelve years."

On the other hand, *The New York Times* reported Dr. John Goodlad of the Center for Educational Renewal at the University of Washington as saying "The research shows that you're better off promoting a child. The promoted group does better academically, socially and emotionally. Keeping kids back in kindergarten is immoral."

What should you do if a teacher wants to hold your kindergartner back for a year?

· You can refuse and tell the teacher, "I simply will not allow you to do this." With enough determination you may win your case, but what if the teacher is right? You may find the following year that you have won only a Pyrrhic victory, as your child founders in first grade.

· You can readily acquiesce and say, "All right. Whatever you say." But what if the teacher is wrong? Your submission will not only create a problem for you and your child, but will indicate your belief that the child's future belongs to the teacher more than to you.

· You can ask for (and demand, if the school gives you any trouble) a conference with your child's teacher and the principal. The point of the conference is not to defend your child or to belittle him; it is to get information. Without hostility, you could begin by saying "I'd like to know why you think my child should be held back."

If they reply, "He seems too immature to handle first grade," you should pursue the question, asking to know specific areas in which he is less mature than his classmates.

If they point out that he has not yet acquired the necessary skills, ask them to identify which skills he lacks.

Then before deciding whether or not to consent, ask the most important question of all: "If he stays back, what do you propose to do with him?"

Schools have met this question in several ways. Small schools often have no alternative to having the child repeat kindergarten year in the same room with the same teacher. Under these circumstances I have known parents who withdrew their children, put them in a different kindergarten for a year, and then let them return in first grade or, in some cases, remain in the new school. It worked.

Schools large enough to have more than one section of kindergarten will have the child repeat the year in a different room with a different teacher. Here he has a new personality with whom to interact and, as a result, new teaching/learning approaches. This usually works too.

Some schools have come up with a still better solution: They have developed an interim class between kindergarten and first grade in which children are given a chance to catch up as they grow up. From this grade, those whose growth has taken a spurt may be able to go directly to second grade the following year, while the rest will advance with their classmates to a first grade whose challenges they can now meet.

Risk is involved in whatever decision parents and teachers make in regard to holding back an unready kindergarten child. If he is held back, it is possible that he could have gone ahead and blossomed the following year; if he goes on to first grade, it is also possible that he may wither in the face of failure.

My own experience over many years has led me to take the risk on what I consider the safer side—holding the child back. If an unready child is held back when he should have been promoted, schools can correct the error with a minimum of woe by advancing him in September or October. Although the switch may entail a short period of catching up, it builds, rather than tears down, the child's self-esteem. However, if an unready child is promoted when he should have been retained, the remedy of returning to kindergarten or repeating a grade later in elementary school creates an enduring emotional trauma.

Grade placement by age is a decision we are slowly coming to realize is arbitrary, for as an English teacher way back in the sixteenth century realized, "Ripeness in children does not always come at the same time."

· 81 ·

"If my child is already reading, should I have her skip first grade?"

Except in unusual cases, I think skipping a grade is not the best way to help advanced children. There is more to be learned in first grade than the three Rs, particularly how to live within a class community of peers. First-grade children put into a grade with older, more mature children may never catch up socially and may find themselves handicapped throughout school. Let me quote an answer I received from a high school boy in response to a question I asked his class: If you could wave a magic wand, what would you change in your past school experience?

> I would not skip a grade, which I did in elementary school. Being with older kids always made me feel like an outsider, and I never had a best friend. When the boys in my class got interested in girls, I was still into

robots, and you can be sure the girls didn't get interested in me. I'm looking forward to college when I can move away and start all over again.

If you have a child whom you or the school thinks should skip a grade, please reconsider. Chapter 19 points out alternative solutions.

"Should I get my child switched if her friends are in a different class?"

On the first day of every school year, as the principal I used to see a handful of elementary children go home in tears because their friends are in another section and they didn't get the teacher they wanted. On the second day the mothers were in my office asking me to switch their child to another class. "None of her friends are in the class with her, and she doesn't think it's fair. I don't think so either," they would say. I would summon up my strength, say no, and strive to explain my reason. Here goes again!

One of the major lessons of life is survival in a world less than perfect, and I sincerely believe that elementary school is not too early to begin learning it. When parents constantly smooth out unpleasant situations for their child—such as a class without best friends or a teacher she didn't want—they deny her the confidence that comes from working out her own problems. Ego strength builds from the exultation of "I handled it alone."

Instead of trying to have your child's class switched, you can give her more solid help by evaluating the situation with her. She knows what's bad about being in a class without her friends or without the teacher she hoped for. You can help her see some advantages that may offset the bad. Try some of these arguments.

- "You'll still see your old friends—at lunch and recess and after school. You're not losing them."
- "You'll make new friends."
- "Give the teacher a chance. Maybe you'll discover you like him after all."
- "Look. You are going to have to face a good many disappointments in life; no one escapes them. Think how getting through this one will help you handle the rest."
- "You'll still have some teachers you're crazy about,

won't you? Like Miss Kramer in gym and Mr. Horton
in art."
· "Wait a minute. Don't all the sections have music together? And gym too? So you'll see your friends in
some classes."

If your arguments fall on deaf ears and your child's complaints
continue to resound in yours, there is only one thing left to say: "I
know you're disappointed, but that's the way it is, darling; let's make
the best of it! You can come to me with your misery whenever you
want, but as the old song says, *Qué será será*."

"When should my child start getting homework?"

In most schools homework begins in first grade, with children
spending ten or fifteen minutes practicing their letters and numbers
and later reading and writing short sentences. I personally don't think
homework is necessary in first or second grade because the children
are still getting used to the rigors of a full day of work, but teachers
have their reasons for giving it. Some think it builds good study habits,
and others think it enables children to learn at a faster pace. I was more
in tune with the teacher who explained, "I give homework because the
children want it; it makes them feel grown-up." And I relived years of
parent confrontations, like a drowning person whose life flashes before
him, when a teacher told me, "I simply got worn out by pushy parents
when I didn't give homework; so now I do."

· *83* ·

Don't complain that a teacher does not give enough, or any, homework. Children in the early elementary grades can learn plenty during
the day in class. A more valid complaint is probably that the homework
is too repetitive: If a child can do three multiplication problems, why
make him do twenty? If he *can't* do one, why give him twenty he can't
do?

I have seen schools that give no daily homework through elementary
school but do all kinds of learning projects in class; others that give
only weekly assignments; and still others that assign work only to
children who have not completed work in class. Parents should not
use big homework assignments as the criterion of a good school any
more than children should use no homework as a criterion.

Like beauty, homework is often in the eye of the beholder. The last
few times I have visited my grandchildren, I have seen Noah busily
working at the computer, surrounded by library books and the ever-

present encyclopedia. "I thought your teacher didn't give homework," I commented.

"He doesn't," Noah took time out to say. "This isn't homework; it's a project."

If you think that your child's school is inadequate, you may have real cause for concern. Take a close look at the curriculum, the teacher, and even at your child; chances are homework has nothing to do with it.

"We're moving; is entering a new school going to pose problems?"

When you move, particularly if you move out of state, your child may find that his preparation from the previous school does not jibe with that of his new classmates. If he has already covered the work and is above the level of his classmates, he may be in for a year of boredom unless the school sizes up the situation and does something about it. If the school fails to take the initiative, it is up to you to insist on one of several options:

- The school can put your child in a higher grade. You should consider this option cautiously because, as I indicated earlier, this might cause him discomfort with his peers.
- The school can arrange for your child to remain in his age group but take his strongest subjects with a higher grade. Most school schedules can accommodate this arrangement, which works well both for the school and the child.
- The school may be able to individualize a program for him in his regular grade. The more open a classroom is, the more flexibility it has to develop programs to meet a child's specific needs.

On the other hand, when your child enters a new school, he may find himself behind the rest of the class, which could cause him to struggle fruitlessly all year or simply give up. Here too you can insist on one of these options:

- The school can place your child in a lower grade. While staying back in the same school may cause embarrassment and defeatism in a child, repeating a year in a new school carries far less stigma. When your child understands that he is repeating not because of any failure on his part but because the new school has different requirements, he will probably adjust quickly. I speak not only from professional but from personal experience, having repeated fourth grade when I moved from a public to a private school.

• The school can design an individualized program to help him catch up to his classmates.

• His teachers can set aside regular hours during the day in which to give him extra help. I have seen this done successfully in the morning before school starts and after school. If the school suggests that he miss other classes, such as art or music, in order to receive extra help during the day, ask for another solution, because those classes are important too.

• If no plan works out satisfactorily, you can always resort to having your child privately tutored. Although this involves an additional expense, it is only temporary and may offer a quicker and easier solution than any other.

"How can I tell if my child is placed in the wrong grade?" • 85 •

Although children mature at their own individual rates, our system of education assigns them to classes at a group rate, using age as the measurement. So insistent are schools in adhering to the age determinant that admission to kindergarten—which is the starting gate of most elementary schools—cuts off at a specific month! It is only common sense that a certain number of children, which educators estimate as high as one in three, do not belong in the grade to which they are assigned.

To complicate matters, despite the fact that boys mature later than girls, both sexes are placed in grades according to the same chronological age. It is no surprise, therefore, that five times more elementary school boys have trouble than girls. If grades were assigned by behavioral age instead of chronological age, the problem would greatly diminish.

If you think your child may be in the wrong grade, look for the following signs.

If your child is in a grade too high for her:

• She may begin acting out in class.
• She may stop trying—refuse to do homework, play truant, and so on.

- She may complain of headaches, stomachaches, and so on.
- She may be receiving comments from her teacher such as "She is not trying" or "She doesn't finish his work."
- She may consistently lose her homework.
- She may hate school.
- She may begin calling herself "dumb," "stupid," "bad," and so on.

If your child is in a grade too low for her:

- She may complain of boredom.
- She may begin acting silly in class.
- She may not do her homework.
- She may be receiving teacher comments such as "She daydreams," "She won't concentrate," or "She doesn't pay attention."
- She may not participate in class.
- She may not want to talk about school at home.

Few children will show all of these signs if they are mismatched to their class. If your child shows some of them over a period of time, though, you may have reason to think she may be in the wrong grade. Talk to her teacher and to the school principal. Talk to your child too because she will know if the work is too difficult or too easy. Misplacement may not be at the root of her behavior; but if it is, the earlier you can rectify the matter, the more easily your child will readjust to another grade.

Selma Fraiberg wrote of early childhood as the magic years, and television has produced a show about junior high school called *The Wonder Years*. Elementary school seems lost in the shuffle. Yet it is these years from six through eleven that children enter as *little* girls and *little* boys and exit simply as girls and boys. In these years they live life in the calm of latency before plunging into the turbulence of adolescence. In these years they play and laugh, exulting in the distances to which they can reach outward with no foreshadowings of the distances to which they will soon have to reach inward. I call them the sparkling years.

CHAPTER 7

Getting Started in Junior High

· Various Types of Schools for the Middle Years ·

One of the most noticeable changes in the structuring of American schools in recent years has been in the education of twelve- to fourteen-year-olds. Until about thirty years ago, educators grouped seventh and eight graders with elementary school children, and even the *Statistical Abstract of the United States* today fails to provide separate figures for that age group. Yet it does not require an advanced degree in child development for anyone to realize that the needs of thirteen- and four-teen-year-olds differ widely from those of their elementary school sib-lings. To lump them all together in one school program denied these differences and set up additional roadblocks for an age group that even under the best conditions has difficulty traveling the road.

After educators acknowledged preadolescents as a separate entity, they began developing schools for them. Nevertheless, as recently as the 1960s there were still only about seven thousand junior high schools throughout the country, almost all encompassing grades seven and eight. Today there are over twelve thousand offering a wide variety of combinations. Because individual differences abound within this age group, schools have developed a variety of groupings, under different names, in their search for the "perfect" combination.

- Junior high school usually includes grades 7, 8, and 9.
- Intermediate school is limited to grades 7 and 8.
- Middle school may include almost any selection and arrangement of grades 4, 5, 6, 7, and 8, although the majority group grades 6, 7, and 8 together.

Administrators may determine their grouping on the mere fact of school-age population distribution within specific districts, or they may decide on more scientific grounds: which age groups adhere most closely. The Board of Education informs me that New York City, which has all three kinds of schools, uses the former criteria, while I know many schools in other parts of the country that have based their school grouping on educational studies.

While I cannot give a specific account of the three kinds of schools because they differ widely among themselves, I can give some broad generalizations:

- Most public school systems have junior high and/or intermediate schools. They feel they can most efficiently prepare children for high school in this way.
- Most parochial schools include grades 7 and 8 within the elementary school. This enables the diocese to control children's education up until high school, at which point they enter either a public or a Catholic private high school.
- Most independent schools have middle schools. They view these years not as a preparation for high school so much as a developmental period that requires a special kind of fostering.

To avoid confusion, I am going to refer to all three kinds of middle years schools as junior high schools.

· The Needs of Junior High Schoolers ·

Years ago there was a book I love entitled *How to Live Through Junior High School* by Eric Johnson (Lippincott, 1975). Parents who have raised children understand why the author addressed the book to them, not to their children.

Children in the age bracket of twelve to fourteen are struggling through limbo, no longer children, not yet adolescents. I think of them as the Almost Children: Unsure of where they belong, they flip between the relatively serene behavior they have *almost* outgrown and the turbulent behavior they are *almost* growing into. Their behavior, surprising to their parents, surprises themselves even more.

While parents rarely know what to expect from these children one moment to the next, they do know the years are difficult for the entire family. As a father of a thirteen-year-old girl said, "I just wish I could go to sleep for two years!"

"Me too," his daughter said with a sigh.

Surprised and pleased to find something—anything—that he and his daughter shared, the father asked, "You mean you want to disappear for two years too?"

"Of course not." She sneered. "I want you to." They both lived through junior high—awake!

Let me identify the chief characteristics of the twelve- to fourteen-year-old. You may find comfort in discovering that your child is not an aberration and in understanding why the years are not easy.

Rebellion is the keyword. Responding to their natural urge to assert themselves as separate beings, preadolescents press their parents to the limit. They reject everything their parents endorse, from manners to morals, conveying a message of hostility and abandonment. Underneath the surface, however, it is as difficult for them to leave the security and protection of childhood as it is for their parents to feel them slip away.

Parents have an easier time though because they can say "I want to hold on to my baby" without a sense of failure; in fact, the words, spoken or not, reinforce the positive parenting they hope they have done. Children, on the other hand, can't say "I want to hold on to my mommy and daddy" without admitting defeat, because what they are trying to do is become independent.

What prevents an easy transition is the ambiguity of a preadolescent's feelings, which, lacking the maturity to confront, she attempts to handle aggressively. If she can't slide out of childhood, she will fight her way out. If you react to your child's rebellion with hostility of your own instead of with grin-and-bear-it patience, you only prolong the period of rebellion and increase its intensity.

Self-consciousness. Preadolescents feel under scutiny and embarrassed most of the time—over the changes their bodies are rapidly undergoing, over the feelings stirring within them toward both their own and the opposite sex, over their weaknesses and inadequacies, over the way they look. It is difficult for parents, especially those whose children are bright and beautiful, to realize the pain they suffer. When I used to tell Darcy at nine, "Gee, you're pretty," she would beam and reply, "I know." Today at thirteen, she stands in front of the mirror making faces and declares, "I am *so* ugly."

Conformity. Preadolescents cope with their self-consciousness by becoming carbon copies of their friends and of the rock stars, sports heroes, and movie and TV personalities they and their friends idolize. Behind the facade of similar hairdos, T-shirts, and sneakers, with borrowed walk, talk, and attitude, they feel comfortable at last. They belong.

Product and clothing manufacturers get rich on conformity, which sends preadolescents in droves to buy the look of everyone else. Parents, on the other hand, get frantic because the look is not what they expected: shirts with wild pictures, tight pants, jackets that would fit their father. A mother picking up her eighth grader after school one day complained, "You all look alike. I couldn't tell you from the other kids."

"Mom," the boy said with a smile, "you've just given me the first compliment in a year."

Sex. Sexual stirrings cause preadolescents not only embarrassment but titillation such as they have never known. They are fearful, excited, curious, experimenting with sex by word and action, bragging about it, lying, hoping. They are in a constant state of budding spring, which arrives about two years earlier for girls than for boys and much earlier for either than parents dare to admit. If you deny a child's sexual stirrings and make him so afraid or guilty that he will deny them too, you do not make what you consider a problem go away. You only make it hide underground until it can erupt later. Sex is a major part of a preadolescent's life; parents have to face it.

Identity. When Erik Erikson introduced the world to the term "identity crisis," he labeled a transition that begins in the junior high years and continues into high school and college and sometimes throughout life. In essence, an identity crisis is the inner search for oneself, undertaken when a child no longer sees himself existing as part of his parents or as part of his peer group, but feels the need to be his own unique person. You might understand the pain and disorientation of the identity crisis better by comparing it to intense labor in giving birth to a baby.

I know a restrictive family that took pride in their trouble-free children all through these middle years. While other parents faced the usual upheavals involving tears, arguments, slammed doors, and death wishes, the family wrapped themselves up smugly in a job well done. Five years later, however, when most parents could heave a sigh of relief at having passed through the eye of the storm, the parents in this family were just entering the hurricane; their daughter, now in college, was on drugs, and their son had dropped out of high school.

The identity struggle is bound to come. Parents can make it easier—and safer—for their children by relaxing their hold so that it can come at a time when children are still at home where they can help.

"What should I look for in a good junior high?"

Flexibility.
Because your preadolescent is in a continual state of flux, the school can best meet his needs when it is structured to give him leeway. Look for ways in which your school adapts, such as these:

· Flexible schedules that do not run by the school bell. English can have a double period when the teacher needs it; math and science can meet together for a joint project; the librarian can have a period or a half period when needed. This provides teachers and students time to finish what they begin instead of being cut short by time slots.

· Some choice in subject matter. While students have certain required courses, good schools give them a choice within the requirements: soccer or football; earth or life science; world history or ancient Greece; and so on. By high school they fill in the necessary gaps.

· Diverse teaching methods—including team teaching, computer programs, individual projects, and theme teaching, in which all subjects focus on one country or one time in history. This overcomes the fragmentation of learning that sets it miles away from a preadolescent's life experiences.

· Interchangeable groupings so that a child is not slotted into seventh grade, but may take different subjects with different groups. In this way particular interests and abilities can be met.

· Hands-on experimentation. This entails learning by doing in place of learning from a textbook, a process of discovery to which this age group responds enthusiastically.

Individualization.
Despite outward conformity, children at this age have an endless range of interests, maturity levels, aptitudes, emotions, levels of concentration, and independence. To expect such a heterogeneous group to learn the same thing in the same way at the same time is totally unrealistic and accounts for much of the failure preadolescents experience in school. The most successful junior high teachers develop in-

dividualized programs for children, alone or with small groups, so that they may not only meet basic requirements but go as far as their interests and ability carry them. (Individualization will be fully discussed in Chapter 14.)

Sex education.

Preadolescents need information on sex to set straight the myriad myths and rumors they have picked up. They also need to learn far more: the responsibility people in a relationship have to each other, the danger of exploiting someone or of being exploited, the strength of marriage, the meaning of friendship. Twenty years ago Dr. Mary Calderon made educators aware that sex education involves far more than what she referred to as "plumbing courses."

Too many school systems used to wait until high school, even senior year, to provide sex education. According to statistics on pregnancy, venereal disease, and the onset of sexual activity, by high school students have already provided their own sex education. The junior high years are the perfect time to clarify information and help students develop attitudes and values on a subject that is all but consuming them. Please understand that I do not mean to eliminate sex education from elementary schools. On the contrary, I think it should begin in kindergarten and continue throughout; I have developed and supervised such a program. I do feel, however, that sex education in these middle years is the most crucial.

Drug education.

Because of the intensity of peer pressure in these years, drug education can have a strong impact. A good program can help children conform to the nonuse of drugs instead of to the abuse of them in order "to be cool." The ready availability of drugs to almost any junior high schooler, plus the tragic impact of the AIDS epidemic among drug users, demands not the perfunctory one-shot schools used to provide but a strong, ongoing drug program.

Stimulation.

Some teachers complain that junior high schoolers "couldn't care less"; other teachers find them so absorbed that they fail to hear the bell ring when class ends, and parents can't get them away from their homework at night. The difference lies not in different children so much as in different teachers. It is true that children this age are easily bored by traditional schoolwork, but when they are turned on, watch out! A teacher who lets students design and execute projects that involve them in real-life situations, who guides students into re-creating history instead of memorizing it, who lets students prepare their own classes to teach, who encourages them to research and write about their own interests—this teacher will have no bored junior high schoolers.

I met a social studies teacher who came to class every Monday dressed as a character in history and answered questions until the first child guessed who he was. There were no bored students in his class. Nor were there in a combined science and math class in which each student had to become an inventor and re-create the circumstances of his invention and his findings. Nor are there now in the hundreds of classes I have never seen, but where I know junior high school teachers have their students so engrossed in projects that they forget to watch the clock.

Student input.

Children in these middle years thrive in a democratic environment and either wilt or turn hostile in a dictatorship. Teachers and administrators in a good junior high school listen to students and let them influence many areas of school life. I have seen successful schools where students handle the discipline of minor offenders; others where they have weekly meetings with the principal to air complaints and offer suggestions; others where they give counseling help to their peers; and others where they write teacher evaluations for the administration.

A parent told me with some concern of the junior high her daughter attended, asking if I thought it could be any good. It seems the girl had brought home her report card and presented it to her parents, who were less than pleased with a row of Cs and C minuses. "This isn't too good," her father said. The girl agreed.

"Do you think the marks are fair?" her mother asked.

"Of course I do. I'm the one who gave them."

The girl's school believes in student self-evaluation as a stronger motivator than the teacher evaluations to which most students are accustomed. I suggested to the parents that they could tell how good the school was if the marks on the next report card began showing improvement. They did.

· 93 ·

"What kinds of junior high schools will meet these needs?"

A school adapted to meet the individual needs of this explosive, heterogeneous group of young people can do the best job of educating them.

Open schools, which may be either public or private, allow students to learn through their own initiative far more than traditional ones. A good example is a seventh grader I knew whom nobody could motivate to study until he was placed in an open class. Realizing his passion for baseball, his teachers let him read and write baseball stories and study math by computing and analyzing statistics. In this way, the open classroom not only enabled the boy to acquire verbal and math skills, but turned him on to learning in a new way that has lasted into college.

While there are fewer open schools today than there were in the sixties and seventies, they still are available in many areas. As educators have found that inner-city nonachievers in a traditional school often come to life under the fail-proof system of individualization, many urban areas have opened alternative schools for just such children.

Under pressure from parents opposed to the academic competitiveness of their schools, some suburban districts also offer open education at the junior high level. Some provide an open school as an alternative for parents, while other smaller schools may offer an open track within the regular school.

Rural schools seem to combine elements of open teaching as a matter of necessity because their population, drawn from a wide area, presents the challenge of great diversity in background and ability. In addition, rural schools have to cope with long distances, troublesome weather, and even intermittent periods of absence when children are needed to work on the farm. The flexibility and individualization of open teaching provide a way for them to reach children who might otherwise be lost in the traditional classroom.

Independent schools operate on either a traditional or open philosophy, with more of them in the former category these days. Parents can usually locate an available open school, though, by contacting the National Association of Independent Schools, as suggested earlier.

Montessori schools usually do not include the higher grades. Many stop as low as third grade; others continue through sixth; some extend through eighth. The most complete Montessori schools, such as Whitby in Connecticut, include grades 4, 5, and 6 in what they call upper elementary and grades 7, 8, and 9 in junior high school.

Children who have begun in a Montessori school or who have had at least a few years in its earlier classes, progressing through their own unique program, continue to do well at the higher levels. They have by this point become self-motivated learners who can develop and complete their own projects toward stated goals and can handle the advanced studies required of children at this age. Children who have not had Montessori schooling, however, may have a difficult time adjusting to it as late as sixth or seventh grade.

Parents considering a Montessori school frequently ask me: "What will happen when my child leaves Montessori and goes into a regular school? Will he be able to handle it?" From follow-up studies educators have done and from my own personal experience, I find that a child who has successfully completed a Montessori school not only does as well in a traditional school as other children, but often does better. He may need about three weeks to get used to new expectations and new teaching methods, but once he has them in hand, he is again a self-motivated learner heading toward his goal.

Public junior high schools offer large heterogeneous peer groups. Not only do these give students a greater choice of friends with similar interests, but equally important, they afford familiarity with a world different from the students' own. On the other hand, because public schools by nature are less selective, some of the peers may have some antisocial behavior problems that parents would like their highly conforming children to avoid.

Public schools may also offer a wider variety of elective subjects than all but the largest private and boarding schools, increasing the chances of matching a student's individual interests. Students in small schools suffer the frustration of not being able to take the course they want "because you have another class scheduled that period." As frustrated as they, I began to regard the schedule as the determinant of a child's entire future! Schools with large student bodies can offer several sections of each class to accommodate almost every child's schedule.

Independent schools, whatever their philosophy and teaching methods, offer smaller classes and a smaller student body in general. The more personal attention they are able to give is a decided advantage to children of this erratic age. So are the increased opportunities afforded the children to experience and learn leadership roles. Too small a peer group, though—under fifteen—not only limits a child's choice of friends but may isolate him from the real world by creating an unrealistically homogeneous environment. Good independent schools, such as the Master's School in suburban New York, overcome the limited numbers of girls in their sixth and seventh grades by including them as part of a sixth-, seventh-, and eighth-grade middle school of about thirty students. While some of their classes are separated by grade, most of their activities include all three.

Church-related schools vary as widely at the junior high level as all others, although in general Quaker schools tend to be more open and individualized. Catholic schools are usually traditional, a notable exception being the Pittsburgh nongraded diocesan schools, which were among the most wonderful, alternatively structured schools I know.

It is impossible to generalize, but personally, I find that the diverse school population Quaker schools attract and the humanistic approach they use serve preadolescents especially well, regardless of religion. I opt for private over parochial Catholic schools for this age because of their nondenominational goals and special junior high units. As for

Hebrew schools, I feel that because of their exhaustive programs and rigidity, they serve best those children who plan a life as rabbis or cantors or as men and women in strict orthodoxy.

Boarding schools, like independent day schools, are enormously diverse and can therefore serve the many different needs of preadolescents. If admission to an Ivy League college is a child's goal, he can try for competitive schools, such as Andover and Exeter, but only after eighth grade because they start in ninth. Lawrenceville and Groton begin at the eighth-grade level, and many less competitive (and perhaps less prestigious) schools admit sixth and seventh graders.

Boarding schools may provide an answer for children whose home has become a battleground. Many boarding schools have built-in guidance and even therapy programs to help children through these difficult years.

I advise parents to consider carefully the stress load a child must carry if he is sent to a boarding school just because Dad and his older brother went there. Unless he is sure of himself as a person separate from them and unless he is a good enough student to succeed, attempting to follow footsteps can lead him right out the door. I know too many children of this age who could not withstand the continual comparisons: "Well, your brother handled that problem without trouble," or "What would your dad say now if that class picture on the wall could talk?" Even when the comparisons were not articulated, they heard them in their mind. Some merely flunked out; others got into behavioral problems. One boy was caught smoking pot. When the headmaster asked him why he did it, his answer told the whole story: "I knew my dad never did."

Coeducational schools, as pointed out earlier, create the real-world situation in which boys and girls eventually must live; so why not get them used to it? Right? Not always. The excitement and curiosity of sex may be so compelling for some at this age that, with the opposite sex at their side constantly, they are able to focus on nothing else. Single-sex schools provide a calm island amid the roaring internal ocean of these junior high years; young people will often be better able to pilot themselves through that ocean later on. For some, however, the hope is unfounded. When they avoid the sexual struggle in middle school, they merely delay it for new agonies in high school.

Parents have to consider two determining factors in making their decision for single-sex or coed education. One is the way their child is interacting with the opposite sex, and the other is their own skills in coping with turmoil. In actuality their geographic location may make the final decision, because these days single-sex schools are few and far between.

Military schools, I feel, are far too inflexible to meet the needs of this mood-changing, interest-changing, ability-changing, self-image–changing age group. Some children of this age, however, long to attend a military school. I say let them try it; if they are unhappy after the first year, they can transfer.

· Special Concerns in Junior High ·

"How is junior high school different from elementary school?"

The transition from elementary to junior high school can be as traumatic for your child as the transition from home or nursery school to kindergarten. Because private middle schools are usually smaller and more personal, I do not include them in this generalization. Junior high creates a whole new world.

· 97 ·

- · The school building is much larger and far more difficult for a student to find her way around in.
- · There are many more students, most of whom your child does not know; the majority of those she does know from her elementary school may wind up in different classes.
- · When she enters, your child will be among the youngest in the school and will find herself struggling with feelings of inferiority. Remember, she has just come from being a senior member of her elementary school.
- · Because the teachers will not even know her name at first, she is apt to feel like a nonperson. As one seventh grader reported home after the first day, "Nobody knew I was there."
- · She will no longer have a homeroom base in which to store her belongings, but a locker in the hall; and no longer a homeroom teacher to act as parent-in-residence, but an attendance-taker and notice-giver. She will feel her new independence at first as both a joy and a fear.
- · She will have harder and longer assignments and have to budget her time with even greater care than she does her allowance in order to complete it all on time.
- · She will have to abide by more stringent rules and regulations.

- She will have to study harder for exams that are more difficult and carry greater weight in determining her final grade.
- She will get caught up in all the girl-talk about boys (and he will in boy-talk about girls), and she will probably attend her first real dance. Because boys are often reluctant to go to dances, some schools make attendance a requirement.

"What if my child can't handle independence?"

Parents whose children enter junior high school without having been given an opportunity to try out their independence may think their children have fallen under an evil curse when the first report card comes home. The previous "Excellents" and "Goods" may have been transformed into Ds and Fs with comments that repeat phrases such as "No homework . . . doesn't seem to care . . . late to class." Parents can help.

Remember, no matter how blasé your child may appear, he is deeply embarrassed by his new failures. Do not attack him with anger or threats. Because your disappointment coupled with his own is punishment enough, you might begin by acknowledging his feelings: "I know this report card makes you feel awful."

Then set out with him to find a solution that will make both of you feel better: "What do you think was going on that kept you from working?" Together you can probe possibilities and find remedies.

For example, if your son says, "I get lost in that big place," have him draw and keep in his notebook a diagram of the school with his classrooms in bright red.

If your daughter says, "Everyone's always talking to me," remind her that it is hard to say "Shh" to a friend, but help her practice a few scenarios in which she postpones conversation till lunch, recess, or a walk to class in the hall.

If the problem is "There's no time to do all the homework," get your son to design an afternoon schedule for himself that assures the completion of homework. This may entail cutting down TV to one show after dinner and none on after-school activity days. If you let him create the schedule, you will meet much less resistance.

If your daughter tells you, "I've got other things on my mind," she certainly has! Assure her that it is perfectly normal and that you understand. Explain, however, that "other things" have to be put on hold during the business of class or her marks will get even worse.

Restore your child's self-esteem by assuring him that you trust his ability to handle the situation by himself.

As a last resort, if she is unable to handle the transition to junior high alone, you will have to take the reins by setting new regulations at home and making sure she adheres to them.

"What should my child do about all the elective courses?"

Because most junior high schools require basic courses in English, math, social studies, and science, you don't have to worry that your child will enter high school with only three levels of basket weaving and a background in organic foods. All schools try to make sure that she takes the courses she needs; that is the job of the guidance counselors and teacher-advisors.

Some schools, however, offer so diverse a course menu of electives that even the most mature students and certainly their parents are befuddled. When parents used to ask their children, "What subjects are you planning to take?" they could understand the answer: "English, math, science, history, and gym." Today it's not so easy because children have a choice of options under each subject heading.

I know a child who announced the subjects she had chosen, among which was Greek mythology. "What, no English?" asked her alarmed mother, who grew even more alarmed when her daughter answered, "Greek mythology *is* English."

"Why not English mythology?" her mother asked.

"I think that comes under Bible."

If you want to help your child plan a program, you might consider the following:

· 99 ·

- · A broad English course that provides a foundation for further, more specialized courses, instead of one that focuses on a limited area: Contemporary Literature, rather than Novels That Became Movies.
- · A math course that allows her to start with the skills she has acquired and continue building toward more difficult skills and concepts. The course she needs might range from Review of Arithmetic to Beginning Algebra.
- · Any science that interests her. Many schools offer a choice of two or even three (if the school year is built on trimesters) science courses during the year so that students may acquire a base in a variety of sciences.

- A social studies course that serves both as a review and an application of the history she learned in elementary school, such as Current Events or Democracy at Work. After years of studying the Greeks, Romans, and American Presidents, a social studies course of this nature brings a student's learning to life.
- A foreign language if it is offered; even two if the child's interests lie in that direction. Children juggle languages with far less confusion than adults would imagine. I advocate a foreign language not only because many undergraduate and graduate college programs require it but because knowledge of a foreign language provides lifelong pleasure. It is easier to begin in the junior high than in high school.
- An arts course, such as theater, sculpture, film, photography, and so on. These are not the whipped cream of education but are as nourishing a part of the meal as any other subject. They develop a child's taste and creativity and self-confidence. I know an eighth grader who worries and struggles to pass her academic subjects and who explodes with talent and joy in the plays her drama class produces.
- A sport or physical education course in which she can participate. Unless your child is a good athlete, restricting her sports activity to a team may deprive her of both the experience and the exercise she wants: Too many coaches aim for team victories with their better players more than for student growth with all players.

"How many extracurricular activities should my child take on?"

At the start of junior high, I think your child should limit himself to one after-school activity, which will probably be a club or a sport. Faced with this new assortment of activities, he will be tempted to overprogram himself. As in all disagreements with this age group, don't insist "You can't," and thrust yourself and your child into a face-to-face confrontation. Reason with him. Try to help him realize that just adjusting to the new school will consume a great deal of his time and energy on top of a heavier new homework load and that overprogramming will only add unnecessary stress.

Don't expect your child to accept these arguments easily. Like a hungry child, he may think he can handle more than he really can. He may protest, "Don't be silly. I have plenty of time."

Point out, "You have plenty of time now because school has just gotten underway. You'll have more work later on."

"But everybody's signing up for things. Clark signed up for three clubs," he may toss at you.

You can't discredit this because you do not know, but you can suggest, "The guidance counselor may make him give them up later if his marks fall. Would you like that?"

He may have to admit, "It would be kind of embarrassing."

Now you can score the winning point: "Why don't you avoid that possibility and sign up for just one activity now. Next semester, if you have things under control, you can add another."

As the curtain falls on that act, you are likely to hear a sensible, "Yeah. I think I'll sign up for the newspaper."

You have avoided both a scene and too much child stress. School is off to a good start.

"How can I be sure my child makes the right friends?"

· 101 ·

I discuss peers in an entire chapter later on, but a word is due here because the question is of grave concern to parents of junior high schoolers. You *can't* be sure your child makes the "right" friends; you can't be *sure* of much about your child from this age on.

By the "right" friends, most parents mean boys and girls who say no to drugs, smoking, alcohol, and sex, who do not get involved in crime, and who do get good marks. Your children will be surrounded by those who say no and those who say yes, and those who take education seriously and those who laugh it off as a joke. You cannot isolate your children. The best protection they have is your trust, their own self-esteem, and the positive influence other role models have had on them up to this point.

Some parents define "right" friends in elitist terms—children who are white, upper socioeconomic class, American born. In the name of protection, these parents make an effort to limit the growth experiences of their children, who, if brainwashed into similar prejudices, may never expand their relationships.

Parents, encourage your children to make friends with children of all races and nationalities in all socioeconomic groups so that they can discover common denominators and widen their perspectives. You cannot safeguard your child by isolating her in an ivory tower like a legendary medieval maiden. You can only make her strong in her values and sure in her self-worth so that she will safeguard herself in the teeming world beneath the tower.

By the end of October, problems of starting school are usually under control. A honeymoon period, similar to the first six months after a presidential election, is probably underway: Friendships have not yet gone sour, report cards have not yet been sent home, and teachers are still hopeful. In November the climate may heat up!

CHAPTER 8

Clear Communications

· The Importance of School Communication ·

The book of Genesis interprets the problem of poor communications in one simple story. The people of the earth, it says, figured out that if they confined themselves to a tower, they would be able to achieve whatever they wanted because, being close together and speaking the same language, they could always understand each other. God took a look at their tower and in His infinite wisdom said:

> Behold, they are one people and they have all one language; and this is only the beginning of what they will do; and nothing that they propose to do will now be impossible for them. Come, let us go down, and there confuse their language, that they may not understand one another's speech.

And so the Tower of Babel was built. As I look back over years of problems among parents, teachers, and students, I think God must have been creating the American school system. There may be an estimated 2.5 million teachers in over a hundred thousand schools in the United States, with some 44 million children, and close to 100 million parents of some kind or other. Each of those schools is its own Tower of Babel.

About 8 million children come to school from homes where languages other than English are spoken. Yet the breakdown in communications does not stem from diversity of tongue but from diversity of viewpoint. The languages spoken by parents, teachers, and children arise not from the ancient roots with which the dictionary familiarizes us but from the feelings and needs of individual people. With no Berlitz phrase book as a guide, people speak in signs as incomprehensible to one another as ancient hieroglyphics. You may recognize this scenario—I know teachers do—as a typical sequence of noncommunication:

> Mrs. Allen is explaining long division to the fourth grade. When she turns her back to write on the board, Brian throws a paper airplane across the room. It hits Wendy on the neck, and the rest of the children break into laughter. As the class explodes, Mrs. Allen spins around just in time to see Brian launch another airplane. "We went through this yesterday," she scolds, "and I told you never to do it again." Brian hides a smile. "Can't you ever learn anything?" the frustrated teacher yells. She writes a note asking Brian's mother to come in for a conference.
>
> When Brian sees his mother after school and hands her the note, she asks, "Why does Mrs. Allen want to see me? Have you done something wrong?"
>
> Brian assures her that he has not and explains, "She thinks I'm stupid. She said so in front of the whole class." The next day Brian's mother storms into the conference with the opening words "How dare you call my child stupid!"

All three of the actors in the scene have important messages, which they send out over crossed wires. Because what each of them receives from the other is garbled by his own feelings and by static created by the others' feelings, none of them hears what is intended. As a result, the student, the teacher, and the parent respond only to what they hear, not to what the others actually say. The result is not communication but anger. Had they been able to interpret the garbled messages, they could have avoided confrontations, begun to know each other's needs, and uncrossed the wires. They might have learned that:

- The child feels like a failure in his studies and tries to win success with his classmates through his antics. In disrupting class by throwing an airplane, he is actually saying "I need to be somebody."
- The teacher is frustrated at her inability to control the child. In screaming at him, she is actually saying "I won't admit I have failed."
- The mother's ego is hurt by her child's misbehavior and low achievement. In attacking the teacher, she is actually saying "My child—because he is my child—is smart and good. You, the teacher, must be at fault."

Their inside voices spoke clearly, but only their outside voices rang aloud, and no one translated. The teacher heard Brian say, "I do what I want, teach!" Brian and his mother heard Mrs. Allen say, "What a dumb kid!" Mrs. Allen heard Brian's mother say, "You should be fired!"

They could no more address the particular situation or solve Brian's larger problem than the residents of the Tower of Babel could resolve theirs. Only when all the languages of school can be deciphered will parents, teachers, and students be able to send and receive intelligible messages and turn their community from Babel into "the one people . . . with nothing impossible to them."

· 105 ·

· Communicating Is a Two-Way Process ·

"No one ever hears what I say."

All of us are quick to condemn our children and often their teachers for not understanding what we say. "You must be hard of hearing," a father shouts at his daughter who makes no move to turn off the TV and go to bed. It never dawns on him that he might be hard of speaking instead.

If the naval radio engineer taps out the letters T-P-T instead of S-O-S, the ship is going to sink because he sent the wrong message. Similarly, if we tell our children yes when we mean no, they will go ahead and do what we don't want because we too sent the wrong message. That's easy to correct because we learn to choose the right word quickly.

A more difficult problem arises, though, because while the wireless sends dots and dashes in a changeless monotone, the words we speak betray their definitions with tones and inflections. The greatest cause of miscommunication often lies not in what we say but in how we say it. Children are well aware of this because they are experienced at interpreting what Mother is *not* saying.

For example, though you may say what sounds generous—"Never mind, I'll do it myself"—you send a message of anger. You won't get a "Thank you" in reply, but more likely "Why are you always so mad at me?"

Though you may say, "Yes, tell me another Knock-Knock joke," you send a message of boredom. You may get only a disappointed face in response.

Your tone of voice will probably determine the kind of response you get from your children's teachers as much as it does from your children. For that reason, let me suggest a few guidelines to follow that might clear the message-sending lines.

- Don't be sarcastic. No matter how negative the message you want to convey, state it candidly. A forthright expression of your feelings and opinions never carries the personal put-down of a sarcastic dig.
- Speak in a normal tone even if you are furious. When you raise your voice, your anger eclipses the point you want to make, and you dispel any hope of dialogue. It is far more effective to express your feelings in calm, well-chosen words.
- Don't assume a superior tone. Even if you are speaking to a teacher whom you consider an idiot, don't patronize her. Your air of superiority will only put her on the defensive and deafen her to what you want to say.

Let's try out a few scenes you might find yourself playing. Your daughter was accused of cheating on an exam by a teacher, who later found he had made a mistake. You are distraught over the hurt and embarrassment he caused her, and you face the teacher, determined to elicit a public apology.

You might say with a sneer, "So, a teacher can make a mistake too, I see." Confronted with your sarcasm, he rises to discredit the insult with something like "Look here, I don't pretend to be perfect, but your daughter has cheated before, you know." You will get nowhere.

Or you might scream. "How dare you accuse my daughter of what she never did. You shouldn't be teaching."

The teacher faces your anger with his own. "I don't have to take your screaming, and maybe you shouldn't wonder about my teaching, but about your daughter." You won't get an apology here.

Or you might look down your nose and say, "I'm sure you don't understand that we don't have children who cheat."

The teacher will be on the immediate defensive: "My dear woman, teachers see children like yours cheat all the time. Don't think your daughter is above it." You won't get what you came for.

Now let's say that you are well aware of the subtleties of communicating and say what you mean in a cool, calm voice: "You hurt my daughter by your false accusation, and she is embarrassed to face her classmates. You can help her feel normal again if you will tell the class that she did not cheat, that you made a mistake."

If the teacher is at all reasonable, he can only concur, and you can chalk off the problem as solved.

Although you may feel that you would never speak in inflammatory tones, anger can twist your intentions without your ever knowing. I was caught short by a student sent to me for a reprimand. "I know I was wrong," she said, "but do you have to sound so mad?" Be aware; I am now.

While your tone of voice can distort the meaning of an intended message, the actual words you choose can play tricks as well. For instance, if you think the work is too easy for your child, don't tell the teacher "He is gifted." The word works like a red flag on a bull because teachers hear it from scores of disgruntled parents. As a teacher said, "With all the gifted children in my class, how come they can't do their homework?" You will get farther if you say "He catches on quickly" instead.

· 107 ·

The same applies to trigger words such as "You lied" and "You didn't explain"; you will come to terms more readily with "I guess you made a mistake" and "He didn't understand."

From the other side of the desk teachers have developed a vocabulary of their own to keep parents from overreacting too. If you want the facts, you may have to dig beneath the words. When you hear such words as "failing," "slow section," "hyperactive," and "low IQ," don't panic; stop and ask precisely what they mean.

I learned the hard way that when a child has an undetermined problem, parents take the suggestion of psychological testing as a personal insult. However, they can accept the idea of less guilt-producing neurological testing, even though one often overlaps the other. The words have different connotations.

The communications plot thickens when you realize that half of the messages we send do not use words at all. The body language of a slouch, clenched fists, half-closed eyelids, and tight lips, for instance, carries on a heated conversation before you utter a sound. The behavior language we examined—the child throwing an airplane, the teacher screaming, and the mother making an accusation—conveys messages so painful and private that the boy, the teacher, and the mother dare not express them openly.

"How can I tell what people are saying when they don't say it?"

Just as some parents fail to send messages clearly because they are "hard of speaking," so others may fail to pick up messages because they are "hard of listening." Heed the traditional railroad sign of "Stop, Look, and Listen," and use its warning to keep you from stepping into the path of oncoming communications. Merely thinking that you are safe may not be enough.

· When a teacher talks to you, *stop* and pay full attention to what he is saying. Don't interrupt, don't fumble for your eyeglasses, and don't plan what you are going to say next.

· *Look* for the nonverbal signals the teacher is sending along with his spoken words. Is he reaching out or pulling back? Is he stiff or relaxed? Are his face and body carrying a different message from his words? Then *look* at *your* nonverbal signals too. Are you shutting the speaker out by locking your arms across your body? Are you fighting him with a clenched jaw? Are you meeting him with eye contact?

· Now *listen*, not only with open ears, but with an open mind as well. In other words, *hear*. If you listen to the teacher with phrases ready on your lips to spill out the minute he pauses for breath, you are hearing only your own words, not his. You can't have a dialogue when you respond only to yourself; you have to hear what he says before you can answer.

· Finally, *understand*. If the railroad sign was in a foreign language, it wouldn't work; you have to understand what it says. The same is true of communicating. Unless you are willing to understand, you won't make contact.

It is not easy to understand a viewpoint different from yours, but you can begin to do it by changing places with the person who holds it. For instance, when a teacher complains that your child disrupts the class, try to suppress your instinctive reaction, "What right has he to say that!"

Step behind his desk in your imagination for a moment and try to teach long division to thirty giggling fourth graders. You will think instead, "Oh, this poor man! How does he do it every day!" From that viewpoint, you can address the problem: "Of course Katie will have to behave in class. Why don't we both speak to her."

If you are trying to convince the reluctant principal to let a doctor talk to the eight grade about contraception, don't tell yourself, "He's a straight-laced old fool who's a century behind the times!"

Mentally sit in his office with a committee of parents irate over their children's exposure to "what they don't need to know till they're older." Tell yourself, "He has so many parents to pacify. He must have ulcers." Then offer a compromise: "Why don't we let the PTA take this up as an issue and see what they can do?"

The best way to know what other people are saying is to apply the old Indian proverb and "walk a mile in their moccasins." The path may be rough, but it will lead you away from oncoming trains!

"How can I improve the way I communicate?"

Even with sincere efforts to send and receive clear messages, static often interferes when people interact with other people. The following suggestions may help you clear the lines:

Ask the right questions.

Scene I: A child enters the house after school with a glum face. The parent asks, "What's wrong?"

The child answers, "Nothing," and slouches off to her room. The parent's question was too intrusive to elicit an answer. Instead of tapping on the door of the child's private world, it attempted to knock the door down and barge in. The child bolted the door to her hurt—and to her communicating—with silence.

Scene II: Another child enters the house after school with a glum face. "You look unhappy," the parent comments. The child listens. "Something must have happened in school to hurt you," the parent continues. The child nods. "I'm sorry," says the parent. "Perhaps if you share it with me, I can help."

Tears and words pour from the child simultaneously: "I forgot my lines at assembly, and everybody laughed." Parent takes the child in her arms, and later they talk. Instead of intruding, the parent gained entrance to the child's feelings and opened the way to dialogue through trust. In this case, the right question was no question at all.

The right question can open communication lines with any member of the school community.

For example, if a teacher accuses your child of copying on a spelling test, don't ask, "Why would he cheat?" That might shut down the line. Try instead, "What did you see him do?" which could open it. *Ask for facts instead of speculation.*

If at a PTA meeting another parent suggests a dress code of which you disapprove, try, "What problems do you think it would solve?" instead of "Why?" *Be specific rather than general.*

If the principal turns down your suggestion that the school have a Field Day, avoid "Is it too much trouble?" Ask, "What has been your experience with a Field Day?" *Elicit observations, not defense mechanisms.*

Support the other person.

I recall my first year of teaching when an irate parent with her eight grader in tow accused me of being unfair because I gave her daughter a B minus instead of a B on an English exam. "You're not helping your daughter by emphasizing marks this much," I replied, probably with too much vehemence.

The mother responded by screaming, and her daughter by being embarrassed. I just stood appalled until the mother left in a fury, dragging the girl behind. Although the child undoubtedly learned a bad lesson from her mother, I learned a good one: Never attack a person who is communicating on an emotional level. Support her feelings instead.

I would have gained far more ground had I answered the woman's accusations with "I can see that marks are really important to you. Let's look at the exam together and see why she got a B minus."

You can use support better than attack when:

- A teacher keeps the whole class in from recess. Don't Say "How dare you?" Try this instead: "They must really have given you a rough time, but don't you think they need the fresh air?"
- Another parent complains that your child used a four-letter word. Not "So what?" Try this instead: "Thank you for telling me. She shouldn't be talking like that, I know, although it's probably only a phase, don't you think?"
- The principal will not see you. Don't call and shout, "I insist." Try this instead: "I know how terribly busy you are, but I have a serious concern and will only take a few minutes of your time."
- You suspect your child of drinking. Not "You are bad." Try this instead: "I'm sure it's a temptation when

your friends are doing it, but you have to remember
that you are your own person, not that of your friends.
We can't allow drinking."

To support a person's feelings is not the same as agreeing with or
condoning his actions. On the contrary, support is an entry into discussion and problem solving that you would cut off by an attack.

Reflect the other's words.

A great deal of poor communication stems from misunderstanding;
it would have to be a rare child who has not said to his parent during
a disagreement, "I didn't say that!" And a rare parent and teacher and
principal too. By reflecting what someone else is saying, you can clear
lines and be able to respond to what she is saying, not what you *think*
she is saying.

For instance, when a child turns on the TV after dinner, her mother
says, "No TV till your homework is finished."

"I think that's a dumb rule," the child answers. "My favorite show
is on now, and anyway, I haven't much homework."

Mother gets angry. "Don't disobey me. Go do your homework."

The child gets angry too. "I'm not disobeying you. I only said . . ."

"I heard what you said," Mother scolds, but she didn't hear. She
heard what she thought the child said and got both of them in an
uproar.

To prevent a scene like that, the mother could play back to the child
what she thought she said, instead of accusing her of disobedience. If
her reflection is accurate—"You're saying that you can do your homework after the show because you only have a little?"—they can deal
with the problem. If her reflection is inaccurate—"You're saying you
won't do your homework?"—the child has an opportunity to clarify
the communication and resolve the problem.

All school communications will be less fraught with anger and frustration if people receive messages as they are sent. Although reflecting
the sender's message can't assure harmony, it can assure discussion
on the same wavelength.

Reverse roles.

Reversing roles, or role playing, is a concrete way to walk in someone
else's moccasins—not simply to look at an issue from another's viewpoint, but to imagine oneself as that person. Because parents are not
in a position to ask teachers, other parents, or school administrators to
role-play scenes with them, the technique can be used only peripherally.

For instance, when confronted with a situation that demands understanding of her viewpoint, a parent might ease the others into her moccasins by asking "What would you do if you were in my place?"

With a child, on the other hand, role reversal is highly effective because it makes a problem concrete rather than abstract. At the same time it eliminates parent-child inequality by giving the child an opportunity to assume parental power and the parent to relinquish it.

While role play is effective, using it too much dilutes its impact. Reserve it for special needs. For instance, if a child balks at wearing a hat and gloves in 34-degree weather, simple logic will probably convince him. However, when a child isn't mature enough yet to see viewpoints other than his own, reversing roles might help.

Perhaps a ten-year-old, feeling very grown-up, can't understand why she has to have a baby-sitter, and logical arguments don't convince her. Try role playing, casting her in your role as a parent attending a party across town and putting yourself in her place at home alone. Any number of scenarios may arise: The "child" becomes frightened by a strange noise; the lights blow out; she falls and hurts herself, and there is no one to help. While all this is going on at home, the "parent" is worrying about the baby-sitter-less child and unable to enjoy the party.

Or perhaps Aunt Alice is coming to visit, and your child refuses to be nice to her. Let him play the role of Aunt Alice, and you become the child. When the "aunt" arrives, the "child" greets her rudely, refuses to talk with her, makes a face, and runs upstairs. After acting out the scene, both the child and you are better able to understand one another's points of view.

CHAPTER 9

Communicating: Parent To Teacher

· In Preschool ·

Parents and teachers are both essential parts of the teaching team, a fact that makes good communication between them essential. No matter how large the differences between you and a teacher may seem, you actually have a similar goal: to foster your child's growth. Faulty communication turns you into adversaries; good communication makes you partners.

"Can a parent communicate too much?"

The answer is yes. Parents who hang around class at the start or come early before dismissal in order to discuss their child block real help from the teacher in several ways. First, they minimize the teacher's effectiveness by taking her away from the children for whom she is there. Second, they focus on so many minor daily concerns that should a major one arise, it might be lost in the shuffle. And third, they make a teacher dread, instead of welcome, conferences. Parents who place too many demands on teacher's time defeat their own purpose: Instead of assuring extra care for their child, they so antagonize the teacher that their child probably receives less.

Instead of demanding teacher time on a free-wheeling basis, you will receive more attention and appreciation by making an appointment ahead of time if you have a real concern to discuss.

"Can a parent communicate too little?"

The answer again is yes. However, it is much more difficult to undercommunicate than to overcommunicate because the teacher will call you in when a school situation necessitates a conference. On the other hand, sometimes something happens at home that you feel will affect your child in school; then it's up to you to initiate a talk. Except for these two situations, there is no need for parents to pelt a teacher with questions and concerns about their children. A simple morning greeting when you drop your child off will remind the teacher of your interest.

"Who should participate in a parent-teacher conference?"

Where there are two parents at home, both parents should sit down with a child's teacher when she calls a conference. In this way the child learns early that school belongs to the whole family, not just to one parent, usually Mother. Whether a young child should take part in a conference can be argued both ways. On the one hand, some people feel the child should realize from the start that his point of view on school matters is essential. Others worry that a young child may be upset by a discussion of his problems.

You might resolve the question by examining the particular problem you plan to discuss at the conference. If it is something over which the child has some control—his behavior, for instance, or his eating or toilet habits—I feel it is useful to have the child share in the discussion and offer his suggestions for a resolution. If, however, the problem is one beyond your child's control—poor coordination, perhaps, or immaturity or suspected hearing loss—then I see no reason to include the child. For this reason, it is wise for parents to ask the teacher to specify the problem when she calls them in.

"How should I prepare for a preschool teacher conference?"

The best preparation for a conference at this level is to go in ready to listen. Your child has taken a big step into a new situation away from home, and you want to learn how he is doing. Do not throw a string of questions at the teacher, such as "Is he learning to read?" or "Can he write his name yet?" If the teacher does not provide an adequate description of your child in school, questions such as the following will elicit more useful answers:

Does he seem happy?
Does he play with the other children?
Who are his friends?
What activities does he seem to like best?
What signs of maturing do you see?
Is he having trouble in any particular area?
Is he handling the bathroom by himself all right?
And most important; What can I do to help at home?

"How much about a home situation should I tell the teacher?"

Fill your child's teacher in on any home situation that the child carries to school: working mother, single parent, handicapped sibling, grandparent living with the family, alcoholism, and so on.

Alert your child's teacher to any changes at home that may affect the child's behavior in school: death, divorce, new baby, sickness, moving, marriage, job loss, and so on.

While much of this information is personal, it is important to remember that because young children cannot explain why they feel and act as they do, their parents must supply information to help their teachers figure out what is going on. Teachers are morally and, in some cases, legally bound to keep what you tell them confidential.

"How can I complain if I don't like the way the teacher deals with my child?"

You know your child better than the teacher does. Therefore, if you think the teacher's way of relating to him is detrimental to his fullest development, you are obligated to say so. If you do not, you deprive the teacher of a chance to do a better job, and you deprive your child of a fuller preschool experience.

Approach a preschool teacher as an equal team member with a joint problem: "Sandy doesn't seem to be responding to school as positively as she might. What do you think we can do?"

Because the teacher will undoubtedly ask why you think Sandy is not responding well, be prepared to give specific evidence. Maybe Sandy cries or says she hates school or calls her teacher mean; or maybe Sandy's behavior at home has changed for the worse in some way you attribute to the teacher. Put the facts as you see them on the table.

At this point you can suggest that the teacher's way of handling Sandy may be at the root of the problem. If she is too strict, you might say, "I have learned that Sandy behaves better when she is encouraged to make some of her own choices. Have you tried it?" On the other hand, if the teacher is too lax, you might suggest, "Because Sandy is used to firmer guidelines at home, perhaps you could set some down for her for a while." In either case, the suggestions will open the door to fuller discussion with the teacher and, with luck, to a better days in preschool for Sandy.

"How should I thank a preschool teacher for doing a good job?"

Nothing makes a teacher feel better about her job than a few words of praise from the parents of her pupils. Once in a while as you pick up or leave your child at school, you might point out the signs of development you notice in your child: He is putting his clothes away or carrying his dish into the kitchen after dinner or telling you stories from a book or sharing his toys more willingly.

A small gift at Christmas or at the end of the year reinforces a "Thank you." I am a strong advocate of children's participation in gift giving above and beyond the mere handing over of a present. For instance, even a small child can help make cookies for his teacher or can draw a picture to tape to the wrapping of a gift. One of the most warming gifts I ever received was a necklace of macaroni with each "bead" separately colored, attached to a drawing of me with the necklace around my neck.

· In Elementary and Junior High ·

"Will the teacher 'take it out' on my child if I complain?"

Many parents feel that their complaints to or about a teacher have made life more difficult for their child in school. If this is true—and I have no doubt that in some cases it is—there are several possible causes:

- The parent may have complained so many times that the teacher transferred his dislike of the parent to the child.
- The parent may have accepted her child's accusations against the teacher without any corroboration.
- The parent may not have brought the complaint to the teacher, but gone behind his back to the principal or to other teachers or parents.
- Angry and hurt, the teacher may unknowingly be wreaking vengeance on the parent through the child.
- Angry and hurt, the teacher may *knowingly* be wreaking vengeance on the parent through the child.

· 117 ·

Any excuse for a teacher's "taking it out" on your child is unacceptable. However, in the first three cases, the parent has brought about the situation by mishandling complaints.

First, teachers react as other human beings do, and when every action they take and every word they speak appear to bring on parental complaints, they grow irritated. It is not uncommon for irritation to lead to irrational responses. You will be more successful if you wait for a serious complaint or else store up a basketful of small ones before talking to the teacher.

Second, when children bring home complaints about their teacher, parents have a responsibility to determine their child's reliability. Is the teacher really at fault? Or is the child using the teacher as a scapegoat for his own difficulties? If you accept your child's accusation without investigation, you may not only be doing a wrong to the teacher, but even worse, you may be encouraging manipulative behavior in your child. The safest way to handle a child's complaint is for you and your child to lay it on the table before the teacher.

Third, teachers deserve the courtesy of honest dialogue with a parent who is displeased. A parent who talks about a teacher behind his back puts the teacher on the defensive and, unfairly, cuts off any chance for him to defend himself. The result is the teacher's self-righteous anger, which may manifest itself in equally unfair attacks on the child. The only satisfactory way for you to register a complaint is directly to the teacher involved.

Whatever explanation fits a case of a teacher's "taking it out" on a child, you must put a stop to it. Parents have said to me, "I don't dare. He'll make it even worse for Susan." If that is true, you must come to Susan's aid. First, you and she have to sit down and tell the teacher what you think is happening. Point out examples of the mistreatment you see. If the teacher has been unknowingly vengeful, the discussion will open his eyes; if he has acted deliberately, he will have to answer for his action. In either case, the mistreatment of your child will probably stop. If it continues, you should not be afraid to take the matter a step further: You should insist that the principal set up an appointment with you, your child, and the teacher to discuss what is truly a serious matter.

You should keep in mind, however, that the majority of teachers do not punish a child for parental complaints, especially when those complaints are presented without hostility.

"If a child has more than one teacher, whom do I see at a conference?"

Unfortunately, many schools schedule conferences only with a child's homeroom teacher. Because many junior high schools eliminate homerooms, regular conferences are often omitted, and parents meet with teachers only when a problem arises. I consider this situation unfortunate because I think parents and teachers must know each other in order to reinforce a child's education in the school and home environments. There are several ways to overcome conference problems if your school does not bring all your child's teachers together with you.

One way is to get the PTA to persuade the principal to alter the scheduling of conferences. Many schools have rescheduled conference times to mesh with the free time of working parents.

Another way is to make a personal effort to see all of your child's teachers together. This kind of group conference is effective because one teacher may see your child's strength or weakness from a different viewpoint and be able to reinforce or contradict it. As a result, both you and the teachers will come away with a better understanding of your child.

A third way is to set up separate conferences for you and each of your child's teachers. These provide a series of pictures of your child, drawn from different viewpoints, which you are then in a position to put together into a full composite.

"Should a child this age be part of a parent-teacher conference?"

Yes, I feel strongly that all three people in the education triangle benefit from a joint conference—parent, teacher, and child.

First, when conferences are limited to a parent and teacher, words they report secondhand tend to lose their impact. It is far more convincing for a child to tell his teacher "I don't understand the questions" than for a parent to say "My child says she doesn't understand the questions." Similarly, it is more convincing for a teacher to tell a child "You don't listen when I explain the question" than for the parent to report at home "Your teacher says you don't listen."

Second, misunderstandings are less likely to arise when parent, child, and teacher discuss problems together. For example, when a parent brings word home from the teacher that her child starts fights, the child can argue, "That's not true. Jimmy starts them." What can the parent do? She wasn't there; she doesn't know who is right.

If, on the other hand, at a three-way conference, the teacher tells the child, "You start fights," he is less likely to pass the buck to Jimmy because the teacher is there with the facts.

Third, children deserve the respect of participating in a conference that focuses on them. I keep thinking how demeaning it would be for a man if his wife and employer discussed his job performance while he waited at home—or worse, in the hall—to learn what they said about him. School is primarily about children. I think they deserve an equal share of listening, speaking, and discussion of their performance.

Some question this point of view on the grounds that what passes between teacher and parent in a conference might hurt a child. I think they don't give adequate credit where it is due: Children have been proven to handle circumstances as dire as terminal cancer with greater fortitude than their parents. Certainly they can handle lesser tragedies. I have actually seen children heave a sigh of relief upon learning that their poor school performance was attributable to verbal or numerical inadequacy or to emotional upset when they had previously thought it was due to something "bad" they did.

· 119 ·

"How can I prepare for a parent-teacher (-child) conference?"

Discussions in a conference at these levels are more specific than at preschool. I suggest three steps to help you get the most complete picture of your child.

First, begin by listening to what the teacher has to say. If the teacher appears to be waiting for you to throw questions at her, you might suggest, "Please tell us how you see Peter in class." As she replies, really listen; don't argue with her and save your questions until she has finished.

Second, ask questions. You might begin by asking questions in response to Peter's most recent report card, if he has received one: "What seems to be his trouble in math?" . . . "What is he doing when you say he is not paying attention?" . . . "In what way does he demonstrate leadership?" and so on.

Bring up any specific problems at this point in the conference. "He seems angry when he comes home; do you think something is bothering him in school?" . . . "Does he have any special friends? He never mentions any." . . . "We have a new baby at home. Do you think his inattentiveness may be related to that?" and so on.

Third, ask for suggestions. Because what goes on at home bears directly on a child's school performance, the teacher is in a position to suggest ways in which you can help your child. Perhaps you need to ease up on pressure for high grades . . . cut down on television . . . read with him . . . acquaint him with local museums . . . allow him more decision making . . . set firmer guidelines . . . invite his friends over to play, and so on.

Parents enter a conference involved in the life of only their child; teachers enter it involved in the lives of many other children. Therefore, keep the teacher in mind and your eye on the clock, and you will prevent the sighs I have heard in the faculty room, "Whew! I thought they'd never leave!"

"What am I supposed to do at Open House Night?"

The most important advice to follow is what you are *not* supposed to do at Open House Night: Don't pull the teacher aside to talk about your individual child. Open House, usually held in October, is an occasion for parents to see their children's classrooms and to become

· 120 ·

acquainted with the school program. Parents may sit at their child's desk, examine her work, and hear the teacher explain what she will be teaching during the year. When your child has several teachers, you will probably be asked to go from room to room. As a rule, the evening ends with refreshments shared by teachers and parents, offering an opportunity to bring the adult school community together informally.

One parent with one child in the school and two parents with two children face no problem in covering their teachers and classes. However, when there are more children than parents to divide, the question is always "Whose class shall I go to?" I think you should go to each child's class for part of the time. Explain before the teacher begins to speak why you are going to have to leave; she will understand. Then slip from the room as quietly as possible.

"How should I confront a teacher when I'm angry?"

Parents do get angry at teachers and, in many cases, rightfully so. I read about a teacher who punished children by making them stay in a cardboard box in the hall, and I have known teachers who were equally outrageous in other ways: one who laughed to his class about having been drunk, one who used obscenities, another who made slurs about a child's religion, and even one who explained to his sixth-grade class that a girl who was acting up "probably was having her period." If the parents of children in those classes did not complain, they should have; children are a captive audience and have only their parents to protect them when exploited by a teacher.

· 121 ·

As mentioned earlier, the first rule to follow in registering a complaint to a teacher is to make sure it is a valid complaint: Did it really happen? Did it happen under the circumstances reported? Therefore, do not attack the teacher with fists flying, but make an appointment for you and your child to see the teacher and then state the charge precisely: "I understand you kept Marcy from having lunch yesterday because she had not completed her homework. Is that true?"

With Marcy facing him, the teacher cannot deny the charge, assuming it is true. The best defense he can put up is an excuse: "That wasn't the first time she didn't turn in homework."

You can cut through his defense: "She is wrong, I admit that. But the school day is long, and Marcy needs some nourishment to get through it. I am not pleased with what you did, and I don't ever want you to do it again. If Marcy fails to do her homework, you can keep her from recess or give her extra assignments over the weekend. But I want her to have her lunch." Handling it in this manner, you will have made your point far more forcefully than if you had lost your temper, and the teacher will have no cause for anger.

If, however, your accusation is unjustified because Marcy colored the situation somewhat, the scene will be played differently. After your accusation, the teacher may say, "I didn't keep Marcy from lunch. I told her next time she didn't do her homework, I'd eat her lunch myself. She knows I was kidding."

Marcy is shifting from one foot to the other, looking down at the floor. "Is that right?" you ask her. She nods.

"I'm sorry for the misunderstanding. Thanks for straightening it out," you say to the teacher. "Let me know if Marcy doesn't bring in her homework again." By not having accosted the teacher in anger, you maintained his friendship, at the same time joined him in solving Marcy's problem with homework, and let Marcy know that she has to face her mistakes.

CHAPTER 10

Communicating: Parent to Child

Children begin life as great communicators: They scream for food and comfort; they bang their heads on the wall in anger; they hit their siblings in jealousy; they twist their hair in anxiety; they hug and pat in love; and they shout in exultation. As they grow up, however, particularly when they enter school, they may withdraw into silences that leave parents feeling baffled and rejected. "What can we do?" they ask.

· With Preschool and Early Elementary Children ·

"How can I get my child to share what happened in school?"

When parents ask preschoolers, "What did you do in school today?" the children are apt to answer, "I don't know." They really do not remember. Their activities during the course of a school day engage them like changing pictures in a kaleidoscope—with excitement and intensity for short periods of time. No more than a parent could re-create a pattern displayed two turns back by a kaleidoscope can a young child pull the day's activities from the whirl of memory. Without a bruise to point out, he may not remember he fell; without a picture to hold up, he may forget he painted.

Parents can activate a child's memory and usually get a lively conversation underway with a few specific questions: "What picture did you paint?" . . . "Did you play with Jane?" . . . "What did you have for snack?" . . . "Did you have something for Show and Tell?" With memory thus refreshed, children this age tend to launch into enthusiastic recountings of their day's adventures.

"How can my interaction extend my child's learning experiences?"

Every interaction between parent and child is a learning experience because learning takes place in all areas of a child's growth, not just in the academic. Drilling a preschool child in letters and numbers and making her learn to print her name or read words in a book serve to extend a parent's ego far more than a child's learning. The real learning experiences at home come through mutual loving and playing that lead to trust and self-confidence. However, you can lay the groundwork of personal growth and skills in countless ways. The following few suggestions are mere starters.

Developing independence

- Let a child select the clothes she will wear each day.
- Encourage her to dress herself as much as she is able.
- Let her extend an invitation to a friend. (You will have to confirm with the parent.)
- Let her tell you stories and "read" books to you.
- Encourage her to pick up her room, put her dirty clothes in the hamper, carry her plate into the kitchen after meals.
- Let her navigate the route when you go for a walk.
- Let her have a say in family decisions.

Developing relationships

- Play games together.
- Plan family activities.

- Watch TV shows with her and discuss them afterward.
- Spend time together with relatives and friends.
- Play dolls and school and house with her (with him too).
- Share her feelings—enjoy her laughter, comfort her tears, acknowledge her anger.
- Let her share your feelings—don't be afraid to show your sorrow or anger or joy.
- Let her see you express affection in your relationships with family and friends.
- Hug and touch and kiss and cuddle her—love is concrete for young children.

Developing skills

- Large motor: encourage bike riding, running, jumping, climbing, dancing.
- Small motor: paint pictures with her, string beads, stir cake batter, make decorations, hit notes on the piano.
- Numbers: count cars and trees and people with red hats, stack playing cards, build with dominoes, play finger games.
- Letters: read stories, look at street signs and advertisements, shape your fingers or body into letters, draw letters and help her turn them into animals and people.

· 125 ·

In addition, help her develop awareness of a larger world by taking her with you to the store, the post office, the bank; of nature by collecting leaves, walking barefoot in grass, planting seeds, making an animal scrapbook; of herself by measuring her height, looking at baby pictures, expressing her feelings in colors and rhythms, making different noises, smelling, touching, listening, tasting, and looking at her surroundings.

Above all, read, read, read. The closeness reading brings about through physical touch and through the shared experience of a story is a far more important foundation for learning than the word skills it develops. Children whose parents read to them associate reading with pleasure and discovery, which, as they grow older, becomes their comfort, their source of learning, their adventures in fantasy. As a teacher I know said, "School is secondhand. To read and look around you is education."

"How can a working mother extend a child's learning?"

While a working mother has less time to spend with her child, she has added opportunities to offer. My daughter, now a mother herself, still talks about the times that I, as a student in graduate school, took her with me to classes because the baby-sitter got sick. She, for the same reason and to the delight of her two children, has had to take them to her office on occasion. Learning experiences come in many shapes and forms—word processors and interoffice telephones, file cabinets, stamp machines and copiers—and in those moments when it is important to sit quietly with a toy or book from home.

Even working mothers have early-morning and evening hours to spend with their children—making breakfast, doing dishes, and setting time aside to read a story, play a game, and listen. I know a mother who lets her child dial whenever she has a phone call to make, another whose son helps her select and lay out her clothes for work the next day, and a father who invents a story about his little girl's pet gerbils every night before she goes to sleep.

Working parents often complain to me, "But I'm so tired when I get home."

I answer the only way I can: "I know."

Still, you cheat yourself and your child of the closeness you both need at this stage if you let the rigors of your work keep you apart. Give your child time—if only fifteen minutes—devoted exclusively to him after you take your coat off. Then include him in cooking dinner, changing your clothes, or whatever your schedule calls for next. If you are fortunate enough to be able to sit down and rest, hold him and talk while you do. One father I know plays the Eyes game with his little boy every day after work: "Let's lie here together and see who can keep his eyes closed the longest." Even five or ten minutes provides a refresher!

Weekends, devoted to catching up on chores, offer endless opportunities for parents and children to play, explore the neighborhood, and go on family outings. There is even a lesson in "Mommy's tired right now; we'll play that later. Why don't you sit by me and look at your book?"

"How can I be sure a baby-sitter is interacting constructively with my child after school?"

The answer has to be "You can't *really* be sure," but you can get a fairly good idea.

Explain to the sitter at the start what her role is and how you expect her to fulfill it. Be sure she understands the kind of activity and interaction you want for your child.

Always keep the house well supplied with crayons, paper, paste, pipe cleaners, buttons, ribbons, and bits of cloth, in addition to dolls, toys, stuffed animals, and so on.

If the sitter is creative, each morning ask her to tell you what she plans to do with your child that day after school. If you are not satisfied, offer your own suggestions.

If the sitter is not creative, suggest activities before you leave. Be specific: not "Make something," but "Create a zoo with pipe cleaners," or "Decorate the window with paper snowflakes."

Suggest outdoor activities too—a walk, a bike ride, a trip to the park, ball games in the yard with friends.

When you come home, check with the sitter and ask your child to tell you what they did—like an interested parent, not like a detective investigating a case.

If you are worried, phone home in the afternoon and find out what they are doing.

Before giving up, keep trying to help the sitter improve with specific guidelines and instructions. Some organizations, such as the Y, offer parent education courses as well as courses for nannies and baby-sitters. In addition, how-to handbooks are available, among them *The Babysitter's Manual* by Sharon Mijares (Grace, 1983), and *The Babysitter's Handbook* by Barbara Benton (Morrow, 1981). You might check these resources if you need help.

Finally, if you feel the sitter is not adding anything but accident prevention to your child's after-school life, get rid of her and get a new sitter if you can. Don't subject your child to five or six hours of passivity before you return home from work. If you cannot find a new sitter, try other possibilities—sharing with a friend, enlisting a grandparent or another relative, joining a play group.

Don't think that I mean for you to keep your child dashing from activity to activity like an animated cartoon. That would be as bad for her as doing nothing and far worse for you when you returned home. What I am trying to avoid is the easy way out that sitters have been known to use, television. When a third-grade teacher expressed concern over the content of some of a child's writing assignments, the mother checked and found that her child and her sitter spent afternoons watching such shows as *Guiding Light* and *Hawaii Five-O*. Don't let this happen to you.

I think it is good for a child to watch an appropriate TV show at five o'clock, but I don't think he should do it all afternoon. He needs to rest after school and play, and I think he needs time to do just plain nothing. What's important is that both you and he feel comfortable with the sitter.

· With Older Elementary and Junior High Children ·

"How can I get my child to talk to me?"

"What did you do in school today?"
"Nothing."
The final thud of that attempted conversation echoes in home after home every afternoon around three o'clock. In despair, parents ask how they can get a child to give a more informative answer than the door-closing "Nothing." Do your children really sit in a vacuum from nine till three?

Children in the upper elementary grades and junior high school do not have faulty memories; they know what happened during the day. Their reluctance to share it stems from ambivalent feelings about independence and dependence, which they want simultaneously. Their need to assert themselves as their own individual beings holds them back from sharing the private matters of school. Yet the not-quite-outgrown need to be a part of Mother and Dad urges them in the opposite direction. The result is a painful dilemma, which they handle most safely in silence and solitude.

You have to understand this situation and refrain from forcing ourself into your child's inner sanctum by nagging her to talk or acting angry or hurt. If the power of your coaxing should succeed in eliciting talk, your child will be resentful; if it fails, she will add a few more bricks to the wall between you.

What should you do?

· Do not greet your child with "What did you do in school today?" Give her a welcome first: "It's good to see you." Then try a question that shows caring rather than prying: "How are you doing?" or "How's everything?"

· If a reply comes in the form of short grunts, accept them and back off. Let your child flop on the couch or go to her room alone, adjusting to the switchover from being an equal among peers at school to being your little girl at home.

· Later on she may be ready to talk. Don't push it. Wait until she is relaxed and back in place—maybe while you share a snack, maybe not till dinner or even bedtime.

· 128 ·

Then you can ask your question. You know the old door-slammer is a strike-out; there is no more Show and Tell to ask about; and "What did you do in math and science?" is too boring to lead anywhere. You need new questions. The following two may help you as much as I have seen them help other parents.

Try asking first, "What was the best thing that happened in school today?" Being specific enough to pique her curiosity, the question is likely to make her rummage through her day's memory and pull out answers as varied as "I was last in the spelling bee" to "We learned a new kind of dodge ball in gym." She has opened the door to the good part of her day at school, which you can extend with further questions.

"What kinds of words did the teacher ask?" . . . "Was it scary being the last one left?" . . . "Who was on your team?" . . . "How can you remember those words?" . . . "What was the hardest word you had?" . . . "I'll bet you felt proud."

And "How do you play the new kind of dodge ball?" . . . "How does it differ from regular dodge ball?" . . . "Did you pick teams?" . . . "I'll bet you got tired from all that running" . . . "What other games did you play in gym?"

With that subject exhausted, you might then ask the second question: "What was the worst thing that happened in school today?" This elicits the hurts and injustices that have always sought solace in a parent and are eager to do so now: "The teacher was so unfair in reading." . . . "Janet wouldn't sit with me at lunch." . . . "We had a boring assembly about telephones." . . . "We had a mean substitute for music."

Although most preadolescent children respond to their independent/dependent ambivalence by balancing both pulls, some feel the need to take a firmer stand on the side of independence. I remember a father who told me that he asked his seventh-grade daughter what she had done in school that day. "Dad," she replied, "school is *my* business. I don't ask you about the office. Please don't you ask me. Okay?" I smile not at the child, but at the father's utter shock at realizing that his "little girl" was suddenly a person in her own right.

These children fight against their sense of powerlessness. Being unable to drive, get a job, stay out late, and make many of their own important decisions, they are left with school as one of few parentless experiences they can have. As a result, school becomes the focus of their independence, and parents have to use extreme caution in attempting to share it with them.

Direct questions come across as threats to their independence, which they put at risk by sharing the best or worst part of their day because

· *129* ·

it is *their* day, not yours. Where questions will not open doors, reinforcement often will. You may be able to draw out even the most reticent preadolescent by expressing your understanding of her feelings and of the problems she has had to face in school. For instance: "I know you had a history test today. It must have been difficult." . . . "I hope the teacher was aware how hard you worked on those math problems." . . . "You must have been nervous when you had to give your oral report."

If your comments elicit a response, your job is to listen, using all the skills of listening as explained in Chapter 8. If they elicit a mere groan or silence, your job is to stop probing and continue giving support with a pat or a squeeze or a suggestion that there is a snack waiting in the kitchen. If the child wants to unload, she will know you are there for her and select her own time and place.

"How can I extend my junior high child's learning beyond school?"

From about ten years on, children are ready to share the world of their parents in a myriad of ways which extend school experiences.

In the games they play. Charades, Essences, Adverbs, Statues, and Dictionary are great family fun and teach lessons of observation, emotional expression, and word consciousness, among others. When my children were small, we played a game by looking in store windows and taking turns imagining the countries that produced each item.

In the trips they take. Everyone knows the educational value of trips around the United States and to foreign countries, and I urge you to include your children whenever possible. However, not everyone knows the educational value of sharing trips right in his own or a nearby city: the variety of architecture to observe, the small specialized museums from which to absorb other cultures, parks to explore, libraries with programs to offer, science exhibits, plays—even adult plays that are appropriate—art, music, lectures. With a little effort and imagination you can open classroom doors and share year-round learning with your children.

In the volunteer work they do. I used to take a group of seventh graders to an old age home every week, where they wrote letters for the blind, pushed people in wheelchairs to the television room, and even fed an old man with Parkinson's disease. Above and beyond such specific help, they sang to those who were bored and talked and listened to the lonely. These children not only learned lifelong lessons, but grew in the confidence that comes from an opportunity to give to others.

Unfortunately, most schools do not afford children community experiences. However, you are in a position to use the community as a classroom in as many ways as your imagination allows. Children as young as fourth grade can make contributions to aged, blind, deaf, and disabled people in local homes and institutions. They can work with political and environmental groups along with their parents. They can make posters and hand out leaflets for health organizations. They can keep their streets litter-free.

Children in upper elementary and junior high, all too often bogged down in tedious worksheets and textbooks at school, long for hands-on learning experiences. You have the classroom of your local community to provide them.

"Is it all right for my child to have secrets from me?"

Children can keep secrets when their maturity enables them to grasp two concepts: one, that they are separate, self-contained entities to whom others may not have access; and two, that they can hold on to an abstract idea in the same way they can hold on to a toy truck or a doll. Young children are incapable of both. When they learn that Mother is giving Daddy a sweater for Christmas, they come right out and tell: "Mommy is giving you a sweater."

· 131 ·

As children develop greater maturity, they begin to realize that they and Mother have information to which Daddy is not privy. Yet they are not yet mature enough to handle the complete abstraction and, in an effort to keep the secret, may tease Daddy by saying "Mommy is not giving you a sweater for Christmas."

By elementary school, while children understand the concept of a secret, as they are still unsure of their own individuality, they find sharing it irresistible. "Promise you won't tell," they may say to Mother, "but Amy told me she hates Lucy."

By preadolescence, however, children have attained enough maturity to deal both with abstract concepts and their own individuality. Furthermore, they have developed a conscience that reinforces their ability to keep secrets; children are notoriously close-mouthed about keeping secrets within their family at this age.

They are also close-mouthed about keeping secrets away from their family. I find two main explanations.

First, as children's loyalties edge away from parents to peers, secrets become an integral part of peer relationships, cementing the sense of belonging essential at this age. Withholding information from parents is an unmistakable way of saying "I have my world, to which you have no access."

A second reason for keeping secrets from parents at this age is that children fear their parents' reaction. Though titillated by their new feelings and eager to experiment with them, they are also uneasy and ambivalent. It is safer to hide the fact that Jimmy brought a joint to school, Mary and Stan "did it" in her garage, or Joe stole a pencil from Woolworth's than to risk sharing it with Mother and Dad.

Obviously parents worry about their children at this age and grow frantic as they read every day's headlines and statistics. While parental worry is par for the course, trying to dig secrets from your children will not eliminate it. They will not tell you what they do not want you to know; they will only become more secretive as you become more aggressive. Children have a right to private thoughts and knowledge, and you owe them the dignity of respecting that right. If communications between you and your children have been kept relatively open from the beginning, they will share their serious secrets.

"How can I be sure my child will tell me when something really bad is happening at school?"

You cannot be sure, but you can encourage a child to tell.

A sixth-grade girl confided in her mother that an older schoolmate had shown them pictures of naked men in a magazine. The mother wisely discussed the pictures with the girl and answered her questions. She ended by saying she was going to tell the principal. The child pleaded with her not to, explaining that the girl who brought the pictures would know and get even with her, or worse, would blame another girl whom she hates anyway. The mother finally conceded and did not tell the principal.

Was she right? Should she have told or not? I think the mother did the right thing in this case because the offense posed no threat: Nude pictures may not be the best medium for sex education, but they won't cause harm. Had the mother overruled the girl and told the principal about the incident, it is probable that the girl would not have confided in her mother next time. And next time might have posed a real threat.

Several *do nots* may help parents handle a similar situation.

First, do not report every offense a child tells you. Keep the child's confidence unless the offense is dangerous. Drugs, drinking, sexual activity in school by teachers or students, weapons, stealing, and so on, are serious and dangerous. Parents must report them to school authorities.

Second, if the offense is serious, do not report it to the school without telling your child. Confronted by arguments and pleas, explain that you have to enlist the school's cooperation in curtailing this activity before someone is hurt. Make it clear that you will exact a promise from the principal not to reveal who told.

Third, do not snoop around your child's possessions in an effort to learn what is going on. Do not read his letters or diary or listen in on phone conversations. Such actions destroy all possibilities of trust.

Fourth, do not threaten to punish a child if he does not reveal information on your suspicions. Instead, continue trying to convince him that if he has information, he could help friends and perhaps even save lives in school by telling it.

Several *dos* might help as well.

First, if you suspect your child's knowledge of or involvement in a negative school activity, come right out and ask: "I have a feeling that there are drugs being passed around in your classroom. Have you seen any of this?"

If he says, "Yes," and confides in you, you can discuss the situation with him and decide how to tell the principal. If he denies it, you should let him know your genuine concern and explain that you are going to talk to another parent about it.

Second, discuss your concern with another parent with whom you are friendly. Do not, however, start a telephone rumor campaign. If the parent corroborates your fears, talk to your son again. Explain that you are not alone in your worry, and give him another opportunity to confide what he may know. Tell him that you intend to ask the principal.

Third, if you bring up the possibility of drugs or some other negative activity with the principal, approach the matter not as a *fait accompli* but as a possibility that gives you concern. Present the data on which your concern is founded, and then leave the rest to the principal.

"How can I stop my child from shutting herself off from me by watching television when I'm home?"

Preadolescents love TV. It's relaxing after their stressful day, and it provides common ground for discussion with their friends. "Hey, did you see *Growing Pains* last night?" begins many a seventh grader's arrival in class.

Of course, you can say "No TV" and turn the knob. If you have planned with foresight, all you may have to do is remind your child that she had better select carefully because she can only watch for an hour. Offering a more appealing alternative sometimes works:

- "Hey, we haven't talked all day. Come, let's have a cup of cocoa together."
- "Who's for a family game of Charades?"
- "Take a look at this article I read. It's just what you were talking about the other day."

I don't promise results, but you know your child's special interests and with a little imagination can probably come up with a good suggestion. Because children often watch TV for lack of anything better to do, all you have to do is provide something better.

If you can't draw your child away willingly or drag her away without a fight, why not sit down and watch the show with her? "Watch those dumb sitcoms?" parents ask me in horror.

Yes, pull up a cushion and get right in there, because while the sitcoms may not contribute to your child's growth, your sharing them with her will. First of all, it will put you together, and just being physically close carries a message. More important, though, it opens the way to conversation, a path that children this age frequently barricade. While you are talking (during the commercials or after the show), you may even help your child develop some insights, maybe even better taste in TV shows. Try a few of these dialogue-openers:

- "Do you think girls really act like that?"
- "What would you do in that situation?"
- "When they laughed at that kid, how do you think he felt?"
- "Would you like us to be parents like that?"

From your child's answers, you may get a few insights yourself.

CHAPTER 11

Communicating: Parent to Parent

"What exactly is a class mother?"

A class mother is the parent of one of the children who has time to take on a lot of extra work. As a liaison between the teacher and the parents, she serves two main functions. When the teacher plans a class activity, she is the one who rounds up chaperones to keep the children in line on trips, bakers to make cookies for parties, and seamstresses to sew costumes for plays. Her greatest aid is the telephone, but when she can't reach parents or at least can't reach parents who accept her call to action, she ends up doing most of the work herself. I know a class mother who made forty-four angel wings, one set of which I feel she certainly earned for herself.

The class mother also serves as the spokeswoman for parents when trouble is afoot. If you feel uneasy about a general situation in the class, bring it to her attention. Maybe you think that the teacher sneaks a cigarette in the classroom or lets the children get out of control. I know class mothers who have handled problems as minor as a teacher's miniskirt that the children could peek under and as major as suspected sex abuse.

The class mother is in a position to discuss your concern with other parents on the phone or to call an informal meeting and then to relay the parents' concern to the teacher or to the principal without personal involvement. In this process, you will be spared embarrassment and the teacher, ill feelings.

You will gain a great deal if you can see your way clear to serve as a class mother or co–class mother for a year; some schools enlist volunteers by assigning them only a half-year tour of duty. You will find yourself on the inside track of whatever is happening in the class; but more important, you will be telling your child "I think school is important." He will feel as proud of your being class mother as he would if you were First Lady. Take advantage of it now because by the time he reaches high school, he won't care.

"What about the PTA?"

"I thought the PTA was just a social club."

At one time when parents felt they should become involved in their child's school, they planned a booth for the spring fair or picked up the phone to pass on some gossip. No longer. Parents still plan and talk together, but now with the more significant goal of improving their child's school and perhaps even the whole American system of education. Their successes, as you saw in Chapter 1, extend from coast to coast.

There is no better way for parents to exert influence on local and national education than by becoming active members of the PTA. This is no longer a social club but an enormous organization dedicated to the number-one cause on your list: your child's education.

When you pay your minimal dues to the treasurer of the PTA at your child's school, you join 6.5 million other parents in a nationwide organization known as the National PTA. Although your own PTA is self-governing, it belongs to a network of regional and state groups, which send representatives to air your voice at the national level.

Founded ninety-two years ago, the National PTA has been the force behind changes in child labor laws, improving school libraries, and establishing a juvenile justice system. Today it spearheads programs to eliminate drugs, teen driving while under the influence, smoking, and AIDS. The nation's awareness of child safety, teacher recognition, and parenting skills has stemmed in large part from the National PTA.

In order to become part of the PTA impact, however, you have to belong. After you belong, you have to believe. After you believe, you have to be active. By using the full force of the PTA, you can strengthen your lone voice by raising it with hundreds of other parent voices in your school, thousands of other voices in your region, tens of thousands of other voices in your state, and 6.5 million other voices in the nation. The result is a shout for better education for every child in the United States . . . and that means yours!

"How can I make my PTA more effective?"

If your PTA hasn't awakened yet—and you will be able to tell from the dull, poorly attended meetings it conducts and from parents' unawareness of its potential—here are a few guidelines for setting the alarm.

Start with a membership drive that will get parents excited. You can get help from the National PTA, which will give you suggestions and material to implement them:

THE NATIONAL PTA
The National Congress of Parents and Teachers
700 North Rush Street
Chicago, IL 60611–2571
(312) 787-0977

· *137* ·

Next, strengthen PTA meetings so that parents will want to attend. Set aside a specific date each month so that parents will reserve it. Plan your meetings around issues that people care about and invite a speaker from the community or show a film for variety (available at your local library or the National PTA). Keep the meetings short—no more than an hour—but always allow time for questions and answers followed by refreshments and informal talk.

Get your PTA involved in the regional PTA so that parents will be able to attend meetings and workshops and bring back workable ideas. Subscribe to National PTA publications (some free, some with a small charge), and make them available so parents can keep up-to-date on school activities in other areas. Instead of having to reinvent the wheel when a problem arises, you may find that another school has already solved it.

Form a PTA committee to work with the principal on drawing parents into the school's educational activities. Many schools use parents as classroom aides, individual tutors, library assistants, and lunchroom supervisors. This has a dual benefit. The school saves money to use on otherwise unaffordable items and parents become part of the school.

"How do I get the PTA to go to work for me?"

When you have a complaint or a suggestion that directly affects your child, you may find satisfaction by taking it through the steps outlined in Chapter 2. If your concerns are broader, affecting the school as a whole instead of just your child, you may proceed in the same manner. However, you will probably be more successful if you enlist the help of the PTA, whose chorus of voices will argue a stronger case than your solo.

Let us assume that you are displeased with the school's writing program. You want the PTA to embrace your cause and use its clout to get more creative writing into the curriculum. Here is a way to go about it.

At the next meeting, when the president asks if there is any new business, tell the group, "I rarely see the children do any writing. They may have a book report now and then, but nothing creative. With so much emphasis on self-expression these days, I think every grade should be required to include creative writing in the curriculum. I'd like the PTA to do something about this."

Discussion will ensue with parents agreeing and disagreeing, and at some point you can say, like a veteran parliamentarian, "I make a motion to appoint a committee to investigate the possibility of more creative writing in the curriculum." If the motion passes, you will undoubtedly wind up as chairperson.

What you want to do now is develop arguments that will convince parents at the next PTA meeting to undertake your cause. Therefore, get your committee members to solicit the opinions of English teachers in the school and find out if other schools have strong writing programs.

With this information in hand, at the next meeting you will present your case to the full PTA, who will vote. If you win, you will probably be chairperson of another committee, this one aimed at convincing the principal to put greater emphasis on creative writing. Your work will be cut out for you, but with the support of the PTA, you have a good chance of reading your child's short stories and poems before another year passes.

There is, of course, the possibility that the PTA will vote against your idea. If this happens, you may find a group of parents who share your enthusiasm to talk to the principal with you, or you may decide to drop the idea and work on creative writing at home. If you choose the latter, let me offer a word of personal advice: A word processor is a great motivator for children.

"Does a signed petition work?"

A signed petition can carry a great deal of weight. Its effectiveness, however, depends largely on how and when it is used. If you want to bring about a change in your school, such as the previous example of creative writing, you don't need a petition; you have parents in person and can use their combined PTA strength to put pressure on the principal and even the superintendent if necessary. If, however, you are concerned about a larger issue, one that involves the outside community, you may persuade the PTA itself to undertake getting signatures on a petition. I know specific instances where by getting hundreds of citizens, many not even connected to the school, to sign petitions, parents were successful in putting a guard at a school crossing, having a traffic light installed, arresting drug pushers, and installing weapon-detecting devices at school entrances.

"What should I do when people call me with rumors?"

Rumors and gossip can disrupt the operation of a school with the force of an earthquake reaching seven on the Richter scale. The tremors begin when one disgruntled parent passes on to another parent a fear or suspicion as if it were a verifiable fact: "Did you know that Mr. Williams is having an affair with one of the girls in high school?"

"No! Wait till Ann hears. She never did like him, you know." And so the story goes from parent to parent until, by geometric progression, what began as a rumor becomes a fact. No one knows exactly how or why rumors start, but once underway, like hurricanes, they feed themselves and do enormous damage. I have seen a young girl destroyed by totally unfounded rumors that she was pregnant, and teachers forced to defend themselves against false accusations from homosexuality to being Communists.

Like the World War I posters that showed Uncle Sam pointing a finger and saying "I want you," every school should point a finger and say, "You can stop the spread of rumors."

First, don't repeat what parents tell you. No matter how juicy a tidbit you hear, let it go in one ear and stay there.

Second, let a rumor-bearing parent know how you feel; don't hesitate to say, "Unless you have substantial evidence for this, I don't want to hear it, and I hope you'll stop spreading it to other parents." While you may lose a friend, you will gain a healthier school.

Third, report rumor-spreading to the principal: "I think you should be aware that there is a lot of talk going around the school that Mr. Williams is having an affair with a high school girl. I don't know whether it is true or not, and I don't consider it my business. I'm telling you so that you can put it to rest." If the rumor is true, the principal will take appropriate action; if it isn't true, she will get it stopped.

"What can I do to stop parents from banning certain books?"

The subject of banning school material has become one of the most heated controversies in American education in recent years. Its roots lie deep within parental psyches and moral judgments too unreachable to deal with here. Parents are what they are—be it fundamentalists or free thinkers, reactionaries or liberals—through psychology more than through politics. They believe what they need to believe.

The parents in your school may be banning books not because they consider them harmful but because they may consider them inappropriate for children of that age. For instance, pressure from parents pushed *Romeo and Juliet* from the fourth grade where it was being taught up into junior high school, because parents felt that if children studied the play before they were able to relate to it emotionally, they would not enjoy it later on. No one suffered from the change; the only one who cared one way or the other was the teacher, who had delighted in the histrionics Shakespeare afforded.

In another school parents objected to a film that the teacher used in an eight-grade sex education course because it showed actors in a position of intercourse. Feeling that such an explicit scene would overstimulate preadolescent children, parents were able to have the film replaced by one that used animation instead. No one objected, and the children still learned.

On the other hand, parents may be banning books because they disapprove of the values they find in the material. The Scopes "monkey trial" in 1925 was brought on by fundamentalists who, adhering to the Biblical explanation of creation, fought a science teacher who taught Darwin's Theory of Evolution. Scopes was tried and found guilty on the basis of a Tennessee law banning the teaching of evolution. Times have changed, and today states realize that the banning of books or teachers on religious grounds is unconstitutional. Still, groups of parents sometimes attempt to pull from libraries and classrooms books that they feel conflict with their personal religious beliefs. For instance, just a few years ago Tennessee heard another book-banning trial; this time, however, constitutional law held firm, and the books remained.

A major focus of education in the past decades has been to open students' minds to a variety of viewpoints on subjects as diverse as Abraham Lincoln and sex. The old-fashioned, simplistic explanations of "good" and "bad" and "right" and "wrong" have been replaced by discussions of ambivalence and relativism, with the result that students are learning to think and to weigh what they read instead of merely to parrot. Even young children are having to consider both sides of a question, as a teacher reported after a child came in without his math assignment. "My dad showed me how to do it on his machine, and my mom showed me with toothpicks," he explained. "I didn't know what was good and bad, so I didn't do it. Was that right?"

In an effort to return to the narrower concept of learning schools had thirty years ago, fundamentalist parents are lobbying from the halls of their children's schools to the offices of their state legislators. Books such as *Catcher in the Rye* and *The House of Seven Gables*, both of which I found captured the interest of even nonreading junior high schoolers, have brought on court cases, and school productions of *Grease* and *Midsummer Night's Dream* have been canceled. Despite constitutional law, even President Reagan put creationism on an equal basis with evolution.

· *141* ·

What can you and parents like you do to stop the sweep of book banning? Because the movement's success came from a strong, united effort on the part of fundamentalists, its defeat demands similar strength from the opposition. Most parents don't want book banning; they want to educate their children under the principles of free and open thinking, but they have not united to speak in one voice as the book banners have. Now is the time to begin.

If parents in your school initiate a banning campaign, call the PTA into action like Paul Revere. Get opinions from teachers, the principal, and the superintendent; find out how other schools in the district have coped with banning.

Form a committee to gather information from your state legislators, a judge, and religious leaders in the community.

Schedule a meeting to present the facts you have gathered. Invite respected speakers who support an antibanning position. After the meeting, send a summary of what transpired to the entire school community.

If the school supports you in preventing the banning of books, the issue may die down, unless the pro-banners take it to court, where it might linger for years through a series of appeals. Book banning is serious business, and the fight against it is worth all the energy you and the PTA can muster.

CHAPTER 12

In School: Teachers

How illogical it is, President Kennedy pointed out, that people pay a smaller wage to those to whom they entrust their children than to those to whom they entrust their plumbing! Money bespeaks American values, and it appears that we view ill-functioning toilets as a greater threat than ill-functioning teachers. Yet teachers influence children, for good or ill, with a character-shaping force second only to that of their parents. When Henry Adams wrote "a teacher affects eternity," his voice echoed what St. Augustine's might have said had he spoken of teachers instead of mothers: Give me other teachers, and I'll give you another world.

· Concerns with Teachers in Preschool ·

"What is a good teacher?"

A good teacher of small children, above and beyond all other qualifications, must love them.

"What do you like best about school?" I asked a four-year-old as I picked her and her painting up one noon.

"My teacher loves me," she answered.

"How can you tell?" I asked.

The little girl thought a moment and then poured out proofs of love: "She liked my picture . . . She kissed my bump . . . She smiles at me."

Because children will not be fooled by pretense, preschool teachers have to match their proclamations to their displays of love: They must really enjoy the children—listen to them, play with them, notice signs of their growth; they must respect their innate dignity and be sensitive to their vulnerability; they must be willing to share, to comfort their hurts and be excited over their excitement; and above all, they must never exploit them for the sake of their own ego.

Until recently, nursery school teachers required no official certification but were judged by their interactions with children. Today preschool teachers, excluding assistants, must be certified by the state in which they teach. Although the ruling assures their having studied early child development and acquired a bagful of games, songs, and activities, there is no way it can assure a caring nature. The love a good preschool teacher exudes grows from her own childhood experiences that helped to form her personality.

Important as love is, it is not enough; teachers of young children need knowledge and skills as well:

· They must understand *how* young children learn in order to provide them with learning experiences. If you are interested in learning more about the stages your child will go through as his learning skills develop, you might want to read some of Jean Piaget's studies of young children, all available in public libraries. They are fascinating, but more important, they will safeguard you against all-American achievement anxiety. Three good works are: *The Origins of Intelligence in Children* (International University Press, 1966), *The Construction of Reality in the Child* (Ballantine, 1986), and *Play, Dreams and Imitation in Childhood* (Norton, 1962).

· Teachers must understand ways of motivating a child's creative expression—in painting, block-building, singing, story-telling, play-acting.

· They must understand how to stimulate a child's social awareness—in group activities and sharing and assuming responsibilities.

· They must understand the kinds of physical activities that promote large- and small-muscle development at this age.

· They must understand the needs of young children in order to create an environment in which they will find satisfaction. Abraham Maslow's *Toward a Psychology of Being* (Van Nostrand Reinhold Co., 1988) is invaluable reading if you are interested in this hierarchy of needs.

· They must understand the fears that haunt children in order to eliminate them from the preschool setting where they could so easily arise—fear of interruption or suddenness or falling, for instance. Invest in a paperback copy of Erik Erikson's *Identity, Youth and Crisis* (Norton, 1968) to get a better understanding of your child's fears and of many other problems you will face in the future.

· They must know how to control young children in a group and individually—attention span, diversion techniques, effective methods of discipline, and so on.

You do not need to be an expert in teacher evaluation in order to determine whether your child's preschool teacher is qualified. You can tell as you visit the classroom. You can tell as you see your child develop. Above all, you can tell as you sense her feelings about school.

"What can I do about a teacher who can't control an aggressive child in the class?"

You are right to be concerned because even one out-of-control child in a preschool can lessen the learning experience of the entire class. He takes more than his share of the attention of the teacher, who because of her frustration is likely to be less effective. More important, he stirs other children into reactive behavior so that they too magnify aggressiveness in the class. If the teacher has complained about your child's aggressive behavior, you may have told the child, "Don't throw the truck at Neil again." With an uncontrolled child in the class, he may have responded, "But he always hits me first."

That is preschool logic, and when a teacher has fifteen children being logical, the class can become a war zone. It is not rare for children to come home with actual injuries—a cut from a thrown block or a bruise from a push into a table. If your child is caught in an unruly class, you owe it to him to try to ease the situation:

· Let the teacher know that you are deeply concerned over what you see happening and that you feel it must stop.

· If the teacher denies the situation, reinforce your complaint with a group of other parents. Ask the teacher to explain her efforts to control the troublesome child and explore with her the possibility of other, possibly more successful, ways.

· Urge her to talk to the child's parents. Perhaps they can work with him at home toward improving his behavior at school. Some schools have even asked parents of an unruly child to stay at school with him for a while to keep him under control.

· 145 ·

· Determine whether the teacher has enough adult help to handle the class effectively, to isolate the out-of-control child from the other children until he calms down. If she needs an additional aide, you should present the problem to the board of directors and suggest that they hire another one. I know a group of parents who, unable to persuade the directors to hire another part-time aide, took on the job themselves. Mothers and fathers who could spare an occasional half day from work—and sometimes nannies, if parents couldn't—took turns helping the teacher on a regular basis. The teacher was delighted; the children were proud; and the parents felt truly a part of the school.

Before mothers entered the work force in the numbers we see today, many nursery schools counted on them as classroom aides, requiring their time as well as their tuition check for their child's admittance. Although mothers are far less available nowadays, fathers with flexible jobs assume the school volunteer role from time to time, and surrogate parents—grandparents, nannies, baby-sitters, and so on—fill in where necessary.

Should all your efforts fail to calm down your child's aggressive classmate, I see only three ways for you to go:

· *146* ·

1. You can move your child to another preschool.
2. You can join forces with the teacher and other parents to have the out-of-control child taken out of school until he is more mature.
3. You can persuade the board of directors to replace the teacher with a more able one.

If the aggressive child who needs controlling happens to be yours, you will find a plan of action in Chapter 18.

"I'm worried: My child's teacher has never taught before."

A new, young teacher may approach the job with all the energy and enthusiasm it demands, may love the children and be highly qualified, and yet, you are right, she may lack enough experience to take hold and do a good job at the beginning. Then again, she may be a natural and step right in and fool you. I know a new teacher who was so flustered the first week that she kept tripping over the toys and the children and on Friday sprained her ankle. When she returned on Monday with a walking cast, she slowed down and turned out to be one of the best teachers the school ever had. You owe a teacher a few weeks' time for adjustment; fifteen jumpy children pose a far greater challenge than the hundred books she may have studied. If after a few weeks, however, she still seems at a loss, get a group of other parents to go with you to the board of directors. Explain the situation to them. If they themselves are inexperienced, they may say, "I guess we'd better start looking for another teacher in a hurry."

Or they may go in the opposite direction with "That's awful, but we're stuck with her till June."

Don't accept either of those responses. What you want to hear, and should hear if they have been around preschools before is, "Too bad. Let's see what we can do to help." If they don't see how to tackle the problem, here are a few suggestions you can give them.

· Why don't they have the teacher attend workshops that may be available?
· Why don't they hire a temporary aide to relieve her burden until she feels more in charge?
· Why don't they ask parents to serve as temporary aides?
· Why don't they ask an experienced teacher—possibly the one who just retired—to work with the teacher until she can handle the class?

· 147 ·

In most cases, when a qualified teacher is eager to learn and is given support and help by the parents and the board, she will be able to take charge in a short time.

"How do I get rid of a teacher who has been there just too long?"

You are talking about burnout, a phrase used a lot these days to describe a teacher who stays too long, both for her own good and for the good of the children. Maybe she is too old to teach preschoolers any more, or maybe she has just used up her creative energy. Whatever the reason, she should have been asked to retire at the end of the previous year instead of taking "one more" class and giving the children less than they deserve.

If your child's teacher is too worn out to provide the kind of program he needs, you—alone or with a group of other mothers—should speak to the board of directors. They should talk with the teacher and, as gently as possible, explain their feelings. They have several possible solutions to the problem.

· They can hire an associate teacher, not an assistant but an equal, with the understanding that she will take over the class when the older one retires in June.

· They can suggest that the teacher retire at the Christmas break and hire an associate to work with her until that time.

· If she clings to her contract, insisting that she remain until year's end, the board may have to pay her salary for the year and ask her to leave earlier. The cost is little compared to the wasted year the children would have if she stayed.

"How hard will it be for my child when a new teacher takes over middle of the year?"

Although circumstances sometimes necessitate a preschool teacher's departure from school before the end of the year, you are right, it can have a near-traumatic impact on the children in her class. As the pre-school teacher is your child's first object of trust in the large world outside the family—actually a mother away from mother—her disappearance will be frightening. Not only will the child have to start all over to build trust in a new teacher, but even worse, he will never be sure this one won't leave too.

I visited a kindergarten class with a new teacher after their teacher had been gone for about three weeks. One little girl with wide eyes told me, "She's dead."

The boy standing next to her gave a fuller explanation of her demise: "Jeffie hit her."

I don't know what preparations that school made—or rather, did not make—but I do know many other kindergarten and nursery school classes that adjusted to a new teacher with no signs of guilt or upheaval. A child in one of them told me, "We got two teachers now, but you can't see her." The difference lies in the planning and care with which the transition is handled.

If your preschooler's teacher is leaving in the middle of the school year, make sure the board of directors lays careful plans.

· They should tell parents as soon as they themselves know.
· They should hire a replacement immediately.
· Several weeks before the teacher's actual departure, they should have her replacement join her on a daily basis in the classroom. In this way, the children will

begin to feel secure with the new teacher, and she, in turn, will begin to understand them.
  · They should arrange to have the new teacher assume more and more of the classroom responsibility so that the departing teacher can ease herself out.

Preparation does not rest solely with the board; you should urge the teacher to do her part too.

Shortly before her replacement joins her in the class on a daily basis, the teacher should tell the children she will be leaving. She must make it clear to the children that she will miss them and continue to love them and be concerned about them. In order to dispel any guilt the children might develop at their being the cause of the teacher's leaving—remember "Jeffie hit her"—she should let them know why she is leaving.

Almost any reason that compels a teacher to leave before the end of the year can be used as a positive learning experience for the children.

The best sex education I ever saw at this level was a pregnant teacher who let the children keep track of the baby growing within her and share with her the excitement of a new life. Her visit to the classroom with the newborn baby was the most talked about event of the children's year.

· 149 ·

I never saw career education in preschool until a teacher who was leaving because of her husband's transfer invited him to talk to the children about his work. They were so interested that he arranged for the class to visit him at his office before he moved.

Even a teacher leaving to undergo an operation was able to use the experience constructively by reading the class stories about doctors and hospitals and inviting the children to share their own experiences of being sick.

After the teacher actually leaves, she still has a responsibility to ease the transition by keeping in touch with the children for a while. They will love drawing pictures and dictating letters to send her and will delight in replies. If she can visit them at school just once after she leaves, the children will have escaped trauma, and she can say to herself, "A job well done!"

When handled with planning and sensitivity, a teacher's departure from the class, rather than causing upset, will be woven in as part of the children's entire experience. They will miss her for a short time, but having been allowed to share in the event, they will not feel abandoned. Attachment to their new teacher will be a normal evolution.

· Concerns with Teachers in Elementary School ·

"What is a good elementary school teacher?"

Some years ago I conducted a workshop for elementary school teachers called "How to Recognize a Super Teacher When You Are One." The material I used was a composite of almost a hundred top teachers from every state whom I had interviewed and observed for fourteen years while collecting material for the Annual National Teacher of the Year Program. What impressed me about the workshop was the number of teachers who registered in order to answer the question "What makes a good teacher?"

Although the characteristics of a good elementary school teacher overlap those of a good preschool teacher, the emphasis differs. A Gallup poll found that half of the general American public consider "ability to communicate knowledge to students" and "ability to motivate students to learn" the most important characteristics of a good teacher. Children, on the other hand, tell me a different story: Caring, they say, is the essential characteristic. With only a third of the general public even mentioning that, it is apparent that daily contact with teachers better qualifies children as evaluators than adults.

When I ask elementary school children to indicate specifically what their teacher does that shows them she cares, I get a series of answers that, like brush strokes on a canvas, paint that one teacher whom those of us who are fortunate long remember:

"She helps me when I don't know what she's talking about."
"He doesn't let the boys scream and yell."
"She lets me write a story in Spanish sometimes."
"He makes me laugh."
"She gets us to act out math problems."
"She said it was okay to not do my homework when my cat died."

As diverse as these examples of caring may seem at first glance, in combination they describe teachers who devote all their resources to children. They are not teaching to impress the principal or compete with other faculty members; they are not teaching because it's a job; they are not teaching to feed their ego. They are teaching because they really care about the children in the class, as learners and as human beings. A closer look at what the children interpret as signs of caring boils down to a list of important qualifications, an answer to what makes a good teacher.

- Willingness to spend extra time and give extra help so that every child can succeed.
- Ability to maintain order so that children can focus, uninterrupted, on their activities.
- Recognition of each child's individual needs and resourcefulness to meet them so that children can learn in their way at their time.
- A sense of humor so that children will see learning as fun.
- Imagination to turn even routine lessons into hands-on experiences so that children will remember by doing.
- Acceptance of their pupils as whole people who grow from their emotional experiences as well as from their intellectual ones so that children will not be compartmentalized.

Children who know their teacher cares about them as people see themselves on the same side, teammates in learning; children who feel that their teacher's interest in them lies only in making them meet her demands see her as a player on the enemy team. I have sat in classrooms where hostility vibrates in waves between teachers and students, where orders are challenged and aims thwarted. I have also sat in classrooms with love and laughter where students work long hours and refuse to stay home even when they are sick. The difference is a teacher who cares.

· 151 ·

A few years ago I visited a ninety-eight-year-old woman who, at seventeen, had been a music teacher in New York when horses pulled trolleys. She showed me a letter she carried with her from a student she had taught years before. "Albert," she said. "was a wild little boy, always jumping around during chorus. The principal wanted to expel him from the chorus, but I thought that would make him even worse. I kept him after school for a week and taught him to play 'My Country 'Tis of Thee' with one-finger. When the class was ready to sing it next time, I called, 'Albert,' and he came to the piano and played perfectly. Do you know what? He never gave me an ounce of trouble after that."

What was in that fifty-year-old man's letter to his old music teacher? "I wish I could say I grew up to be a concert pianist," he wrote, "but I didn't. I grew up to be a math teacher. Without you I wouldn't have grown up at all. Thank you. I told my students what you did, and they thank you too."

Caring regenerates itself. It cannot be taught, along with lesson planning and class trip procedures, in schools of education. Caring grows from having been cared for—by a parent, by a teacher. Not everyone has. That's the bad news. The good news is that teachers can be taught many of the practices of caring teachers—how to keep order without screaming, how to individualize, how to make lessons interesting. In addition, they can be required to give extra help to students in trouble.

I suspect that the humorless cannot be taught humor in college, nor can they be instilled with respect for the totality of human beings. However, they may learn that responding to the humor children create for themselves makes teaching more fun and that accepting children as whole beings, not just minds to mold, makes learning more possible. In that knowledge, they may eventually find themselves caring.

"What if my child has a 'bad' teacher?"

If you ask an elementary school child why she thinks her teacher is "bad," the answer most likely will be "He's boring." Perhaps he is— too many teachers are—but then again, perhaps your child means that the drudgery of learning multiplication tables and spelling rules is boring. So "boring" is a moot point.

There are, however, less questionable characteristics of the "bad" teacher: He may not know his subject; he may scream at the children; he may be lazy; he may lack enthusiasm; he may play favorites; he may belittle children in front of their classmates; he may be impatient or unclear in explanations; he may have such a large ego that instead of caring about the children, he exploits them for his own ego gratification. I have seen examples of them all, and more. Because parents usually know who these teachers are before their child reaches their grade, some ask the principal to assign their child to another teacher. Maybe they are lucky.

Then again, maybe not. What do you do if your child is stuck with a "bad" teacher?

· *Don't* follow your first impulse and demand that your child be switched to another class. Chances are the principal will not make the switch, and even if she did, it would not be the best solution for your child (as I shall explain in the next section).

· *Don't* try to fool your child. Be honest. Admit that she is going to have to spend the year with a far less than perfect teacher, but assure her that she will survive. Your understanding and support will go a long way toward seeing her through.

· If the teacher's liabilities are qualities such as being unenthusiastic or boring, you and your child might seek to discover some of his assets. Does he know a lot more than the book says about his subject? Does he plan interesting field trips? Is your child learning skills that will help in other classes? Does he really care about the children? I have seen a few affirmatives to questions like this turn a bad year around at least 90 degrees and result in what one child referred to as "an okay year."

· If, however, the negatives of a bad teacher stand in the way of a child's learning, then it is time to see the principal. You may want to go alone or with a small group of other parents who feel as you do. Approach the principal with determination, but not hostility. For instance, don't say, "Miss Walling keeps destroying the kids in her class, and you've never done anything about it. This time we insist that you stop it." That will create an additional problem with the principal instead of solving one with the teacher.

Try an approach that might lead to action rather than an argument: "I know it's hard to get a teacher removed, but Miss Walling shouldn't be in a classroom. She doesn't teach; she destroys the children. We have compiled a lot of examples of what she does, and when you hear them, I know you will agree." Then give him as many specific examples as you can collect: precisely whom she belittled in front of the other children and how she did it; the exact times when she was unprepared for class; definite ways in which she manifests laziness and impatience; details of her exploitation of children, and so on.

Here are two goals for your meeting with the principal.

First, you want to bring about a change in the teacher's behavior. This may come about by the principal's speaking with the teacher alone or by setting up another meeting with the parents that includes the teacher. An unimaginative teacher cannot turn into a creative artist overnight, but she can learn to plan more interesting classes or to control a sarcastic tongue.

Second, you want to overcome the damage done to your child by the teacher. If the damage is academic—for example, if material upon which future lessons depend has not been taught—you have a right to ask for extra help for your child and for all the children until they are caught up. If, on the other hand, the damage to your child is emotional—perhaps she has been scapegoated or belittled—it is essential that the teacher make amends by an apology to the class. Of course, a teacher who abuses children in this way—or in any way—should not be in a classroom. However, rules of tenure being what they are, it is often extremely difficult to get a teacher removed. It can be done, however, as parents in Chapter 2 demonstrated.

It is important for you to remember that in most cases, your child can shrug off in a day or two the hurt you assume will last a lifetime. I remember one of my sons coming home in shame after a teacher made fun of his outfit, which he considered cool. I didn't mention it the next day, but the day after that I asked, "Are you feeling okay about Mr. Barrow?"

"Sure. Why not?" he answered me in total incomprehension.

Therefore, while you work to offset the effects of a "bad" teacher, avoid turning it into a *cause célèbre*. If you make too much of it, the child may begin using it as an excuse for any school problem that arises.

"What if the teacher picks on my child?"

It is a rare child who doesn't come home some day complaining that her teacher singles her out from the entire class for scoldings and punishment. The question for you to determine is "Is my child just imagining this, or does the teacher in fact pick on her?"

How do you get the facts?

First, you ask your child to explain specifically what the teacher has done to her. Answers will probably cover a wide variety of abuses, such as "She kept me in from recess," "She didn't scold anyone but me for talking," or "She tore up my painting."

Next, you ask, "What had you done that made her do that?" Your child's explanation may readily offer a solution: "I didn't do anything. I didn't mean to throw the eraser across the room; it just slipped out of my hand." No further questions. You can handle that one with the child in a discussion of intent.

"If I grab a stick and hit you because I'm mad, will it hurt?" you might ask.

"It sure will."

"What if I'm just swinging a stick around for fun and hit you by mistake, will that hurt?"

"Well, yes," your child will have to concede.

Now you can warm up to the point: "Can you see that whether you throw an eraser on purpose or by mistake, you still disrupt the class, and the teacher still gets mad at you?"

"I guess, but she always picks on me, not just this once."

"Maybe you do things that cause trouble a lot of the time, not just this once. Is that possible?"

"Yeah, but I'm only fooling around."

"If that's so, what can you do so the teacher won't pick on you?"

"Stop fooling around, I guess."

Don't expect that your child will never get into trouble again; words do not transform children into angels. She may, however, have somewhat deeper insights into the cause and effect of her behavior, and that beats being an angel.

If your child feels that she is totally innocent, hasn't caused trouble even by mistake, the only person who can solve the problem is the teacher. The teacher can't solve it alone, though, because she can give you only her version. It takes teacher and child together to get at the facts here.

Because most elementary school children are neither secure nor mature enough to ask a teacher "Why do you pick on me?" it is up to you, the parent, to orchestrate a teacher-child talk. Make an appointment for you and your child to see the teacher, and don't back down from including your child in the meeting if she balks at being there—as she probably will. Explain that she is the only one who can present her side of the story.

Don't go into the meeting angry, and don't go in apologetically. Be up front in presenting the situation: "Jackie feels that she gets punished more than the other children. Since she doesn't know why, we thought a talk between the two of you might clear things up."

In 90 percent of the cases, it does. The teacher assures Jackie that she likes her and refreshes her memory by pointing out that four other girls also missed recess that day because they were pushing in the hall. "Oh, yes," Jackie remembers sheepishly. They clear the air, and Jackie may say on the way home, as one of my own sons did, "Gee, I didn't know she was so nice!" Or even: "Boy, that Anne. She really gets in trouble!"

There are two other possible scenarios, however.

The teacher may confront Jackie with a series of other past actions that warranted the discipline she meted out. You had not heard about these. "Do you remember doing that?" you or the teacher may ask. "Well," Jackie may drawl reluctantly, "sort of." With that admission, the teacher and Jackie set the scene to explore her behavior, probe into reasons for it, and come up with some solutions. Again they have cleared the air so that Jackie can start anew tomorrow.

On the other hand, the teacher may attempt to defend a totally unjustified disciplinary action. Teachers can be wrong, remember. When one of my sons was in the third grade, his teacher had the children make Mother's Day cards. As each child completed his card, he showed it to the teacher for approval. When Chris presented his card, the teacher tore it in two saying "This is no good. Make another one." He did not make another one, but gave me the two pieces stuck together with Scotch tape. When Chris and I spoke to the teacher the next day, she admitted she should not have torn his drawing, but explained that because it wasn't very good, she thought he could do better. He never did do better; if fact, to this day he does not draw at all.

If you find yourself in a similar situation, I think you have every right to demand an apology to your child. If, however, the teacher does not even feel she made an error, then I think you and the teacher should have a little conference together with the principal.

A teacher's ill-advised action cannot be undone. However, it can serve to teach a child the painful lesson that grown-ups too can make mistakes, and in that knowledge she may gain strength to accept her own.

"What if my child hates his teacher?"

Like adults, children too run into personality conflicts, one of the most troublesome of which can be in their relationship with a teacher. As a parent, you find yourself in a frustrating situation: In the next classroom is a teacher your child adores, and here he is doomed to spend the year with one he can't stand. What should you do?

· *Don't* try to get him switched to another class. As I pointed out earlier in the book, throughout life your child is going to find himself having to get along with people he does not like—classmates throughout school, bosses and coworkers later on, neighbors, community members, even relatives and in-laws. If you teach him early on that the way to handle the situation is to run away from it, you have set the stage for future trouble. Finding a way to survive the year with a teacher he dislikes is a far more valuable lesson.

· Let your child know that you understand his feelings and that it is all right to dislike a teacher. "You don't have to like everyone, dear!"

· Ask him to define, if he can, what he doesn't like about the teacher. Children often dislike people who are different from those to whom they are accustomed merely because, inexperienced as they are, they see difference as a threat. If your child explains dislike for a teacher because "She's old-fashioned," or "She has a dumb laugh," or "She talks funny," take the opportunity to explain the value of diversity among people . . . and of tolerance.

· In addition, explain that, although life is more enjoyable if he likes his teacher, he can learn even if he doesn't. Point out that learning, not liking, is the business of school.

I have observed that in most cases, a child who begins the year hating his teacher reaches a state of peaceful acceptance within a month or so. As my own grandson told me just the other day. "She's not so bad after all."

"Is it bad for my child to be the teacher's pet?"

As enviable as the role of teacher's pet may sound, in truth it is highly damaging.

· It makes the other children dislike your child. I heard children chanting this ditty to a classmate who apparently never got punished:

> "Teacher's pet, teacher's pet,
> You ought to have what you never get."

· Being teacher's pet encourages hypocrisy in your child. She plays the goody-goody role in school and another part when her teacher can't see her.

· 157 ·

· In providing special allowances and favors for your child, the role of teacher's pet deprives her of experience in handling the pains and problems that the other children face. She may find out the hard way that she isn't every teacher's pet.

· I think the most damaging thing about being teacher's pet is that it encourages your child to believe her worth depends upon being good. She has to be good—or at least *act* good—or no one will like her. How this warps the wonderful, fallible person she really is!

If you think your child has become teacher's pet, go see the teacher. Explain that you think your child is being catered to excessively, pointing out specific instances to support your claim. "The other children are beginning to tease her about it," you might say, or "She feels you scold other children even when she has been at fault."

The teacher will undoubtedly reply, "But she is such a darling child. I never need to scold her."

Stand your ground. You might try, "Thank you. We think she's pretty terrific too, but we make her toe the mark. I hope you will too."

Although the teacher may not say words to the effect of "Okay, I will change," chances are she will make an effort.

Meanwhile back at home, you might have a talk with your daughter about her responsibility in being teacher's pet. Ask her to examine her behavior to see whether she encourages the teacher's favors. For instance, does she volunteer for every job that comes along? Does she always defend and agree with her teacher in contrast to the rest of the class? Let your daughter do a little self-observation.

"What should I do about a teacher who can't handle religious differences?"

Fortunately it is a rare teacher who is either so foolish or so cruel as to deliberately hurt children by mishandling religion. It happens occasionally, though. I know a child whose teacher called her a "kike." The mother learned of it when her daughter, never having heard the word, asked, "What does it mean to be called a *kite*?"

No excuse is acceptable, and no allowance can be made for that teacher or for any teacher who displays bigotry. When a principal saw sixth graders taunting a classmate in the hall, he was surprised at what they were saying: "You're dumb, and your dad's dumb if he said you didn't come from a monkey, 'cause you did. Maybe they're still monkeys!"

Deeply concerned, he questioned the teacher, who admitted she was discussing evolution with the class and perhaps had gone overboard in saying that people who don't accept it in the face of evidence are just not very smart. The child from a creationist home was probably less permanently hurt than the others who witnessed the teacher's bigotry: He found protection in his parents' teaching, but they found a deadly weapon for future use. The role model gave it legitimacy.

If a teacher disparages your child or any other child because of his religion, you have a right to be outraged and should waste no time confronting the teacher. Should the teacher ever do it a second time, you should advise the principal, the superintendent, or the Board of Education, and insist that they take steps to remove either the bigotry or the teacher.

More often religious mishandlings come about thoughtlessly: a teacher involves the whole class in making Easter baskets or shoebox crèches, or plans a class trip on a Jewish holiday. If this is the case in your child's class, speak to the teacher, who may be totally unaware of the hurt he is causing. I know a school where the PTA took steps to assure that no child would feel hurt or left out at Christmastime. They got volunteers to tell children about the legend of Santa Claus and read the Christmas story from the Bible, and they also had volunteers teach children how to make dredels and sing a Hanukkah song; when Passover and Easter came around, they conducted a Seder for the children and also discussed da Vinci's "Last Supper."

Making room for Christian and Jewish religions may not be enough any more. With the growing diversity in American schools, it is not uncommon to have Moslem, Buddhist, and Hindu children, whose parents can bring great enrichment to the class in discussions of their religion, rituals, and holidays. These children, like children raised in homes with no religion, should not be forced to participate in the generally accepted Christian activities at holiday times. You can insist that your child's teacher find nonreligious alternatives such as holly wreaths, snowmen, bunny rabbits, spring flowers, and so on.

While Christian holidays overwhelm the country's stores, main streets, and media, teachers have a responsibility not to let them overwhelm the classroom. When teachers forget, parents like you must remind them.

· Concerns with Teachers in Junior High ·

"What is a good junior high teacher?"

· 159 ·

A good teacher of preadolescents is one who, in their vernacular, turns them on. Although teachers have individual ways of accomplishing this feat, the common denominator is an ability to turn cut-and-dried material into a personal adventure in learning for each child. You can find examples of this kind of teaching as various as the imaginations of the teachers themselves:

· Instead of assigning her students to memorize the Greek gods and goddesses from Bulfinch's *Mythology*, a teacher I know had her class rewrite familiar fairy tales using Greek gods and goddesses as characters. The class selected several of the plays for production and, years later, still remember Hepaestus as Rumplestilskin and the Furies as Cinderella's stepsisters!

· An English teacher lets her class learn the metrical feet used in poetry by choreographing dances to the different patterns.

· A science teacher introduces biology by having each child keep a chart of his weight changes, blood pressure, temperature, and liquid intake and output for a week. One of the parents told me that his daughter had so much fun with the project that she undertook to monitor the whole family's bodily functions.

· A math teacher raises money with his students through a cake sale. With the proceeds the class purchases a share of stock, measuring its ups and downs throughout the year in fractions, decimals, and percentages. What a way to learn math . . . and maybe even future financial wizardry!

· A social studies teacher asks each child to select a disadvantaged group to which he will belong for a week—blind, mentally disabled, old, homeless, unemployed, non-English speaking, and so on. During that week, through dress and behavior, students re-create the person they have chosen, recording the reactions of other people to them, their own feelings, and their ways of responding. Although he has not conducted a longitudinal study, the teacher is convinced that his students' empathy will lead to greater social awareness when they grow up. I once visited a class where the teacher made the majority of her students a status "green," while the remainder were a less enviable "blue," in order for them to experience how prejudice affects interactions.

The appearance of simulation games on the educational market testifies to the value of learning by doing. These kits provide teachers with materials and directions for setting up experiential learning situations similar to the social studies examples just described. One of them turns the class into a working community in which each student undertakes a job in retailing, wholesaling, insurance, government, police, and so on. One of my granddaughters, who was the town banker, came away not only with a knowledge of checking, savings, loans, and interest but with new respect for the interdependence of people and their enterprises.

Admittedly it is difficult to spark academic ardor in preadolescents whose minds whirl with rock music, ball games, and sexual fantasies. Yet teachers can do it, and when they do, "There's no stopping those kids!"

"My child feels ignored."

Your child is not alone; many children in a large junior high school complain, "No one even knows I'm alive." I know children who feel it even in smaller schools, and they all deserve your empathy. Put yourself in your child's place. He has left an elementary school where he had a room in which to hang his coat and a teacher who counseled and kept track of him; now he has a locker in the hall and a homeroom teacher who just takes attendance. Before, he and his friends had the same classes together with just one or two teachers; now he faces six or seven different teachers and rarely sees his friends till lunch. In elementary school the principal used to greet him by name; now the principal doesn't even recognize his face. One child explained his sense

· 160 ·

of being nobody this way: "I saw a big cornfield on television once, maybe with a million plants growing in rows. Well, I feel like one of those corn stalks right in the middle of the field."

How can you help?

Begin by acknowledging his feelings. Don't tell him, "That's silly. Of course the teachers know who you are." Most of them probably don't, and even if they do, he *feels* they don't. That is what matters. His sense of being nobody is far more real than a statistical count of the teachers who do and do not know him. Don't take his feelings away; let him have them.

In addition, assure him that it's all right to feel like that; under the circumstances, it's inevitable. If you tell him, "I can see why you feel like that," he will begin to feel less invisible.

Go on to explain that with 125 students in their classes, teachers can't devote time to personal relationships as they did in elementary school, "but the reason they are there is that they *do* care about you. Your growth and learning are a measure of their own self-esteem."

Explain too that growing up, as he will come to understand, brings not only many new people into his world, but many new kinds of relationships with them—some more personal than others. "It's hard because you have been thrust into this all at once. It'll get easier when you get used to it. And I promise you that even in a big junior high or high school or college, you will have a teacher or two who become a close part of your education. The other teachers you learn from. Those teachers you remember."

· 161 ·

One final word: Keep in mind that even though your junior high child may have shot up six inches and show signs of adult budding, he is still a little child in many ways. One of those ways is his need for love and acceptance, which may be harder to give now than when he was an acquiescent three-year-old. Give it anyway—abundantly.

"My child's teacher seems too interested in her."

A teacher who shows a special interest in your preadolescent can motivate her with horsepower that you never knew was there. In place of invisibility, your child feels like a shining star in the school's vast firmament, and you see her rays spark new interests, new projects, new discussions at home. Would that every child could be so blessed!

Yet even the moon has its dark side, and as the teacher's interest in your child develops into a closer relationship with more time spent together, you may begin to ask, "Is this normal? Is this healthy?" In most cases, the answer is yes. Occasionally, however, it is no. When can you tell the difference?

In the normal turmoil of preadolescence, it is easy for children to develop a strong attachment to a teacher who encourages it. Unlike a parent who seems always to find fault, this teacher recognizes the best in her, denying her sense of inadequacy and nothingness. The child thrills to the special attention she receives and feels like Wonder Woman. As a result, it is easy for a teacher to exploit children for his own emotional needs, which are usually satisfied by a coterie of "worshipers," who work harder than they ever have and eventually outgrow him. Sometimes the teacher's needs are more intense, and the exploitation becomes sex abuse.

To tell the difference between a teacher's productive and unhealthy interest, parents must rely greatly on their own intuition. However, a few suggestions may help:

· Start by sharing your child's enthusiasm for her teacher. Avoid prying, but express your interest and encourage her to talk about what she and the teacher do.

   Not: "Is anything funny going on between you and Mr. Golding?"
   But: "Mr. Golding must be wonderful; I've never seen you so turned on by a subject. What kinds of things do you do together?"

· Don't be jealous of the attention you may feel your child is taking away from you to give to the teacher. At this age it is far more normal to wax enthusiastic over a teacher than over a parent! You probably can recall a teacher you adored, can't you?

· Don't let your child engage in activities with the teacher outside of school unless other children are included. But find a way to put your foot down without making accusations: "No, I don't think any teacher should do things with a student outside of school unless the whole class is involved. It muddies the student-teacher relationship."

· Don't allow your child to go to the teacher's home unless the whole class is invited.

· Have the teacher to your home for dinner. This way you will get to know him better, and you can observe his relationship with your child.

· If your concern grows, discuss it with your child. Explain that you feel the teacher has gone beyond the usual boundaries of a relationship with a student. "I really feel there is something unhealthy in the way

Mr. Golding feels about you. Don't you sense it yourself? Does it make you uncomfortable too?"

· Don't talk to other parents about your concern, because rumors will begin to fly and damage your child as much as the teacher. Above all, it will break down trust in your relationship with your child.

· If you feel you can—and this is not easy—have a talk with the teacher. Don't accuse him of anything, but don't mince words either. "I'm sorry I have to say this," you might begin, "but I think the closeness you and my child have developed is not in her best interests. We both think you are a wonderful teacher, but I wish you would put more distance between you and have a more usual teacher-student relationship."

· If you don't get anywhere with the teacher and you feel the situation is potentially serious, talk to the principal. She is in a position to investigate the teacher without making accusations and to take appropriate steps should your concerns prove to be founded. I know a case where parents reported their suspicions of sexual involvement to the principal, who admitted that the teacher had been suspected of misconduct at a previous school but had never been actually accused. I know other cases where principals were able to put a stop to excessive interest in students by merely speaking directly to the teachers.

· 163 ·

"My child's teacher acts like one of the kids."

Some teachers, usually inexperienced ones, feel that the way to make students like them is to adopt manners and mannerisms that cater to their preadolescent tastes. He may use obscene language or sexual allusions; he may be lax in homework requirements and classroom behavior; he may discuss off-limits elements of his personal life—sex, drinking, drugs. The result is inevitably little order and less learning. While preadolescents are titillated by this kind of teacher, at the same time they resent it, having little respect for someone who so condescends to them.

I think the best course of action for you in this case is to speak to the faculty advisor, who in some cases is a vice principal or dean of faculty or perhaps even the principal herself. Because the teacher is most likely new at the job and misguided in his eagerness to "relate" to his students, what he needs is not a reprimand but help. I have seen schools overcome this problem by assigning teachers with this problem a more experienced teacher as a mentor who will sit in on a few classes and suggest changes for improvement. If the teacher is serious about implementing the suggestions, he can master the techniques in a short time. Unfortunately, when a teacher has played the teenager with his class, he is going to have to work hard to change the image, and that may take a long time.

"Do I dare make my child confront a teacher alone?"

At junior high a child should be able to handle problems that arise with teachers without your intervention. He should be able to ask for extra help, explain why he couldn't complete a homework assignment, protest his innocence when the teacher accuses him unjustly, and so on. If he is shy, however, or lacks self-confidence, he may suffer the agony of a Roman prisoner tossed to a lion if he has to face a teacher alone. You can help.

- Begin by encouraging him to speak to the teacher by himself: "I know it seems scary, but remember, she can only understand what happened if you tell her. If you don't, she has to go on what she supposes. She really *wants* to know."
- If he still can't brave the lion, then go in with him to see the teacher, but let him know beforehand that he has to explain the problem to the teacher, not you. You will be there, but you are not going to do it for him.
- At the meeting, lend moral support, but don't take over. Let the teacher and your child do most of the talking.
- After the meeting, compliment your child on the way he handled the problem, and point out that he really did it by himself even though you were there.

When the next problem arises, he may have enough confidence to do the job himself. If not, repeat the process above until, like a fledgling sparrow, he can wing it on his own.

CHAPTER 13

In School: Grading

· Marks ·

"Why do children need marks?"

I am speaking to a group of parents and teachers at an independent school in the Midwest. I say, "In the hands of schools, marks become poison darts aimed at a child's life center. He feels the sting as the dart hits, but not yet downed by its venom, he continues to stagger and struggle until he can muster no more strength and prop himself up with no more hope. Then he dies."

The audience sits aghast until a parent asks—I can't tell whether in shock or anger—"Why do you hate marks?" I have heard the question before.

I don't hate marks. Marks are a helpful tool for students to see what they have learned and for teachers to see what they have taught. What I hate is the way teachers and parents often use marks.

As a teacher, I have always explained to my students that grades are simplified codes delivered to them like rolled-up messages in the foot of a carrier pigeon. At a quick glance, marks tell me the degree to which I have or have not taught my students what I am supposed to teach them; at the same time, they tell my students the degree to which they have or have not learned what they are supposed to learn. Some other teachers, however, communicate a different message with grades, which students quickly pick up. As William James phrased it, they "worship the bitch-goddess success."

Students get the idea—and not falsely—that marks evaluate them as people— measure not how far they have come in math or English but how far they will never go in life. This destroys their self-esteem. They also understand that teachers use marks to motivate them, holding them like a sword of Damocles over their head to make them study. This destroys their own inner push toward the thrill of learning.

"Why do grades kill when used for evaluation?"

As I return papers, the classroom inevitably hums with frantic whispers of "What ya get?" I see students with broad smiles flaunting their papers, along with those who lower their eyes and shamefully slip theirs between pages of a looseleaf notebook. I see children glow or pale into shadows.

I sent innocuous messages. The As and Bs and Cs told students, "You and I can go on to something new"; the Ds and Fs say, "You and I have some more work to do here." Both messages steered the students and me in a direction for learning. That's all.

Yet the majority of students missed the point because they don't understand marks as a language of learning; they translate the signs into personal success and failure. In the As and Bs they read, "I'm a winner"; in the Ds and Fs they read, "I'm a loser"; and in the Cs they read, "I'm not good enough." The grades on their papers don't fly to them on pigeon feet, but instead charge into the classroom on the claws of a tiger.

Year after year I have seen the self-image of young people destroyed. When they say, "I got an F in math," they mean, "I am an F person." Although I know, and try to convince them, that some extra help in fractions may strengthen them but that even if it doesn't, they are still all right, what they know is more final: that they will never be all right. They are F people, and F people lose out on more than math; they lose out on life.

When the kindergarten teacher sticks the first gold star on a child's forehead, marks become the measurement of worth: "I'm good because I wrote my letter in the line . . . or didn't spill my milk . . . or wrote my first name." But what about the child with no gold star? "I must be bad because my Ts jumped up too high . . . or I got milk on the table . . . or I wrote 'FRIC' instead of 'ERIC'."

From the beginning children learn that stars and smiles and high marks reward "good" and that starless foreheads and blank looks and low marks punish "bad." No one sits down with a lesson book to teach them; they learn through subtler means: teacher's tone of voice, parents' joy or sorrow, classmates' pride or shame. The system is designed for marks because they fit on report cards and because they are quick and easy to understand.

When teachers use marks to evaluate a child, they replace the self-evaluation he has struggled to develop from infancy with an arbitrary one of their own. Therefore, not only do marks infect a child's self-image like a metastasizing cancer, but they block his personal growth as well. He can no longer discover what is important to him in the long years of learning; he has to respond to what is important to his teachers. He can no longer search for his own values; he has to accept those of the teacher. Now that a teacher holds the yardstick, he has to lay aside the measurements by which he could evaluate himself and accept instead evaluation by her yardstick. As a result, he has to grow into what she considers important and live by what she values.

Marks lie to children about what they are. Marks limit children in what they can become. That's why marks kill like poison arrows.

· 167 ·

"Why do grades kill when used for motivation?"

The voice of a first-grade teacher rings harshly in my ears. "Everyone who gets an A can go out on the playground after lunch," she announced before a spelling test. As the children poised their pencils, they knew why spelling was important: It gave them privileges.

Using marks to motivate students begins early in school and continues throughout. The "good" students get to carry messages to the front office . . . and join the Honor Society . . . and be in the play or on the football team. They also get accepted at Yale and Vassar . . . and into status graduate schools . . . and finally into "top" jobs. The privileges of working to get high marks are obvious.

The damage, though less obvious, is also taking place. Many students study hard because they are eager for new experiences; they are curious and stimulated by the thrill of discovery. I am not concerned with these students because they do not need marks to motivate them. I am concerned with those students who study hard only to get good marks and the rewards they bring. They miss the value of learning in two main ways.

Learning involves risk taking—venturing into the uncharted territory of long division and French and Shakespeare in order to discover it. Memorizing facts, repeating lecture notes, and waiting for a teacher to provide the "right" answer is a sure path to good marks. On the other hand, individual probing and problem solving may lead to "wrong" answers and not-so-good marks, which, I might point out, is the usual course of genius and invention.

The mark-motivated student cannot be a real learner because she dares not take a risk. She must play it safe, like a worker bee in a beehive in order to assure an A. As a result, she misses the thrill of learning, described by many educators as the "wow! experience." She does the drudge work, but never becomes the queen bee.

More important, the mark-motivated student fails to become a life-long learner. Eventually—after she has won all the diplomas and degrees and there is no one around to give out marks any more—she can't find a reason to reach out and learn. So the student who worked for marks stops learning, stops growing, stops living in the fullest sense.

A feeling of emptiness, psychiatrists report, is the major cause of depression in the United States: People have no reason to wake up in the morning. They go to work, they come home, they watch TV; but nothing matters. They are bored. Lifelong learning precludes boredom; mark-long learning invites it.

· 168 ·

"Is it better to use no marks at all?"

For me to answer that question is like a minister answering "Which is better, religion or atheism?" My life has convinced me of a point of view just as his has. I suffered through the trauma of marks as a child, doing well but always frightened and anxious. As a teacher and counselor I saw marks defeat children, and as a principal I determined that no more children in my school would die. I gave up marks in favor of comment slips for many reasons.

1. The descriptive comments on nongraded report cards pinpoint a student's strengths and weaknesses with far greater accuracy than objective marks can. What does an A or an F tell you about your child's interests or personality or motivation as they relate to his learning?
2. Because one single percentage point can make the difference between a C plus and a B minus on a student's report card, a child's academic rating hangs on a thread. I've heard parents yell because their child got a B instead of a B plus.

3. In a nongraded system, students dare take the risk of original thinking because they have space to work through errors without being penalized. In a graded system, where errors result in big, red Fs, students are more likely to play it safe by giving the teacher the answers she expects. They remind me of Czechoslovakian students suddenly released from Marxist propaganda, who explained their previous school behavior to The *New York Times*: "Naturally we all lied. You had to copy ideas from textbooks that you don't agree with, and sometimes you even had to pretend that you agree with it." They too were afraid to question and debate.

4. The excitement and personal satisfaction of learning are in the long run stronger motivations for learning than the competitive struggle for marks. The loss to students deprived of opportunities to realize this struck me dramatically when one of my students at the university admitted he could think of no reason to study besides marks. When a fellow student, almost as stunned as I, pointed out that he has studied many subjects just for the fun and satisfaction of knowing, the first student rationalized, "It must have been to make you more interesting at parties."

I wonder and worry: What will happen to this student when he graduates from marks?

"Can marks be used constructively?"

Yes, marks can be used and sometime are used constructively. You can check your school and give it a mark yourself.

· Have the teachers made it clear that they give marks only as a form of abbreviated language to tell both students and teachers what they still have to do? After I return the first college freshmen papers, which are usually pretty weak, I love to see the surprise on their faces when I say, "If you failed, great! Now we know what we have to work on." In high school they saw no connection between "failed" and "great."

· Does the school keep marks private? I know a school that posts them on the bulletin board!

· Does the school deemphasize marks by not having prizes and honor rolls? While these serve as great status symbols for students and give parents plenty of brag material, they make personal evaluation by mark a central focus of the school. When one of the schools where I have worked wanted to give an annual prize in my name and asked me to determine the category, I suggested a prize for the student who took the biggest risk in learning and failed. The school abandoned the idea of a Mary Susan Miller award.

· Do the teachers discuss marks personally with each student? Even a five-minute conference can put marks in perspective.

· Does the school explain the significance of marks to parents? I know one that sends a note home with each report card, urging parents to regard the marks more as signs of progress than of achievement.

· Does your own child feel as one I know who said, "They're not all that important"?

· Do you?

If you tally a lot of yes answers to those questions, you can be pretty sure that your child's school is not hitting him with poison darts.

· Constructive Evaluation in Preschool ·

"When should I expect the first evaluation?"

There is little value in a parent-teacher conference to evaluate nursery school or kindergarten children until your child has had ample time to adjust to the experience of new teachers, new friends, new regimen. While a week or two may suffice for some children, others need months in order to develop enough trust and confidence to go about the business of growth and learning. Many children actually regress when they begin preschool because they feel they have to rely on the babyish behaviors they used before school to get attention—crying, temper tantrums, clinging, wetting. You will have to rely on your own judgment and the teacher's to know when your child has settled into a pattern.

An initial preschool evaluation should have some validity by Thanksgiving because your child has had time to adjust and the teacher time to observe. While most nursery schools rely on verbal evaluations in a meeting of parent and teacher, your kindergarten may send home a formal sheet with written comments by the teacher, or even a printed form with the teacher's checks in boxes labeled "Gets Along with Peers," "Follows Directions," and so on.

As Chapter 5 pointed out, if your child's changed behavior at home indicates an incipient problem, don't wait, but take the initiative to explore it with the teacher. Relax though; if the teacher senses a problem developing, she will rarely ignore it, but will call you in for discussion. Preschool teachers, like casting agents, work best under the principle of "Don't call us; we'll call you."

"What do I do after a conference?"

A preschool teacher complained to me one day that although parents could not wait to hear how their children were faring in school, they rarely put the information to use. "It's as if I hand them a cement block," she said, "and they just sit there holding it instead of using it to build a foundation."

"What a waste of material!" I agreed. Parents need to understand that a teacher's observations are for the child's benefit, not for the parents': not to swell the parents' egos if the child is doing well, not to shame them if he is having trouble, but to guide them in ways of reinforcing his development. You can put what the teacher tells you to the best use for your child with a few simple guidelines:

· First, let your child know that the teacher likes her and is pleased with how much she contributes to the class. A simple "Your teacher says you're wonderful, and she is happy you are in her class" will do.

· Then share the teacher's comments with the child. If she has not participated in the teacher conference (see Chapter 9) tell her what the teacher said—the areas in which the teacher said she is doing well and those she might work on. For instance, "Mrs. Jackson is thrilled that you know all the songs and that you can push yourself on the swing." Stop here and give your child a chance to discuss her prowess. Then: "But she says you spill your juice a lot. Do you? What do you suppose makes that happen?"

· Make efforts to help the child strengthen her areas of weakness not by scolding or lecturing but by introducing appropriate activities. For instance, if she has trouble playing with other children, create structured games for her and her friends at home, instead of just letting them fend for themselves. If she has trouble concentrating, engage her in an activity with you—building blocks, listening to a story, and so on—for longer periods of time each day. If she clings to dependence, make a game of her dressing herself, picking up her room, and so on.

· If the developing problem appears more serious—such as excessive fatigue, speech difficulty, or motor inadequacy—don't discuss it with your child at this time. You and the teacher should decide how to handle it, as we shall discuss in detail in Chapter 18. You will probably involve her at that point.

· Avoid labeling your child in response to the teacher's observations. Whatever a child is at four or five has every chance of altering as she matures: The rest of the class may catch up to the "bright" child, and the "slow" or "lazy" child may grow to be a star. Help her remain a whole person.

· If your child's school has sent evaluations home, save them. Not only will they serve as points of reference in judging your child's progress, but they will provide fun and enlightenment for your children as they get older and look back on themselves. There was great amusement in the voice of a six-year-old who reminded his father, "Remember when I was little and got my Zs backward?"

"How telling is a preschool evaluation?"

Because the source of a preschool child's behavior is usually his level of maturity, how he functions in school rarely indicates his innate ability as a student. If he has begun school too early, however, the problems he encounters at three, four, and five may continue all through school. (This is fully discussed in Chapter 5.)

On the other hand, if a child is gifted, a teacher can usually tell from indications beyond those of maturity. A gifted child will show longer-than-usual periods of concentration, more intense curiosity, more adept skill at taking things apart, a larger vocabulary, among other signs. You will probably notice these signs at home as well. If you do, I urge both you and the teacher not to make an issue of it. Do not have the child tested at this point. Instead, create a stimulating environment for him to play and grow in and enjoy him as he does.

Keep whatever assessment the teacher makes of your child in perspective.

No matter what the teacher sees in school, the picture is never complete. While the teacher may record daily observations of your child's behavior, she cannot know the internal processes that lead to his behavior nearly so well as you do. For example, the teacher may be aware of his inability to tie his shoe or get along with classmates, but you are in a better position to know why. Seeing him only in school, the teacher is privy only to what the psychologist Jung called your child's "persona"—that part of the Self which people want the world to see, not the part allowed to act in the privacy of family. As a result, the preschool darling may be a hellion at home . . . and vice versa. The teacher has only a partial picture.

On the other hand, the teacher sees your child in relation to other children in the class and to others in many classes before while you see your child alone or in relation to siblings and occasional friends. Therefore, although the teacher may not have a complete picture of your child, she has a picture that compares him against others. For instance, you pour your child's juice at breakfast automatically and think nothing of it when he sits back and waits. The teacher sees him at snack time as the only child among fifteen who doesn't know how to pour from a pitcher. In this case you have only a partial picture.

It is only through the combined viewpoints of you and the teacher that you are able to see a complete picture of your child. Therefore, don't interpret the teacher's evaluation as the finished portrait without adding the lights and shadows you see at home and in a variety of other settings, along with your greater understanding of the causes of his behavior.

"How should I react when my child earns gold stars?"

Fortunately, no nursery schools and only a scattered few kindergartens (and those only at parental insistence) give marks as such to the three-, four-, and five-year-olds in their charge. They often do, however, give equivalents: gold stars and, if a child doesn't quite make it, silver. I shudder to recall a teacher who gave chocolate kisses instead! The "good" children surely developed cavities and the "bad" ones, ego problems.

Children at this age, as they have since birth, develop self-esteem almost wholly as a reflection of their parents' response to them. Gold stars, while acknowledging their mastery in a diversity of areas, have little effect on a child's general feeling of worth unless teachers and especially parents make the connection for her. "I stood the quietest in line," a kindergartner announces proudly as she hops off the school bus, patting the star on her forehead. She may not yet have broadened its significance to "I am the best kid in class," but she surely will when her parents equate "gold star" with "good girl." Then the trouble begins.

You can prevent your child from falling victim to mark abuse when she gets older if you begin now to keep gold stars in their place.

· Praise your child's achievement when she comes home with a gold star, but don't praise her as a person. For instance, don't say, "What a good girl you are to stand still so long. I am proud of you." That extends the gold star too far. Say instead, "I'll bet it wasn't easy to stand still in line so long. You did a hard job." That keeps the gold star where it belongs. In making this distinction, you will let her know that being wonderful does not depend on winning or not winning gold stars, but simply upon being her own self, which nothing can change.

· Compliment her as she displays her prize, but don't harp on it. If she wants to tell someone else about it, all right; but don't urge her to "show Uncle George what you got today," and don't show him yourself.

· Avoid asking her as she comes home from school, "Did you get any gold stars today?" Just hug her and be glad she's home.

"What should I do if the teacher praises my child too much?"

Some teachers are so smitten with a child that they set him up as an example for the other children. "Terry is the best worker in the class," one kindergarten teacher repeated almost daily, as Terry began to see himself as some kind of Wonderkid. Although such singling out may inflate parental pride, it distorts a child's self-perception, often placing upon him the burden of always having to be best. What should you do?

· Go see the teacher. Explain what you see happening and ask that your child not be singled out for more praise than other children. "I'm thrilled that you think he is as wonderful as we do," you might say, "but I'm afraid he'll begin to think he's the only wonderful one in the world."

· If your child tells you, "I'm the best in the class," explain that you are very proud of him but add that most children are best at something. I heard a mother discussing with her little girl what each child in the class was best at, and after completing a list that included "bests" from coloring to putting away blocks, the mother asked, "What are you best at?" She was duly distressed to hear, "Oh, I am best at being best."

· How to Use Elementary and Junior High School
Evaluations Constructively ·

"What kinds of marks do schools use at these levels?"

Although some schools continue to give comment slips in the primary grades, most schools grade students with marks as soon as first

· 174 ·

grade, and almost all schools use marks by third grade. These may be the traditional A, B, C, D, and F or the more subtle E (Excellent), G (Good), S (Satisfactory), and N (Needs Improvement).

Whatever symbols a school uses to grade students, children cut through the softening efforts right to the cold, hard facts. An E by any other name is an A; a G is a B; an S is a C; and an N is a big fat F. Educators do not fool children. They may call Laurie's reading group the Blue Birds and Billy's the Chickadees; but when asked, Laurie says, "I'm in the smart group," and Billy says, "I'm in the dumb group." Winners and losers balance on threads as tenuous as letters of the alphabet and bird names. Remembering that may keep a Chickadee or an N from destroying your child's self-esteem and a Blue Bird or an E from destroying someone else's.

"What can I do to help my child keep marks in perspective?"

You can do a great deal to offset the damaging effect of marks to which your child may be subjected in school.

· 175 ·

· Don't be among those parents who consider their children's high marks as status symbols, like mink coats and shares in blue-chip stocks. When you accept the idea that marks are merely teacher-student messages of progress, you realize that they can't do a single thing for your ego. Of course, you are proud of your child when she receives an A, but you can be proud of her when she receives an F as well. The difference lies in the object of your pride: because of the A, you are proud of your child's *progress*; regardless of the A or the F, you are proud of your child's own *self*. When you honestly believe that, you have taken step one in the constructive use of grades.

· Let your child know that you think grades are important as a way of diagnosing how far she has come, but not as a way of measuring her. If the school looks on marks differently, stand firm and explain that you consider the school wrong. That is not heresy, nor is it the first and only time you and the school will have different values.

"How do I handle report cards?"

· When the report card arrives, go over it with your child. Be interested. Listen to her comments. Avoid judging a whole report card as "good" or "bad," but discuss individual marks instead. For instance, don't say, "This is an excellent report card" but rather "You must feel good about your progress in math."

· If you are facing a row of As and Bs, you might comment on how much your child appears to have learned and discuss the material she covered: "You must know an awful lot about the Sumerians. What parts of their culture did you study?"

· In the light of Cs, make it clear to your child that C means average, despite the sense of failure with which teachers and students often view it.

· With Ds and Fs, your child may arrive with either tears or defensive excuses, neither of which will profit. You can help her see those marks more positively by analyzing rather than judging them: "It's clear that you need some work here. What do you think is the problem? Can you correct it, or do you think you should talk to the teacher about it?"

· If your child receives low marks, investigate her effort and study habits with her. Often a new homework routine can set her on a more successful track. (Chapter 15 discusses this.)

· 176 ·

· If she is deeply distressed over low marks and sees no way to improve, despite your suggestions, urge her to sit down with her teacher(s) to work out a plan. Often a different seat in class, a new method of note-taking, or some periods of extra help will solve the problem. If your child can't handle a teacher conference on her own, go with her, but let the teacher and her do the talking.

· Avoid the temptation to tell a child with a B that she can pull it up to an A next time. A B is a sign that she learned a lot; let her know that and be happy with her. When I ask students what they consider their greatest problem with parents, over half usually reply, "No matter what I do, I can't ever seem to please them." Be a parent your child can please.

"Should I give any kind of reward or punishment for marks?"

· Don't reward your child for getting high marks. You will take away any other motivation he has for learning. I think of Julian who used to burst into his home after school with cries of "You'll never guess what I learned about the ocean today," or "I'll bet you don't know what a circumference is!" He did well in school because he was excited to learn, but his parents missed the point. "We'll give you a dollar for every A and fifty cents for every B," they told him. By the end of the year Julian was more excited about tallying up money for his piggy bank than learning. He still got As and Bs, but he lost something more important.

· Be wary of overpraising your child for high marks. Let him know he did well and let it go at that. Too much praise places tremendous stress on a child to keep doing well and better and best. He becomes terrified of not living up to the image. Some children give up and completely stop working rather than continue in the parental pressure cooker; others bear the stress load but cheat for fear of not doing well enough.

· Don't deprive or punish your child for getting low marks. Because the shame he feels is far worse than any punishment you can heap on him, your job is to alleviate the shame, not to reinforce it. Punishment makes him feel like an even greater failure, and failure is a sure path to turning off.

· If your child blames the teacher for low marks, saying she wasn't fair or didn't cover the material, drop the subject for the time being. Later, after he has recovered from his hurt and shame, you will be able to handle the situation more productively. (The first part of this chapter discusses how.)

· Just as Fs do not make a child an F person, neither do As make him an A person. If your child brings home top marks, while not belittling academic achievement, you can help him realize the great diversity among people and the diverse areas in which they make outstanding contributions. Intolerance and intellectual snobbery, which are sometimes by-products of straight As, limit opportunities for real learning.

· 177 ·

"What if the school and I differ about marks?"

Because schools are not designed to fit parents, nor parents schools, as snugly as foot sizes and shoes, frequently their conflicting values pinch. Low-key parents often find their children in highly mark-competitive schools, and achievement-oriented parents find their children in schools that downplay marks. If you are one of them, what are you to do?

During my six years as director of an independent school, the faculty and I shifted the goal from an emphasis on marks to an emphasis on noncompetitive learning. We eliminated academic prizes and honor rolls; replaced traditional marks with Pass, Fail, and, in some courses,

High Pass; replaced report cards with descriptive comments by each child's teacher. Children now had an opportunity to learn for learning's sake and parents, to watch their progress in terms of growth rather than achievement.

Installing the new philosophy split the school population down the middle. One group embraced it for freeing students to learn, while the other opposed it for removing their motivation for learning. The faculty and I strove to educate parents and students, pointing out the benefits children reap from nongraded learning. Although we were able to convert some parents and students to the new philosophy of grading, with others we failed.

There are more mark-competitive than noncompetitive schools across the country today, reflecting the fast-track values of their communities. In these schools the honor roll brings status, paid for with anxiety; learning equates with homework and with tests graded in percentage points. I know these schools: I attended one. I know the sleepless nights before exams on which I might get a B instead of an A; I know the feeling of failure at seeing an 81 percent at the top of a history quiz; I know the hysterics over not understanding long division; I know the panic of a mental block in English. Worse than all these memories, I know the years of wasted time it took me to discover what real learning was all about—the absorption of it, the excitement, the discovery, the joy! Years beyond high school, years into college still straining for marks instead of education, like many of the young men and women in my current university class.

If your child is in a school you consider too competitive, what should you do?

· You can remove your child from the school. This is a sure cure if you can find the school you want.
· You can keep her in the school and accept the competitive system. This subjects her to the anxiety and waste I suffered.
· You can work through channels to soft-pedal the school's emphasis on marks. This takes time.
· You can offset the pressure from school by keeping marks in their place at home. I have heard many a parent, including me, say, "I know your teachers push you hard for good marks, and I know how bad they make you feel when you don't get them. But I don't feel that way. What's important to me isn't what mark you get, but what you're learning and how you feel about it." You will have to say it more than once and believe it and above all, live by it. This works.

Although it may be more difficult to find a school that has abandoned marks or puts little emphasis on them, if you find one, you will walk into a different atmosphere. Instead of the tension of children struggling their way up the bell curve, you will feel a greater sense of community: fewer tests and more group projects. You probably won't see any mimeographed worksheets or anyone answering questions in the back of the book. There will be more talking in class and less note-taking and never a voice asking "Do we have to know this for the test?" There won't be tears and sleepless nights before exams or panic over report cards. There will be fewer strained faces.

If your child is in a school you consider too noncompetitive, what should you do?

· You can take your child out of the school and find one of the many that are mark-oriented. This option refocuses learning from growth to performance and adds great stress.

· You can work within the system to change it. You may succeed, but I doubt it because a noncompetitive school finds its *raison d'être* in its philosophy.

· You can keep your child in the school and counteract its philosophy by setting up your own pressure system at home. I suspect a few parents in the school I ran told their children, "I don't care what the school thinks. I think marks are important, and they are going to stay important here. You'll know what that Pass means." This places an unnecessary burden on your child.

· You can keep your child in the school and set about learning the benefit of markless or less mark-focused learning: Talk to the principal and teachers, have them explain it at a PTA meeting, let your child explain it to you. This option works.

As you find in most matters of school, the difference between a positive and a negative experience for your child is you more often than the school.

· 179 ·

"What do I do about a poor student who can't do better?"

To children who try and still do poorly, "What ya get?" resounds like a death knell. Yet children ask it in school and parents ask it at home, and each answer breaks the hopes and the heart of the child a little bit more.

Some children are poor students and remain poor students despite their efforts. What can you do to ease the pain when your child sees herself as a failure in a world that worships success?

· Accept her as she is. Acceptance means more than merely echoing Mr. Rogers's "I love you the way you are"; it means believing it. Welcome your child as the multidimensioned person she is, not a stereotype, but a one-of-a-kind, never to be replicated.

· Help her accept herself as she is. Let her realize that "poor student" is only one side of a many-faceted person who sparkles and shines from other angles. Your acceptance of her is the stamp of approval by which she will accept herself.

· Encourage her to develop other abilities in which she can excel. I know poor students who feel like Vanessa Redgrave at a curtain call, Mickey Mantle when they touch home base, Julia Child when they bake a cake.

· Be honest with yourself and with her about her school performance. I know a family who adopted an attitude that said "Okay, so you're not a great student. So what! We'll help you get through and go on to other things in life." They provided extra help in math and reading, and their daughter was able to pass with low Cs and finally graduate. She went on to a junior college, where she made the dean's list and was proud.

· If the school is so demanding that she is unable to pass even with extra help, put her into a different school. You may locate an independent school with a geared-down program that will enable her to achieve its goals and develop self-esteem, or you may demand that your local district provide for her special needs. If only an independent school is available to meet her special problem, your local school system, responsible for the proper education of every child in the district, may be required to pay the tuition. Check with the district.

"What do I do about a child who fails and doesn't care?"

Despite appearances, no child enters school with the desire to fail. Even those children who year after year bear the labels of Fs and Ds on their report cards walk through the classroom door in September with the feeling of "This year it will be different!" Too often it is the same.

You may read a variety of signs that you think indicate not caring: Your child doesn't do his homework; he turns in papers late; he waits till the last minute to undertake a project; his work is hurried and sloppy. When you berate him about his poor performance, his very words convince you: "I don't care," he snaps.

Don't be fooled by what he says and does. Know one thing for certain: He *does* care. That is why his actions and words say he doesn't; he cares so much that he won't even try for fear of failing. While he snaps and shrugs his shoulders outside, inside he is weeping. How can you help?

- By not scolding, nagging, punishing, or threatening, all of which will reinforce his failures.
- By acknowledging the feelings of disappointment and hopelessness that failure brings.
- By working out a schedule together that will enable him to complete his work more effectively.
- By talking with him and his teacher to ascertain what kind of help he requires.
- By asking the school to send home weekly comment slips that will keep you and your child in touch with his progress.
- By arranging for extra help outside school if he needs it.
- And always by reassuring him of your love for him and of your respect for his competencies in other areas.

· *181* ·

"What do I do when my child pushes too hard for good marks?"

Children learn from all sides of their environment that life is competitive and that winning matters. While some require an outside push to keep them in the game and others give up and drop out, many children internalize the competitive drive, becoming their own team coach. These children, in spite of everything you do to get them to relax, are so caught up in a determination to win that they can't stop pushing themselves. I have seen them every year—single-focused children who miss the fun of friends and extracurricular activities and play and doing nothing in order to have time to study. Unhappy children who do not know they are unhappy. Workaholics in the seventh grade. Nervous wrecks in college, such as the student who told me, "The only thing that matters to me is getting good grades for my parents."

Although the problem is far more difficult to tackle than the one just discussed, it is just as serious. Don't neglect it.

- First, recognize it as a problem. You are undoubtedly pleased to see your child working hard and doing well; so you instinctively praise him and don't see a reason for concern.

· Take a look at pressure that might be coming from home: Are you sending signals that high achievement is the way to win your acceptance? Do you praise your child's successes too much? Do you give him rewards for getting high marks? Do you compare him to other children? Do you set yourself up as a model of success for him to follow? If so, put on the soft pedal.

· Talk to your child's teacher about this problem as you would any other, and make sure your child is with you. Find out if teachers are putting too much pressure on him, and if so, ask them to ease up. "He doesn't seem to be interested in anything but getting As," you might explain. "Can you suggest some ways he can get himself to relax?"

· Talk about values at home. It's easy to point out the success values that surround him: He is as aware of them as you are—money, power, popularity, and so on. Ask him to examine other kinds of values—generosity, caring, cooperativeness, and so on—and see if he finds evidence of them in school, at home, and in the larger community. You might even suggest he read biographies of such people as Eleanor Roosevelt, Albert Schweitzer, and Martin Luther King, whose contributions to civilization relied far more on interpersonal than on academic success.

· Plan new family activities in which your child will participate: Take up a sport or music lessons together, jog, go for hikes, for instance. New challenges may make him more aware of other, nonacademic areas of excellence.

Although you will not find a quick and easy solution to this self-made overdrive, you will notice gradual changes as you continue to work on it.

· Tests ·

The use and abuse of testing is one of the most controversial subjects in education. You should know what tests your children take and how the school uses the results because if you don't know, you can't lend the help and support your children need.

Because testing policies differ widely by state, you will have to contact your state Department of Education or your district school superintendent to learn which tests your children are taking. You might suggest that the PTA bring in someone to discuss testing at a meeting. Until you obtain more specifics, the following general information may help.

"What different kinds of tests does my child take?"

Your child probably takes three different kinds of tests.

One is the kind his teacher makes up to see if he has learned the material she has covered over a period of time—the quizzes, tests, and exams you probably help your child study for at home.

A second is the standardized achievement test given in a variety of forms, often by state mandate. This kind of test, such as the Education Research Bureau's test (ERBs), measures your child's performance level in comparison to other children in the same grade all over the country and reports the results in percentiles or stanines, which may seem confusing. If your child ranks in the 85th percentile, that means that 15 percent scored higher than he and 85 percent scored lower. If he ranks 5 in stanines, it means that he is right in the middle from 1 to 9.

A third is the standardized aptitude test, which measures not your child's achievement but his ability. This kind includes the famous Scholastic Aptitude Tests (SATs), which measure aptitude in specific areas, and different kinds of IQ tests, which measure certain kinds of intelligence.

If you want more detailed information on standardized tests, you can contact the Department of Education in your state capital or the following organizations:

· *183* ·

CENTER FOR RESEARCH ON EVALUATION,
STANDARDS AND STUDENT TESTING
University of California at Los Angeles
Los Angeles, CA 90024
(213) 825-4321

ASSOCIATION OF AMERICAN PUBLISHERS
Test Division
1 Park Avenue
New York, NY 10016
(212) 689-8920

THE NORTH DAKOTA STUDY GROUP ON EVALUATION
Center for Teaching and Learning
University of North Dakota
Grand Forks, ND 58202
(701) 777-2674

"How can I help my child when tests are coming up?"

The best way to prepare your child for any test is by maintaining a calm attitude about it yourself . . . by helping your child feel relaxed about it . . . by explaining that the test is not a competition, but a way of identifying her personal strengths and weaknesses . . . by neither rewarding nor punishing her when the mark comes back.

When your child is faced with standardized tests, you can help her further by keeping in mind the limitations of such tests. Don't get the idea that test results are a life-or-death sentence; they are not.

First of all, standardized tests are made to fit computers rather than children, and answers to objective questions are often arguable. For instance, who is to say that a child who checks off "scary" instead of "huge" when asked to describe a giant is wrong?

Second, IQ tests measure only three kinds of intelligence—verbal and mathematical reasoning and the ability to recall—but researchers have identified between fifty and a hundred different kinds.

Third, standardized test scores may differ widely, not only year to year, but week to week. There is the oft-quoted case of a child testing 50 on the IQ scale and, shortly afterward, when he retook it, testing 114. I personally know of a child whose IQ dropped twenty-seven points during a temporary period of emotional turbulence.

Emerson saw the true test of civilizations not in the statistics of their census or cities or production but "in the kind of man the country turns out." Perhaps one day parents and teachers will take his wisdom to heart and know that the true test of education is not in the statistics of its marks or test scores or IQs but in the kind of person the school turns out. On that day children will begin being educated.

CHAPTER 14

In School: Curriculum

Although you may feel you have little expertise in evaluating a school's curriculum and, as a result, little say on the subject, curriculum raises concerns that directly affect your child.

· Curriculum Concerns in Preschool ·

"How much playtime should a preschool have?"

Play is the curriculum of preschool. Through play children do their learning of skills, of life roles, of relationships. Through play they learn to think and express feelings and use their five senses. Through play they begin to develop a sense of who they are. Play is a preschool child's three Rs.

I wish more parents understood this. A mother applying to the school I ran told me she was removing her child from his current preschool because all he did there was play. "What do you think he should be doing?" I asked her.

"Learning letters and numbers, writing his name," she answered.
"Why?" I asked again.

"So he'll read and be ready for school," she said.

I explained that readiness for school lies far more in *wanting* to read than in already *knowing how* to read and that pushing reading too early often turns off the wanting. "Your child will play all day here too," I added. She left in search of a more academic preschool, which I am dismayed to realize she and other misguided mothers can easily find— in the United States, that is, not in Denmark, which has one of the highest literacy rates in the world and legally forbids teachers to teach reading in kindergarten.

If you are concerned that your child's preschool is nothing more than baby-sitting, you can check it out by asking a few questions.

- Does the teacher introduce your child to new activities when your child is ready?
- Does the teacher encourage both group and individual play?
- Does the teacher introduce new materials to the class-room in order to pique the children's interests?
- Does the teacher read to them and sing with them and listen to them as they speak?

A good preschool teacher keeps in touch with your child's growth: Are his skills improving? Is he becoming more independent? Is he more able to work in a group? Does he express his feelings more constructively? She provides play opportunities that foster growth at his level.

"Will preschool eliminate a child's speech problem?"

Depending on the nature of the problem, a preschool experience may or may not be able to overcome a child's speech problem. Most children lisp or mispronounce words at this age, usually to the delight of their parents. Who cares if the "fwowers are wed" and the "yemons are lellow" when the child is communicating! In a year or two the average child, whether she is in preschool or not, will speak more maturely, but preschool may speed up the process by providing more motivation.

If, however, a child has a real speech problem, she may need specialized help, not just time, to overcome it. Sometimes a child fails to outgrow her baby lisp, or she speaks her *l* from the glottis or her *m* and *n* through the nose. These kinds of speech problems may need corrective attention later on. However, professionals advise:

· Do not make an issue of your child's speech in these early years.

· Never laugh at a child's speech, no matter how "cute" or funny it may sound.

· Instead of correcting your child each time she mispronounces a word, repeat the word correctly in talking to her. For example, if your child says, "I want some lello," do not jump in with "The word is Jell-O, not lello." Instead ask, "You want some Jell-O?" This approach lets your child hear the correct pronunciation without developing a feeling of inadequacy.

· Explain to your child's teacher how you handle mispronunciations and ask her to handle them the same way.

· If your child gets upset because other children cannot understand her, listen and respond to her feelings. Do not let her view the situation as a tragedy, however. Explain that people often say words differently until they grow up. Let her know that most of the time children correct their own speech but that sometimes they need help, and assure her that she will get help when she is older if she needs it. Pressure from other children can act as a great motivator for children who cling to baby talk; unfortunately, it can be an equally great frustrator for those with a real speech problem. If this latter is the case with your child, advise the teacher, who can make a point of reading stories and discussing with the class the many differences that exist among children in an effort to help them become more accepting.

· By second grade, if your child's speech has not improved, you should discuss the problem with her teacher. At this point, you should probably have her undergo testing by a speech therapist.

"What do I do if my child is out of step with her classmates?"

It used to take me half an hour to cover a city block with my four-year-old granddaughter, who stopped to sound out letters on every sign; I expected "Coffee Shop" to be the first words she read aloud. It took me half an hour with my grandson as well; although letters on signs remained meaningless squiggles to him, he played ship's captain at every fire hydrant. Both are avid readers now in elementary school.

Yogi Berra observed, "It ain't over till it's over," and many a ninth-inning surprise has proven him right. Similarly, in considering the process of learning, it ain't starting till it's starting, and if parents would heed that wisdom, it might start sooner.

Children defy classification. Although psychologists identify average levels of development, they recognize their shortcomings and provide great leeway. Like the man who drowned in a stream that averaged only two feet deep, they know averages can play tricks. Many parents, however, regard the stages of growth as categorically as they do shoe sizes, insistent on getting the right fit: Their child must walk at a year, be toilet trained at two and a half, read at whatever age the current fashion dictates. When their child is behind the developmental chart or worse, behind someone else's child, they panic. Because preschoolers, on the other hand, neither read developmental literature nor judge their classmates' progress, in sane ignorance they go on growing at their own pace.

Your child's teacher is aware of your child's development. If he is ahead of the group and seems ready to read, she will afford him opportunities to go in this direction. If he is behind the learning level of the group, she will provide support to get him ready. Your child's teacher is a far better source of information about your child's progress than all the averages you can line up . . . and certainly better than other children's parents.

· 188 ·

"How does a preschooler learn socialization?"

Children learn to be social creatures in two interrelated ways: by trusting themselves and by trusting others. Both kinds of trust develop through loving nurture at home that conveys the message "I must be wonderful because they love me," and at the same time "They must be wonderful because they love me." With the sense of trust that grows from self-acceptance and acceptance of others, children are ready to reach out confidently. The job of preschool is to provide a conducive environment and a group of peers to receive and respond to their reach.

If a child is not ready to socialize when she enters preschool, she will be unable to function in the group and will disrupt the functioning of others. (Preschool readiness is discussed in detail in Chapter 5.) As a result, she may lash out aggressively or withdraw in a traditional fight-or-flight response to the stress she feels. Instead of helping her develop social skills, the preschool experience will actually have retarded them. For this reason parents should not force a child into preschool too soon, but arrange for home-based child care, if necessary.

In most cases, parental support and the passage of time will lead a child to social readiness.

When a socially ready child enters preschool, the activities through which she interacts with other children are designed to develop her skills further: sharing toys, listening and presenting at Show and Tell, playing group games, concentrating when the teacher talks, eating together at snack time, cleaning up and putting away. The child who enters preschool in September with herself in the center of the universe is able to emerge in June with others in her galaxy.

· Curriculum Concerns in Elementary School ·

"What should elementary school curriculum cover?"

The curriculum of elementary school should provide children with the tools of learning. It fits between preschool, which prepared them to handle tools, and junior high, which will help them start using the tools.

What are the tools of learning that an elementary school should provide?

· *189* ·

· Obviously, children need reading, writing, and arithmetic for starters, but the school can't stop there. Children have to *understand* what they read and then go further and understand what they don't read but infer from their reading. Children have to write in correct sentences and unified paragraphs, but they have to go further and *think* so they will have ideas to write about. Children have to decode the language of numbers, but they have to go further and use the *logic* of the minds and the *technology* of the computer to reach beyond themselves.

· Children need to learn problem solving in order to save themselves and the world from a quandary. Like apprentice Miss Marples and Hercule Poirots, children should be given a chance to track down answers to questions in libraries and museums and through interviews in the far corners of their community.

· Children need social studies that provide a foundation for understanding how the United States works as a nation and as a member of the world of nations. That's not enough: They need to learn when it fails working and why.

· Children need exposure to the arts so they can develop tastes and interests that reach beyond television, rock music, and the movies and so they can set themselves free to create their own arts.

· Children need sports to develop their bodies and the belonging that comes from a team.

When an elementary school puts these tools into the hands of its children, they will have no trouble using them in junior high. The problem is this: How can you tell whether your child's school follows a curriculum that gives him these tools? Asking doesn't offer a solution: "Does this curriculum prepare my child for junior high school?" No school is going to answer "Well, actually, no."

You need other means of investigation.

· Check students' achievement scores (see Chapter 13) against national norms. Because these include scores from inner-city problem schools, your school's scores should be way above average. Although any single child's score may be misleading, scores of the whole school present a fairly accurate picture.

· Appoint a PTA curriculum committee to study the school curriculum from first grade through sixth. The principal will probably assign an assistant to work with the committee.

· Talk to the dean of students at the junior high that most of your school's graduates attend. When you explain that you are investigating, not complaining, he may give you a general idea of the performance level of students from your school.

· Best of all, see what your child is learning year to year and how competent he feels.

· Your school may be accredited by a regional school association. (Not all elementary schools are.) If yours is, ask the principal to let the PTA curriculum committee see the last accreditation report; it will give you an accurate judgment.

"What can I do if the curriculum is too easy for my child?"

If your child continually finishes her work before the rest of the class and sits around bored or gets into trouble, you should talk to her teacher and suggest several ways to handle this situation.

The teacher can let your child design a long-term project to work on when she has finished in class. One teacher let a child write and illustrate of book of haiku poems; another put two children to work on making a salt-and-flour model of an early Roman town. Because you don't want to sound pushy, use a soft approach.

Don't tell the teacher: "Jill says the work is too easy in your class and she is bored to death. Can't you move ahead faster?"

Try this instead: "Jill loves the unit you are doing on Greece, but she finishes her work before the others. Could you have her do something more, like build a paper model of the Parthenon or illustrate some of the myths?"

The teacher can keep a box of puzzles and learning games from which your child could select one to challenge her while the rest of the class completes the work. This isn't especially creative, but it will at least keep your child's mind clicking.

The teacher can send your child to the library for independent study on a subject they have jointly selected. Sometimes a child becomes so absorbed in an independent study unit that she works on it all year, gaining new study skills in the process.

If the school has a computer room, the teacher can have your child work there on a series of available programs.

At the very least, your child can keep a non-school book in her desk to read when she has finished her work.

"What can I do if the curriculum is too difficult for my child?"

If your child is unable to keep up with the class, he, his teacher, and you should work out a plan of reinforcement. What it entails depends on the seriousness of your child's problem. The teacher may:

- Give him extra help during school.
- Assign another student to work with him.
- Give you work with which to help him at home.
- Suggest outside tutoring.
- Suggest summer school.
- Feel he needs to repeat the year.

The important thing is not to let your child keep falling farther and farther behind. He may be able to fill in the academic gaps during the summer, but he may never be able to rebuild his damaged self-esteem.

"How important is sex education in elementary school?"

Because the purpose of sex education is to help children understand themselves as people and as partners in different kinds of relationships, I think an elementary school curriculum is not complete without it.

Sex education should begin in the early grades asking the question: "Who am I—the person, the son or daughter, the sister or brother, the friend, the pupil in school?" With this kind of foundation, it should then proceed to explore the roles and responsibilities children have in their various relationships with family members and friends: "What do I give and what do I expect to receive?"

In the higher grades of elementary school, as children enter puberty, sex education should guide children in the discovery of difference and sameness between girls and boys, men and women. Children should learn body functions and the changes that both sexes undergo.

Teachers disagree on whether children should have sex education in single-sex classes or together; both have their merits. My own experience has led me to believe that teaching boys and girls together makes more sense because sex involves a boys-and-girls together relationship. However, because embarrassment silences talk of especially personal subjects, such as menstruation or wet dreams, single-sex classes on particularly sensitive topics usually are more productive.

· Curriculum Concerns in Junior High School ·

"What is a basic junior high school curriculum?"

Every state requires English, math, science, and social studies in junior high. Upon that base, schools provide other subjects as their district requires. When educators realized about twenty years ago that preadolescents study harder and perform better when given a choice of their own, they added elective courses at the junior high level. A student can't skip required English, but he may take a course entitled Women Poets or Science Fiction instead.

Many schools offer electives, but others hold firm to the belief that children need more rigid guidance at this age. If they don't get a foundation of comprehensive literature or basic science now, they may never get it. Chapter 7 suggests ways in which you may help your junior high schooler choose electives and still have a solid academic base.

"What is all this talk of year-round schools?"

Year-round schools are one of many innovations in school scheduling.

For years schools operated on the basis of semesters with the school year divided into halves—one half from September until January and the second half from February through June. As new ideas about education emerged, schools began to break from tradition in order to accommodate them. Today you may run into a variety of other schedules.

Trimesters. Many schools divide their year into three parts—the first ending before Christmas, the second at spring vacation, and the third in June. This works particularly well in a junior high school with electives because students can take three trimester-long courses each year instead of two, thereby broadening their range of learning experiences. I like trimesters because they allow students to complete exams before going on vacation and to return to a new, clean slate.

Theme scheduling. This divides the year into seven- or eight-week units, each unit built around a theme, such as the Middle Ages or Heroes. The teacher of each subject develops the curriculum around the theme during that period. The advantage to theme scheduling is that it eliminates the fragmentation children are subject to in the ordinary course of skipping from one subject to another with no thread of continuity.

Subject scheduling. This divides the year into a unit for each major subject, during which time children study that one subject in all disciplines. For instance, during a unit on science, social studies classes focus on forces leading to scientific discoveries; English classes read biographies of scientists and science fiction; math takes up computations used in different scientific disciplines. While subject scheduling has the advantage of unifying a child's learning experience, it falls short in subjects that require continuity. Children tend to forget how to speak French, for example, once they put the unit aside until the following year.

Six-day scheduling. Every school administrator comes to the realization that there are not enough days in the school week to provide all the programs he wants. The six-day school week offers a possible solution. It does not return to Saturday classes of earlier years, but adds a sixth day to each week by "stealing" it from the week to come. For instance, the first week is Monday through Friday with the following Monday added; the second week is Tuesday through Friday with the following Monday and Tuesday added; and so on round and round. Because classes meet four or five times a week, more classes can be fitted in; but confusion reigns in this schedule, and at the end of the year no one can identify an actual gain.

Year-round schools are something else. They have arisen not only to accommodate education theory but also to make better use of edu-

· 193 ·

cational budgets and meet the growing needs of working parents. "Look at all those buildings standing empty all summer," city officials said. "Let's make use of them, save money, and solve a problem in the bargain."

"Look at those empty schools," working parents said. "Why can't they keep my children there when I'm not on summer vacation?"

Some schools have tried year-round scheduling and either kept or dropped it; many more are trying it now. Some schools divide the whole year into quarters. Students must attend three of the quarters, but they are allowed to attend the extra quarter too. Thus they can speed up their education by three months each year if they want or receive extra support in the fourth quarter if they need it. Teachers must teach at least three of the quarters but may add a fourth if they wish. The advantage to them is that they can work all year if they wish instead of supplementing their salary with unrelated summer jobs. Other schools divide the year into an eight-weeks-on, four-weeks-off schedule, or six-weeks-on, three-weeks-off for the whole year.

Year-round schools solve the original problems as well. Working parents can keep their children in school during the summer months while they still have to work, and the city saves money by being able to educate more children in fewer schools and by avoiding vandalism on the usually empty buildings.

With so many benefiting, it appears that year-round schooling may be riding the educational wave of the future, despite the confusion of class scheduling and mismatched family vacations it may cause.

"Is tracking good or bad?"

The answer to that question is yes: Tracking is good or bad, depending on how you view it. Tracking, of course, is the practice of grouping students in classes according to their ability, the opposite of heterogeneous grouping. The average junior high school has a low track for poor achievers, a middle track for average students, and a high track for students who perform well. Advantages and disadvantages exist side by side in tracking.

Proponents of tracking point out these advantages.

· Students are able to work at a pace best suited to their learning abilities. Students in the high tracks speed ahead, while students in the low tracks are provided more time. As a result, the high tracks are able to offer constant challenge without penalizing slower students, and the low tracks are able to provide additional help and practice without holding faster students back.

· In heterogeneous classes bright students tend to take over from less able students who are too insecure and embarrassed to participate. On the other hand, in homogeneous, or tracked, classes less able students need not compete with their more stellar peers and can participate and ask questions no one will think are "dumb."

· Teachers in tracked classes have more leeway to gear material to the special interests and abilities of their students. As a result, students in all sections are more likely to become involved in learning.

· Teachers of tracked classes tend to become less frustrated because their goals can be set according to realistic expectations in each track. They know they do not have to hold able students back from their potential nor demand more than less able students are capable of giving.

Opponents of tracking focus on these disadvantages.

· Once students are placed in low tracks, it is difficult for them to move up—first because they have not completed higher track work and, second, because labels tend to become self-fulfilling. As a result, just as the kindergarten he attends may determine a Japanese child's future and the national exams at age eleven that of a British child, so the seventh-grade track in which he is placed may set an American child on a course for the rest of his life.

· No matter how subtly schools handle the labels of tracking, students know who is in the "smart" section and who is in the "dumb." "Dumb" undercuts the basic motivation for learning—self-esteem.

· The greatest danger of tracking is that it does not allow for children to develop at different rates. A poor student in the seventh grade may not necessarily be a poor student forever: He may be a late bloomer, maturing more slowly than the average; he may have emotional problems that time will help him overcome; or he may be unable to focus himself temporarily amid a sea of personal troubles at home. Instead of allowing for the removal of temporary learning blocks, tracking consigns students to the eternal damnation of being "dumb."

· The labels of tracking can be equally harmful to students in the top track who, in accordance with the American value system, may easily believe that "better student" is equivalent to "better person." Tracking deprives them of an opportunity to learn that most people are "better" at something than they are, a fact that, if taken seriously, could give the word "equality" new impact.

· The scheduling in many schools, particularly smaller ones, makes it impossible to track a student at different levels according to his performance in different subjects. For instance, a student weak in English but average in math might wind up in a low track in both subjects, or a low-track student in both subjects in September might be unable to switch to a higher track midyear as his performance improves in one. Scheduling flexibility is limited, even with the advent of computers.

· In large urban areas a unique problem with tracking arises: black and Hispanic students make up a high percentage of the low tracks, while white and Asian students swell the high-track ranks. While this apparent inequality stems from environmental, not hereditary, factors, it magnifies already existing discord.

Even a careful weighing of the arguments on both sides of the tracking question fails to provide a definitive answer. Is it good or bad? Yes. Should you push for tracking in your school? That depends on . . .

· Your child. Additional support from a low track will probably be helpful if your child has enough self-confidence to accept her academic weakness without a personal stigma. The challenge of a high track, on the other hand, may be equally helpful if your child has perspective on academic achievement.

· You. If you are embarrassed to have your child in a low track, or if you find yourself bragging about a child in a high track, either track will do more harm than good. If your child announces that she is in a low track, tell her, "Good. You'll be able to go slowly and work through those awful decimals and percentages. You won't be so frustrated over your homework either." If your child announces she is in a high track, tell her, "Good. You won't be bored this year and I'll bet you learn some study skills to get you through the extra work."

· Your child's teachers. Children become the images of them that their teachers bring to class everyday—the "dummies" they resent teaching, the "bright kids" whose section they requested. A study in which teachers were assigned two equivalent classes but told that one was "bright" and the other "slow" revealed that at the end of the year, the "bright" classes received far higher marks than the "slow" classes. If your child's teachers feel like this, they won't help your children. Tracked classes will work only if their teachers look at tracking as an opportunity to give all kinds of students the kind of education they need. You can't always determine this from talking to them, but you can surmise it from their attitude.

· Your child's school. If your child's school wants tracking to work, it has to function on the underlying philosophy that all children are equal members of the community. If the principal establishes that philosophy and you and your child feel its presence, tracking has a good chance of working.

"How do I get outside help for my child?"

· Ask the teacher or the principal, either of whom might be able to refer you to a former teacher or a tutor who has worked with students before. Don't ask your child's current teacher to take on the job, though; your child needs a different viewpoint.

· Contact the principal of your district high school, where you may be able to locate a student who wants to earn additional money by tutoring.

· Check the yellow pages of your phone book to see whether your community has a tutoring school or service that could meet your need.

· Be sure to let your child's teacher know that he is being tutored. Explain that the tutor will keep in touch with her to determine the kind of help your child needs and the progress he is making. You keep in touch with the teacher too, so that you'll know when to terminate the tutoring.

"What if sex, drug, or guidance classes upset my child?"

· 197 ·

If your child seems distressed over classes in these sensitive areas, you have to look for several possible causes.

The teacher may have used material that was overtitillating or frightening for your child—pictures of sexual intercourse or of people dead from a drug overdose, for instance. If this is the case (you should check it with the teacher as well as the child), you must let the teacher know that you think the material was inappropriate. If she indicates that similar material will be presented in future classes, you have three options: Prepare your child ahead of time; ask the teacher to excuse your child from those classes; or ask the principal to tone down the course.

The distress may be yours, not your child's at all. While he may have reported what happened in that class as matter-of-factly as he did what happened in math or social studies, you may have reacted in horror. Lay your shock aside and draw your child out to see how *he* feels about the class.

When I taught sex education, a mother told me that her eighth-grade son came home talking about condoms as a deterrent to AIDS. Horrified, she had said, "That's awful. The teacher shouldn't fill your head with fears like that when you're only thirteen."

"Look, Mom," he reassured her, "if Thunder Mountain at Disney World didn't scare me, how could this?"

It may be that your child has discovered a new way to get your attention—coming home with a story that will leave you aghast: "You won't believe what Mrs. Hollins showed us in class today! I almost passed out it was so awful!" How can you resist? If you react with the alarm your child anticipates, he will probably repeat the performance, especially if you do what he dares not—go to school and get his teacher in trouble. What you should do is stop being shocked. Don't overreact, but listen calmly to your child and, when he has finished, discuss the matter with him. When your child realizes that sex, drug, or other material he anticipates as inflammatory sets off no sparks in you, his "distress" will cool down.

CHAPTER 15

At Home: Homework

An eighth grader I know was severely chastised by his teacher for having failed to memorize an assigned list of vocabulary words. Upon the teacher's demand of an explanation, he admitted with embarrassment, "I forgot. I was too busy reading."

A third grader, who had asked permission to go to the lavatory, failed to return to class within the time designated by the teacher. Retrieved by a messenger and scolded by the teacher, the little girl replied, sobbing, "But I saw the snowflakes falling."

Over many years of hearing children's explanations of their sins, I have come to understand the good news and the bad news. The good news is that children nourish themselves with learning, as hummingbirds do with sweet nectar, discovering it by instinct and naming it simply "fun." The bad news is that teachers and parents mistrust the environment's gardens where children roam free to learn, calling them back instead to the restrictions of the structures they themselves erect.

School is one small area in which children learn. The larger places begin with home and neighborhood and extend as far as their minds can travel.

· The Purpose of Homework ·

Homework is for learning.

I have never yet spoken to a group of parents without one of them asking "How do I make my child do her homework?" It sounds familiar, doesn't it?

My answer creates momentary shock: "Don't."

Most children dislike homework. The extent to which some dislike it was studied recently by researchers at two universities—Illinois and Loyola. They discovered that the older the child, the more intensely negative is his response to homework. The fact that homework puts 11 percent of ninth graders into a black mood (only 6 percent of fifth graders) and enables a mere 12 percent of them to feel good while doing it (25 percent of fifth graders) helps explain the nightly scenes with which so many parents are confronted. If teachers assigned more creative homework than most of them do, black moods would drop and "feeling good" would rise sharply. However, because parents are powerless to activate a teacher's creativity, they have to either live with the misery or look elsewhere for a solution—to themselves.

The fundamental reason that so many happy homes become what I call Homework Hell after dinner each night is that few parents understand the purpose of homework. Homework is not for earning an A. Homework is for learning. Parents who allow a home to sound like the agonies of the damned because their child faces an assignment are blocking the learning experience for the child and are sometimes even jeopardizing their marriage. (I know a father who for years refused to go home until his child's homework was finished!)

Homework is the basic tool for a child's learning experience. The teacher has explained something in school—let's say long division—has done some problems on the board, and has asked your child to do some. Ten problems are assigned for homework. If she does them correctly or makes mistakes and corrects them herself, she is successful: She has learned long division. However, if she does them incorrectly and cannot find her errors, she is still successful. She knows what she doesn't know. More important, her teacher will know what she doesn't know and can help her learn long division tomorrow or next week.

Children live in the same success-oriented world we do, where mistakes bring shame and fear: The two-year-old cries when he wets his pants; the ten-year-old invents excuses when she can't find her library book; the eighth grader blames a teammate when he misses the ball. Children can't make mistakes without humiliation, and so their homework must be right to avoid their teacher's anger. Right? Wrong. The teacher will be angry if a child doesn't *do* homework, but she won't be angry if the homework is wrong. Let her homework speak for her: "I worked on this, but I couldn't do it."

"Weren't you listening in class when I explained?"

"I was, but I just didn't get it. Would you explain it again?"

The shame of mistakes is in the child's head. And in the parent's head. It is not in the head of the teacher unless she is so hung up in her own defenses that she shouldn't be in a classroom . . . and Chapter 9 can help you handle that problem. To hand in homework with mistakes is not only acceptable but downright wonderful because it enables the teacher to identify and correct the child's problem. Mothers and fathers in Homework Hell have certainly not communicated this truth to their child and have probably not even perceived it themselves. If they had, there would be no need for hysterics over a misunderstood assignment and a possible F. Do you know why teachers bother to put grades on homework? Let your child in on this secret if you want to calm his nerves: to motivate their students to do it at all!

Homework is for responsibility.

· *201* ·

Homework is a tool for another kind of learning as well—in the long run more important than long division—the tool for assuming the responsibility of good study habits. When a child tackles his homework, he schedules his time, organizes his work, ignores distractions. In short, he learns self-discipline. After a child struggles through his homework, he turns it in the next day with the pride of knowing "I did it." Right or wrong as his homework may be, he gains self-confidence in knowing that from the chaos of mind, notes, and looseleaf binder, despite temptations, frustration, and boredom, he found a way to get his homework done on time. Good study habits not only get his job done; they make him feel good about his ability to do it.

· Homework In Preschool ·

"Should teachers give homework?"

A kindergarten teacher I know was beleaguered by a mother for not assigning the children homework. Overly ambitious for her little boy, she berated the teacher each morning as she dropped him off, until one day the weary teacher asked, "You really think I should give him homework?"

"I certainly do," the mother replied.

"All right," the teacher said. Then turning to the little boy standing between them, she added, "Learn to tie your shoes."

In answer to the question: No, preschool teachers shouldn't give homework. Play is a child's homework; support him in that.

"How can parents help at home?"

Truth to tell, preschool teachers would far rather have children come to class knowing how to tie their shoes and put on their snow suits than knowing their letters and numbers. It is only when insistent parents wear down administrators or teachers that they back down from their principles and send home worksheets.

Homework, as most parents think of it, is irrelevant in preschool because the job at hand is not to learn academics but to learn living: a child getting a sense of herself as an individual and as a member of larger communities; learning to use her body; learning to relate to others; learning to play; learning sizes, shapes, and distances.

Preschool children do their homework as they interact with their environment. Parents, siblings, other family members, friends, and parent substitutes are in a position to stimulate children toward this end.

- Play, read, talk to children; listen to them. Make things with them. (There is more detail on this in Chapter 16)
- Take them on walks and excursions. Take them shopping.
- Sing, dance, listen to music.
- Take them to visit old people, babies.
- Let them play with animals.
- Let them select the clothes they want to wear and let them dress themselves as far as they can—even when shirts end up backward.
- Encourage them to undertake activities alone, even when it means more work for you.
- If the teacher has asked them to bring in something from home, let them find what they want.

These are the kinds of homework assignments preschoolers and their parents should be working on, without ever considering them work. Play is a child's work.

Above all, do not start pushing a preschooler into reading, writing, and arithmetic. The happy, emotionally healthy child will catch on to those soon enough and skillfully enough when the time comes. Avoid flash cards! They reinforce rote learning; they force the acquisition of skills for which a child may not be ready; they are dull, dead boring; and in the long run, they tend to retard rather than accelerate a child's verbal and numerical development.

· Homework In Elementary And Junior High School ·

Setting the stage for homework

First, make sure that your child has a quiet place in which to work. If a small apartment or a group of noisy siblings precludes this, it is worth getting the other children away for a few hours or else finding another place for homework to be done—a grandparent's or aunt's home, for instance.

Next, make it clear to your child that homework is a serious matter; it is work you expect him to complete just as his parents complete their work. Express interest in his assignments. Ask whether you may see them when finished, but do not insist if he is reluctant (unless, as we shall discuss later, his teacher has asked you to).

When your child arrives home from school, allow him time to unwind and relax, to have a cold drink and a snack, to discuss his day. Do not insist that he tackle his household chores or his homework immediately. He has had a physically, mentally, and emotionally wearing six hours and will benefit from an hour or so of play or listening to the radio or just lolling around.

Radio, television, telephone, and homework

The radio, as you may know, is a controversial subject in many homes, perhaps in yours. I am constantly asked whether a child should be allowed to have music on while doing homework. Having been raised at a time when music was relegated to leisure times and dances, my first reaction used to be a decisive no. Today, however, I reconsider.

Music is such an integral part of the lives of children now that many of them actually work better with music in the background. If your child wants the radio, I suggest that you allow it to be on, though more softly than usual, and see what happens. If homework gets done and done adequately, then the radio does no harm. If, on the other hand, it distracts your child from her homework, ask her to keep the radio off until assignments are completed.

Television is another matter because the visual attention it demands precludes its use as a background accompaniment to homework. Make it clear to your child and stick by the rule that TV is out of the question until homework is done. Without strict adherence to this rule, a child can too easily keep postponing homework until suddenly it is bedtime. At that point, you and your child are caught on the horns of a dilemma: undone homework or exhaustion. Neither is conducive to learning.

Similarly, telephone conversations can easily use up the hours of an evening with no time left over for homework assignments. Make a hard-and-fast rule that your child can make or receive only short phone calls until all homework is completed.

· 204 · Ways of helping

When your child settles down to homework, she may ask for your help. Keep in mind, however, that while asking for parental *help*, children are experts in getting parental *doing*. Don't get caught in the trap. Here are some specific ways to provide real help.

· Listen to spelling words after she has studied them. Jump around the page, rather than asking them as they appear, in order to break the pattern in which she learned them.

· Make up and ask a child questions from notes taken in class or from her textbook when a child is preparing for a test.

· Suggest that she herself make up questions or problems she would ask if she were the teacher and then listen to her answers.

· If she does not understand an assignment in a subject as specific as math or grammar, for instance, try to explain the principle behind the assignment. Do not do any part of the assignment for her, but make up a few similar problems or sentences for her to practice on. If that helps, she can go on to do her homework; if she is still confused, reassure her that it's all right, that the teacher will go over it with her tomorrow. If she is stuck with a lax or lazy teacher, you might send a note asking the teacher for extra help.

· If she is having problems with a reading assignment, avoid summarizing it for her. You will help her more by explaining how to pick out main ideas and letting her try it for herself and report back to you with the results.

· If she has a paper due and asks you to proofread it, only go so far as to read it and say that you found, for instance, three spelling errors and two missing commas. Let her locate them for herself.

When a child won't do homework

When a child will not enter what may turn out to be a battle with his homework, deciding instead to retreat and watch TV or play ball, parents have a tendency to get in there themselves and fight the fight for their child.

Do not nag your child into doing homework.

Some parents nag a child until, worn out and sullen, he flops at his desk. What they have done, though, is take the responsibility away from him and assumed it themselves. A nightly pattern develops then in which homework becomes the parents' responsibility, not the child's; if they don't do their job of nagging, he won't do his homework. In this situation, both long division and study habits are lost, often with disastrous results. I know more than one child who was nagged into doing his work through elementary and high school and flunked out of college because he was suddenly on his own.

Do not use punishment as a threat to make your child to do homework.

Other parents threaten their child with punishment if he fails to do his homework. He is then put into the position not of assuming responsibility for homework but of making a judgment on which is worse, doing his homework or receiving his parents' punishment. The danger in this practice lies in the resentment the child feels at being forced to live under the sword of Damocles, resentment often deep enough to lead as far as truancy or dropping out of school. Certainly not to learning.

Do not do your child's homework for him.

Some parents—far more than I thought before I started teaching their children—find the easiest and safest way to handle a child who balks at doing homework is by doing it themselves or by doing so much of it that it no longer represents their child's effort. I have seen many a social studies project that Mother did because she had more time to spend in the library or that Dad's secretary typed because she does more words per minute. I have seen math worksheets written in several different hands and English papers no eighth grader could possibly have written, despite a spelling error here and there that I was almost embarrassed to correct. Obviously, when parents do their child's homework, they prevent his learning what he is supposed to learn from the assignment. Just as obviously, and far more seriously, they also teach him to plagiarize. You get kicked out of college for plagiarizing . . . and out of the presidential race, if you remember!

Do not cover up undone homework with excuses.

Finally, do not write excuse notes for undone homework unless a catastrophe arises or your child gets sick or so fatigued that he falls asleep. You won't fool the teacher anyway if your notes become a regular practice, but you certainly will have fooled your child—fooled him right out of learning what his homework was designed for and fooled him into learning that he can count on you to get him out of hot water.

Not helping with homework

With this long list of *don'ts* to warn parents, the question arises as to whether there exist any *dos* when children drive their parents crazy over homework.

"Is there anything I can do when my child won't do her homework?"

"Yes."

"What?"

"Don't make her do it."

Not playing the homework game is a real and positive way to help a child who will not do her homework. It is not easy, and it is not painless, but it is the most constructive help you may ever give her.

If you have a child who puts you through nightly Homework Hell, stop becoming part of the setup. Tell her that homework is her responsibility, not yours. Wash your hands of it, but keep the television and the phone turned off, as advised earlier. Let her go to school with her homework undone. Reaction will be forthcoming from the school sooner or later. Maybe not the first time she fails to hand in an assignment. Maybe not even the second time. But soon she will fall behind in her work and be required to make it up. At the least, she will have to stay out of recess or after school and do the work. Maybe the teacher will suggest that you find a tutor to catch her up to the rest of the class, in which case you should insist that she pay for a good part of the cost from her allowance or babysitting income. She may be required to abandon previous plans and attend summer school, which is a last-resort option. At the worst she may even have to repeat the year.

None of these options is attractive to either parent or child because the scenes and screams that ensue could have been avoided. It would have been far easier for the child to have done her homework in the first place or, if not, for her parents to have found ways to get it done.

Remember, however, homework is your child's responsibility, not yours, and you are seeking a way to help her, not to assure that the homework gets done. When you gave your child the responsibility of doing her homework, you also gave her the freedom of choice: "Will I or will I not do my homework?" Of her own free will she made her decision and went to school assignmentless. By not doing her homework for her, by not coercing her into doing it, and by not making excuses for her, you have enabled her to learn a valuable life lesson: When she makes a decision, she has to handle what comes as a result it. She has learned accountability.

While it is true that your child has fallen flat on her face, she has fallen knowing that it was *her* face. You have given her the dignity of that lesson. Years later, or maybe just next year, when she confronts the weightier and more life-threatening decisions that surround her, she may be able to protect herself with the lesson of accountability you taught her in the shared pain of homework.

· 207 ·

"I did my homework in school!"

Your child excuses herself from the dinner table and, instead of heading toward the desk in her room, switches on the television with a carefree air. "No television until you've finished your homework," you remind her.

"Oh, I did it in school." Now what?

Some elementary school children always complete their homework in school. Quick to understand the lesson and finish their practice sheets or projects before the rest of the class, they are told to work on their home assignments until the teacher is ready to go on. These children truly "did it in school."

Other children occasionally complete their work before their classmates and, therefore, from time to time really do have an opportunity to do their homework in school.

A few children who cannot face the boredom or fear of homework take the I-did-it-in-school way to avoid it. They lie to their parents.

Many children, however, lie to themselves. They may have glanced through an assigned story or rushed through math problems on a worksheet. More probably they convinced themselves that they have already studied for the test the teacher assigned for tomorrow.

How are parents to determine the situation that actually exists? Because only their child knows for sure, ask her what the homework was and when she did it. Answers with the ring of legitimacy sound like:

- "It was only reading, and the teacher kept me in from recess because of my sniffles."
- "I did the dumb multiplication worksheet while the other kids were practicing their times tables."
- "I got to school early and didn't have anything else to do, so I went over my social studies notes for the test tomorrow."
- "We only had science. I did it in study hall."

Answers that call for further investigation sound like:

- "We didn't have much."
- "She didn't give any—just the same old stuff for a test."
- "It was just a worksheet. I did it in class while Tara was reading her story."

What can parents do?

· If your child occasionally completes her homework in school, rejoice with her and enjoy the evening together.

· If your child always completes her homework in school, talk to her teacher with her. Perhaps she would like to undertake a long-term project to work on when she finishes before the rest of the class, or maybe she could assist classmates who need help, or just read a good book of her own.

· If your child deceives herself about completing homework, you will have to help her develop more efficient study habits at home. Have her explain her assignments to you every evening as a way of clarifying them for herself, and have her show you the finished homework to reinforce her feeling of completion.

· If, however, your child deceives you about having completed her homework in school, you have two problems. The lesser one is structuring a system in which she will develop study habits, as suggested earlier. The major one is dealing with the lie.

Why does a child lie about having done her homework? One reason is that she hates doing it, would rather watch television, and is too immature to foresee the consequences of not doing it. Yet the consequences will come. If they come in the form of harsh words or disciplinary action from the teacher or in a note to her parent, she will have learned a lesson: While a lie may postpone consequences, it does not prevent them.

Another reason for a child's lying about having done her homework is that she feels incapable of doing it and would rather be caught in a lie than in what she interprets as "being dumb." This child needs no harsh words or punishment, but rather support from school and home to build confidence and self-esteem: her teacher to provide extra help; her parents to relax pressure and reassure her of their love; and both to reinforce acceptance of failure, not as a stigma, but as a positive step toward learning.

Too much homework

Children in the early elementary grades, if they have homework at all, should have to spend no more than fifteen minutes on it; third and fourth graders, perhaps thirty to forty-five minutes; and fifth and sixth graders, no more than an hour. Junior high schoolers may be required to spend as much as two hours on assignments.

If your child is consistently spending more time on homework, there are several avenues you can follow to reach the source of the difficulty.

First, your child. Is he using his homework time efficiently? If he is, you will see him at his desk applying himself to the assignments until they are completed. If he is not using his time efficiently, you will notice interruptions for a look in the refrigerator, a conversation, and maybe even for a stolen look at a TV show. Should you discover the problem to be not too much homework but too little concentration, some simple guidelines may help: Suggest a five-minute break between assignments and have him begin his homework early enough to finish before his favorite TV show comes on. When he realizes that the possibility of happier evenings rests in his hands and not the teacher's, the problem may disappear.

Next, the teacher. Is she aware how much time children spend on their homework? There is one way for you to find out—ask her. If excessive homework turns out to be a common problem in the class—and she will know by asking the children—she will be able to adjust her assignments. If, on the other hand, your child alone is struggling with an overload, she will be able to relieve his burden in two ways: either give him the extra help he may need to understand the assignments better, or ask him to put the assignment aside after a certain time, whether he has finished or not. If she fails to do either, you may have to take the initiative to get him extra help or to set a deadline on homework hours. A parent has a right to say "I made him stop working and go to bed. He was exhausted."

Third, the school policy. Does the school operate under the principle that long hours spent on home assignments demonstrate good teaching? Some do. If your school is one, the best you can do is undertake the slow process of effecting change, beginning with the principal, as outlined in Chapter 2.

Too little homework

While students are more stressed over too much homework than over too little, their parents reverse the stress factors. "Eric never brings work home from school," a mother complained to me recently.

"What grade is he in?" I asked.

"First," she answered. Then, feeling somewhat abashed at what might be contrued as pushiness, she added in justification, "But his sister in second grade never has any either."

The most restrained answer I could give was "That's nice."

Children in grades 1, 2, and 3 need no homework because a full school day provides all the studying they can handle. They will learn more in the home hours through play, relaxation, and interaction with the family than through an extension of school work. Most teachers know this. However, many of them give even young children homework in order to quell the tide of parental complaints.

In grades 4, 5, and 6 children can handle limited amounts of homework. If your child has no homework or less than you think she should, before registering complaints, discuss homework with the teacher. Maybe your child is a quick learner and finishes her homework in school; maybe the teacher builds homework time into the day's schedule; or maybe a twenty-minute assignment is all the children need to reinforce their school work.

You should make your final judgment not on the amount of time spent on homework, but on its value. If your child comes home with two hours' drill on solving base 5 problems in base 10, that is too much homework and too boring. If, on the other hand, your child comes home, as one of my grandchildren did, with an assignment to begin a story and stop after the first page, her frustration proved to me that that homework was too limited. Like Goldilocks, children deserve assignments that are just right: skill drills limited to the extent of determining their mastery level and creative challenges open-ended enough to let them work as long as they want.

"Should children do homework together?"

Studies have found that when two or three children work together, each learns more than he would if studying alone. In the light of this, many schools have abandoned individual desks in favor of tables or clustered desks that allow group study. My heart leaps up, as Wordsworth's did over rainbows, when I enter a classroom abuzz with children's hushed voices, their heads bent together over their work. I see them, more than learning their lessons, learning the impact of cooperation in a far too competitive world.

Children can benefit similarly from working together on many home assignments under two conditions. First, they have to be mature enough to address their work instead of using their time together in play and fooling around. For this reason, working in twos tends to be more profitable for upper elementary and middle schoolers than for the average younger child. Second, their work must be shared equally by both children, not undertaken by one and copied by the other. I still chuckle over seeing two boys "working together," with one poring through pages of the *World Book Encyclopedia* and the other reading *Sports Illustrated.* The moral of that story is that a parent may have to check out the teamwork from time to time.

· 211 ·

Forgotten homework assignments

Every night the same child used to call my daughter to get homework assignments. "I'm sick and tired of that kid's voice," my husband finally said.

"Would you rather have my friend's dad sick and tired of *my* voice?" she asked in reply. Touché!

If your child is the one calling a classmate every night to get homework assignments, discover the reason and help to curb the habit.

> · Is she so disorganized that she really fails to keep track of her assignments? If so, get her an assignment pad, show her how (and why) to use it, and check it every night until she organizes herself more efficiently.

- Is she using homework as an excuse to talk to her friend? If so, remind her of the no-calls-till-homework-is-done house rule and stick to it.
- Is she afraid that she may have the assignment wrong and calls her friend for reassurance? If so, understand her fear, but strive to build her feelings of competence. In the meantime, suggest that she check her homework assignments with her friend before leaving school in the afternoon.

"Should a child use a calculator?"

To the ears of a teacher this questions is as absurb as "Should a child drive a car instead of learning to walk?" To the ears of a child, however, it has a different ring: "Do I have to walk to California when I can drive there in a car?"

The answer to both sets of ears is no: "No, you can't drive a car instead of learning to walk; and no, you don't have to walk everywhere when you know how to drive a car. You can do both."

Children should learn addition, subtraction, multiplication, and division in order to understand what math means. Not learning basic arithmetic because we have computers is like not learning to read because we have tape recorders. Yet because calculators can shortcut the endless drudgery of arithmetic in problem solving, children should not only be allowed to use them but should be taught how to use them. Parents can help by teaching them and by providing practice through playing math games and letting them work out figures on trips to the bank and market.

"What about taking my child out of school for trips?"

As a young teacher, I used to resent bitterly a child's missing school because she was accompanying her parents on a trip. I learned, however, that parents could turn the trip into a learning experience with a few guidelines.

- Let the teacher know well in advance when the child will be leaving and returning.
- Ask the teacher what work the rest of the class will be covering during your child's absence. Don't phone or send a note asking her to

write it down, but go see her in person, and *you* write it down. Why should she put in extra time for your vacation?

· Make it clear to your child that she is expected to complete the assigned work, and see that time is set aside for that purpose.

· Make new learning experiences part of the fun you and your child share on your vacation: as you discover the history of the place and enjoy its arts and culture, as you look around at its flora and fauna, as you listen to its people.

· Suggest that your child keep a journal of the trip, writing in it each night before bedtime, so that her memories will stay fresh. Children forget quickly.

· Buy your child an inexpensive camera and let her take photographs, her own photographs of sights that capture her interest. They may turn out to be quite different from those you take—few churches and museums, but some wonderful dogs, boats, and policemen!

CHAPTER 16

At Home: Play

· The Importance Of Play ·

The importance of play has been stressed for years by leading authorities on children, from Bruno Bettelheim to Dr. Spock, with whom generation after generation of parents have practically lived. In an interview a few years ago, Dr. Spock reiterated to me what he has said in books and speeches for over forty years: "Play is the most important way children learn. We ought to give it a different name so that parents would take it seriously."

Surely he is right. Because play means something different to parents than to children, parents tend to trivialize it. To them play is a means of temporarily dumping the burdens of responsibility that come as part of the job of adulthood; through play, they become children again. To children, on the other hand, play is a rite of passage to growing up; through play, they eventually become adults. In *Childhood and Society* (Norton, 1986), a book every parent would gain a great deal from reading, Erik Erikson explains the difference between adults' play and children's play by saying "The playing adult steps sidewards into another reality; the playing child advances forward to new stages of mastery." That is why for children, play is not "child's play," but the important business of work.

Young mammals, be they lion cubs, kittens, or children, are born knowing how to play. As instinctive to them as eating and sleeping, play serves the same basic purpose of assuring their survival. Let us examine some of the basic lessons that children, along with their less developed animal relations, learn as they play.

• Play provides training in life skills. Lion cubs learn attack and defense as they scuffle with each other in mock biting and clawing. Kittens acquire stealth as they lay in wait for the dangling ball of wool. Children also learn in play what they need to know as adults: By re-creating life situations—playing house and store and fireman—they test different roles; by using their whole bodies in jump rope or small parts of their bodies in marbles, they develop coordination; by seeing who runs the fastest, they learn to compete; by putting on a play with friends, they learn to cooperate; by solving a puzzle alone, they learn to struggle. You can add endlessly to the list by observing your children the next time they play.

• Play helps build relationships. Just as young animals in play reinforce the family group as a unit of defense against intruders, so children strengthen bonds with their family and friends as they play together. The unifying force of shared play, which adults are aware of in their own golf foursome and bridge club, brings parents close to children, whether in a game of Candy Land or baseball. Similarly, play brings children close to friends in bonds that often last a lifetime.

• Play helps children master the environment. Young animals stretch their playing field as they become more secure, learning to judge the distance from new territory to safety should the the enemy appear. By playing, children too learn to handle their environment—first to roll over in it, then to sit, to stand, to walk, to run; soon to climb its rocks and trees, to dive into its waters, to leap through its air. They learn to build castles in it and to dig deep holes, to use it to grow flowers, fly kites, and launch fleets of sticks that sail to the sea.

• Play helps children know themselves in their environment. As baby animals find their own strength in the enemies that stalk them and the shelter that protects them, so children also discover themselves in relation to their surroundings. They are king of the mountain, master of all they survey as they race to the hillock and look down; they are a single pebble on the vast beach as they stand in the battering surf. As leaders and as followers, they find they have a place.

• Play helps children deal with the stresses of life. When kittens grow tired of nursing or lion cubs of sleeping, they pounce on each other to play. Children also instinctively turn to play as a way of relieving stresses that will recur from boredom, loneliness, hurt, anger, and fear for as long as they live. In the relaxation of play they will find new strength to cope and learn the greatest life lesson of all—that they *can* cope.

· Playing with a Preschool Child ·

"What toys are educational?"

On my oldest child's second Christmas, when he was sixteen months old, I timed his attention span with different toys; it ranged from ten seconds with a stuffed animal to sixty-three seconds with a push toy filled with rattling balls. After a while I followed as he toddled into the kitchen, where he spent over half an hour banging spoons and spatulas on pots and pans that he pulled from the lower oven drawer.

The trouble with many toys on the market is that in trying too hard to *be* fun, they deprive children of *having* fun. By electrifying the car and the clown, they deprive the child of his own pushing and twirling; by making the doll talk, they prevent the child's bringing it to life himself. As technology gets better, toys seem to get worse, which accounts for the everlasting appeal of pots, pans, and spatulas.

In selecting toys for a preschool child, keep several points in mind.

Do they let the child create his own fun with them?

Balloons and balls do, art materials do, building equipment does, dolls and stuffed animals do, puzzles do, push toys and pull toys and games he can play do, and musical toys let him dance and sing. You get the idea.

Are the toys appropriate for the child's age?

If the toys offer him no challenge, he will become bored, and if they are too advanced for him, he will become frustrated; in both cases, he will toss the toys aside in search of greater satisfaction. While you do not want to keep your child at the baby level and must be aware when he outgrows pull toys, neither do you want to push him into Erector sets or Lincoln logs when he is happy building with Duplos.

Do the toys address the child's interest and yet carry it further along?

You do not want to buy toys the child does not enjoy; for example, if your children, like many others, are totally turned off by jigsaw puzzles, do not force puzzles on them. However, you do want to build on your child's interests and still afford her new play experiences: If she likes dolls, for instance, buy her a simple weaving set with which to make covers for her doll beds or clay to make cups and saucers for doll tea parties.

Can the child play with some of the toys alone?

It is important for a child to spend part of his play time in amusing himself so that he will build the inner resources that lead to independence and self-confidence. If your child has not yet mastered this ability, find toys with which you can initiate play that he will then be able to continue alone.

Among the most educational toys are those that you do not buy but make from bits of materials around the house and scraps of imagination that you and your child put together. Here are a few ideas for starters:

· Put the dining-room table or chairs back to back and cover them with sheets. They become houses, stores, forts, tents—whatever you need for your impromptu plays. They also become private places for reading or a nap.

· Collect grocery boxes until you have enough to build a fort or to line up as cars on a train. If you are desperate on a rainy day, empty some dresser drawers and use them instead.

· Use old clothes and jewelry to dress up as queens and teachers and nurses and mommies and daddies. Make up plays or act out stories you know.

· Make masks from paper bags or from sheets of paper and string. Invent monsters and new kinds of animals and clowns and princesses.

· Use shoeboxes to make basinets for dolls and teddy bears. Line the inside with cotton, and cover the outside with material and ribbon.

· Tell stories and sing songs into a tape machine. Then play them for the family.

· Make and illustrate books on notebook pages tied together with ribbon: an alphabet book to begin with, a child's autobiography told through pictures and stories that a parent can write from dictation, an animal zoo, a community directory.

· Think of books as educational toys too. Read to your child every day, letting her select the book.

· *217* ·

You and your child can quickly add to this list as you walk through the house, pulling ideas along with the contents from old boxes stored in the attic or in the back of closets. What turns up will be fun for both of you, and you won't even know it is education.

Family games

When a family plays games together, the fun mounts, and so does the solidity of relationships. In addition, games give children a chance to share equally in a democratic situation where all players are equal. Try to pull your family together for games several times a week.

· Read a story together.
· Play any of the hundreds of games for preschoolers you find in toy stores, from the tried-and-true Candy Land and Picture Lotto to new ones that appear each year.
· Play physical games such as hide-and-seek, ball, tag, jumping and skipping games, Take a Giant Step, A Tisket A Tasket, and so on.
· Play sit-down games, such as I Spy or Who's Got the Button?
· And best of all, invent your own games. Our family had great fun trying to throw a ball into the wastebasket, bowling with milk cartons, guessing moods from the faces we made, trying to make each other laugh, and seeing how many fruits, candies, vegetables, and so on, we could name. Try it—inventing the game is fun in itself!

· 218 ·

· Playing with Elementary School Children and Junior High Schoolers ·

"What toys and games are educational for elementary schoolers?"

Children in elementary school are the greatest game-players of all. They love games—any kind, any time, with anyone—and they can invent their own with no more than a bottle top and a few pebbles. Doubters should have seen a little group I watched on a playground, taking turns tossing pebbles in the air and seeing who could catch the most in the top of a Pepsi bottle. With this frame of mind, the whole world is a game, and your only concern is in not stifling the inventiveness.

· Buy building toys that let children make their own choice of the finished product—not a kit designed to build a specified object, but a variety of materials that can result in robots or rockets as weird and wonderful as the child imagines.
· Find stuffed animals that do not replicate the ones your child

already has. I've seen everything from anteaters to zebras, with rare birds like penguins and macaws as well.

· Dolls are still wonderful for girls and some boys. Get baby dolls and little boy and girl dolls that let children be their parents, cuddling them, feeding then, and putting them to bed. It is difficult to play Mommy and Daddy with Barbie and Ken or similar dolls that look capable of handling today's problems with plastic cool that precludes parents. Most of their fun lies in their wardrobe and cars and boats, which offer far more materialism than education. In addition, they serve as role models of good looks and sexuality that differ sharply from the reality most boys and girls will face.

· A dollhouse often becomes a lifetime treasure. Let your child make curtains and redecorate the rooms from time to time and add occasional new family members and furniture.

· Board games of every kind delight children at this age—both the old ones, such as checkers, Parcheesi, and the Game of the States, as well as more recent additions, such as Clue and Go to the Head of the Class. No child should be without Monopoly, an endless source of fun and learning. I recall driving my children to Atlantic City years ago just so they could check the street names with those on the Monopoly board!

· Fleets of cars and trucks provide fun, especially when you help children make garages and firehouses for them under chairs and tables.

· Question-and-answer games are an endless source of fun for children, even when they have used all the cards and start over on questions they have already answered. The bits of trivia they learn are not the chief value, although I must admit my eight-year-old grandson stuck me on the capital of Bulgaria the other day. What proves a longer lasting result of Q&A games is the mental stimulation that spills over to other areas as well.

· Children in the upper elementary grades can begin experimenting with simple science sets, under adult supervision, of course. The easiest and least dangerous seem to be sets for exploring geology, biology, and weather.

· Because elementary school children are physical dynamos, encourage them to play baseball, soccer, and basketball, even to practice alone. They love dodge ball and prisoners' base and the other school gym favorites. Give them opportunities for ice and roller skating, bicycling, skateboarding, swimming, cross-country skiing, canoeing. And be sure they have jump ropes, hoops, and pogo sticks.

· Homemade games, like the bottle top and pebbles, invariably prove to be the most involving at this age. Children can experiment with different kinds of paper airplanes, color them, name them, and time them for speed. They can make a relief map of a country in which

· 219 ·

they are interested or of one they invent: build mountains of clay or a salt, flour, and water mixture; use mirrors for lakes and arrange grass, sticks, grains, and sand for the landscape; paint winding rivers a bright blue. They can act out a play or put on a puppet show, using a shoe box with painted walls and costumed pipe-cleaner figures. They can make stilts from tall juice cans and string. They can turn their book-shelves into a library, cataloging and arranging all their books, maybe even yours. You and they can take it from here and surprise yourselves with the excitement you can find around the house.

· Don't forget to provide an abundance of books: ones suited to their skills that they can read alone, and longer, more difficult ones that you will read to them.

"What are some educational games for junior high schoolers?"

Junior high schoolers are far less involved in playing games than their younger siblings. They prefer listening to music, talking to their friends, and, if you are lucky, reading. Still, there are some surefire hits.

- Board games such as Monopoly and Risk; you might even try chess.
- Games of skill that they can play alone—Hi Q, Laby-rinth, and so on.
- Word games such as Scrabble and Boggle.
- Science experiments in chemistry, astronomy, biology, electricity, computers.
- Card games. While Go-Fish, Hearts, and all the vari-eties of Solitaire are still fun, poker and Twenty-one soon become favorites. Some parents let their children use toothpicks as currency in these games, but I avoid even a semblance of gambling by having children score points instead of winning bets on the cards they hold.
- Physical games are probably the most popular—the seasonal ball games; Ping-Pong; pool; contests in jumping, throwing, and running; table soccer; and hockey.
- Homemade games are less popular with this age group, although my children have had fun making

their own experiments—watching a candy thermometer rise to 212 degrees as the water begins to
boil, and testing different foods for starch when iodine
turns purple. In addition, they have set up golf putting
on the living-room carpet and restaurants in the dining
room, complete with menus and home-cooked meals.
They have staged productions of musical comedies
they have seen and done imitations and made up their
own versions of *Name That Tune*. A no-fail favorite is
Hangman.

Family games for this age group

I have grouped elementary and junior high school children together
because a family activity usually involves children of both ages. Even
the family preschooler can join in the fun by becoming partners with
Mom, Dad, or big brother or sister. The point is to have everyone play
together. While there is no end to a list of possible games, the following
suggestions may get you started:

· Board games. Monopoly is one of the best if you have time.
· Ball games and other physical games.
· Guessing games like Twenty Questions and Who Am I? Essences
is one of my favorites: One player thinks of someone they all know,
whom the other players try to guess by asking questions such as "If
he were a color, what color would he be?" . . . "If she were a book,
what book would she be?"

· Acting games—Everyone knows how to play Charades, but are
you familiar with Adverbs? Our family loves this: One person goes out
while the others choose an adverb. Upon returning, he has to guess
the adverb by asking the other players to perform actions "adverbi-
ally"—dance, read a book, comb your hair sleepily, enthusiastically,
angrily, or whatever the adverb dictates.

· Games for sharing feelings. In one game, players take turns selecting a category—happiest day, most embarrassing moment, biggest
wish, accomplishment of greatest pride, favorite book, and so on. Each
player shares her answers with the rest of the family. Another worthwhile game in this category is Statues, in which players take turns
shaping another player's face and body into an emotion, which the
others have to identify—sorrow, embarrassment, joy, fear, and so on.

· Books are important here too. Select a book on which the whole family agrees—*Treasure Island*, *The Scarlet Pimpernel*, *Oliver Twist*—and read a chapter together several nights a week, if possible. Let each member of the family who is old enough have a turn reading.

· Special Kinds Of Play ·

Games that actually teach skills

By now it must be clear that I do not believe in forcing skill instruction on children, because it frequently retards real learning. Still, there are games that stimulate interest in the three R skills.

Despite the popularity of educational electronics, which sold $375 million worth of games in 1988, I think an inexpensive deck of cards is just as effective. Preschoolers can develop number awareness by sorting cards by color, suit, and matching numbers. I invented a game in which older children can learn sequential basic arithmetic by adding, subtracting, multiplying, and dividing cards that they are dealt. Allowed three turns to select from the remaining deck, they try to finish with a higher score than their opponent.

Junior high schoolers can learn fractions with cards: Dealt ten cards, they have to arrange them into five fractions that add up to more than their opponents'. They can learn algebra as well, setting up a problem with the joker representing X: for example, X plus 7 minus $2X$ times 3 minus $5 = ?$ Players draw cards from the pile until they draw a card that identifies X and gives the answer.

As a deck of cards is the most open-ended game on the market, parents can use it to lead children into far more number awareness and problem solving than the usual electronic questioning of "What is 63 plus 14?"

Many games on the market, such as dominoes and bingo, teach number skills to children as they play. In addition, they afford parents and children imaginative opportunities to invent and solve their own math problems and puzzles. Similarly, word games such as Scrabble and Boggle reinforce word skills; Game of the States and Risk teach geography; Masterpiece introduces children to works of art.

A typewriter can provide hours of fun at many levels. Preschoolers learning letters and numbers are excited to recognize the ones they know and to type them on rows across a page. The simple sentences that first and second graders have fun writing become full-blown stories and plays as they get older. Junior high schoolers take pride in mastering touch typing, which they can teach themselves with simple instructions. Because typing frees children from the physical and emotional strain of printing and script, many schools make typewriters available to children whose progress appears temporarily blocked.

I have always found a small cassette tape recorder not only a way to enjoy a long rainy day but a source of many kinds of learning. One of our favorite uses is to have someone begin to tell a story into the tape where no one else can hear; then have everyone else follow suit one at a time. When the last one has finished, we play the tape . . . and have a good laugh over our composite creativity. Use of a cassette player encourages children to put on a variety show, complete with homemade commercials, in which they sing, read poetry, play an instrument, tell jokes, and act out scenes—all in anticipation of hearing themselves later. I saw children develop a game in which they taped each other speaking a single sentence as a variety of different people might— teacher, politician, and so on—and then asked whoever would listen to identify them.

A discarded telephone, two if you have them, is obvious fun for preschoolers to use in their adult-imitation play. Even older children can use them, though, in "What Would You Do If . . ." play; for instance, ". . . if you wanted to turn down an invitation?" ". . . if you smelled smoke?" ". . . if you called a wrong number?" and so on.

· 223 ·

"What about electronic games?"

Thousands of electronic games glut the market, from the simple ones that teach colors and shapes to preschoolers all the way to personal computers installed in 58 percent of middle-income homes on which millions of elementary and junior high school children spend hours playing video games.

Almost as much material *about* electronic games has come on the market as well. They aid learning or they destroy learning, depending on whom you read. Let's look at both sides. Because practically no one disparages the simple hand-held preschool toys, let's focus on the more controversial video games.

"What is said to be good about video games?"

· They refine eye-hand coordination. This is undoubtedly true, which is why the young usually beat adults. If you have tried to beat your fourth grader at Mario Brothers on the Nintendo, you know what I mean!

· Many of them communicate a storehouse of facts. This is also true although a question arises as to whether accumulated trivia is beneficial. Still, Apple's "Where in the World" and "Where in Time" provide a lot of history and geography.

· They keep children involved for hours—a definite plus for many parents—although I think there are more creative ways.

· They introduce children to the growing electronic world of today and what will be the full-grown one tomorrow. True.

· They involve children in active play, unlike their passive role while viewing television. I question this argument on two points: (1) How active is their mind during a video game? (2) Does television *have* to be passive? We shall discuss both points later.

"What is said to be bad about video games?"

· They have a mesmerizing effect. True. The flashing lights, the clicking and buzzing put children in a near-hypnotic, not-in-this-world state while playing. Contrary to the argument above, while this may require moving eyes and fingers, it deadens mental participation.

· They are addictive. True. Children have to have their "fix," as any parent who has a video game knows. Of course, the parents too may become addicted.

· They replace involvement in other activities. Studies show that avid video game players read less and spend less time on sports and on homework.

· They give children a false idea of what learning is, and herein, I believe, lies the real damage. Children think the little bits of information they learn—such as the percentage of married men who like their mothers-in-law, a synonym for "ghoul," and even the capital of Bulgaria—is what knowledge is all about. When the goal is to collect unrelated answers to un-thought-provoking questions, how are you going to convince children to think? Will they ever believe that knowing is not a collection of trivia but, as Jacques Barzun explains it, "the ability to summon up an organized view of some topic"? I worry.

I am not being such a heretic as to suggest that parents rid their home and their child's life of video games, although I know a family who gave their Nintendo to the Salvation Army Thrift Store, and their son survived. I am merely urging parents to use caution by limiting the time their children spend on video games—half an hour a day, perhaps. Furthermore, until they kick the video game habit, suggest some fun substitutes—a family game or book or a chance to lie down, listen to their tapes, and do absolutely nothing.

"What about television?"

Watching television, to paraphrase the opening of Dickens's *Tale of Two Cities*, is the best of times and the worst of times. Through television, children can be exposed to the world's great thinking and artistic creations—Socrates and Joseph Campbell, Shakespeare and Eugene O'Neill, Beethoven and Aaron Copland. They can attune themselves to nature at its eagle-soaring best and understand its environment-polluting worst. They can feel good about themselves with Mr. Rogers and laugh with Bill Cosby and cry over Lassie. They can learn, acquire taste, and simply relax, as we all must at times, over nonsense.

On the other hand, they can tune in to violence, sex, and terror, be overstimulated, have nightmares, and get ideas that even some judges have said lead to criminal acts. Children have been reported to watch television thirty hours a week; some even spend more time in front of the TV set than in back of a school desk.

How should parents handle television?

According to the late pioneer in children's television, Dorothy Cohen, until children are five years old, parents should be highly selective about the programs they watch. After five, when children become less impressionable, the normal run of television programs will not damage them.

Television does have a deadening effect, however. Kindergarten teachers notice that children who watch excessive TV are less imaginative and less able to follow directions; teachers of older heavy TV viewers speak of less curiosity, lower concentration, and less creativity. Parents should, therefore, limit television time to no more than a hour a day, perhaps somewhat more on weekends.

Whenever possible, parents should watch television with their children, and not only watch, but initiate discussions about the show.

You can make violence less damaging by triggering your child's thinking with a question: "Can you think of any other way he might have handled the situation?" or "Why do you think he grabbed a gun instead of trying to work out the problem another way?"

You can help your child put the idealized world of TV in perspective by considering "How do you think you and I would have acted in that same situation?" or "Do you see anything unreal about the way she behaved?"

You can help him explore emotions: "How did that make you feel?" "How do you think that person felt?"

You can extend his imagination: "How else could it have ended?"

"If the story hadn't ended, what do you think would have happened next?"

You can help him develop taste: "What was good about the show?" "What would you have changed?"

Do not get children their own television set to watch in their room; use television to unite, not isolate, members of the family. A valuable lesson in give and take can be learned when all members of the family take turns selecting a show to be watched.

Instead of watching the same old situation comedies or mysteries on weekend evenings, rent a film if you have a VCR. Many of the classics, such as *David Copperfield*, *Dr. Jekyll and Mr. Hyde*, and *Vanity Fair*, are available, along with most of the great musical comedies, which families can enjoy together.

Don't let television become the family fight ring: Set up your ground rules and stick to them.

A great deal of information on television programming, on new legislation governing children's television, and on ways to make television more constructive for your child is available through the following organization:

· 226 ·

ACTION FOR CHILDREN'S TELEVISION (ACT)
20 University Road
Cambridge, MA 02138
(617) 876-6620

"What about war toys?"

War toys pack the shelves of stores coast to coast—from the discount chains that sell G.I. Joe and his equipment from prices as low as $3.95 to the elegant F.A.O. Schwarz in New York with several-hundred-dollar space suits and lasers to shoot children who don them. I recall the sight of a little boy walking from a toy store with his Rambo submachine water gun, a smile on his cherubic face. I shudder remembering a shopping trip last Christmas where, in a store strung with garlands of holly and resounding with piped-in carols, a woman pushed a cart filled with an Evil Horde Fright Zone set, a Cobra Hydrofoil with its push-button missile rack to release depth charges, and two packages of plastic hand grenades. Merry Christmas!

How can parents buy such toys for their children? I ask myself, and then I answer: Because they are advertised, because their children want them, because it is easier than saying no. I have read enough studies and conducted enough of my own to believe that war toys stimulate aggressive behavior in children: Children who wear camouflage suits and play war games with war toys do more hitting when they are little and get into more crime when they are older. The world's great war lovers, like Tzar Ivan, Peter the Great, and Napoleon, devoted their childhoods to tin soldiers and toy guns before they became big enough to play with real ones.

Certain psychologists believe that violent toys serve as a release valve for a child's repressed anger. They do no harm, they say, and may actually do some good. I disagree. Children find many other ways to let off steam : sports, play-acting, competitive games, for instance. Putting weapons into their hands sends the message that war and violence are okay; otherwise Mom and Dad wouldn't encourage them. Children don't need guns; they shoot just as accurately with their thumb and index finger. When Noah was four years old, he invented a new weapon. "Hey, Mom," he asked. "Can I shoot with a carrot?" Why not? Let him release repressed anger with imagination!

Even if you cannot be convinced that war toys lead to violence, you have to agree that they do not lead to peaceful development. Therefore, stay away from them. There are enough other kinds of toys to keep your child supplied, even though you may have to hunt to find them.

· 227 ·

Chicago boasts a Peace Museum, the only one I know of in the country. "Toys of Peace" is one of the special exhibits they send around the country to let parents know of alternatives to war toys. If you are interested in learning more about peace toys, contact the museum:

CHICAGO PEACE MUSEUM
430 West Erie Street
Chicago, IL 60610
(312) 440-1860

You might also want to contact a man who has started a movement to demilitarize toys. He conducts workshops for parents who want help in saying no to war toys and has established a movement to build a monument to peace from war toys that children relinquish and send him. For further information, you can write Frank Asch:

THE WAR TOY DISARMAMENT PROJECT
c/o R.R. 1, Box 10100
Wells, VT 05774

I would like to leave parents with two further comments on home play as part of a child's learning. The first is a scene I witnessed in which a six-year-old boy was playing with his nine-year-old sister—she with three Barbie dolls; he with He-Man and three of his most gruesome adversaries, Skeletor, Beastman, and Clawman. My first reaction was one of horror, because I consider Barbie less than a valuable role model and the other four action toys downright destructive in their teaching of violence and "evil empires." Furthermore, knowing the parents of these children to be gentle people, I was shocked to discover such toys in their home.

However, as I watched—unobserved because the children were totally engrossed—I soon realized that they were not using the dolls as they were designed to be used. In the hands of the little girl, Barbie had no sex appeal, and in the hands of the little boy, He-Man and his troupe waged no war. On the contrary, the children had paired them off with the three Barbies as mothers and the He-Man collection as their children (Beastman and Clawman were twins). On the living-room rug they were merrily having a picnic!

What does this story prove?

· That children's imaginations are far greater than the confines set by toy manufacturers.
· That while the up-to-the-latest-weapon realism of G.I. Joe and his equipment can lead only to the war games they are designed for, fantasy toys can fly to yet unimagined and peaceful worlds.
· That children nurtured in nonviolence play in nonviolence.

My second comment is an observation made by author Eda LeShan. "Fun," she says, "is when you feel challenged to do your best, when somebody needs you and when you are proud of what you are doing."

What that quotation proves is that parents are in the driver's seat when it comes to providing fun for their children and, if you will look more closely, in providing education at the same time.

CHAPTER 17

Extracurricular Activities

The value of extracurricular activities

Extracurricular activities are essential to a child's development and learning, whether they be those offered through school and community or those put together haphazardly by the child himself.

· They develop new interests. Without outside involvements, children miss opportunities to broaden themselves, to let curiosity lead them, to refine their taste—to become the interesting people we and they themselves enjoy.

· They reinforce established skills and develop new skills. Whether a child plays tennis, works at the recycling center, or takes singing lessons, regular involvement makes her more proficient. As her expertise increases, her self-confidence in one area extends further, instilling her with the I-can feeling in the face of other challenges that face her.

· They set goals. Like school, extracurricular activities enable children to strive for higher accomplishments—more difficult compositions to play, a faster swing with the bat, a new cake recipe. In this way, they establish a motivation for learning that schools, with their emphasis on marks, too often fail to provide: self-satisfaction.

· Above all, they are relaxing and fun. Like all of us, children need to escape the responsibilities that family relationships and school impose on them. Their absorption in extracurricular activities allows this on a regular basis.

The major guideline for parents in selecting extracurricular activities is to insist that children make their own choice—not piano lessons because Mother plays or wishes she could play; not soccer because Dad remembers his days on the high school team; not art lessons because it would be easier to take him to class with his sister. Children should be encouraged to choose what pleases them without guilt over not pleasing someone else. In cases where children cannot make up their mind, parents may be called upon to help—not by making the decision, but by encouraging their children to explore their feelings and examine their confusion until they reach a decision themselves.

The overprogrammed child

· 230 ·

When my children were in preschool, securing a friend for an afternoon of play took no more than a quick phone call to the mother. Today the process involves a social secretary:

"Can Tara come over and play tomorrow?"

"Tuesday? Sorry, no. She has ballet."

"How about the next day?"

"Oh, no. She goes to that French group."

"Maybe Thursday?"

"I wish she could, but that's Gymboree day, and Friday she goes to the father-daughter play group with Jim."

Then, just as Mother 1 despairs, Mother 2 suggests brightly, "I just remembered. Gymboree is called off a week from Thursday. How about then?"

Like millions of other children from upwardly mobile families, Tara is on the fast track. As she gets older, she will enroll in figure-skating classes, Suzuki violin, gymnastics, jazz dancing, and ceramics and continue to need a social secretary to unearth a free afternoon for friends. Her parents will hold their own with other parents, boasting of her accomplishments and pay the bill for lessons, guilt-free in the knowledge that they have insured their daughter's success in life.

What else have they done?

- They have taught her that satisfactions derive from the world outside, not from her own inner resources.
- They have taught her that "success" is counted in the acquisition of miniskills in competition with her friends.
- They have put her in a pressure cooker and convinced her that she likes it.
- They have robbed her of doing-nothing time, in which children engage freely in what their parents no longer remember—the act of wonder.

It is my belief that children should have extracurricular activities no more than one day a week on school days and, if they choose, when they reach elementary school, one activity over the weekend as well. Parents, give your children the freedom to play. Give them the gift of leisure, from which they will derive benefits lasting farther into adulthood than the accumulated skills of their lessons.

Give your children the initiative to create their own after-school activities and pursue them according to their own schedule. For instance, if they take ceramics lessons, provide supplies so they can teach themselves oil painting when they want to; if they play baseball Saturdays in Little League, let them organize their own soccer or field hockey teams with their friends; or if they take lessons on an instrument, let them teach themselves a second instrument if they are interested. A mother I know whose eleven-year-old takes oboe lessons and also is teaching herself piano told me, "I'm afraid if I start her on piano lessons, she'll be turned off. Now she plays all the time."

· 231 ·

· Outside Activities in Preschool ·

"What should a child do after school?"

The stimulation of preschool is an enormous drain on children: friends to play and fight with, toys to choose from and put away, activities to engage in, directions to follow. Physically, mentally, and emotionally, it is exhausting. The first thing children need after a morning of preschool is lunch and a nap, which is always scheduled in a full-day nursery school. After that, children need relaxed play with a neighborhood friend or with parents or caregivers. By 5:00 or 6:00 it is time for a bath and supper, perhaps a TV show, family play, and a story before bed.

I see no time for organized after-school classes or activities for pre-schoolers during the week. While I personally consider Saturdays spent with Mother or Dad in a round of routine chores or in specially planned family activities of greatest value, if parents are determined to keep up with the Joneses' preschoolers, Saturday is the time to do it. Use three criteria in selecting an activity:

- Let it be noncompetitive and non-achievement oriented.
- Let it be physical (dance or gymnastics, perhaps), but not overstrenuous.
- Let it be an activity the child wants.

Activities that fit the preceding criteria are those such as dancing, singing, art, and free creative play, rather than French, violin, or gymnastics.

"What about Sundays?" parents ask me, traumatized at the prospect of twelve unplanned hours for their preschooler. That is the time for walks, picnics, games, visits, puppet shows, and lending a hand as Mother and Dad cook, fix the car, shovel snow, walk the dog, and go about what needs doing. Working parents in particular can put Sundays to constructive use by sharing time that is deprived them on weekdays.

Weekends present parents with the choice of watching a ball game on television or spending time with their preschooler. The former, reminiscent of past single or newly married days, provides entertainment; the latter leads to growth—theirs and their child's. Parents and children need each other at this stage to build nonpostponable bonds and to learn who they are in each other's eyes and in their own. Weekends will become free again soon enough as children grow into watching ball games too or escaping from the house with friends. Then they will need you in different ways, but now while they are little, they need you to see and touch and be near because that is how they define love.

"What about Sunday school for preschoolers?"

While all Sunday schools I know (they go by many names) have preschool classes, most of them are gentle baby-sitting groups to accommodate parents attending religious services. Materials may include Bible stories and crafts designed for special religious holidays, but in general the religious training tends to be low key. Religious indoctrination at this age is better done through play and role modeling than through strict instruction, both for the benefit of the child and the success of the religious teaching.

Although Sunday schools do present one more organized activity for children, they usually last no more than an hour and are free of stress. Furthermore, the family group going to church or temple together finds another opportunity for unity. Corny as it may sound on the bumper sticker of a car, "The family that prays [and let me add 'plays'] together, stays together."

· Extracurricular Activities in Elementary and Junior High ·

"What about children who want no extracurricular activity?"

There is nothing wrong in a child's not wanting to become involved in extracurricular activities. In fact, it may be a constructive sign that the inner resources he has developed keep him adequately occupied without reliance on planned activities from the outside. If your child seems happy, healthy, and busy without extracurricular activities, back off and let him be

· 233 ·

However, if his lack of involvement appears to indicate trouble brewing, you might consider several possible causes:

· Perhaps he finds all the offered activities boring. In this case, try to ease him into one of them. Point out how he might enjoy pursuing it during the summer on his own or suggest that he sign up with a friend. If he remains negative toward organized activity, you might be able to stimulate his interest in an individual endeavor such as music lessons, swimming at the Y, jogging, volunteer work, and so on. Avoid excessive pressure, though, because your child may be at a stage where he requires free afternoons to compensate for what he feels is a heavily scheduled life. Let him play or read or sort out his baseball cards or follow you around and talk; just do not let him find escape all day in the great American drugs—television and video games.

· Perhaps he is too fatigued to do anything but lie down or loll around when he returns from school. As this is not a normal condition for children of this age, you should check out the health factors. Is he eating properly? Getting adequate sleep? Is he in a sudden growth spurt? Discuss the situation with the child's physician, who may want to test him for anemia. Examine any emotional factors that may be draining his energy—difficulties at school, family upsets, problems with his friends. You may want to discuss the possibility of drugs or depression with the school or an outside counselor.

· Perhaps he just wants to be with his friends. If he and his friends spend after-school time playing together, know where they are and what they are doing. If the former is safe and the latter constructive, stop worrying and let him and his friends create their own extracurricular activities. Constructive play doesn't have to be playing chess or building model airplanes; it can range from listening to music and reading magazines to just plain talking. If, however, you do not approve of where they are "hanging around" or what they are doing, then you need to take some steps. These are discussed in detail in Chapter 22.

"Should a poor student have extracurricular activities?"

Some parents adhere to the belief that extracurricular activity and poor school performance exist in a cause-and-effect relationship. As a result, if their child is doing poorly academically, they remove her from the basketball team or the class play so that she will have more time for her studies. While I have on occasion seen an overprogrammed child pull up her schoolwork by being deprived of extracurricular time, the usual child makes no change at all.

Extracurricular activities provide mental relaxation, a valve for releasing pent-up frustrations, and a source of self-esteem, all of which are conducive to a child's healthy growth. In fact, studies have shown that children involved in outside activities perform better in school on the average than those without them. When parents, therefore, use the removal of extracurricular activity as a means of either punishing a child for poor grades or of motivating her to produce good grades, they actually defeat their own purpose. While their child may gain additional time, she will lose an experience that enables her to put whatever time she has to constructive use.

As a school director, I encouraged weak students to undertake an outside activity and persuaded some adamant parents that success in a nonacademic area could spill over and give children a whole new outlook on themselves and on school. I particularly remember a boy who, in a vicious cycle of failures, had abandoned all hope until he joined the photography club and had his photographs displayed in a club exhibit and admired and written about in the school newspaper. For the first time he knew the feelings of accomplishment and pride; and although it was a great surprise to his parents, it was no surprise to me that his next report card for the first time sported glowing teacher comments.

The only time I think parents are wise to deprive a child of extracurricular activity is when she has overprogrammed herself and may be too exhausted or literally have no free time to study.

Extracurricular pressures

Outside activities should be fun. Children should have fun doing them, and parents should have fun watching them (plays and ball games, for example), hearing about them (book clubs or service projects), or viewing their finished products (ceramics, art, or creative writing). When previously enthusiastic children no longer enjoy extracurricular activities, chances are they have been put under kinds of pressure that preclude fun. Let us consider four types of pressure.

Status pressure

In certain communities selected activities become the "in" thing. Everyone who is somebody has her child take Suzuki violin or ballet from Madame Kay or prehockey at the independent school ice rink. Even though your children may have no interest in violin, ballet, or ice hockey, they may find it difficult to resist pressure from their peers. Even though you may not want to push your children and, furthermore, may not want to spend the amount of money required, you too may find it difficult to resist pressure from your peers, the mothers and fathers of your children's friends.

Don't give in to it. The lesson your children will learn from conformity for conformity's sake is a destructive one that may develop into a lifelong habit. Let them know it is too expensive and find one that better suits your budget. Or point out that because their interests lie elsewhere, it would be foolish to spend their limited free time in an activity someone else enjoys. Finally, give your children an opportunity to learn that pursuing an individual interest—such as being the only girl in school who plays the oboe or the only boy who plays golf with his father—will in the long run prove more rewarding than conforming to a noninterest.

Pressure to win

Scores of parents have spoiled developmental baseball and Little League for their children by turning a game into a life-and-death competition. Are they using their children to compensate for their own failed hopes? Are they seeking status through their child's win? Or are they simply unaware of the pain their children endure for fear of losing? The answer may be yes to all three questions. However, cause is not the issue here—not *why* parents pressure their children to win; *how* is the issue—how to prevent them.

If you find yourself more determined to see your child's team win than to see the eagerness with which your child plays, you may be responsible for the pressure that is depriving him of a rewarding experience.

"That was a dumb play," a father calls to his son, who missed the catch at second base.

"You guys beat those show-off Orioles, and I'll give you each a dollar," urges a father-coach.

"For God's sake stop crying and act like a man," a mother stage-whispers to her eight-year-old, who is struggling to hold back tears after striking out.

"What do you mean 'out,' you bum?" screams a father to the umpire as his son walks back to the bench, more embarrassed by his father than by his third strike.

Are you those parents? Behind all your "team spirit," are you really telling your child "If you don't win, I'm ashamed of you"? Tune in to yourself next time and find out.

Pressure to be athletic

The agony of this kind of pressure manifests itself most often in boys who fail to fill the male model of masculinity. They are the ninety-pound weaklings in whom years ago Charles Atlas discerned the yearning to be turned into muscle men, the unloved on campus aching to be the football heroes of adoring Betty Coeds, the bespectacled skinnies immortalized today as "nerds." Despite the proliferation of science prizes and literary awards, success for many boys in school still comes packaged in a gym suit; and when the suit is ill-fitting, it may not come at all.

How can parents help their nonathletic son cope with the pressure to make a school team? No magic wand will erase his longing; no magic word will bring comfort. Can they help at all? I think so. First, they have to acknowledge the pressure in order to open the sluice gates through which the child can release his dammed-up pain. To pretend that either the pressure or the pain is nonexistent will merely increase both, often to unbearable proportions.

Second, they can help their son deal with reality, a lesson that will probably become a trusted ally on many future occasions in his life. He is not athletic; that is the cold, hard fact that all his self-flagellation and wishful thinking will not change. Not until he accepts that realization will he be in a position to confront it constructively.

Third, he can take several coping routes.

1. He can forget athletics and seek success in nonathletic areas—theater, debate, music, and so on.
2. He can undertake a training course—either by himself or through an organized program—to overcome his physical inadequacies and still aspire to heavy sports.
3. He can enter sports competition in fields that require qualities other than machismo muscle—Ping-Pong, badminton, and so on.

A boy's ability or inability to cope successfully with being a nonathlete in an athletic world rests a great deal on his parents' attitude. If they themselves define masculinity in terms of muscles, no matter how many words they speak to the contrary, their son will receive the message and feel like a failure. If, however, they see masculinity in far broader terms that include courage and empathy and doing one's best, then their son will grow through the pain into real manhood.

· 237 ·

Pressure to practice

"Should I make my child practice the piano, or should I let her drop it?" This is one of the questions parents ask me most frequently. The answer depends . . .

Is the child taking lessons because *you* think she should or because she is interested? If you forced lessons upon her in the first place, and she was not interested to begin with and still is not, then I think you should back off and let her drop piano.

On the other hand, if she was eager to take piano lessons but now finds that practice is harder work than she anticipated, I think she is obligated to give the piano a fair chance. Point out that it becomes more enjoyable as she becomes more proficient and that she will feel proud when she can play a few pieces. Because you went to the trouble of locating a teacher and scheduling and paying for lessons, she should be responsible for living up to her end; that means practicing without making your home resound like Dante's Inferno. I have found that practicing three days a week instead of daily is far more palatable to most children.

I don't advocate making a child practice piano any more than I advocate making her do her homework, mainly because when you come right down to it, you can't "make" her do either. You can only make her go through the motions. I do suggest using a little more pressure with the piano than with the homework, though, because the classroom teacher has clout to hold her accountable, and the music teacher hasn't.

It is possible that your child wants to abandon piano because one of her friends has started guitar or drum lessons, and they seem more fun. Don't let her become an instrument hopper. Suggest that when she masters the basics of piano, you will let her add guitar or drums or even give up piano at that point. With the background in music piano affords, she might even be able to begin self-teaching on other instruments at a later date.

A child's negative feelings about her teacher may be a cause for balking at practice and wanting to quit. Observe the teacher yourself and talk to your child about her. An instrument teacher has to understand that a child's interest may wax and wane and will rarely, as in the case of little Amadeus, have number-one priority. The teacher has to be flexible enough to accept weeks here and there when practice has been inadequate or nonexistent, and creative enough to select music the child will respond to. If your child's teacher falls short of these criteria, give up on that teacher and try another before giving up the lessons.

· Summer Activities ·

Gone are the Norman Rockwell summers when boys in tattered overalls waited for the tug of a fish at the end of their poles and jumped naked from a rock into the old swimming hole . . . when girls played jacks on the porch and rolled hoops . . . when fathers chatted on the steps and mothers set pies on the kitchen window sill to cool. Today's children undergo the rigors of sleep-away or day camps that keep them occupied and safe while Mom and Dad work for a few weeks of vacation in July or August.

The important question in this new setting is, therefore, "What shall I do with my children this summer?"

For preschoolers

I think the most constructive summer activities for young children revolve around friends and family. Because they have just completed nine or ten months of organized activity at school, they need to relax.

· If Mother or Father is home, now is the time for trips to the zoo, playing in the park, going on picnics, swimming, and sharing all the fun of nothing to do and warm days to do it in.

· If Mother or Father is at work, grandparents or other relatives may enjoy breaking the child-caretaker routine with special trips and visits.

· Children should have time to play with their friends, casually if they live in the same neighborhood, by prearrangement if they need to be brought a distance. It is a particular treat for a child to include a friend on some of the special excursions he takes.

· If parents work and children must be placed in day care over the summer months, parents should make a special effort to plan family activities over the weekend, even if some chores get overlooked. Summer is the ideal time for strengthening family bonds because people are less tired, the weather is conducive to good dispositions, and work pressures often drop off. Take advantage of it.

For elementary school children

Children in elementary school need to be involved during the summer months.

· They may find their involvement at home with family and friends, where horses, streams, meadows, or farm animals offer daily adventures.

· On the other hand, they may need scheduled activities to afford the involvement they need—day camps, church or youth groups, 4-H, and so on. Because special-focus camps exist in many areas, parents often can match a camp to their child's interests for the happiest experience.

· I think children benefit enormously from assuming responsibility for some kind of project over the summer. I know a ten-year-old who grew vegetables in his backyard and sold them in the neighborhood from his red wagon. Another baby-sat with the neighbor's four-year-old two afternoons a week. You can help your child select a pursuit that will interest her and at the same time develop self-confidence and a sense of responsibility, with the range as varied as knitting a sweater, reading biographies of Presidents, or teaching a group of younger children to play baseball.

· Although I am not a great believer in sleep-away camp for this age group, I recognize occasions—and children too—that call for it. Do not send a child to sleep-away camp who is less than enthusiastic to go because she will feel you are getting rid of her and, in many cases, be so upset that she will have to return home anyway. If your child really wants to go to sleep-away camp, for the first year sign her up for the shortest time period allowed—usually two weeks or four. If she wants a longer stay the following summer, you will have a better idea of her ability to handle it.

Three cautions:

1. A month should be long enough for your child to be away. A month at home has its benefits too, remember.
2. Do not plan to take a distant trip the first time your child goes to sleep-away camp. Let her know you are home and there if she needs you.
3. Write to her at camp several times a week, and do not expect letters as frequently from her. Keep your letters newsy and cheery, not filled with pictures of your loneliness, which will make her feel guilty.

For junior high schoolers

At this age, children need their peer group. Therefore, unless there are friends and supervised activities for your child nearby, you are probably better off with an organized program.

· Day camps abound in most areas. Let your child select the one he wants based on the criteria most important to him: what activities the camp offers and which of his friends are going.

· Sleep-away camps may be very good for children who *want* to go. If they have been before, they may even begin to assume duties as counselors-in-training. A month may be adequate for many children, while others may enjoy the full two-month program. Let your child decide, both on the camp and on the length of his stay.

· A possibility for junior high children who want no part of camp, day or sleep-away, is a summer course. Given by a local high school, by community centers, and even in some areas by science institutes, these courses are designed for fun and stimulation. As they give no homework or grades, there is no pressure, and children can involve themselves in subject matter as varied as birds and stars, pottery and weather, handwriting analysis and acting.

· At this age, most children who stay home for the summer are eager to earn extra money and, by putting their creative thinking to work, are usually able to find ways. I know one who washes "dishes" in her father's science lab, another who does the marketing for an elderly lady. There are lawns to be mowed, wood to be stacked, rooms to be dusted, babies to be sat with, newspapers to be delivered, furniture to be painted. You and your child together can discover the endless et ceteras.

· Travel ·

As the offspring of a so-called child-rearing expert, my children are occasionally asked to describe their childhood. As I look back now, I recall hundreds of my mistakes they could bring forth in answer, but instead all three of them reply with great enthusiasm, "We traveled all over the world!"

The enthusiasm is genuine, and even "all over the world" has the ring of sincerity when I realize it was viewed through little eyes. Yes, we traveled a lot. As a teacher, I had time; and as a born adventurer, I had curiosity. We took a freighter through the South Pacific and drove into the highlands of New Guinea; we climbed Alps to walk on the falling stones of ancient castles; we camped on reindeer hides in Lapland; we got lost in Turkish bazaars; we froze on the North Rim of the Grand Canyon and roasted potatoes in a fire on the shore of Lake Erie. Halfway through each wondrous adventure, we met my husband in civilized spots like London, Paris, Oslo, or Washington and toured world capitals for two weeks.

The children attribute their worldview to their early travels. If this is true, I am grateful, for the world needs their view to begin to understand and accept people and ways different from our own. For my part, I look back on our travels as I imagine the princes of Europe must have looked on their Grand Tour before settling down to the job of reigning: It showed me what I could become if I kept trying.

As far as I am concerned, no excitement compares to traveling with children: discovering the world together; uncovering laughs in odd little corners; relishing discomfort because you know it will end; and learning, learning, *learning* together! I urge hesitant parents to try it. Here are a few guidelines that might help:

· Infants are easy to travel any place with. Hang them in a pack in front or back; nurse them so you don't have to carry bottles and formula; carry cloth diapers, which you can wash and dry and reuse, instead of suitcases full of paper diapers, which you cannot replace everywhere.

· Toddlers are the most difficult to travel with because they always run off and are too heavy to carry and too young to be interested sightseers. Try camping or stay in small towns where playgrounds and swimming pools are available. Take picture books and toys flexible enough to be used in different ways.

· Preschoolers are good travel companions when you settle down in a single spot that has some of the conveniences of home. They love zoos and picnics and taking walks, all of which are quadruply exciting in foreign towns. They like making friends with local children too.

· Elementary school children, especially if you have given them previous travel experiences, can go anywhere. They love adventure; so let them be map-readers and troop leaders as you hunt out castles and cairns. Don't expect them to like, or even try, exotic foods, though; carry along a large jar of peanut butter. In cities, limit your time in museums and art galleries, selecting the areas to visit according to the children's interests: One of my children who loved boats handled Turner beautifully but balked at Rembrandt. Take them to plays—musicals particularly and mysteries.

· As junior high schoolers are highly peer-oriented, I used to let them invite a friend along at the parents' expense, even to places as far away as Fiji or Israel. It is not a necessity, but it helps. Let your children study the brochures you get ahead of time and have a major role in planning your itinerary; just as in school, when a subject turns them on, they throw themselves into it fully. They can assume a good part of the responsibility of a camping trip, and although they cannot drive, they are usually excellent navigators and sign-readers. Communicating with people who do not speak English, via charades and a phrase book, challenges the problem-solving skills of these preadolescents and provides great stories afterward.

Here are some general suggestions for traveling with children:

· Have them keep a journal if they are old enough. If they are not, then you keep it for them.
· Let them take photographs of what they want. They might want to leave space in their journal for the photographs they take.
· Do a lot of walking. The children will benefit from the exercise and will see a great deal more too.
· Resist the temptation to turn every occasion into a "learning experience." My eight-year-old grandson Noah brought this warning home to me a few years ago as, walking around Westminster Cathedral in London, I overzealously pointed out and explained the memorial of each famous person. As we entered the room where Queen Elizabeth I is buried, he noticed a printed sign directed to tour leaders that read, "No lecturing here, please." With a look of relief, Noah pointed out the sign to me and, putting his finger to his lips, whispered a knowing "I think you'll have to wait till later."

CHAPTER 18

Your Unique
Child's Problems

· Each Child's Individuality ·

When I was a child, a teacher explained infinity to me. "Picture a granite rock a mile high and a mile wide," she said. "Then picture a sparrow flying to the rock once every hundred years. It pecks at the rock once with its tiny bill and flies away. When the rock has been pecked away ...that is infinity." While purists may find fault with the teacher's image, for a child whose mind could conceive of nothing longer than the night before Christmas, it worked well. Even today I return to that picture when I run into the idea of endlessness.

I think of human individuality in terms of that rock and sparrow, and I hear echoes of my old teacher as I try to make young people grasp the infinite uniqueness of each of them. Never in all past ages and never in any future time, I tell them, never in any spot on earth or over it or under it will genes and circumstances come together to form another you...even when the sparrow has pecked the rock into dust. Even when we learn to clone each other.

The limitlessness of human individuality awes me. I wish every child saw it as I do so that he would prize his worth, use his body and mind and feelings as nonexpendable treasures. I wish too that parents saw their child's individuality as I do so that they would let him be what he is instead of misshaping him in a mold of their own design.

The source of individuality

At first glance, it appears that fate has conspired against human uniqueness: Evolution endowed each of us with the same physical equipment, while the process of maturation arranged for us to develop our body, intellect, attitudes, and moral sense in the same sequences. At this rate, one person might be as interchangeable with another as anatomy diagrams in a science textbook. Therefore, why, instead of being like the Stepford wives, are we all so wonderfully, so terrifingly different? A quick dash through one track of the process of personality development may shed some light.

The wise and wry psychiatrist R. D. Laing believes that parents serve as an "identity kit" from which their children piece together a picture of themselves. On one hand, they imitate their parents: Don't we all know the boy who struts just like his father and the girl who flies off the handle like her mother? On the other hand, children react against their parental models: How else is a boy able to break that birth bond with his mother? How else are boys and girls able to establish their separateness from Mother and Dad? In the reacting against, the search for uniqueness begins.

Another tool rests in the bottom of that parental identity kit, one more sensitive and potentially dangerous than both imitation and re-action against. It is called identification, a process in which children become their parents: the abused child becomes the abuser; the loved child becomes loving.

It appears that the die is cast early . . . or is it? Despite our shared biological inheritance, each of us enters the world with a genetic pattern duplicated by no one else. Despite the processes of imitation, reaction against, and identification that each of us undergoes, our individual relationships with our individual parents produce responses so varied as to defy replication. As a mere twenty-six letters can be arranged to produce works as unique as *Hamlet* and *Mad Magazine*, how much more unique are the works produced by the infinite patterns of DNA combined with parenting!

Forces against individuality

It is not easy to grow up an individualist with pressures for con-formity pushing in from all sides. With the teen stars of television and film sporting faded jeans and oversize shirts, those are what your chil-dren want . . . and what stores see they can get. In fact, as I learned in a shopping trip with my granddaughter recently, that is about *all* they can get, way down to size 2. Advertising compounds the problem with the demand for name labels on the faded jeans as an entry permit to the in group. Language becomes a label too, with even the youngest calling someone "bad" when she means "good," and "rad" when she means "cool," or what used to be "hot."

Sure, we had peer codes when I was young; we wore saddle shoes, cardigans, and page boys, but the world was bigger then, and only *Life* magazine let us glimpse each other. Television began narrowing the world when my children were young, and their whole generation adopted long hair, love beads, beards, and holes at their elbows. The youth cult was born. Today it is full grown and living in a small world where news spreads as fast as gossip in a small town. Along with Michael Jackson's white glove, *Police Academy VI* and Alf's "No prob-lem" catch-all phrase, signs of conformity have taken a more ominous turn as sex abuse, crack, handguns, gang rape, and mass murder look like the latest fad.

Parental support of a child's individuality

One of the most loving fathers I know explained why he was de-termined that his son graduate from Exeter and Harvard Law School and enter his law firm. "I know he will like it," he said. After a pause in which I remained silent, he asked, "Don't you think so?"

"I know *you* will like it," I replied.

It is difficult for parents to dissociate themselves from their children, who are bound to them not only through their bodies but as much through their self-images and dreams. Yet unless they do, they cheat children of their birthright to be themselves. A few suggestions may help you support the individual growth of your child:

· Don't make her fulfill your dreams; encourage her to dream her own.

· Don't make her be the kind of person you like; instead, like the kind of person she is.

· Don't be a conformist yourself; set a model of individualism for her.

· Don't criticize and belittle and harp on her faults; let her know how wonderful her unique self is and how much you love her. When you are angry, scold what she does, not what she is.

· Above all, release your child little by little as she tests her separateness from you. Independence does not arrive full blown when a child enters high school or goes away to college; it has been building from the moment she pushed away from your breast, rolled over, learned to walk, ran to her room and slammed the door, slept at a friend's house, rode the bus alone, earned money. If you try to hold your child back out of fear or ego needs, you are doomed to fail because she will leave anyhow. Try instead to equip her with coping skills so she can judge life's odds and risk them when they are in her favor.

· Finally, keep your eye on the large picture without focusing on minutia: Let her conform to the little things to which she and the peer group attach significance, but which really make no difference. Let her wear the in styles: untied sneakers, shorts that all but glow in the dark, jackets three sizes too large. Put up with in language like "dork" and "dude" if it makes her feel cool, but restrict the obscenity. Let her see the senseless movies made for young people that they consider hilarious as long as they are rated no worse than PG. Check the PG-13s yourself before giving consent and avoid the Rs, even if "Everyone else in the class saw it."

If you work at strengthening your children's sense of self, chances are they will outgrow their need to conform and eventually have enough confidence to be what is right for them. They are not going to call people "nerds" or consider Pee Wee Herman the height of humor forever. When you weather peer conformity successfully, you may be like a mother I know who exclaimed in surprise to her teenage daughter, "I think you're wonderful, but you're not at all what I expected!"

When you weather it successfully, you may also hear what she heard in reply, "You're wonderful too, but you're not what I expected either!"

An old Yiddish proverb says, "Little children, little problems; big children, big problems." Assuredly, because each child is born human, he will have problems; and because each is designed as an individual, he will come equipped with his own special brand.

· Problems Developing in Preschool ·

"My child wets her pants in school."

Wetting her pants in school is a great embarrassment to a preschool child, whose classmates invariably respond with uninhibited pointing and stares, proud that they are not responsible for the puddle. A child I know reported his accident to his mother when she took him home, explaining in exasperation that his "dumb" friend told the teacher and adding, "She knew. Her shoes got wet."

The first problem to address if your preschooler has a wetting problem is to assure her that it is no big deal. A hug, a kiss, and an "Oh, that happens to everyone once in a while" should ease her embarrassment. The second problem to address is *why*. A child may be unable to control her bladder in school for a variety of reasons.

· She may be afraid to ask to go to the bathroom. You can determine this possibility by asking the teacher to take the child to the bathroom once or twice during the morning or afternoon for a few days. If your child's wetting stops, you will have found the cause of it and may prevent its recurrence by bathroom reminders at regular intervals during the day.

· If your child wets her pants at home as well as at school, she may still be too immature to control her bladder. In this case, ask the teacher to take her to the bathroom at regular intervals in hopes of preventing an accident, but let her wear diapers in case the teacher's timing is off. Because toilet training is a prerequisite of attendance at many nursery schools and at all kindergartens, your child may have to put off school until she is trained.

· Frequently when a child begins wetting in preschool, a situation has arisen that is too stressful for her to handle. She may not be ready to separate from her mother or, with a new baby at home, she may be fearful of losing mother's love and is coping by reverting to baby behavior, which previously succeeded in bringing comfort. If you are aware of the development of a stressful situation, make an effort to give your child extra attention and reassurance. See Chapter 5 for details.

· On the other hand, your child may be angry and getting back at you or her teacher in the most vengeful way she can devise: "You're so insistent on my toilet training? I'll show you!" Discuss this possibility with the teacher and see whether you can identify the cause of her anger—perhaps a feeling that going to school is a rejection from home or that lack of the teacher's individual attention indicates noncaring. Give your child the reassurance she needs in knowing that she is loved both at home and at school and help her find alternative ways of venting her anger. If wetting persists, have the doctor examine your child. There are physical causes as well as psychological ones, and lack of bladder control can be medically treated.

What to do about the "bad" kid in school

Chapter 5 discussed aggressiveness in preschool—your child's aggressive behavior to other children and other children's to yours. However, there is another kind of aggressive child in school who may appear during these early years. You may hear about him when your child comes home one day: "Boy, George is bad. You know what he did today? He hit Marcy with a fire engine and made her cry." You are duly horrified.

A few days later you hear even more. "George wrote all over Allie's painting with red crayon and spoiled it." And the following week: "George kicked Roger in the leg."

· 248 ·

Finally, fearful that your child will become George's next victim, you speak to the teacher: Can't she do something to control George? "George?" the teacher asks.

"Yes, the little boy who kicked Roger and hit Marcy with a fire engine and ruined Allie's drawing."

The moment of truth arrives: There is no George in the class. Two possible scenarios follow. In one scenario the teacher says, "Your son Billy is the one beating up on the other children." Billy, it turns out, has been acting out his aggressions on his classmates and, feeling guilty about his behavior, clears his conscience without fear of recrimination by confessing his transgressions in the name of George. In this way, Billy is able to continue ridding himself of angry feelings and still not get into trouble at home.

The teacher could have prevented the play-acting—and probably the acting out too—by alerting you to Billy's behavior at the start. Because she did not, it is urgent that you, the teacher, Billy—and George—face the situation together. You can make it clear to Billy that such behavior is unacceptable. The three of you should try to discover the cause of Billy's aggressiveness, eliminate or at least minimize it, and present him with alternative behaviors for ridding himself of angry feelings.

In the second scenario, the teacher stops after explaining "There is no child named George in the class." Billy is not misbehaving either. Instead, he has created George from his own secret wishes and has set him on the rampage he himself dares not take. Billy is angry and would like to be George, kicking and hitting and destroying children's paintings. His conscience or his fear of punishment prevents the switch, though; so he merely relates George's outrageous acts with glee. Here too you and the teacher should try to discover the cause of Billy's anger and help him deal with it.

CHAPTER 19

Your Unique Elementary and Junior High Schooler's Problems

· Behavioral Problems ·

Aggressiveness

Children in elementary and junior high school rarely hit and kick as their younger schoolmates do, not because they feel no anger or insecurity—on the contrary, they probably feel a great deal more—but because they discover other ways of acting out. More sophisticated than preschoolers, they are aware of a greater variety of options through which to release their repressed feelings. In elementary and junior high school, aggressiveness assumes many guises.

Teasing

Children lash out at each other through teasing in an attempt to overcome their anger and frustration. Little boys notoriously tease little girls to affirm—both for themselves and for others—their masculinity, just as preadolescent girls tease boys to hide their emerging fears of sexuality. Children tease "Fat Stuff" and "Dumbo" and "Teacher's Pet"· and "Fag" in order to build themselves up by putting someone else down. As they do it in the name of fun, with pokes and laughter, they spare themselves the additional pain of conscience pangs or teacher trouble.

Bullying

When teasing removes its costume of verbal fun and games and reveals its physical naked self, it becomes bullying. The bully does not pretend to be playing but, like a terrorist, exerts his power through fear. "If you walk through the door before me, you'll be sorry." . . . "Give me your homework to copy, or I'll break your finger." . . . "Don't tell who did it unless you want to get beat up again." The bully keeps his targets like hostages, silenced and afraid, operating out of sight of anyone except other potential targets who, to save their own skins, also remain silenced and afraid.

· *251* ·

If your child is the object of teasing or bullying, do not assume that it will go away: Studies reveal that teasing and bullying usually do not disappear with the passing of time, but more often turn into scapegoating. According to Dr. Sandra Sexson, director of training in child psychiatry at Emory University, even one year of being a scapegoat can categorize a child and destroy her future at school. Furthermore, do not assume that your child can handle the problem alone: Targeted as the object of teasing or bullying, a child loses the very self-confidence and self-esteem that would enable her to cope. Therefore, step in to help. Alert the teacher to what is happening and urge her and/or the guidance counselor to address the subject with the whole class. Meanwhile do all you can to reestablish your child's self-worth by confirming your love and pride in her.

If, on the other hand, your child is not the target but the perpetrator who teases or bullies, you have an even more serious problem to contend with. Why is he doing it? Why does he want to hurt other children? What is he feeling? When did it start? Is he compensating for a lack or a perceived lack within himself? Obviously you will have discussions with your child. You and he will discuss the situation with his teachers and the guidance counselor, if the school has one. If the problem persists, I suggest you seek family counseling from an outside professional. The dynamics of the home situation may be creating stress of which you are unaware.

Clowning

Like the circus clown who hides tears behind a painted smile, children who play the clown hide aggression behind their antics. To amuse their classmates, they shout out silly answers to the teacher's questions; they make faces behind her back; they draw mocking pictures on the chalkboard. Because everyone but the teacher laughs, the clown is an acclaimed success. Why does she choose that role? Because as a clown she feels free to hurl insults at the teacher, the authority who underscores her inadequacies and impotence. She realizes, of course, that although even the clown does not act with complete impunity, she receives less stringent disciplinary measures than she would were she to hurl the insults herself. Therefore, she deputizes the clown to stand in for her.

Vandalizing

Destroying school property is a way of destroying school itself, what psychologists call displacement. It is a child's way of eliminating not only the school building and the whole institution of education but all the bad feelings about himself that school creates and, even more broadly, all other authorities in his life whom he resents. By cutting into desks, writing four-letter words on the walls, breaking windows, stuffing toilets to overflow, and drawing on chalkboards with indelible markers, children shout a loud "Go to hell." In being heard but not identified, they vent their rage safely, not in a single shout that dies in the halls but with a permanence that enrages their teachers.

Breaking Rules

When a child breaks school rules, she uses undisguised antisocial behavior, which may be as minor as repeatedly coming late to class or as major as smoking or drinking; as minor as throwing food in the cafeteria or as major as carrying a switchblade knife. Like vandalism, breaking rules is a way of lashing out through destruction, not of school property but of the school system and the community it holds together. Unlike vandalism, however, it makes no effort to shield the offender but lets her stand arrogantly in the glare of her actions. Because it is overt and so easily punishable, many psychologists regard rule breaking as a cry for help from a desperate child who sees herself out of control of her feelings.

* * *

If your child is acting out through clowning, vandalizing, or breaking school rules, she needs help. Help includes what some parents call punishment, but what I see as accountability for the child's behavior: apologies to teachers whose lives she has made miserable by clowning, payment for destroyed property by earning money, acceptance of disciplinary action from the school for having broken its rules. Discussions among parents, child, and school personnel may unearth the causes of such behavior, which can subsequently be dealt with. If the behavior persists, you should seek professional help.

Dishonesty

Dishonest behavior takes many shapes and springs from many sources. A new study aired on national television in a show called *See Dick and Jane Lie, Cheat and Steal* reveals that a third of the children questioned had lied to a friend, half had stolen, and three-quarters had cheated. Parents have cause for alarm.

Lying

It is important to realize that lying or what we may call "making up stories" is a highly creative process, for which novelists and playwrights win Pulitzer prizes. Imaginative children frequently let their fantasies run rampant with tales of danger and heroism and of netherworld creatures they conjure up. They may be totally unaware of having crossed the line between truth and fiction with events that are as real to them as the fear-created tigers in their closet. Parents want to avoid quashing their child's creativity and, at the same time, do not want her to fall into a habit of lying. The question is "How do I succeed in the juggling act?" The answer lies in discovering the reason for the lies.

The child who lies for the sheer joy of turning the world into a storybook adventure will outgrow or channel the habit as her process of maturation enables her to distinguish truth from fiction. Parents can recognize these lies because they are pure fun with no ulterior motive.

However, a child may lie for other reasons.

- To protect herself after an act she knew was wrong— "I did my homework but lost it."
- To wreak vengeance on someone who has angered her—"My teacher uses bad words in class."
- To make herself feel important or appear important to someone else—"I got 100 on the test."

These kinds of lying indicate a child's feeling of helplessness in facing an unpleasant situation; unable to cope directly, she copes with a lie, that age-old defense not only of children but even of the leaders of nations. Although parents will be hurt and angry over being lied to, they must realize that screams, yells, and punishment will not solve the problem but only magnify it and make the child hone her lying skills to avoid being caught next time. What they have to do is give the child alternatives—an alternative to the behavior that got her in trouble in the first place and an alternative to lying as a coping technique. Because the myriad of behaviors that might require alternatives are discussed throughout this book, let me suggest only some alternative coping devices parents might present to their child.

First, help her realize that because lies are usually detected, she will be in trouble anyway. That is, if she is lucky. If she gets away with the lie, even worse, she will be in trouble with herself, carrying around a dusty, ashamed feeling inside and losing the self-respect that makes her like herself.

Then help her see a better way of protecting herself after a wrong-doing than by lying: Owning up will enable people to continue trusting her instead of doubting what she says.

· 254 ·

Also suggest a more constructive way to handle people who have angered her. Let them know how they made her angry and tell them not to do it again; if they continue, avoid further contact with them.

Finally, convince her that she does not have to lie to feel important. Remind her of the many ways in which she *is* important.

If you are successful, she may still resort to lying occasionally when she finds herself in a tight spot. Most young children go through a period of lying, which you may be able to handle more calmly if you realize that in most cases it is a stage, not a trend, that you can help your child through with love and constructive suggestions.

Cheating

Parents are usually surprised to learn that students who cheat are more often high achievers than low achievers. Most of the so-called poor students have given up trying to get good marks and, having thus accepted their part in the failure syndrome, have no reason to cheat. Good students, on the other hand, not satisfied with being less than best, may resort to cheating as a way of assuring success, with which they dare take no risk. I have seen A students plagiarize term papers on which they would have probably gotten an A anyway, copy notes on their hands and arms for exams that they would have easily passed, and check answers against their neighbor's when theirs were right in the first place.

What causes such irrational behavior? The answer is usually over-pushing on the part of parents who focus on academic achievement as the major criterion of worth. Their children, either rightly or wrongly growing up with the idea that acceptance by their parents hinges on their school performance, take any steps to assure an A. The epidemic of cheating that rages in schools across the country shouts a warning to parents: Stop pushing your children to the top of the class; establish such values as honesty and courage and kindness, which mean more than success; and stand by your children with love even when they fail.

Stealing

A child may steal for any number of reasons, and your greatest hope is that she gets caught so that you can discover the reason and help her. If a child steals an item from a classmate because she knows you will not buy it for her, you should ask yourself why she cannot cope with nongratification. Have you overindulged her? Is she so accustomed to getting everything she wants that she can't handle a sudden no? If so, it is none too soon to alter the pattern and let her learn that she can not only survive, but will grow into a more self-fulfilled person by learning to do without.

If a child steals in order to hurt somebody, out of jealousy or malice, you need to draw out her feelings. Only when you know why she wants to punish the other person are you in a position to begin helping her. As always when confronted with your child's feelings, acknowledge them instead of giving in to your immediate reaction: "That's ridiculous!" Jealousy and malice are valid feelings; your job is not to deny them but to help her deal with them in a more constructive way.

Some children steal as a way of exerting control in a situation in which they feel powerless—that is, school. While these children, like all others who perform antisocial acts, need to have it made clear that stealing is not acceptable, they need also to be apprised of areas in which they *do* exert some control. For instance, point out that your child exerts control in school by selecting her friends, her clothes, her lunch, and by deciding how to do her work. Because a teacher can assign students control in many other areas as well, you might speak to your child's teacher. I think you have to be honest, though, and agree that most schools are not organized as democracies but rather as authoritarian states. Point out that you lived through the experience and will help her while she does the same. Meanwhile, see whether you can democratize your home enough to turn part of her life over to her control.

Stealing from a store becomes for some children a rite of passage.

I taught in a school where a group of seventh-grade girls gave weekly lists to their boyfriends, who then went to the local discount store to shoplift items on the list. Any boy who refused was dropped from the group and labeled a "fairy." These children proved their "manhood" by shoplifting in the same way adolescent boys in preliterate tribes proved themselves by their first animal kill. Fortunately the boys were eventually caught and disciplined both by the school and their parents, who did not celebrate the rite of passage with tribal pride. My disappointment lies in the fact that while the guidance counselor made stealing the subject of a rap session with the whole seventh grade, few parents followed through individually at home.

If your child is caught shoplifting, insist that she return all the stolen goods in person to the manager of the store and write a formal apology. If any of the items cannot be returned—such as food that has been eaten—see that she pays for them from her own earnings or allowance. You might, in addition, assign her a research paper on the subject of shoplifting to assure her doing some in-depth thinking on the subject. If shoplifting continues, you should seek outside help; it may indicate kleptomania or some other emotional disturbance.

· 256 ·

"Should a child tell on a friend?"

One of the most painful dilemmas in which your child can find himself is to discover a good friend in a bad act: He hears his friend lie to the teacher; he sees the ring his friend stole; he watches his friend reach for his homework to copy. What should your child do, caught between Scylla and Charybdis as he is? If he takes one route, he loses a friend; if he takes the other, he hurts his conscience. History has put its greatest heroes in similar situations, forcing them to make choices that were no more painful—Joan of Arc, Galileo, Socrates, Jesus.

If your child is asked by his friend to become part of the crime—to hide the stolen ring or give him the homework to copy—a strong superego may help him say no or find other words that say as much:

"It wouldn't be fair."

"It would get you in trouble."

"My mother would kill me."

"I don't think we should."

Even "I have no place to hide it" or "I haven't got my homework."

If, however, he finds himself pushed by a more abstract code of honor, should his conscience make him tell on a friend? It is not easy. If the teacher asks, "Who stole the ring (or told the lie or copied the homework)?" should he raise his hand and tell? Or slip up to the teacher in private? No, his job is not to set the world—or even the classroom—aright, but to urge his friend to go about it.

"Why don't you give it back and tell the teacher?" he might ask his friend, adding supportive arguments: "She won't be mad if you tell, and you can promise never to do it again." He could end with a clincher like "Think how bad it'll be if she finds out herself!"

Don't urge your child to become an informer. Help him instead to be a persuader.

· Emotional Problems ·

Exam anxiety

Examinations put even adults under extreme stress: Remember the last time you took a driver's test? There are few situations in which people feel so vulnerable as when they face an examiner in control of their future, and school tests and examinations regularly put students under what they perceive as life-and-death stress. While some children pass through exam periods with a minimum of anxiety, others become total wrecks. What makes the difference? A look at that driver's test you took indicates three variable factors that might provide an answer.

A feeling of competence

If you have been driving for years and need a retest only because of a recent move out of state, you will hop behind the wheel with self-confidence. Your children in school are almost the same: When they enter an exam sure of what they know, like you, they will hop behind the desk in command of the situation and of themselves. Literally, as they put it, no sweat. The difference between you and your children, however, is that most of the time they are not as sure of themselves or of what they know as you are, with the result—plenty of sweat!

The school's attitude

If as you begin your driver's test, the examiner looks over at you, smiles, and assures you that you are doing fine, you will relax and think, "This isn't so bad after all." If, however, the driver scowls, stiffly directs you to "Turn right," "Park here," "Back up," without comment, you will probably feel your blood pressure rise in fear.

Your child's teacher can be like either of those examiners. If he considers examinations the focal point of the year's teaching, he will put your child under tremendous pressure. In many schools the final exam, for instance, counts for a half or a third of the year's grade, and I even know schools that fail a student who does not pass the final exam. On the other hand, if the teacher considers an examination simply as a method of self-evaluation for both students and teacher, the stress level will drop. Some teachers actually assign grades for the year before students even take the final exam; others allow students to retake exams until they pass them, saying, "If we want them to know what's on the exam, why not let them study the material until they know it and can pass?"

The parents' attitude

Try to imagine that you are sixteen, your family lives in a city and has no car, but you are taking a driver's test anyway. Unpressured, you feel no anxiety. Now try to imagine another situation for that sixteen-year-old, you, who, one of the last in the crowd to drive, is panting for a license. Your worried parents tell you as they let you off at the test site, "Remember, if you make a single mistake, we're not going to let you drive." In a state of full-blown anxiety, you sit down in the test car.

· *258* ·

Which kind of parent are you? If you have been sending your child the message—whether in words or mere vibrations— that she had better do well on exams, or else . . . you are a parent in the second scene. If, however, you have let your child know that exams are just part of the entire learning experience, on which to do the best you can, then you are a parent in the former scene. The scene in which you place yourself has a great deal to do with the degree of anxiety with which your child faces school examinations.

What can parents do to alleviate their children's exam anxiety?

- · Help them keep exams in perspective; do not let them overmagnify their importance.
- · Offer to help them study for exams by hearing vocabulary, asking history questions, and so on, but do not force yourself on them.
- · Try to limit the amount of time they spend on cramming for exams. They need the relaxation of outdoor play, perhaps a family game or a TV program, and a good night's sleep.
- · Realize the stress they are under during exams and

avoid confrontations. Try to keep the environment conflict-free.
· Acknowledge their anxiety over exams so at least they will not have to suffer in silence.
· Let them know that the results of exams, whether good or bad, in no way change who and what they are.

Shyness

In the American competitive culture that rewards aggressiveness and popularity, shyness tends to be viewed as an aberration. Parents and teachers alike seek help to reconstruct the personality of children who don't raise their hands in class or join the group at recess or struggle for leadership roles in school. Shy children speak softly and carry no stick, preferring anonymity to acclaim, shadows to the spotlight. Were you to transplant a shy child to Victorian times or earlier to colonial America, she would be viewed as a model of perfection—a child seen but not heard. Today, instead, we look at her and ask, "What's wrong?"

Perhaps nothing is wrong. According to Dr. Philip Zimbardo in his book *Shyness* (Jove Books, 1987), 42 percent of upper elementary school children and 54 percent of junior high schoolers consider their classmates shy. Two-fifths of all adults admit they were shy as children, with tests revealing that all but a fraction of a percent either outgrew their shyness or were able to handle it and build constructive, fulfilling lives. Sometimes the most bombastic children in class are play-acting in order to hide their shyness, just as the famed Greta Garbo concealed hers behind the mask of sexuality in the movies.

Whether a child's shyness should be viewed as a worry depends not on how you or his teachers feel about it, but on the child's own feelings. Some shy children are happy with themselves as they are— quiet, retiring, more sensitive than their classmates. Introverts in the true Jungian sense, they do not require stimulation from other people and activities in order to be alive and growing; they turn inward to discover stimulation within their own depths. While they are friendly to their classmates, they may have only one friend. While they avoid class participation, they cause no trouble and do their work satisfactorily; even the teacher who complains would willingly exchange a few other students for more like them. Shy children march to a different drummer from the stereotype . . . and march on tiptoe. As long as they are happy with their own rhythm and keep in step with it, parents should let them be.

· 259 ·

On the other hand, some children hate themselves for being shy. Although withdrawal into shyness offers them security in the face of the frightening world of school, they long to burst out and be part of the crowd. However, the specter of failure, which they see hovering around them, freezes their will, forcing them into permanent, lone silence. This is the shyness parents should address, first by discovering what the child fears.

· Does he not raise his hand in class for fear of giving a wrong answer? If this is the case, probe his feelings by asking what he thinks would happen if he gave a wrong answer: Would the children laugh? Would the teacher get angry? Would he be made to feel dumb? If he just imagines a yes to these questions, you might urge him to try and see what happens. If, however, he has actually experienced the yes, you should discuss the class attitude with the teacher and ask her to take steps toward changing it.

· Does he withdraw from other children for fear they will reject him? You can probe into this possibility in the same way—by discovering whether he is imagining or has actually experienced rejection. In either case, suggest that he select one child with whom he feels comfortable and try to make friends with him—sit together at lunch, play at recess, or ask him to the house after school. As his confidence grows, even though the single friendship may well branch out into others, do not push him to win a popularity contest.

Children who crawl into shyness for escape from danger, as animals crawl into their holes, find themselves caught in a vicious cycle: Low self-esteem may nudge them into shyness in the first place, where shyness reinforces their low self-esteem. They hate what they are and see no way to become what they could be. While parental intervention as just suggested may alleviate their misery to a degree, it will not reach into the depths of the problem, which is less how to raise your hand and make friends than how to feel secure enough to want to. Parents whose children have reached this painful extreme of shyness should seek guidance from a professional.

Depression

Psychologists have been alarmed to note a marked rise in childhood depression, an emotional disorder once associated mainly with adults. While statistics are not available, it is estimated that as many as one in anywhere from five to ten preadolescent children suffers from varying degrees of depression. However, despite the epidemic, few parents understand the nature of the problem.

Depression results from what psychologists call "a loss of self." A child suffering from depression feels that, swept along by the endless demands and expectations of his parents, he is, like a small boat in heavy seas, swamped. "Where am I?" he calls, and his drowning cries echo, "Lost, lost, lost."

Like all children, depressives will pay any price to keep their parents' love: do and say whatever pleases their parents, regardless of how false they are to themselves. They will smile when their hearts are raging, pretend to love what they loathe, be the child of their parents' blueprint. Fawning and faking and filling their parents' dreams are their tools of survival. Their reward: parental love. The cost: loss of their self.

Depression, like shyness, is a defense mechanism, a subconscious adjustment children make in order to live through a painful reality. Were they to confront themselves with the Faustian truth of having sold their soul for a prize, the resulting anguish would be unendurable. Falling into a state of depression is far safer and hurts less. Like the river Lethe, which obliterates memories of life in the mythical Land of the Dead, depression makes the pain of having once been alive go away. Despondent and fatigued, without appetite or interests, the depressed child gives up his usual pursuits and isolates himself from his friends and family. As he has relinquished the Self that made life worthwhile, he is only half alive.

Some guidelines will help you identify depression in your child:

· Sorrow is not necessarily a sign of depression but instead may indicate a healthy reaction to a loss, such as death, sickness, or uprooting.

· Signs of depression may include insomnia, withdrawal from people and former interests, pessimism, self-criticism, guilt over past actions, exhaustion, noncommunication, lack of vitality—a general feeling of melancholy. A depressed child is more apt to seem permanently "out of sorts" than sad.

· Some depressed children show none of the aforementioned signs but display what is called "masked depression"—restlessness, overactivity, and malfunctioning in social situations.

· Do not jump to the conclusion of depression immediately; a child may display all of the above signs for other reasons for short periods of time—a recent disappointment, heavy stress in school, moving to a new home, physical changes and/or problems, and so on. If the child's mood persists for a couple of months, then you might seriously consider depression.

· 261 ·

If you suspect your child is suffering from depression:

· Talk to him. See if he is aware of his altered behavior and mood and can offer any explanations.

· Talk to his teacher to ascertain whether she has noticed a change.

· Ask the school guidance counselor to meet with your child.

· If the depression continues, seek professional help.

Some psychiatrists put children on antidepressant drugs, which personally I would try to avoid. Other kinds of help are available: individual counseling to help the child work though his depression and family therapy to identify and form new patterns from which the depression may have arisen. Nonverbal therapies are being used increasingly to treat depression in children, especially those who are blocked from discussing their feelings but can actively express them through paintings and sand play.

Because depression often results from a child's unconscious bargain to give up his Self in order to keep his parents' love, the cure must begin with parents taking an honest look at themselves. Are they—consciously or not—forcing their child to conform to their image of what a child should be instead of supporting him in his quest to become what he is meant to be? Are they, like Procrustes, lopping off parts of him so he will fit the bed they have made for him instead of giving him room to stretch into a bed of his own design? If so, stop. Look at your child. Listen to him. And give him back himself.

Without being an alarmist, I want to say a few words about suicide, which became what some psychologists call a teenage epidemic two decades ago. Among middle-class high school students, suicide became the second leading cause of death, the first being accidents, which are in many cases subconscious suicide. Statistics indicate that suicide is becoming a problem among younger children as well, mainly preadolescents, although incidents of children as young as four have been reported. More girls than boys attempt suicide, but because as they use less immediate methods such as sleeping pills and wrist slitting, the girls are more frequently discovered and saved. On the other hand, while fewer boys attempt suicide, those who do are more likely to use violent methods of shooting and hanging and actually kill themselves.

The tragedy of a child's suicide is that when it is successful, the child has failed. Children who attempt suicide do not want to die; they cannot articulate the pain that overwhelms them and are screaming for help in the loudest voice they can muster. Childhood depression is their whispered cry; unheeded it grows louder until a parent hears, sometimes only in the sound of death. Suicidal children almost always give some or all of the following signs:

· A sudden change of mood. The morose child about whom you have been worried will suddenly become happy, almost serene. It is at this point, psychologists feel, that the child has made the suicide decision. Seeing light at the end of her tunnel of sadness, she is relieved of the prospect of unending pain.

· Tying up the loose ends of her life. Like a person with terminal cancer, the suicidal child wants to set her life in order. She may give her prized possessions away, finish a book she has begun, express her love for her family.

· Play-acting suicide. Parents should take a child's pretend suicide seriously, for by doing so they could prevent the real thing. The girl who scratches her wrist with a pin and shows it laughingly to her mother and the boy who ties a rope around his neck for a joke may be rehearsing the first act of their tragedy.

If parents see these signs developing from a child's depression, they should act immediately.

· Talk to the child about her actions. Express your worry, and let her know how much she means to you. In a family counseling session, a young boy told me that he was seriously considering hanging himself on the shower rod in despair over being unable to live up to his parents' expectations of him. Much to the boy's surprise, his father said, "You know, if anything happened to you, I don't think I could go on living."

"I never knew that," the boy said, amazed.

· Get professional help. If the child is self-destructive, she will probably be hospitalized for her own protection or put under careful surveillance at home.

· When your child returns from the hospital, her therapist may ask you to back off so that he can establish a private relationship with your child. Do not assume that he wants to take over your parental role, but understand that what takes place between the child and the therapist belongs only to them. The greatest help you can give is trust, support, and love . . . and a great deal of money to continue treatment as long as necessary. If finances are a problem, check your area for a free psychiatric clinic or one that charges according to family income.

· Remember, children live in the immediate present more than adults do. What is misery now seems like misery forever with no chance of abatement. Yet the suicidal child today is not necessarily the suicidal child tomorrow when the sun rises on a different view of life. While you should not despair, neither should you assume that the problem will vanish by itself. Magical thinking cannot replace

· 263 ·

professional help—sometimes of long duration—in healing a suicidal child.

· Physical Problems ·

Sickness

The ordinary colds, flu, and chicken pox that beset children, though debilitating for them and troublesome for their parents, pose no real problems, because time and modern medicine offer cures. Physical problems arise in several more complex forms.

Pretend illness

Few parents have not heard "I have a headache" or "My stomach hurts" from a child who hopes he can be convincing enough to miss school that day. Because nobody can actually feel anyone else's pain, parents are never sure whether the pain is real or whether they are witnessing an Academy Award performance. If the child is truly sick, he should be home; if he is faking, he should be in school. Parents face a dilemma: If they send the child to school sick, he will probably get worse and infect other children too; if, on the other hand, they keep him home when he is not sick, he will learn to lie and manipulate in order to achieve what he wants. With the consequences of an error in either direction looking pretty bleak, what are parents to do?

· Always take a child's temperature when he complains of an ache or pain before school. If he has a fever, keep him home; watch him and, if the fever persists, call the doctor.

· If he has no fever but shows signs of acute pain, keep him home and call the doctor.

· If he has no fever and shows no signs of acute pain, insist that he go to school. Like most children, with the hope of staying home gone, he will probably chalk up a loss, accept your decision, and go about his daily routine.

· If he continues to complain, insist that he go to school, but allow him to take a note asking the nurse to send him home if he develops a fever during the day.

· The hard part comes if he not only continues to complain but works himself into a state of rage and self-pity, hurling accusations of your being mean and unfair and not loving him. Resist the temptation of taking the easy way out by giving in to his temper tantrum. Insist he go to school.

· Try to find out what may be happening at school this day that is upsetting—a test, undone homework, a report in front of the class, and so on. Talk with him—listen to him—and try to reassure him.

· Suggest that he might feel better if you drive him to school this morning instead of his taking the bus, but he must go to school.

· If pretend illness persists day after day, maybe it is not pretend; take him to the doctor for a checkup.

· If the doctor finds no physical cause, talk to the child's teacher to discover a possible cause at school. Are classmates teasing him? Has he hit an academic snag? Is he in some kind of trouble?

· Some children develop a real school phobia, using feigned sickness as a way of avoiding attendance. Because promises, threats, nags, and coaxing are ineffective against the all-controlling power of a phobia, parents will need professional advice.

· One last word: The stress on schoolchildren is tremendous, and sometimes they need a break, as all of us do. Although I think it is disadvantageous to let a child succeed in tricking you into letting him stay home, there is a way to concede. Once or twice a year plan with him ahead of time a day that he can take off from school. Choose a normal day with no horrors at school to avoid and no special treats at home to glean—just a day in which he can benefit from staying home and doing absolutely nothing. You will be amazed how it lifts his morale! Not every teacher sees eye to eye with me here, but I have learned that one day off can lead to many days'—and months'—benefit.

· 265 ·

An incident my daughter had recently with her third-grade son Noah might see you through a difficult morning of headaches and stomach pains. Noah developed a stomachache upon learning that his sixth-grade sister was being kept home with a runny cold. His early pleas turned to tears of self-pity and finally to anger. He tore up the note his mother had written asking the nurse to send him home if he developed a fever, and finally without the note, which she refused to rewrite, off to school he went. When she picked him up at school that afternoon, with fear and trembling she ventured, "How do you feel?" Without time to answer, he launched into an account of all the day's excitement. During a pause she asked again, "How do you feel?"

Looking at her as if she should be addressing some other child, he said, "Great. Why?" Why indeed!

Imagined illness

Children who imagine illness differ from those who pretend illness in that they do not use aches or pains as a ruse to escape school. On the contrary, they really believe they are sick, usually with a serious disease. The problem stems from two main sources.

First, the child may have been frightened by a sudden confrontation with a disease: she may have read a story about a child with a brain tumor or leukemia; she may have overreacted to a school program involving lung cancer or anemia; or she may know someone seriously ill with cancer or heart trouble. Overly sensitive, she may have developed a fear of having the same disease.

You should discuss her fear with her and give her what information you have concerning the particular circumstances of the sickness that has alarmed her. If her fear persists, enlist the help of the doctor. A thorough examination will reassure the child that she is healthy, and a talk with the doctor about her imagined illness should eliminate her fear of contracting it in the near future.

Second, children sometimes imagine illness when they are suffering either from depression or overanxiety. Elimination of the underlying causes of the depression or anxiety, which probably stem from the home and are reinforced at school, may make the imagined illness disappear. If they continue, parents should seek professional help in order to prevent the development of full-blown hypochondria.

Psychosomatic illness

When my father began practicing medicine, he wasn't able to send a child with headaches for a brain scan; with a skin rash, to a dermatologist; with a stomachache, to an internist. He treated the diseases medically and their causes psychologically. In today's age of specialization, however, doctors like my father no longer exist, with the result that children's headaches, stomachaches, and rashes are treated far more frequently—and unsuccessfully—than the stresses that cause them. The tide may be turning, though, as indicated by recent findings that relate asthma, stomach ulcers, canker sores, and trench mouth in children to emotional rather than biological causes.

Psychosomatic illness, unlike pretended or imagined illness, is real: The psychosomatic stomachache leads to vomiting just as food poisoning does; the psychosomatic mouth pain indicates swollen gums; the psychosomatic asthma can suffocate a child. When children's diseases persist despite medical treatment, or if they recur regularly, parents should consider the possibility of underlying stress factors. What is going on at home? What attitudes and relationships exist? How is the child feeling about her parents and siblings? What is going on at school? How is the child performing? How are peer relationships? How does the child feel about school?

Parents should discuss the problem with the doctor, who may be able to do what my father and doctors like him used to do: Help the child work out the underlying causes of her illness. If the doctor is unable to help in this way, he may be able to suggest a professional counselor, or you may find one through your local family counseling agency.

Prolonged illness

If a child is ill for a long period of time, the problem is how to keep her abreast of her class when she cannot attend school. Unless the illness is so debilitating that it precludes the child's ability to do school work at home, she is far better off to keep up with her work: first, because it maintains a connective link between her and school; and second, because it prevents her having to repeat a year or spend the summer in summer school. There are several ways parents can help children keep up with their class work:

· By agreement of the principal and your child's teachers, you can arrange to pick up new assignments and turn in completed ones every week. Often a neighborhood classmate will serve as messenger, filling your child in on class activities and personal goings-on as well.

· You may be able to help your child with the assignments. If not, you may have to hire a tutor.

· 267 ·

· Because schools are responsible for the education of all children in the community, you may be able—either through the school or the district office—to secure a home teacher for the duration of your child's illness.

· You will find that work at home is most successful when a certain time is set aside for it every day. Mornings are often best because the child feels least fatigued and the prospect of a work-free afternoon lies ahead.

· Arrange for school friends to visit your child once or twice a week if possible. They will help her pass the time while maintaining her place in the peer group.

Pretending to be well

Strange as it may seem to some parents, many children lie to their parents not to stay home from school but in order to go to school. They hide the headache, deny the stomachache, and cover up the sniffles in order to sneak out without detection. Instead of holding the thermometer against a light bulb to get a 102-degree fever, they slide it under cold water, trying to lower the temperature to 98.6.

I applaud both the school and the home that fosters such a sense of fun and enthusiasm for learning, and I fantasize a day when everyone of the 44 million American schoolchildren will try to outwit the staying arm of parents in order to run off to class. I think children should not let every little ache and pain serve as an excuse to avoid school but should learn that even feeling less than perfect, they can still carry out their responsibilities. However, if a child is really sick, he must stay home in order to get well; and if he only has a cold, he still must stay home to prevent infecting other people.

Parents, stand firm! A fever indicates infection in a child's body, and a runny nose at the end of a cold indicates lingering germs. If your child's temperature hovers around 99 degrees or if his nose never seems to dry up, consult your doctor before taking a chance and sending him to school.

Accident-proneness

Every school, despite the most careful precautions, encounters children who are constantly injuring themselves. My school had a junior high school student who in one year broke her ankle in a fall down the steps, broke her wrist as she made a turn in a swimming pool, and suffered a fractured skull when she ran into the gymnasium wall. For years the school community rarely saw this child without bandages and casts.

Some children continually injure themselves because they have poor coordination, due to physical causes such as slow eye-muscle development or to a neurological dysfunction. Tests are able to indicate problems of this nature, and treatment for them is available. In order to help a poorly coordinated child, parents should take several steps.

- Do not make fun of him, and do not be angry. Both responses will lower his self-confidence, put him under extra stress, and, as a result, increase his accident-proneness.
- Do not overprotect him by prohibiting his participation in sports. This response will make him feel even more incapable than he does now. Instead, teach him caution and provide what physical protective devices are available—arm and leg supporters, knee protectors, shin guards, and so on.
- Discuss his problem with the physical education teacher who, having seen many children over the years, is in a good position to evaluate your child's

situation. If the teacher suggests neurological testing,
go ahead with it.

Other children become accident-prone from less definable emotional causes, however. At the simplest level the child may have feelings of inferiority that he attempts to overcome through the extra attention his injuries create.

At a more complex and dangerous level, the child may feel totally worthless and, without hope, subconsciously seek self-destruction through repeated accidents. If your accident-prone child manifests symptoms described earlier under "Depression," consider the possibility that the accidents may not be accidental but may be cries for help. Talk to the child and the school and follow the guidelines suggested.

Eating problems

Anorexia and bulimia, two serious eating disorders, used to be seen mainly among adolescent girls but lately have spread downward into younger children, both boys and girls, in junior high and even elementary school. Both of these disorders manifest an obsessive overemphasis on food: anorexia, by deprivation; bulimia, by indulgence and regurgitation. Overeating has joined the other two as a third serious disorder; a reported 25 percent of children of both sexes are overweight. While psychologists offer numerous explanations of all three eating disorders, they generally agree on the basic underlying factor: a child's inability to cope with excessive stress.

Because giving milk is a mother's main means of nurturing her child and demanding milk is a baby's main source of need gratification, eating disorders in schoolchildren may indicate a regression to infancy. They may be a subconscious means to deprive the mother of the fulfillment that her basic nurturing role affords, or a way of making infantile demands for her attention and care. They may also result from succumbing to societal pressures that equate thinness with social acceptance and eating with personal gratification. Whatever their cause, eating disorders are physically destructive through nutritional deprivation and psychologically destructive through the cycle of guilt they set in motion.

Help must come from five sources.

· A medical doctor, who will check the child regularly
for weight, blood count, and so on.
· A nutritionist, who will design a diet for the child and
check her progress in adhering to it.

· 269 ·

- A psychologist or psychiatrist, who will try to work through the underlying stress factors and help the child find more constructive coping methods.
- The parents, who will work with the others to alleviate stress factors at home. They must not nag or scold the child about her weight and her eating but support her in her efforts to overcome the problem. In the words of a nutritionist I know, "Put a large helping of love in her diet."
- The school, which will also make an effort to ease the stress level by giving the child additional help and support both academically and personally. I have seen a child make great strides when a teacher or a classmate assumes the responsibility of helping her eat what she is supposed to.

· 270 ·

Eating problems can become very serious, turning into lifelong habits or ending in serious illness and even death. It is amazing to me that more children do not develop eating disorders in the American culture, which bombards them with mixed messages—Eat, Eat, Eat and Be Thin, Be Thin, Be Thin. Parents need to be very careful not to add to their child's confusion and guilt with their own mixed food messages.

A variety of books available in libraries offer advice and support in dealing with all three kinds of eating disorders. Among the most helpful, I think, are *A Parents' Guide to Eating Disorders* by Brett Valette (Walker, 1988) and *When Food Is a Four-Letter Word* by Paul Haskew and Cynthia Adams (Prentice-Hall, 1984). For further guidance you may want to contact:

THE AMERICAN ANOREXIA/BULIMIA ASSOCIATION
133 Cedar Lane
Teaneck, NJ 07666
(201) 836-1800

· Financial Problems ·

Private school scholarships

Many parents who find their local schools inadequate to meet the needs of their child eye a private school with longing, yet never approach it as a possibility. Independent school tuitions are high, reaching ten and twelve thousand dollars in some cases; and the general impression is that only the rich and "snobby" attend. "That's not for my child."

Perhaps it is. If you are dissatisfied with the public schools in your community, there are several ways to overcome the problems of cost and imagined elitism.

First, investigate the independent schools in your area and boarding schools as well if you are interested in sending your child away. Also inquire about religious schools that you would consider appropriate, remembering that some of them take children of diverse faiths. (See Chapter 4 for details on nonpublic schools.)

Include the following questions among those you ask the school in your investigation: (1) How large a scholarship program do you have? and (2) How diverse is your student body? On the basis of the answers, you may be able to eliminate your preconceptions of private schools as havens for the rich and elite.

Then apply to the school or schools that you and your child like. This entails filling out forms, visiting, and taking tests. In most schools, you do not apply for financial aid at this time.

After your child has been accepted, ask for information on applying for financial aid and fill out the necessary papers. Because most schools use an outside agency to determine financial need and allocate the amount to be given, the school will not make the decision. It will be made instead by a computer programmed to assess an applicant's financial need based on income, holdings, and expenses. Full scholarships are rare; so even with financial help, you will be expected to pay a portion of the tuition.

· 271 ·

If you do not qualify for aid on the basis of need, inquire about academic or special scholarships. Some schools grant tuition aid on the basis of a child's academic ability or of an outstanding talent she may have demonstrated.

If you and your child do not qualify for financial aid, one path is still open. Some schools will accept the part-time services of a parent in exchange for tuition aid. Therefore, if you are able to offer the school help in an area they seek—secretarial, teaching, and so on—it is possible that they will provide financial help.

Children and money

I know a wealthy man who sends his son to the local public junior high school not only because it is a good school but because he believes "mixing with the public" is good preparation for life. I also know a man, a social worker with a moderate income, whose son is on almost a full scholarship in a prestigious independent school. He sends him there because he considers a superior education a lifelong inheritance for his son. The father of the public school boy asked me, "How can I keep Peter from flaunting his money?" The father of the independent school boy asked, "How can I keep Alan from feeling inferior to all his rich classmates?"

As different as the two men are and as diametrically opposite as their questions were, I had to give them both the same answer: "You can do it by teaching Peter/Alan to keep money in its place." Its proper place, should anyone need to ask, is at the far corner of human worth.

If a child like Peter feels superior to his friends because his home is more elegant, his parents' cars more expensive, his vacations more luxurious, his clothes more fashion-labeled, he is equating his personal worth in terms of his family fortune. Having no need for goals in terms of himself and his community, he limits his opportunities for growth and fulfillment. As if it were a ready-made suit, he dons self-esteem without the pride of effort, of failure, of success, unaware of the thin threads that money weaves. If money brings Peter self-worth, with the loss of it, is he worthless? If money brings Peter self-worth, with the gain of it, where is the real worth of Self he has missed?

At the other extreme is Alan, poor in terms of his wealthy classmates. If he feels inferior to them because his parents drive a Ford, he has never been to Europe, his home is a split-level ranch, and his clothes come from Sears, then he too is equating his worth with money. What good are personal goals to him—academic achievement, community service, fulfilling relationships—when his self-esteem is already established on the comparative financial scale he set up alongside other boys? If he makes money some day, will his worth as a human being automatically increase, despite his lack of personal growth? If he remains middle class, will he always be without worth?

In evaluating themselves in terms of money, both Peter and Alan are living under false pretenses. If their fathers want the help they asked for, they have to guide their sons into realizing that individual worth is not drawn in dollar signs. True, many Americans set off on careers believing the opposite and may not discover the real source of self-esteem until years later when feelings of emptiness engulf them . . . or may never discover the real source. The fathers of Peter and Alan sensed trouble and sought help.

If your child is Peter or Alan, you can help him keep money in its place.

· Don't use your money either to set the pace or to keep up with the Joneses. Use it to live comfortably.

· Don't overindulge your child by buying every expensive outfit and toy he wants...or by feeling guilty over not being able to. He will benefit by your saying "No, you don't need that" or "Sorry, we can't afford it."

· Limit the allowance you give your child—a dollar a week in the lower grades, two dollars later on. Encourage him to save a part of it for buying gifts and for special treats he wants for himself.

· Assign your child household chores that he is expected to do in turn for receiving an allowance. Let him earn extra money for doing special jobs.

· Open a small bank account for him and encourage him to contribute some of his own money every month.

· Make him aware of community needs around him—the homeless, the aged, the handicapped, even pets at the animal shelter, and so on—and encourage him to contribute to their care time and money of his own.

· Limit the amount you spend on presents for his friends' birthday parties; ten dollars should be enough.

· Above all, as in every other case, serve as a role model for your child. He will assimilate your values. Make sure, therefore, that they are values which will provide a foundation for self-esteem built on growth and for self-confidence in any financial community.

· 273 ·

· Special Problems in Junior High School ·

Cutting school

Because elementary school children live their lives both at home and at school under varying degrees of structured supervision, it is not until the relative freedom of junior high school that the option to skip school presents itself. While truancy is rife in high schools throughout the country, rising above 35 percent in urban areas, it is becoming increasingly common in junior high schools as well. Skipping school comes in various forms.

Cutting classes

Junior high schoolers move from class to class throughout the day. Therefore it is easy for them to check in, attend a few classes, and then cut one or two later on. Although teachers are expected to report any absences, frequently they do not; and just as frequently, when they do, the office is apt to overlook an inconsistency in morning and afternoon class attendance. As a result, the child finds it easy to cut classes with impunity.

If you have reason to suspect your child of cutting classes—poor performance, lack of homework, and so on—ask her. Give her the first chance to admit and amend her actions. If you continue to find evidence, go with her to talk to the teacher or teachers involved. If she has been cutting class regularly, ask them to alert you to any absences in the future. Under this system, her attendance should improve without delay.

Cutting a day

Tom Sawyer called this "playing hookey" and caught many a fish on his bamboo pole while engaging in it. Although missing a day of school per se is harmless, succeeding at it through deception teaches a destructive lesson; being caught and held accountable teaches a far better one. Therefore, if the school reports an absence for your child when you know he headed for the bus, do not ignore it. Confront him with the evidence and ask for an explanation. I knew a parent who not only condoned her daughter's school cuts, but even lied to the school to keep her out of trouble!

The average child will cut school for a day for one of three reasons: to flex preadolescent wings, to attend a function outside of school, or to avoid an unpleasant situation. If your child offers an explanation that sounds something like "Everyone does it at least once," or "What's the big deal? We only hung around," chances are his is the first reason. Cutting school was his rite of passage to independence, a far less hazardous one than some others children choose.

If, however, his explanation is more like "We wanted to see the new movie," or "It was the only chance to get Dwight Gooden's autograph at the mall," his reason is more likely the second. In this case, you have to ask yourself a few questions too: Have you so fulfilled his every wish that he is unable to put off gratification? Have you limited his ability to seek alternative solutions to problems? Have you been a role model of the acceptability of white lies? Some serious soul-searching may prevent a repetition of his actions.

If, finally, he has no explanation beyond "I just didn't feel like going," try to find out why. Is he having academic or social problems? Are he and the teacher in conflict? Is he bored? Is the work too hard or too easy? Is he in trouble? You, he, and the teacher will have to work together to get to the problem and solve it.

In the meantime, make it clear that cutting school is unacceptable on two scores: first, he deceived you by pretending to go to school, and second, he missed a day of classes. While I do not believe he should be punished for his actions, I believe strongly that he should be held accountable for them. In the first case, his deception broke down the trust you had in him; in order to help him to reestablish it, you might suggest he write an essay for you on the subject of trust or read a book concerned with trust and discuss it with you. You might even explain that you feel you have to call the school every morning for a week or so to assure his attendance. In the second case, in missing a day of classes, he fell behind in his work; in order to catch up, he will have to ask his teachers for supplementary assignments. In the third case, he made a decision to escape a problem rather than confront it and find a solution. The problem will be there tomorrow too, however, and he will have to face it anyway. Your support is essential in giving him the confidence to do so. Unless "playing hookey" has become a regular habit with your child, handling the situation with a mixture of firmness and compassion should put an end to the practice.

Truancy

Truancy, the habitual practice of cutting school or actually dropping out, is rife in large urban high schools and exists to some extent even in junior high schools. Smaller schools, which report attendance carefully and question parents about a child's absence, find few such problems. However, because truancy is often the outgrowth of other problems, parents should be aware of the possibility.

Studies reveal a close correlation between truancy and drug/alcohol abuse and minor crimes in a cyclic pattern: A child skips school to find drugs, steals money to pay for them, loses interest in school because of drug addiction, and continues needing money, stealing, and skipping school. Truly a vicious cycle.

Parents who suspect their child of truancy are facing a serious problem. They should:

· Contact the school at once for an attendance report. If the school is lax in its record keeping, insist that the principal ask each of your child's teachers to check her attendance daily and let you know.

· If truancy is in fact a problem, begin by facing it with your child: How long has it been going on? Why? What does she do when she is not in school? With whom? Is she aware that attendance at school is a legal requirement for her up to age sixteen (or whatever your state requires)? How does she view her future without an education?

· If drug or alcohol abuse is the basis of your child's truancy, get her into a rehabilitation program as soon as possible. (See Chapter 24 for a full discussion.)

· If problems at school have led to her truancy, go with her to discuss them with the principal and look for a solution. You must realize, however, that the principal has no magic wand with which to erase problems: The principal may offer a way out of the tangle, and you may support your child in her efforts; but it is ultimately the child herself who must struggle to the clearing.

· Let your child know how deeply her behavior has hurt you, and set up an ongoing system of checking with the school to prevent truancy in the future. However, do not withdraw your love or support, and do not send any vibrations that make her think you have withdrawn from her. She is in trouble; she needs you.

Suspension

Suspension is the last measure a school takes before actual expulsion and is, therefore, used only in cases of serious infractions of school rules. In order to avoid legal battles with parents of suspended students, both public and private schools must make their rules and regulations clear to all students, along with ensuing disciplinary action. In most cases student handbooks, given to the entire school population, explain this information clearly.

If the school suspends your child, you must face the question of what to do with him for the two days or week or two weeks he is at home. If he sits around and watches television and movies on the VCR, certainly he will miss the lesson suspension is supposed to teach. He can't spend the whole day doing the schoolwork the teacher sends home. He won't benefit from wandering the streets all day. What should you do?

· Have him devise a plan of activities that he thinks will be constructive, subject to your approval. These might include research and a report related to the behavior that led to his suspension, volunteer work in the community, and so on.
· Have him undertake a household project that needs doing—waxing the car, painting the garage, whatever.
· See that he has time to keep abreast of his classwork.
· Allow him free time for reading and for television with the family in the evening.

- I see no reason to cut off contact with all of his friends, only with those who are involved in his suspension. Contact with other friends should be limited to short periods of time after school and to short phone conversations.
- Because he is serving his time, do not add your hostility to the sentence. Love him while letting him know you are disappointed in his behavior and supportive of the school's action.

There are occasions when parents cannot support the school's decision to suspend their child. I know of a case in which twelve boys were suspected of smoking marijuana in the lavatory. Eleven of them lied, denying their involvement; one told the truth. He was suspended, while the other eleven were let off. "The school taught him a valuable lesson about lying," the boy's parents told me bitterly. "It works." While they agreed that their son was wrong in his pot smoking and deserved punishment, they applauded his courage in being honest and protested against the school's injustice in holding him alone of all the twelve boys guilty.

CHAPTER 20

Your Special Child

· Physical Disabilities ·

"Who is disabled?"

I know a man who was born blind. After finishing school, he graduated from college, earned an M.A., and is today a senior executive in a large firm. "What was it like growing up handicapped?" I asked him.

"I don't know," he said. "I never felt handicapped."

His answer reminded me of a young woman who, deaf from birth, had completed school, college, and graduate school, had become a teacher and gone on to win the New York State Teacher of the Year Award. When she spoke at the state capitol, accepting the honor in her typically distorted speech, not one person in the audience saw her as anything but a master professional. She was not handicapped. Like beauty, handicaps are in the eye of the beholder.

As the first beholders of their dreamed-of infant, parents teach their child how to behold herself. Some parents are able to accept a disability as part of the wholeness of their child and see possibilities as limitless as those for all other children, see her as capable, beautiful, wonderful, and wanted. This child, viewing the reflection of herself in the mirror of her parents' eyes, grows unencumbered by self-pity, resentment, and feelings of unworthiness. Other parents cannot look beyond their child's disability to see their child at all. In their disappointment and shame their child sees her reflection, as if in a mirror in the Fun House: an ugly distortion, helpless and hopeless. The outcome is that millions of children, be they blind or deaf or retarded, grow up whole, as all children are whole at birth; while other millions, denied their birthright by parents, are doomed to live handicapped half lives.

When parents have to face a child's disability not from birth but later on as a result of an accident, excessive pity, not shame, may become the child's greatest liability. Here is their beautiful daughter who plays basketball, dances at parties, and ice skates; she has lost a leg in a car accident. Here is their son, top student, baseball player, bowler, just learning to play the guitar; he has lost his eyesight through retinitis pigmentosa, a disease his parents had never heard of. Destroyed children, lost lives, they think.

While both tragedies resulted in disabilities, with parental help they can avoid resulting in handicaps as well if, after weeping together, parents will dry their tears and redirect their child into the business of living. Doctors consistently find children more resilient than parents, reporting that they are far more ready to get on with their lives after a disabling accident than their parents are. Yet too often parents hold them back through guilt, which attempts to compensate for the accident in pity and overprotection.

Tests indicate that a child's basic personality does not change in the face of even serious disability. If parents have made their children dependent, unsure, and easily defeated by protecting them from pain and solving their problems for them, they will be no more able to cope with a disability than with any other stressor. They will become handicapped.

If, however, parents have enabled their children to develop independence, self-assurance, and a degree of determination by letting them find their own solutions and survive their own troubles, they will cope with a lost leg and blindness. Working around their disabilities, they will still work for goals and have fun and friends in the process. Children in the Special Olympics prove that . . . and a kindergarten girl in leg braces holding hands with a friend as they play Follow the Leader . . . and a sixth-grade deaf boy teaching his classmates the hand alpha-bet . . . and thousands of other children who refuse to be handicapped.

Choosing a school

Until recently parents of disabled children were given little choice in the education of their children. Reflecting societal prejudices and fears, schools automatically excluded those they looked on as "crippled" in some way. While the school system abandoned those they considered uneducable, they relegated others to inferior education in segregated schools. The racial integration of schools, however, paved the way for some integration of children with disabilities into the wider educational system, and today mainstreaming underlies the basic philosophy.

Blind and deaf children can be mainstreamed, attending with the regular student body those classes they can handle and being segregated in classes that require specialized instruction.

Children with disabilities such as epilepsy, physical handicaps, speech defects, emotional handicaps, minor brain damage, and learning disabilities can also be mainstreamed in most school systems. The determination is dependent on the severity of the disability and the child's ability to cope with it in a normal school setting.

Children who are disabled by psychosis or mental retardation and those with multiple handicaps are usually not able to be mainstreamed.

Parents of a disabled child find themselves facing a difficult educational decision: Should they send him to a regular school or to one designed especially for children with a similar handicap? Because no single "right" answer exists, parents can only base their decision on a group of evaluations.

The child's physical condition. Is your child able to handle himself in a regular school situation? Your doctor is in the best position to know your child's capabilities and limitations.

Conditions in the regular school. Does the building provide for the needs of handicapped children—ramps, elevators, teacher aides, and so on? What is the teaching staff's attitude toward mainstreaming? Do they consider it an opportunity for learning, or are they resentful of the extra effort it may require? I have seen teachers with the former attitude design innovative programs and create understanding and acceptance among the entire class; and I have seen those with the latter attitude reinforce prejudice and despair.

Assessment of the special school. If a day school can be reached without too much difficulty, the only decision you have to make is whether or not it would meet your child's needs better than the regular school. Does the special school have the same philosophy of teaching and the same goals as you have? For instance, do they teach lip reading or sign to nonhearing children? Do they believe in medication for emotionally disabled children or not? What are their expectations for your child? These are important questions you must answer only after a great deal of information gathering and discussion with the school and with your child.

On the other hand, if no day school exists, you have an additional decision to make about whether or not to send him to a boarding school. Is he ready to live away from home, or will he feel that the family is abandoning him by sending him away? (See Chapter 4.)

The child's emotional condition. Which school does your child want to attend? Does he opt to feel more comfortable with other children who have similar handicaps, or to struggle through the problems of being different in a real world situation? While you cannot base your decision on your child's feeling alone, you must certainly take it into serious consideration if the choice of schools is a toss-up.

Which is better for a handicapped child: a regular or a special school? Experts provide evidence on both sides of the question, pointing out strongly that a disabled child's needs are no different from those of other children—just more intense. Like every child, he needs acceptance and a feeling of success in order to develop a sense of self-worth, which is more difficult to establish in the face of society's stereotypes.

In a special school, a child immediately belongs because he is like everyone else. Learning in a specially created program and competing with others similarly disabled, he has an equal chance of success. His growth struggles become, therefore, no different form those of any other child in school, because in this world, disability is the norm. Many educators agree with Joseph Cappello, special services superintendent in Trenton, New Jersey, who strongly advocates special education for handicapped children as providing "a comprehensive, predictable and stable program."

On the other hand, other educators express an equally strong belief that the Land of Oz and Narnia are no more unreal than the environment within special schools. Here children have no opportunity to cope with prejudice and pity, the two walls that disabled children must learn to climb: No children tease them or turn away in disgust; no teachers look sadly at them and overprotect them with special privileges. Only in a regular school setting, these educators believe, where disabled children learn to withstand the slings and arrows that people hurl at them can they develop strength to build fulfilling lives in the real world they will eventually have to enter.

Arguments on both sides of the question are right; I see children in special schools suddenly sprouting up like plants released from under a rock, and I see children in regular schools—if I may stick to my simile—growing as strong as any flower in an English garden. Of the approximately 2 million disabled children in the United States, only about 10 percent are unable to attend regular schools because of the severity of their disabilities: The trend is in favor of mainstreaming.

Still, in just the last few years, schools designed for the handicapped have made such tremendous strides that they are drawing greater enrollment. Halls are wider, lockers are more accessible, doors open electronically, voice-activated computers abound—all with the aim of making students more independent in handling their lives. In addition, recognizing the drawbacks of a segregated learning environment, special schools are beginning to desegregate by including regular students among their population, especially the gifted, whose needs also require special care. Similarly, regular schools are retraining teachers and redesigning space in order to provide more and better mainstreaming opportunities for the disabled. My hope is that eventually all children will learn together in a school where none is considered disabled.

As schools make greater strides, parents of handicapped children find many more options available to them. The mother of a Down syndrome child who had been educated up to age twelve in a special school nearby explained to me recently why she and her husband made the decision to send him away to a special boarding school. "We realized that we had given him all we could at home. He had grown to need the social life and broader experiences of the boarding school." She paused and added, "It was hard, though."

If parents of disabled children will make their decisions about school with that mother's attitude, I think they cannot go wrong. Her concern, like yours, was her child's growth. Like her, try to base your decision on meeting the individual needs of your child, not on having the child meet yours. And remember, the right school today may not be right in a few years.

"How can I help my disabled child?"

The following suggestions stem from the belief that all disabled children, with their parents' help, can grow up whole.

· Begin by being honest about your own feelings. Every parent dreams of a "perfect" baby, and so when awakened to the reality of a baby with a disability, parents are hit by some strong emotional charges. "How could this happen to us!"—anger. "What did we do to bring it about?"—guilt. "We'll put her in a home."—rejection. "What will everyone say?"—embarrassment. You have to realize that these reactions are normal and acknowledge them. If you deny or repress them, the feelings will not go away; they will only creep out in other far more destructive disguises.

· Once you accept your feelings, the next job is to work through them. "Of course it could happen to us; we're no different from other people." ... "We didn't bring this on; it happens once in every so many births." ... "She's ours; let's see if we can provide for her at home." ... "The neighbors will just have to learn to accept her." It is not easy to work through these feelings, and even as you are trying, it is difficult to know whether you are merely hiding them. For this reason, many parents seek short-term professional help from a family service center or from a self-help group of other parents in a similar situation. Associations devoted to the disability that afflicts your child will be able to direct you to a self-help group.

· Siblings are often deeply affected by a child's disability. Parents may notice withdrawal or acting out in school and at home. Over-solicitousness toward the disabled child often may mask intense jealousy and rage. While it is possible that parental reaction to the disabled child may lie at the heart of a sibling's distress, it may also stem from normal sibling rivalry intensified by the situation. In either case, I advise short-term family therapy as a way to understand and repattern the dynamics.

· As early as possible, get your child to accept his disability, rather than to fight it. Because his self-acceptance is a direct reflection of your acceptance of him, build it on the theory that disability is only one part of a child. Just as it is important for a child to know that his achievement in academics or sports or any other area, be it high or low, does not determine his identity, so must he—and you—realize that while his individuality includes a disability, it does not take shape from it.

· Professionals advocate a regular preschool for any disabled child whose limitations do not preclude it. While you may ache when you see your child struggle as he participates with his classmates, he will feel more joy than pain. More accepting of differences than older children, preschoolers will accommodate to his needs as a matter of course. Your preschool child will have fun and friends and begin to make his way in the world that awaits him.

· Every year that your child has new teachers in a regular school, explain his condition to them. Make it clear what he is capable of doing and insist they allow him to do it rather than step in to do it for him. Make it also clear what he is not capable of doing and insist that he either get help or be excused and given an alternative.

· From the start obtain as much information as possible on your child's disability. You can get some from your doctor, a great deal from books to be found in the public library under the subject heading of the particular disability, and perhaps the most from societies and/or associations organized for research and information on particular disabilities. Many of these conduct workshops and publish regular newsletters and magazines with the aim of improving parenting, education, and public welfare of the disabled. While the public library has lists of all existing associations, to which you may refer for addresses and phone numbers, I have included some of the larger ones here:

AMERICAN SOCIETY FOR DEAF CHILDREN
814 Thayer Avenue
Silver Spring, MD 20910
(301) 585-5400

ASSOCIATION FOR CHILDREN
WITH RETARDED MENTAL DEVELOPMENT
162 Fifth Avenue
New York, NY 10010
(212) 741-0100

· 284 ·

EARLY CHILDHOOD DIRECTION CENTER
525 East 68 Street
New York, NY 10021
(212) 472-6535

NATIONAL ASSOCIATION FOR PARENTS OF THE VISUALLY IMPAIRED
P.O. Box 180806
Austin, TX 78718
(512) 323-5710

NATIONAL INFORMATION CENTER FOR HANDICAPPED
CHILDREN AND YOUTH
P.O. Box 1492
Washington, DC 20013
(703) 522-3332

UNITED STATES DEPARTMENT OF EDUCATION
Department of the Handicapped
Washington, DC 20208-5641

An important resource for preschool children is the Early Child Direction Center, a federally funded service that locates schools for children with all kinds of disabilities. Both the service and the school are provided without cost. In addition, when the child is five years old, the service will arrange, with parental permission, for an evaluation on which to determine the child's future schooling. You can contact the center at 525 East 68th Street, New York, N.Y. 10021. (212) 746-6175.

· Learning Disorders ·

"What is a learning disorder?"

An attempt to define a learning disorder is like trying to grasp Proteus, the god in Greek mythology who changed shape at will: If you encircled him in your arms, he turned to water; if you scooped him up in a pail, he changed to air. Learning disorders or disabilities, as they are frequently called, are as elusive as Proteus, not only because they change shapes but, to add to the puzzlement, because educators change definitions. Including such names as "brain damage," "minimal brain damage," "communication disorder," "perceptual defects," "dyslexia," and "hyperkinesia," learning disorders are better recognized by their signs than by their definitions.

· 285 ·

Statistics on the number of children with learning disorders vary so widely as to be virtually meaningless. While the U.S. Department of Education defines a learning disorder as neurological in origin, thereby excluding emotional, physical, and economic causes, not all states base their reports on the federal definition. As a result, nobody knows for sure whether there are 50,000 children with learning disorders or 7 million. The figure generally used by professionals in the field today is close to 2 million.

"How can we detect a learning disorder?"

For parents whose child is not keeping up with his class in school, statistics on learning disorders, be they high or low, are irrelevant. "What can we do?" is far more to the point.

Before looking for possible signs of a learning disorder, parents should bear in mind some basic information.

> · Children with learning disorders are not mentally retarded. They have normal or above-normal intelligence.

· The majority of learning disorders stem from a physical malfunction in the brain, a group of neurons that
do not make contact as they are intended to—somewhat like electrical wires in a toaster hooked up wrong
or batteries upside-down in a camera. The circuits cannot be completed, and so the toaster does not heat up,
the camera does not flash, and the learning process
jams.

· There are, however, other causes leading to a fewer
number of learning disabilities: severe emotional problems that block a child's development; early deprivation of stimuli, such as being talked to and playing
with skill-developing toys that promote learning; possibly hereditary factors; and, according to some, nutrition and food additives.

· Five times more boys than girls have learning disorders.

I remember the first time I was asked by a parent what signs to look
for if a child had a learning disorder. I rattled off all the signs I could
pull from my head, upon completion of which the woman gasped and
exclaimed, "But all my children have those!"

So do mine . . . and probably yours. Parents must be extremely cau-
tious before tagging the label on their child, because any number of
the following signs of learning disorder can be manifested by millions
of perfectly normal children as well. If you or your child's teacher
suspects a learning disorder, look for not one or two of the following
signs but groups of them.

· School performance two or more years behind developmental expectations or, what may be easier for you to detect, behind the majority
of his classmates. For instance, preschool children may be unable to
match shapes or colors; first and second graders, unable to read; older
children, unable to write legibly. Report cards and teacher comments
are the best source of this information.

· A lack of motor skills resulting in poor coordination. Learning-
disordered children may be clumsy and often accident-prone. You and
his teachers will notice his inability to throw a ball, ride a tricycle, even
run, skip, and crawl as other children his age do and to color, string
beads, and so on.

· Short attention span. Because a learning disorder prevents a child
from screening out interfering thoughts and outside stimuli, he is easily
distracted.

· Impulsive behavior. A learning-disordered child seems less mature than other children his age. Easily overstimulated, he lacks control and runs around destroying things or hitting people.

· Memory difficulties. He may be unable to repeat what he has just seen or heard, not because of eye or ear weaknesses but because of inadequate brain processing. Similarly, he may be unable to recall abstracts, such as relationships and experiences.

· Effort—frustration—behavior problems. Children with learning disorders start school with the same high expectations as their classmates. They work hard to do what is expected of them, and when they find themselves unable to succeed, they work harder. And harder. Unable to understand their inability to perform as other children do, and upbraided by teachers and parents for "not trying" or "thinking of other things," they become frustrated. Finally, to end the pain of frustration, they give up and stop trying. While some may withdraw, most act out their hurt and anger, becoming behavior problems in the classroom.

"What can I do?"

· 287 ·

If you are aware of a consistent pattern of behavior, from your own and the teacher's observations, that indicates a possible learning disorder, talk to the teacher, the guidance counselor, and, if the school has one, the reading teacher. In addition, I suggest you talk with a teacher of learning-disordered children to obtain his response to what you see as a possible problem.

If you still feel your child may have a learning disorder, ask the school to evaluate him. A thorough evaluation includes neurological, psychological, and educational testing, which the school may or may not agree to do. If the school will not undertake the testing, even after you exert pressure through the district and state education departments, you may have to pay an outside qualified psychologist for the testing yourself. Many schools believe that parents are quick to cry learning disorder when a child fails in school because, like pneumonia or a broken leg, a learning disorder leaves them guilt-free.

On the other hand, discussion of a possible learning disorder may originate from the school, with the teacher asking you for a conference. Discuss the possibility with the teacher and with the other personnel just suggested, but keep in mind that a child's failure in school may be due to other problems or to a teaching disorder rather than a learning disorder.

If, after your discussions, you feel there is no evidence to indicate a learning disorder, you may refuse an evaluation. Some parents believe schools are eager to label children as learning disordered and place them in special education in order to rid themselves of responsibility.

If your child is properly evaluated and diagnosed as having a learning disorder, do not panic. Tens of millions of American adults have learning disorders and are holding good jobs, contributing to their communities, and raising happy families. You probably know some of them without even being aware of their problem. Although most learning disorders cannot be "cured," children can be helped to overcome them and work around them in a variety of ways.

If the disorder is minimal, your child will continue his education as usual, receiving supplemental help from a teacher or an aide. You may want to augment the help through a private tutor.

If the disorder is somewhat more extensive, your child will remain in his regular school, taking most classes as usual, but be assigned to one or more special classes in the area he needs.

If the disorder is major, your child will be assigned to a special school with programs designed for his special needs and teachers trained to teach them. There are two main ways of helping learning-disordered children. One is to take a child back to the level at which his learning circuit became jammed and then to retrain him in developmental stages—like sliding down a banister and then climbing back up the steps one by one. The other is to teach a child to use his existing skills as a way of getting around those he lacks—like taking a detour around a roadblock in order to reach the main highway. Special educators will decide whether one or the other or a combination of both will work best for your child.

Accept your child's disorder as one part of a total child, just as you should any other problem he may have, without using it to label him. With his self-image besmeared by school failures, parental disappointment, and peer rejection, he needs a great deal of love from his family and reassurance that he will overcome this problem.

Two common learning disorders

Dyslexia

Dyslexia is a special kind of learning disorder, a condition in which children are not able to learn or use language as their age and basic intelligence indicate they should. They may read from right to left, be unable to detect differences and similarities in letters such as *d* and *b*, and lack the ability to sound out words phonically.

Parents should be aware of the following signs of possible dyslexia.

· Delayed or poor speaking in preschool children.
· Difficulty learning and remembering printed words as early as grades 1 and 2.
· Throughout elementary school: Reversal of words ("was" for "saw") or sequences of letters ("oganre" for "orange"). Confusion in determining distances and time lapses and in the directions of both space and time. Difficulty in finding the right word when speaking. Difficulty in telling right from left.

When parents and/or teachers notice signs that could indicate dyslexia, they should follow the procedures outlined for any other learning disorder.

Hyperactivity, Hyperkinesia, or Attention Deficit Disorder

There has been a great deal of research lately into minimal brain dysfunction, known more familiarly as MBD. With only slight damage to the brain, the misconnected neurons produce symptoms often so subtle as to be unrecognizable. As explained to me, the behavior of a minimal brain dysfunctional child is like that of a normal child . . . only more so.

Hyperactivity, also known as Hyperkinesia or attention deficit disorder (ADD), is thought to be one kind of MBD, originating from the same sources as other learning disorders but evidencing different signs. Anyone who has raised a hyperactive child needs no one to point out the signs; she has lived through them.

· The hyperactive child is a child in motion. Many children jump and bounce around, but not like a hyperactive child. Some hyperactive children *absolutely, positively* cannot sit still for a moment of their waking hours. Others, however, can remain still for short periods of one-on-one attention from a parent or teacher, but go into the characteristic spin when on their own or one of a group. Furthermore, unlike the movements of most active children who move with goals in mind, the hyperactive child's movements are random and erratic.

· The hyperactive child has a low attention span. Unlike other children, who can watch a TV show or play a game to the finish, he cannot concentrate for long even on activities he enjoys.

· The hyperactive child demands undivided attention, going to antisocial lengths when necessary to get it. While all young children crave attention, the hyperactive child's attention needs are insatiable.

· The hyperactive child has learning difficulties, particularly in the areas of conceptual thinking and recall. This symptom he shares with other learning-disordered children, although he is less apt to have their classic reading and writing problems.

· The hyperactive child acts on impulse. What he feels like doing, he does on the spot, unable to consider either alternative actions or consequences resulting from his act. While young children make instant decisions and follow through on impulse, even they learn—through trial and error along with the maturation process—to weigh their behavior more circumspectly. The hyperactive child does not learn.

· In addition to these five clustered symptoms, the hyperactive child is apt to have trouble sleeping, talk incessantly, have unpredictable mood swings, be poorly coordinated, have poor peer relationships, throw temper tantrums, touch everything in reach, have headaches, and be sensitive to noise.

Some years ago teachers and parents began using hyperactivity as a catch-all word to pin on jumpy troublemakers who paid no attention to the direction "Sit still." It became the in disorder and the easy way out, with the result that many merely "wild" children were being treated for hyperactivity. Today, fortunately, parents and teachers are beginning to understand more about hyperactivity and to seek a professional diagnosis before labeling a child.

If you or your child's teacher suspects your child of hyperactivity, follow the process outlined for other learning disorders. The evaluation process will be similar. The treatment of hyperactivity, however, while following along some similar lines, veers in a different direction as well.

· Treatment of hyperactivity, like that of all learning disorders, includes establishing new behavior and learning patterns and also focuses on academic reinforcement.

· In a large number of cases, treatment also includes medication with a stimulant called Ritalin. While this drug is a stimulant to adults, it calms hyperactive children and actually encourages positive social behavior. For children who do not respond to Ritalin, doctors often recommend a tranquilizer such as Thorazine for the same calming effect. Although the use of drugs for hyperactivity remains somewhat controversial, test results indicate no ill side effects, and because most children outgrow hyperactivity by puberty, medication is only a temporary treatment.

· For a while it was a fashionable belief that sugar caused hyperactivity in children because it was observed that hyperactive children consumed more sugar than the average child. In light of new studies, however, many have cast aside this theory, although adherents of Dr. Benjamin Feingold, the father of the theory, still believe in it. The fact that hyperactive children eat more sweets than other children may be due, it is suggested, to a greater need to replenish the energy they expend in their greater movement.

Parents who want further information on any area of learning disorders will find a large selection at their local library, listed either under the individual disorder or under the general heading of learning disorders or disabilities. I find the following particularly good: *The Learning Disabled Child: A School and Family Concern* by Jeffries McWhirter (University Press of America, 1988); *Learning Disabilities: A Family Affair* by Betty B. Osman (Random House, 1979); *Learning to Parent a Hyperactive Child* by Claire Hafner (G. P. King, 1987); *Your Hyperactive Child: A Parent's Guide to Coping with Attention Deficit Disorder* by Barbara Ingersoll (Doubleday, 1988).

You might also contact your state Education Department and the following organizations for information, speakers for PTA meetings, and regular publications:

· *291* ·

ASSOCIATION FOR CHILDREN WITH LEARNING DISABILITIES
4156 Library Road
Pittsburgh, PA 15234
(412) 931-7100

FEINGOLD ASSOCIATION OF THE UNITED STATES
P.O. Box 6650
Alexandria, VA 22306
(703) 768-FAUS

ORTON DYSLEXIA ASSOCIATION
724 York Road
Baltimore, MD 21204
(301) 296-0232 or (800) ABCD-123

UNITED STATES DEPARTMENT OF EDUCATION
Department of Learning Disorders
Washington, DC 20208-5641

· Gifted Children ·

"Who is gifted?"

A public school in New York City called Hunter educates gifted children from preschool through twelfth grade. The first criterion for acceptance is that the child have an IQ of 150 or above. So eager are parents to enroll their children, a former headmaster told me, that each year prior to acceptance announcements, many whose children had fallen far short of the 150 mark barraged him with threats and bribes. As he explained it, "They wanted their children to be gifted."

Another headmaster I knew, understanding clearly how much parents want gifted children, used what you might call parent psychology to boost enrollment in his independent school: He announced that his school would accept only gifted children. As predicted, parents flocked to apply for admission. Every child accepted was, upon receipt of notice, suddenly gifted; every parent's ego need was suddenly filled.

Both headmasters ran excellent schools. The only difference was that Hunter offered a special program designed for gifted children, while the other school offered a good program for all children. I commend New York for providing gifted children, rich and poor, with the kind of education they need. I am disappointed, though, that a headmaster has to deceive parents by pretending their children are "gifted." I have always tried instead to show parents the truth—that all their children *are* gifted—and help them nurture that gift.

Signs of giftedness

Although parents usually think of giftedness in terms of intelligence evidenced in strong academics, there are other kinds as well: A child can be creatively gifted with a vivid imagination and original thinking; she can be kinesthetically gifted with psychomotor abilities in athletics or the visual and performing arts; or she can be psychosocially gifted with leadership strength. In most cases, a child shows giftedness in a combination of areas and rarely thinks of herself as different from her classmates unless her parents or teachers misuse her.

Studies have shown parents to be more aware of signs of giftedness in preschool children than their teachers are, perhaps because parents have a greater emotional stake in discovering them. If you observe a consistent pattern of the following characteristics in your child at any age, they may be signs of giftedness.

- Curiosity. Your child will be an explorer, reaching into new areas both physically and mentally. She will ask endless questions.
- Language adeptness. She will speak early and develop a large vocabulary for her age, understanding the subtle differences in the meaning of words.
- Reading ability. She may learn letters and teach herself to read before entering school. She will love books, read material way beyond her years, and often immerse herself in reading to the exclusion of other activities.
- Memory. She will not only be able to remember past experiences but will use them with hindsight in making current decisions and with foresight in future planning.
- Reasoning. She will see relationships and be able to arrive at conclusions by both induction and deduction. She will enjoy grappling with philosophical questions.
- Moral maturity. She will display an intuitive sense of right and wrong and make moral decisions far above the average for her age. As a result, she will show empathy for others.
- Concentration. She will focus her attention intensely on what she is doing and stay with it, even as a young child.
- Individualism. Although she will be popular with her classmates and have a few close friends, she will not be a conformist. She is happier going her own way than following the crowd.
- Humor. She may develop a wry sense of humor at a surprisingly young age, skipping over traditional children's jokes to inventions of her own.

"How can I help?"

The aim of raising a gifted child should be to help him grow to his fullest potential in every aspect of his life, the identical aim of raising every other child. When that aim is met, children, gifted and not gifted, grow up trusting, loving, productive, and self-accepting—in short, happy. The trouble is that many parents of gifted children lose sight of the goal, focusing on the gift instead of on the child. In reaction, the child's personality, instead of growing full and round like a basketball, ends up distorted and lopsided, like one of those balls used for lawn bowling. The gifted child then becomes the "creep" his classmates and their parents whisper about.

Although parents may recognize giftedness in preschool, I advise against testing until the child is older. Instead, keep her in a stimulating environment both at home and at school. Alert the teacher and ask her not to push the child but to make challenging play available to her. Meanwhile at home, play with your child—word games, pretend games, number games if she wants them; read to her; surround her with materials for art, building, and outdoor play, but *do not push her*.

By first grade you and the teacher should discuss the possibility of your child's being gifted, and at this point she should be tested if you concur. A variety of tests are used these days, all or any of which your child may take. Among them are:

- Stanford-Binet IQ Test or, with younger, less verbal children, the Wechsler Intelligence Test for Children (WISC).
- Creativity tests, which try to probe more deeply than intelligence tests by identifying original thinking and personality.
- The Krantz Test, which seeks a still more rounded picture of your child by looking for ten different kinds of giftedness instead of the usual two or three.
- The Renzulli-Hartman Scale, which aligns your child on a scale of giftedness to measure her in relation to other gifted children.
- A Parent Form, on which you are asked to rate certain characteristics of the child, providing the examiners with a viewpoint that they could not otherwise see.
- A Peer Form, on which your child's classmates are asked to rate certain of her characteristics, providing still another viewpoint.

If tests indicate that your child is gifted, in most states the school district is obligated to provide for her special needs. This may be offered in four different ways: enrichment, acceleration, semiseparation, and total separation.

In enrichment, your child will continue with his class in the regular school program but be given supplemental courses in free periods. This approach works only if the school sincerely develops an enrichment program for gifted children. Because this costs money and usually applies to a mere handful of students, too many schools merely talk a good line of enrichment while providing little.

In acceleration, your child will either skip a complete grade or will continue with her class for some subjects and take other subjects daily with a higher grade. Full acceleration rarely works for a gifted child, because she catches up to the higher grade quickly and finds herself right back where she was. If she continues skipping—as we see occasionally with children entering college at fourteen—the danger exists that she will become the school "creep" and miss the social experiences vital to her rounded growth. Acceleration in certain subjects may fail for the same reason full acceleration usually does. If, however, the school is able to accelerate your child not by placing her in a higher grade in math or English but by individualizing a program for her, it should prove highly effective.

In semiseparation, your child will remain with her class for part of the day (or week, in some cases) and be taken to another school the rest of the time. Because programs in this school are designed especially for gifted children, your child is able to receive the special education she needs and at the same time maintain her social relationships in the regular school.

In total separation, your child will leave the regular school and attend a full-day program in a special school for gifted children. The advantage is that your child will learn in a richer environment equipped to stimulate and challenge her; the disadvantage is that she will be isolated from the diverse world of which she must eventually become a part.

When you learn what the school is going to do for your child, you have three options. First, if you are satisfied, you go along with the program. Second, if you do not think their program is adequate for your child, you can make the decision many parents of gifted children feel forced to make: to leave the school system for either a private school or another school district into which you have to move. Third, you can gird yourself for battle with the school and the district to demand an adequate program. Some parents have won; others have lost. Guidelines and a step-by-step process are suggested in Chapter 2.

No matter what kind of gifted program your child sets sail in, you are in the best position to help him maintain an even keel. Don't let him list to the side of the boat that indicates "I am better than other people." Understand and help him to understand that gifted means different, not better, and that every child has his own way of being gifted. Don't let him list to the other side that says "Gifted, smifted. Who wants extra work!" Help him to see that his special qualities are just what the word says, a gift, not to be misused but to be nurtured as a responsibility and finally to be paid back to society.

Parents wishing further information should contact their state Education Department and the following organizations:

AMERICAN ASSOCIATION FOR GIFTED CHILDREN
15 Gramercy Park South
New York, NY 10003
(212) 473-4266

NATIONAL ASSOCIATION FOR GIFTED CHILDREN
5100 North Edgewood Drive
St. Paul, MN 55112
(612) 784-3475

UNITED STATES DEPARTMENT OF EDUCATION
Division of the Gifted
Education Building
Washington, DC 20208-5641

I also suggest they read some books on gifted children, available in libraries under the heading "Gifted" or "Exceptional." One of my favorites is *The World of the Gifted Child* by Priscilla L. Vail (Walker and Co., 1979).

No child is average; each is exceptional—gifted in some ways, disabled in others, altogether beautiful and wonderful. The individuality of your child makes her special from the moment she begins to grow within you, screams her way to recognition, and then fills your life with joys to share and problems to solve until you draw your last breath. She is born a star. You can keep her shining.

CHAPTER 21

Classmates:
The Value of
Peer Relationships

"How important are peers?"

From the earliest days of colonial America, Parents (with a capital *P*) have been assigned the responsibility of training their children (with a small *c*) to fit into society. Adjustment has been the name of the game, with mothers and fathers instructing their offspring in the social rules to which they must conform. Children who have learned and obeyed and shaped themselves to fit a predesigned pattern have been considered good children; those who could not—or would not— have been called bad. I can't help thinking that people like Thomas Paine and Virginia Dare, rebels of the first order against the establishment, must have been "bad" children.

Well into the present, parents have continued to bear the burden of socialization, assuring society that children will perpetuate its values, attitudes, and patterns of behavior. "Nothing ever changes"—we have heard that before and seen decades of "bad" children who bobbed their hair and danced the Charleston, marched for women's vote, copied Elvis Presley, grew straggly beards, and burned their bras and draft cards.

In some homes a child "adjusts" in order to escape parental threats and punishment. While he appears "good" on the surface, inside he is stifling his rage to forestall a rebellious explosion. Although in his heart he rejects social norms, he conforms to avoid trouble. In other homes, however, a child "adjusts" in response to the more subtle coercion of parental love: He becomes "good" not to escape reprisal but to win approval. He makes social rules his rules, and himself, a willing member of society.

Whichever motivation parents rely on, the fundamental practice is the same: training the child to fit into society by imposing its rules upon him. Adherence to the rules earns a child the key to personal and, later, professional success; revolt against them casts him, like a leper, out of the mainstream. While no one can deny that the system has worked moderately well in maintaining social order, there are those who feel that a far more effective process has been ignored—the socialization of children by their peers.

· 298 ·

Although parent-child and sibling relationships have provided fertile ground for students in the social sciences, until fairly recently few have thought to till the field of peer relationships. Among the earliest and by far the most thorough who were aware of the developmental impact of peer relationships were the psychiatrist Harry Stack Sullivan and the psychologist Jean Piaget. Studying children in pairs and in groups, these two pioneers discovered that children interacting among themselves adjust to society's rules far better on their own than when their parents set out to train them. There are several reasons.

First, children together learn as equal partners. Within the traditional family, children, having less knowledge and experience than their parents, are given little voice and virtually no power. As a result, they regard themselves as inferior beings and, as we have seen throughout the book, need to work hard—with their parents' help, we hope—to establish self-esteem. The parent-as-trainer socialization process reinforces children's feelings of inferiority with parents correcting them at every turn: "Share your toy." . . . "Don't chew with your mouth open." . . . "Stop teasing her." The pupil learns because the master knows.

Among peers, on the other hand, there are no pupils and masters; all are equal, and when left to themselves, they teach each other not by command but by cooperation. For instance, when two children want to play with the same toy, without the intrusion of an adult they are left with no choice but to find a solution. While this may entail many tugs of war and bangs on the head, they will eventually learn that anger and tears do not solve their problem because they do not enable either child to play with the toy. Taking turns with the toy or playing with it together will eventually emerge as a solution from which they will learn the rule of sharing far more indelibly and with greater self-esteem than if their parents had made them share.

Second, in the interaction of peers children learn not by rote but through discovery. When parents carry out drills in the dos and don'ts to which society demands adherence, their children's altered behavior is as perfunctory as a memorized Latin declension: "*Amo, amas, amat*...I have to share my toys." The actions are there without meaning.

When children learn among themselves, however, they do not even know they are learning the rules of society; they only know they have to find a way out of problems. For instance:

- · If preschool Jimmy knocks Johnny's castle of blocks down and Johnny says, "You're not my friend anymore," Jimmy will learn something about aggressiveness.
- · If elementary school Lisa chews her peanut butter and jelly sandwich with her mouth open and Susie moves to another seat saying "That's yucky," Lisa will learn something about table manners.
- · If junior high Marcia and Ginny stop being best friends because Stan said Ginny was prettier, both girls will learn something about jealousy.

James Youniss explains both processes of socialization—through parent training and through peer interaction—in his book *Parents and Peers in Social Development* (University of Chicago Press, 1982), which I recommend highly as informative and absorbing reading. He concludes that children are socialized by both parents and peers, pointing out that from parents they learn what is acceptable and develop self-confidence in a social environment, while from peers they learn what works and develop self-esteem.

"What do children learn from their peers?"

If you observe a group of children over a period of time, you see a microcosm of society: children fighting and helping each other; leaders

· *299* ·

emerging; in groups and out groups; competition and cooperation; winning and losing; rejection and fun and friendship. It is in this miniature panorama that children not only learn how to get along in the world but begin to create the world they are going to get along in. Sullivan and Piaget leave one with the feeling that if left to their own interaction, children might do a better job of creating society than the generations of parents before them have done.

What do children learn from each other?

Communication skills

The child who enters nursery school talking unintelligible baby-talk soon learns that the others will not play with her because they can't understand her. She begins to speak more clearly. Similarly, an older child who monopolizes the conversation with no concern for what others have to say finds herself without friends. She begins to listen. In no way can children learn better that two-way communication is the foundation of a relationship than in their early attempts at friendship with peers.

Coping with conflict

· *300* ·

Because conflict is inevitable when children come together, learning ways to resolve conflict is also inevitable. A preschooler refuses to share the tricycle and gets pushed off by her friend; there must be a better way. Next time she says, "You take a turn after me." My eleven-year-old granddaughter Darcy and her best friend Ruth underwent the same process in selecting the summer day camp they wanted to attend together. With Ruth wanting tennis camp and Darcy baseball camp, they discussed and argued for weeks—a difficult problem because Darcy does not play tennis and Ruth dislikes baseball. Finally, placing their friendship above their athletic inclinations, they decided to attend two weeks at each camp. They have come a long way together since tricycle-pedaling days. And so do most children as they grow through stages of hitting, crying, teasing, and tattling to discover a more successful method of conflict resolution.

Empathy

In their relationships with each other children learn how to crawl into another person's feelings. They cannot understand, much less empathize with, their parents, whose stature and status set them at an opposite pole. Their classmates, however, are like them. When the teacher yells at their friend, they shrink in embarrassment with him; when he falls off the swing, they too hurt. The dream of "a kinder, gentler nation" will begin not with a President's political rhetoric or legislation, but, as the late Joseph Campbell believed, with a rebirth of empathy. Studies support his theory, reporting that empathetic children, quick to offer help and comfort to their classmates, create a kinder, gentler classroom.

A sense of belonging

From our animal forebears, be they fish or baboons, humankind has inherited a need to belong. Alone we die, not physically perhaps as they do; but, cut off from belonging, we die emotionally. Evidence is the walking dead among us.

Family is the first group to which a child gains membership, clinging for security to "My mommy and daddy . . . my sister . . . my house . . . my room . . . my dog." By two the child becomes aware of a larger world, and by three or four, when he enters nursery school, he discovers it. He belongs to a new group, a group of his peers, extending membership to "my school . . . my teacher . . . my swing."

As early as nursery school, smaller groups within the class begin to form as three or four little buddies seek each other for consistent play. They feel comfortable together, secure; they know where they belong when they leave the security of home for the classroom. In the class and in these small groups, with no one teaching or preaching, children begin to prepare themselves and each other for the society that lies twenty years in the future.

· 301 ·

· "You can't play with us." They learn that exclusivity will always bond their in group more closely—like the New York Mets and the D.A.R. and the marine corps. They learn that being left out always hurts and creates anger—like Jews refused membership to a country club and blacks with a burning cross in their yard. And they may even learn that the classroom becomes a happier place when everyone plays together—the way the United States is supposed to be.

· "If you don't do it my way, I won't be your friend." Children learn that conforming will make their whole life easier—like going to Yale because Dad went there—but they also discover the don't-like-myself feeling it creates when you really wanted art school instead. They learn that it feels good to "do it my way"—such as not drinking with the rest of them—but that the consequences may hurt—such as losing your friends.

· As the year progresses and children grow more sure of their place in the class, they become aware of feelings that boast "My school is better than your school"—group pride—and feelings that threaten "Don't you dare say that about my school"—group loyalty. They are getting themselves ready for patriotism and national defense and their chauvinist and aggressive extremes.

The lessons that children begin to learn among preschool peers strengthen as the years go by. They hone social skills and expand belonging. By discovering what it means to live among others, children discover themselves. According to psychiatrist Harry Stack Sullivan, friends, aware of the distorted self-image families may create, often actually save a child. Classmates set it right. They will not cater to the whims of a spoiled child or be bossed by the family's young dictator; on the other hand, they will listen when families are deaf and teach love to those who come to school loveless. Bouncing self against others, children compare and evaluate themselves, experiment, and finally find the quintessential social "grace"—identity. With this securely in place, they will be able to grow into relationships of friendship and into the intimacy of love.

"How do children make friends?"

· 302 ·

Just as children learn to move and think developmentally, so do they build friendships in successively maturing steps. As parents learn when they put babies together to play, friendship does not begin in the playpen: Each baby goes his own way in parallel play with virtually no interaction. Like two little amoebas, they crawl around, to bump now and then unintentionally.

By age three or four children begin to interact in play. They are able to share a toy—pull a wagon together or roll a ball back and forth—and to take turns in an activity such as holding a doll or jumping. When your child begins to develop a preference for certain children—usually those who are amiable and nonaggressive—over others, he is ready to climb the steps of friendship-building.

Robert Selman of the Harvard Graduate School of Education believes that from this point on, a child's friendships mature in four distinct stages; and although other professionals hesitate to compress the process to such an extent, the four-stage theory provides a comprehensible overview.

0 Stage

In preschool a child's friendships are of short duration—a coming together for a few minutes of fun. Although, as we have seen, groups form easily, they do so with little emotional involvement, being able to break apart and reform as new possibilities for fun appear. Dr. Selman considers this a zero stage because a child's lack of selectivity and involvement lead to interactions rather than friendships.

Stage 1

A child in the first or second year of elementary school selects her friends on the basis of who does what pleases him most, caring little whether it is a boy or girl. If a classmate will throw her a ball when she wants to play catch, that classmate is her friend. When the classmate tires of throwing balls day after day and switches to roller skating, the two are no longer friends; one looks for a ball-thrower, the other, for a roller skater. The six- or seven-year-old who sustains a friendship of long duration has probably found a friend willing to throw that ball all year.

Stage 2

In the latency period, generally considered from about eight to eleven, friendships involve an even exchange. A child is learning that in order to have a friend and be a friend, half of the time is devoted to taking and the other half to giving. Unless a classmate is able to walk this two-way street with her, a friendship will not develop. While friendships at this age provide both joy and emotional growth, children are still not mature enough to sustain them for long. "Best friends" may switch in the course of a school year and are rarely carried over to regrouped classes in subsequent years. At this age, not only do girls and boys stick to their own sex in friendships, but they actively avoid the opposite sex, taking pride in their disdain. I overheard a fourth-grade girl excoriate a classmate by pointing out to a friend, "She doesn't even mind sitting next to boys!"

· 303 ·

Stage 3

By junior high school a child grows into friendships that may last a lifetime. Based on common interests and shared values, rather than on the give and take of play, these friendships provide the first intimacy a child experiences outside her family. While they are usually girl-girl and boy-boy friendships, they have increasingly in recent years moved toward cross-sex relationships as well. Even distance does not break a strong bond of friendship at this age, as the lengthy letter exchange and week-long visits between Darcy and her best friend indicate after Ruth moved six hundred miles away.

CHAPTER 22

Classmates: Problems

· Peer Problems in Preschool ·

"What if my child has no playmates?"

Playing is the major occupation of preschoolers. Although they show little discretion regarding whom to select for a playmate, there are children whom they avoid: "Go away. I don't want to play with you." Preschoolers are not subtle. The child with no playmates usually displays one of three characteristics: aggressiveness, shyness, or nonconformity.

A preschool child who acts aggressively to his classmates is bound to be unpopular. Children avoid playing with a classmate who hits and shoves just as much as an adult does with a golf or tennis partner who screams over a poor shot, for the simple reason that he spoils the fun.

On the other hand, if a child is shy and withdrawn, other children may not make the effort to play with him, especially if they have tried and failed. Surrounded by eager playmates, children will turn to the ones engaged in activities that look like fun rather than seek out a reluctant child with whom to initiate a game. Without the intervention of a teacher, the withdrawn child remains alone.

A third possible source of a preschool child's inability to find play-mates is nonconformity. Already insecure in their early away-from-home experience, children are at first put off by a child who seems different—especially one with a physical deformity. With just a little reassurance from the teacher, however, preschoolers are quick to risk the unknown and make friends.

While parents can offer some degree of help to the friendless child—mainly support and understanding—the onus falls mainly on the teacher. It is up to her to redirect the aggressive child's behavior, to draw out the withdrawn child by pairing him with a friend, and to point out the individuality of each child in the class so that everyone—and no one—feels different. One of the great beauties of preschool children is the speed with which they forget another child's past faults and willingly welcome him into the fun. The child who hits yours today is likely to be the one with whom he wants to seesaw tomorrow.

If your preschool child is having trouble making friends, see the teacher. She is in a better position than you to understand the obstacle and help him overcome it.

· 305 ·

"How much social life is enough?"

A child's emotional gauge determines the right time to "say when" to peer play. After a morning of nursery school or kindergarten, a child has probably had enough; a nap and time alone are what she needs. In the suburbs she might spend an hour outside with the neighborhood children, but in city or rural areas, where friends are apt to be distant, arranged visits would be superfluous. She needs time to absorb the interactions she has already had that day.

Even on weekends many children, content playing alone or with siblings and accompanying a parent on errands, require no prearranged play with classmates. Others, however, who want to have a particular friend over or to go over to her house should be allowed to do so, but only for a limited period of time; all day is too long at this age.

Unfortunately, many parents fear that if they do not push their child into an active social life at the earliest possible age, she will grow up a wallflower, no candidate for Miss (or Mr.) Congeniality. To ward off this ominous threat, they fill her after-school hours, like dances at a debutante ball, with an endless array of partners. The result is a stress overload, which fatigues the child and fills her with such anxiety that in acting out, she is apt to lose the very friends she might make under more relaxed circumstances.

Parents, do not push your children socially. Let them make friends in school, and let them extend their friendships to the degree that they want to. Your intervention should come not to push but rather to pull, to pull them back from an overabundance of peer interaction that their enthusiasm may have led them into. Just as their eyes, which when settling on a plateful of cookies, are often larger than their stomachs, so their joy in play may at times be larger than their endurance. When they have had too much and can't say "When"—you recognize the irritability of overexhaustion when it sets in—you will have to say it for them.

· Peer Problems in Elementary and Junior High School ·

Although the specific tensions that arise in peer relationships during the elementary grades differ from those during junior high school, the problems that lead to them are for the most part similar. In fact, problem signs can be detected as early as preschool and, unless successfully addressed, may magnify and continue throughout a child's school years. Therefore, except for a few specifically preadolescent problems discussed at the end of the chapter, peer problems arising in elementary and junior high school will be dealt with together.

"Nobody likes me."

Older children develop likes and dislikes for their classmates in much the same way preschoolers do. They select as friends those children who are friendly to them personally and cooperative in a group, and who are able and willing to communicate. They avoid troublemakers and teacher's pets and, studies indicate, prefer playing with children who are average to good students.

Yet even meeting these criteria, a child can find himself ostracized if he appears different from the other children. "He's not normal," a second grader explained when I asked why no one liked Robbie. Normal was upper-middle-class suburban; Robbie was a Mexican maid's child. "Not normal" in another school was a sixth-grade girl from a musical family who left early for flute lessons and gave boring recitals. In a junior high it was a girl who wore old-fashioned pinafores instead of dungarees. "Normal" conforms to the shape and size of the group that packages it.

The child who stands apart from the rest of his class walks one of two paths: He may rise as the self-sufficient loner admired by his classmates, or he may shrink as the "creep," the "bore," or the "snob" rejected or scapegoated by his classmates. Parents may be able to prevent misery for their nonconforming child.

If your child is different from her classmates and a loner by choice, parents should not only stop worrying but should rejoice over having raised an individual who accepts herself. Don't spoil her sense of self by pushing her to make friends or chiding "Why can't you be like the other kids?" Don't make her give herself away in order to please you. Keep her as she is to please you both.

Frequently gifted children, more mature children, or children with special talents find themselves regarded differently by their classmates, who like them and admire them but do not feel comfortable with them as friends. In most cases, this kind of child accepts her role, aware that she is unlike her classmates. Although she gets along with them, finding few common interests, she is content to go her own way. No problem exists unless her parents are less content than she and try to force friendships with which neither she nor her classmates are comfortable.

If, however, a child is a loner not through choice but through rejection by other children, you might be able to step in and alleviate her pain. Be gentle when you broach the subject though.

"It's an awful feeling when kids don't want to be friends with you," you might begin. "Do you think you did anything to make them angry?"

"No. I didn't do anything. They're just mean."

"Who specifically was mean to you?"

"Well, Doris for one. When I started to sit next to her at lunch, she said, 'No, thank you, Miss Snob. I'd rather sit with Lucy,' and moved away."

"Miss Snob. Why did she call you that?"

"I don't know. I'm not snobby. You know that. I just don't talk to the other girls like the rest of them do."

"Why is that?"

"I don't know. I'm kind of embarrassed and afraid I'll say the wrong thing and they'll think I'm stupid. So I just walk away from them."

"The way Doris did from you?"

"Well, yes. I never thought of that."

"Maybe you can figure out a way to act so Doris won't think you're a snob."

"I guess I could try to talk to her. Tomorrow maybe before school. She's always there early, like me. What do you think?"

"I think you're on the way to solving your problem, that's what."

A low-key conversation like this may lead you—and your child— to the root of whatever causes underlie her classmates' rejection of her. Does she act bossy? Is she unable to share? Can she listen to others, or does she hog the conversation for herself? Is she a sore loser or a boastful winner? Is she honest? Fair? Can she work and play as a team member, or is she too personally competitive? Because it is almost impossible for a child to see herself as others see her, you may be able to provide a new viewpoint.

Discuss with her how other children make friends.

Ask her what classmates she most admires and then see whether she can identify the qualities she admires in them.

Ask her what she considers her best qualities and contribute your own assessment. Does she put them to use?

Set up some role-play situations with your child in which she can experiment with new ways of interacting with her peers. Give her some new strategies to try; if she is not comfortable with them, let her try others.

When your child feels better equipped to handle a social situation, suggest that you take her and a friend on a special outing—to a play or movie, on a hike, for a swim, and so on. You might plan a small party with her—for a birthday if the timing is right; if not, perhaps for some other occasion. Encourage her to invite friends over to play, but avoid pushing her. Let her make friends at her own pace.

If she cannot seem to find even one friend among her classmates, you might investigate the possibility of a nonschool group or club where she would meet children with similar interests. Community organizations such as the Y, Girls' and Boys' Club, Scouts, and churches offer a wide variety.

Keep in mind, however, that a child does not need a crowd of friends in order to feel accepted; one or two good friends will do.

Throughout your efforts to ease her feeling of isolation, reassure your child of the treasure her individuality truly is. Like Eleanor Roosevelt, who as a shy and unbeautiful girl spent a lonely childhood, your daughter too can tread her own upward path.

If your child is not only a loner but has become firmly established in the role of class "weirdo," there may be a problem of scapegoating.

Group dynamics in almost every class interact to select one child as the projection of everyone else's fears and insecurities. The pain for that child is extreme as day after day she is the butt of jokes and taunts. Whatever she does and says is viewed in the framework of the part into which her classmates have cast her: While another child tells a "rad" joke and does a "cool" dance, your child's joke is "nerdy" and her dance "out of it." She cannot win in the eyes of her classmates.

There is very little you can do to alleviate the situation as long as she remains with the same group of children. Even if you ask the teacher to intervene, the scapegoating will continue in whispers and out of her sight and in most cases will increase with passing years. Psychologists point to lifelong damage that has been done.

The greatest help you can offer might be to move your child into a new group at the end of the school year—a different school if possible or a class with children who do not know her. Give her the chance to shed the old image and begin anew, particularly in a large group where, should the scapegoating begin again, she can find one or two other "outcasts" as friends.

Even if you are able to provide a new start with different classmates, your child will probably find herself right back in the same painful social situation unless something changes. Perhaps she should dress differently or pay more attention to her personal hygiene. Perhaps you treat her too much like a baby and should let her grow up. Maybe she talks too much or reacts inappropriately in a situation. You and your child together might discover ways in which she could create a new image that would be more acceptable both to her classmates and to herself.

· 309 ·

I know parents who faced up to the problem directly with their daughter by pointing out "You know how irritated the whole family gets when you begin asking dumb questions? Maybe the kids in your school feel the same way. Think about it now that you're going to a new school." The girl not only thought about it, but did something about it. With new classmates and a new image, she had a chance to reestablish herself as part of a group.

Some children spend their whole childhood feeling like aliens among their peers. Not until they become adults do they find a niche in which they are comfortable enough to be accepted as they are and grow into what they were meant to be. Anyone who has ever attended a high school reunion must know the thrill of seeing the successful, self-possessed classmate who was once the class "weirdo." I think of all the pain we could have saved her if we ourselves had been mature enough then to value what we value now.

Best friends

Parents frequently bring me the concern that their child turns down invitations to play with a lot of classmates who call: "She sticks around with this one kid all the time."

Best friends play an important role in the social and emotional development of both boys and girls, although each sex uses the relationship for different purposes. In the later elementary years, girls pair off in close one-on-one friendships that introduce their first experiences of intimacy. They sit together in classes, they walk holding hands, they whisper, they tell secrets, and after six hours in school together, they still find enough to talk about on the telephone for as long as their parents allow. They argue too and grow jealous when one or the other becomes friendly with another girl, acting with the same cattiness adult women are accused of. Stepping unknowingly onto the threshold of an adult relationship, they love and hate and hurt and comfort each other with mutual trust and shared confidences. That the bond may last no more than a few weeks or months in no way diminishes its intensity.

· 310 ·

Boys, on the other hand, make best friends in action-oriented groups rather than in the intimacy of one on one. Psychologists believe that genetics may have preconditioned girls for the intimacy of motherhood while preconditioning boys for the teamwork required of their male roles, which began as protectors and providers. Sociologists, on the other hand, see no predisposition, but rather the urging of parents and other social forces as the explanation of girl twosomes and boy group friendships.

Whatever the reason, boys bond in threes and fours with far less talk and more action than the best-friend dyads of girls. They don't whisper; they shout. They don't tell secrets; they tell jokes. They don't hold hands; they wrestle. They don't talk on the phone; they play ball until dark. Their bonding draws a line between "them" and "us," circling around into a wall, within which the group gains strength. In their bonding, boys too are stepping on the threshold of adult relationships they will experience on war teams and work teams with little practice in the intimacy demanded by the marriage team. As the merging of male and female stereotypes into androgyny takes hold, the bonding patterns of boys and girls may change shape as well.

While best friends for both boys and girls are valuable, they may cause problems that call for guidance from parents.

If you find your child clinging to a single friend, not for mutual growth and pleasure but out of fear, there is reason for concern. Is the friendship equal, or has your child assumed the role of disciple to a stronger personality? What does she gain from this friendship, and what does she contribute? Is your child socially insecure? How does she feel about the other children, and how do they feel about her? These are questions you and your child can probe in a gentle, non-threatening dialogue.

"You seem to have a lot of fun with Julie, but you never have anyone else over to the house."

"I like her best."

"Do you play with some of the other girls at school?"

"Not really. They're stupid."

"All of them?"

"Yeah. All they talk about is boys and who's going with who and that stuff."

"That must get kind of boring. What do you and Julie do instead?"

"See, she's like me. She likes animals. Remember we made that horse scrapbook? And we have pretend dog shows, and we play this game where you have to name an animal for every letter of the alphabet. Stuff like that."

"I get you. It does sound like more fun than just talking about boys."

If that's the way your conversation goes, you don't have to worry about your child's special friendship. She is wisely selective. It might go another way, however.

"You seem to have a lot of fun with Julie, but you never have anyone else over to the house."

"I know."

"Do you play with some of the other girls at school?"

"No."

"You don't like them?"

"They're all right, I guess, but they stay together."

"You feel they don't include you?"

"They don't; they never do. They're real snobs. They won't play with Julie either. They say she tries to boss them around all the time."

"Does she?"

"Well, yes, but I don't care. I have to have someone to play with, don't I?"

This sounds like a child clinging to an unsatisfying friendship rather than going under in a maelstrom of loneliness. If this is your child, talk to her teacher or the guidance counselor and see how together you can help her.

Cliques

Almost every year sixth- and seventh-grade girls form exclusive cliques. They may begin with two sets of best friends and add another set, all six girls drawn together by a common interest, which is usually boys. While the rest of their classmates continue their age-appropriate rejection of boys, the clique displays a precocious interest. Their whispers and secrets turn into gossip about who loves whom; they may sneak lipstick to school, attend school fairs and parties "on dates," and even "get engaged" by having the boys give them rings. By aping what they consider grown-up behavior with special knowledge and privileges, the clique establishes itself as the in group. Its aura permeates the social life of the entire class.

· 312 ·

Each year that I taught I saw the clique develop. I was helpless to stop the pain it wrought as, like a war tank, it kept those within invincible while destroying those who dared approach. The boys in the class were safe because they didn't know what was happening. Most of them still avoided girls, and the few who found themselves "dating" and getting "engaged" cooperated even while longing for the football or baseball field where they would rather be.

It was the girls who suffered. All longed for admission to the in group, especially the socially borderline girls who had long felt insecure, but even those whose friends suddenly paled alongside members of the clique. The harder they tried to join, the more the in group flaunted its exclusivity, deigning occasionally to invite a nonmember to a birthday party, but never as an equal. The clique destroyed hearts and egos, some remaining in tatters for years.

My experience, unfortunately, is not unique; the clique syndrome existed in all but the most unusual schools and continues to exist today. The secure nonconformists, happy by themselves or with a friend, escape damage, along with the boys; but the majority of girls—both those in the clique and those longing to be in it—learn negative lessons.

The in group learns that popularity grows in conjunction with sexuality, a lesson that spells trouble later on. Too young for the emotional impact of sex, they use it as a status symbol and begin to establish themselves on the fast track. They become what David Elkind calls "hurried" children, playing an adult game before they know the rules. When they become old enough to know how to play, many of them have already lost. Year after year I saw the high and mighty of sixth- and seventh-grade cliques fall into obscurity—or worse—in high school, while their rejects grew into leadership and learning.

The out group learns a lesson that their parents and teachers should have been trying to make them disbelieve for years: that they are no good. Rejection by the in group offsets any and all previous successes, be they social, academic, creative, or personal, because in-group acceptance is the measurement. It is not social status they have lost but something far worse—self-esteem.

Parents are in a position to help children unlearn the false lessons taught in the clique experience.

If your child is a member of an exclusive clique:

· Do not encourage her. Too many parents consider precocious sexuality cute and foster it without realizing the damage they can do. Do not arrange boy-girl dances at home or even parties at this age: The girls regard them as an endorsement of teenage rituals for preteens, and the boys usually race around together and tear the place up anyway. Dances and parties at school have far less impact.

· Do not allow your boys or girls to "date" at this age. If they talk about going to a movie or a school fair with a date from the class, explain that they are too young to date but that you will be happy to take a group of their friends. (Dating is discussed more fully later on in the chapter.)

· Try to make your daughter understand the hurt that she and her friends inflict on other children when they exclude them from the clique they have formed. Some role play might help her experience the hurt. Furthermore, explore her reasons for enjoying the exclusivity of a clique and suggest other ways in which she could realize similar satisfactions—by taking the lead in befriending other, less popular children, for instance.

· Encourage her to include other children in group activities she arranges: a cookout or Halloween party with all the girls in her class, perhaps.

· Suggest that you take her and a nonclique friend on a special-occasion trip. She may say, "I can't; they'll think I'm a nerd." If so, remind her that she used to like that girl and might be able to tell her new friends so.

· If the clique activities continue, discuss your concerns with the mothers of the other girls. They may feel as you do and have some helpful suggestions.

· 313 ·

· Look for high school role models whom you can point out to your daughter, school leaders who have many friends, athletes in team play, older girls who handle themselves with social maturity.

· Sixth- and seventh-grade cliques often break up by eighth or ninth grade. If you have supported the exclusivity and the sexual overtones of the clique, your daughter will probably have residual effects. If, however, you have guided her in the directions just suggested, even without immediate success in dislodging her from the clique, she should emerge unscathed.

If your child is excluded from an exclusive clique . . .

· Give her a great deal of emotional support. Although you may be delighted that she is not in that peer group, she is hurt and ego-wounded. Let her know how wonderful she is in as many ways as you can, but don't expect miracles: Nothing you do or say will make her pain go away overnight.

· Do what you can to have her stop trying to get into the clique. Encourage her to invite her friends over to the house; be welcoming and supportive of them; let her know that you like and respect them. When she can accept the fact that she is not in the clique and stop banging her head against their stone wall, she will have eliminated much of the pain.

· Plan special activities for her and a friend or two—picnics, parties, movies, cake baking, and so on. Help her learn that she and her friends can have their own kind of fun.

· Talk to her about the clique syndrome. Explain that it forms when girls who are unsure of themselves band together for reinforcement; it operates by giving those girls a feeling of power; and it finally breaks apart when the girls are mature enough to stand on their own. Let her know that you understand the hurt she feels, but that in not being one of the in group, she has a headstart over them on maturity.

"Is peer pressure as strong as they say it is?"

Preschoolers and children in the primary grades feel little need to emulate their classmates because they are still attached to their parents closely enough to want to emulate *them*. Wearing Jordache jeans and Reeboks matters little so long as they can look like Mommy and Daddy and try on their attitudes and mannerisms too. By fourth grade the picture starts to change.

A great deal has been written about peer pressure. That it is a major force in the life of preteens and teens is indisputable because as children get older, their search for identity leads them away from dependence on their parents to interdependence among their peers. Therefore, as they transfer the locus of self-esteem from home to peer group, they adhere to the standards of acceptance set up by the group. Because to be different is to be rejected, conformity is a major goal.

What I think has been exaggerated in discussions of peer pressure, however, is a parent's helplessness against it. According to some reports, parents lose all control of their children when the group takes over, throw up their hands, toss in the towel, and echo words heard nationwide, "I can't do a thing with him!" Nonsense! More likely, "He can't do a thing with you!"

The relationship between parent and child, built from birth, does not undergo a mysterious metamorphosis suddenly at age ten or eleven. Two types of child rearing actually may lead to the feared situation in which the peer group calls the shots, replacing parental authority. One is practiced by parents who, as their three-year-old throws blocks at a classmate, as their six-year-old tears up a book, as their eight-year-old commands them to shut up, watch, sigh, and murmur permissively, "Boys will be boys," or "She's only a child."

If parents adopt an attitude of resignation when their child is that young, obviously the child has the upper hand. He knows who has control, and he has no inclination to relinquish it until forced to. Therefore, when the peer group determines criteria of behavior no more acceptable to his parents than throwing blocks, tearing books, and yelling "Shut up," the parents will still be helpless.

The other child-rearing philosophy is practiced by parents who, relentless in their determination to keep children under control, rule them like a top sergeant in a marine barracks. Their word is law, any break with which leads to sure and often harsh punishment. When these children get a little older and find themselves less dependent on parental control—emotionally if not physically—the will of the peer group becomes an outlet for rebellion. While still paragons of morality and obedience at home, they may follow the group even into criminal acts if necessary; and if caught, they laugh the last laugh as their parents exclaim in shock, "But he was always such a good boy!"

On the other hand, if parents from the very beginning walk the thin line between permissiveness and authoritarianism, they need not fear peer pressure. Establish guidelines on two bases: the safety of your child and other children and your own sanity. While the former can be considered universal—not hitting or throwing rocks, not running in the street, and so on—the latter depends on your personal threshold. I know parents who verge on insanity at the sight of their child's messy room and others who merely close the door and don't look, parents who forbid loud music on the radio and others who enjoy it with their children, parents who separate children in a verbal battle and others who let them scream it out. I even know a mother who lets her children draw and write on their bedroom walls, while others get upset at fingerprints.

The important point is to insist on consistent adherence to the early guidelines you lay down so that your child avoids the limbo of not knowing who controls what. In this way, you set a pattern for the more serious guidelines that will have to be laid down as children grow into situations with more serious consequences.

In addition, leave your guidelines open to discussion with your children instead of imposing them arbitrarily. Let them question: "Why can't I go to a rock concert?" . . . "Why can't I shave my head?" . . . "Why can't I wear a see-through blouse?" Have reasons and give them: "Rock concerts often get out of hand." . . . "You're so handsome this way; I couldn't stand looking at your shaved head." . . . "A see-through blouse is too sexy for your age."

Don't be afraid of an open discussion with your child: It does not mean you have to concede, although you may be overruled by superior logic occasionally. What it does mean is that your rules are made with sound reason behind them and that your child understands why, though unpleasant perhaps, they are necessary. With that kind of mutuality, the rules you lay down will build a strong wall to withstand peer pressure.

A certain degree of peer conformity is essential to a child's development. It is a sign of asserting independence by belonging to a group outside the family. The question parents face is "Where do I accept my child's conformity to the group and where do I take a stand?" The rule-of-thumb answer is that you accept conformity when it does not run counter to basic family values, and you stand your ground when it does.

In the early sixties, I was speaking at a junior high PTA meeting when an executive-type father in a dark suit and striped tie asked a question. "My son wants to wear an earring," he said. "Should I let him?" Without hesitation, thinking of my son as much as that father's, I answered a definitive, "No."

A second father stood up, calling out "Why not?" He was dressed in a loose African shirt, wore a large wooden pendant, and—of course—an earring, an outfit neither I nor the PTA was used to in those days. I am grateful to that man for an important lesson: that in family affairs there are few definitive answers.

In many areas, conformity depends on what is acceptable to you and your family. For instance, I personally do not approve of ear-rings for children—boys or girls—until they are sixteen or so be-cause to me they are a sign of hurrying children out of childhood; yet millions of people pierce the ears of tiny babies. On the other hand, I accept rock music and guitar lessons for children although many parents, associating those with drugs and danger, respond with a horrified no.

While the final say on peer conformity in areas such as dress and music lies with the parents, there are obviously other areas where the line must be drawn.

· Obscenity. Do not accept use of the four-letter words. Children will use them among themselves to prove they're cool, but unless you endorse them with passive acceptance or use them yourself, the words will not become a habit of speech.

· Drinking. Do not allow your children to drink until they reach the legal age. Some parents consider it cute to give their children sips of beer or let them empty cocktail glasses at parties, but recent studies report that the majority of teenage alcoholics began drinking that "cute" way at home.

· Drugs. Do not take drugs and do not condone them, even mari-juana, if you hope to withstand the peer pressure your child may be exposed to. I know parents who have smoked pot with their children "because he is safer doing it at home than someplace else." No. He is safer doing it no place. Your job is to teach him that.

· Smoking. Antismoking campaigns in the media and courses in school have at last made a dent in American smoking habits, which for the first time have begun to decline. Don't smoke and don't condone your child's smoking. If you have smoked all these years, let your child bring the message he has learned in school home to you.

· Conformity for conformity's sake. Don't let your child develop what I call the mirror mentality, the feeling that she has to do and be and have whatever her friends do and are and have. Give her the assurance to know that she can set her own course and still maintain friends. On the other hand, help your children avoid the antiestablish-ment mentality that turns every mainstream movement into a rebellious *cause célèbre*—nonconformity for the sake of nonconformity. Find, in-stead, the fine line parents so often seek and walk it once again. Send the message that selectivity in conformity is what matters: to conform to what meshes with their taste and values and to stand alone when the crowd taste and values veer in a different direction. Communicate that message while the taste of your children's crowd involves only dungaree labels and their values no more than movie ratings, and you will be able to rest secure when the taste involves cocaine and the values a matter of law.

"What about friends who are older or younger?"

There are times when children become close friends with either an older or younger child, frequently a neighbor, whose proximity expedites daily contact. Because the American system of education focuses on grouping children according to age, parents may express concern when their child steps outside the customary group to make a friend. Yet such friendships are part of normal development and can add to it in several ways.

· A cross-age friendship may serve to equalize the abilities of two children. For instance, if an older child is less physically developed than her classmates, she may play more satisfactorily with a child a year or two younger and avoid painful derision form her own age group. On the other hand, if a child is a more skilled athlete than her contemporaries, she will have more fun and find greater challenge playing with an older friend from time to time.

· A cross-age friendship helps eliminate the competitiveness that is built into play between children of the same age. Knowing she is unable to win against an older opponent, the younger child has an opportunity to play for the sheer fun of playing; while the older child, aware of her superior skills, is willing to direct energy toward helping and teaching the younger one.

· A cross-age friendship establishes a role model for a younger child—not an unapproachable one like a movie star or a parent, but one almost within reach. The values and attitudes of the older friend frequently are incorporated by the younger.

· On the other side of the coin, a cross-age friendship enables an older child to hone his nurturing skills. Just as older siblings develop empathy and tenderness, so older friends begin to test the skills that will enable them to become nurturing adults.

Despite the numerous benefits, however, a cross-age friendship can also have a negative effect on a child when it serves an ulterior motive.

· An older child may use a younger child as a target for bullying and bossing, with the younger one holding on to the friendship from fear or from a deeper psychological need.

· An older child, insecure with same-age friends, may cling to a younger child for ego reinforcement, thus depriving herself of a chance to work through her problem toward personal growth.

· A younger child may be pulled by an older friend into experiences for which he is neither emotionally nor physically ready and which may diminish those experiences at a later date.

Observant parents can assess the quality of a cross-age friendship over a period of time. If it appears to be having a negative effect on their child, they should discuss it with her, for she herself may feel uncomfortable in the relationship. Remember, however, by being too adamant you may in fact actually solidify the friendship further; you can rarely break it off by prohibiting it. Your best bet is to help your child see the effect the friendship is having on her and at the same time encourage her to play with other children.

In recent years the media has alerted the public to incidents of sex abuse of younger children by older ones. If your child is regularly sought out by an older friend; if the two engage in play alone; if they play out of sight; if your child seems unusually preoccupied with sex; if she is secretive about her friendship, you may have to consider the possibility of sex abuse. Although you may feel unconcerned if your child's older friend is a girl, recent knowledge challenges the old belief that only boys are sex abusers.

· 319 ·

If, on the other hand, your older child plays excessively with a younger child; if they never play in your house when you are home; if she seeks few other friends; if she seems inordinately interested in sex magazines and sexy movies, you too may have to consider the possibility of sex abuse.

· In both cases, speak to your child first. She may be crying for release from an activity that fills her with guilt.

· If you receive confirmation of your fears, speak to the parents of the other child. Even without confirmation, if you are relatively sure, ask the other parents whether they have any reason to suspect an unhealthy involvement between the two children.

· Depending on the depth of the sexual involvement, a physical exam by your family physician may be in order.

· If your child is either the abused or the abuser, she will benefit from professional help, both to overcome feelings of guilt and to establish new patterns of friendship.

· Keep in mind that not all sexual play between children is sex abuse. In normal development children experiment with sex, looking, touching, and talking; and while you should not encourage sexual play, neither should you panic when faced with it. Explain to your child that although sex is a wonderful experience for adults in an intimate relationship, children lack the emotional maturity for it. In addition, consider how you might arrange for closer supervision of their play.

"What happens when a child loses a friend?"

The loss of a close friend has a significant impact on a child, particularly on a teenager who, struggling with the stress of newly tested independence, is most vulnerable to feelings of insecurity. Nonetheless, friendships are ripped from children with so little understanding of the ensuing pain that parental reassurance may be tossed off with a mere "Oh, you'll make new friends." It is not new friends the child needs, however; it is the old friend, the friend she trusted and shared her life with, the friend torn away to leave her alone.

The loss of a close friend sets in motion for a child a process not unlike the stages of grief, which are familiar to any adult who has suffered a deep loss. The child's immediate response is depression, a sadness that permeates her entire life: She may sleep poorly, have no appetite, lack energy or enthusiasm for play; she may simply loll around or lie on her bed and stare into space. To the question "What's wrong?" she will probably reply "Nothing," because her pain hurts beyond explanation.

You can help by giving love and understanding. Do not deny or belittle your child's feelings, which, even if short-lived, are intense. Do not nag her to "stop moping around," and try to avoid conflicts; at the end of a very frayed emotional rope, she will be quick to explode at what would ordinarily be only a minor upset.

At the second stage, the child may struggle to restore the friendship—to keep in touch through letters and phone calls if the breach came about through the family's relocation; to try to win her friend back through gifts or special invitations if it came about through rejection. While the child appears to have overcome her depression at this stage, she is probably even more miserable under the stress of an internal emotional battle between hope and desperation.

You can help by supporting her efforts to put the friendship back in place. If you have moved a considerable distance, let your child phone her friend from time to time, encourage her to exchange photographs when she writes, and invite her friend to visit on a weekend or during vacation. If, on the other hand, the friendship has broken off through

· 320 ·

a fight or through her friend's acquisition of a new best friend, you are in a position to give far less active support. You might suggest she talk to her friend and see whether they can resolve their differences; but don't *you* talk to her friend or to her friend's parents.

Although you know that losing her friend is an experience from which she will gain maturity, don't try to teach and moralize at this point; save that for some future time. Right now help her realize that the value of a friendship does not depend on how long it lasts but on what each has given to it and received from it. Help her let go of it, while knowing it was not a waste.

In the third stage the child finds the peace that comes from acceptance of reality: She has lost her friend; now she is ready to make new friends.

You can help by encouraging her, as suggested in Chapters 6 and 7. Invite a friend over, plan a special trip or a party. Avoid pushing her, though, so that she will not think she has let you down if miracles of new friendships do not suddenly burst through her shell. Just be there for her; don't make her be there for you.

"What about the child who gets teased?" · 321 ·

A junior high school girl I know had looked forward all year to a part in the sixth-grade play, which was a school highlight each year. This year it was to be *Cinderella*. Shortly before tryouts, however, she announced at home that the play was stupid and that she wouldn't be in it "even if they force me." Suspecting more than met the eye, her mother did some investigating and found that her daughter's classmates had begun teasing her about being overweight. "You should try out for the pumpkin," one of them had suggested to resounding laughter.

"The prince would never get a slipper to fit your foot," another said with a giggle. The die was cast: The play was stupid.

In a somewhat similar situation, a fifth-grade boy I knew faced continual derision from his classmates over his lack of coordination. Skinny, shorter than the other boys, and poorly coordinated, he not only failed to cut the much-admired athletic figure but fell while dribbling a basketball, rarely hit an opponent in dodge ball, and always got caught first in prisoner's base. As captains selected members for their teams, the others in gym giggled, "Hey, what lucky team gets you today?" On gym days he tried to be sick.

What recourse have parents when they see their child suffer under the pressure of teasing from peers? What can they do to help?

· Admit that it hurts. Don't brush it aside with "Oh, they don't matter. Ignore them." They *do* matter, and your child has probably tried and *can't* ignore them. Share the hurt instead and let your child know "Kids can cause a lot of pain."

· Explore with your child any possible ways he can alter the situation that elicits teasing. For instance, in the former case the sixth-grade girl was finally motivated to stick to a diet that the doctor had put her on the year before. Her mother broached the subject this way:

"Kids love to find something to tease about, don't they?"

"They sure do," her daughter answered, "especially me because I'm fat."

"I don't think you're fat, but I do think you'd feel better about yourself if you lost a few pounds."

"See, I *am fat.* You just said so."

"No, I said what Dr. Masters told you last year, that you'd be better off if you lost five or ten pounds. That doesn't mean you're fat. Fat would mean losing twenty pounds, and if you did that, you'd be invisible."

They both laughed. "Do you think I could stay on the diet Dr. Masters gave me?" the girl asked.

"Sure I do. I'll even go on it with you since it wouldn't hurt me to lose a few pounds either."

The mother turned the child's painful experience into a positive step to eliminate the possibility of future teasing from her classmates.

The father of the boy used a similar approach.

"Boys can be pretty cruel, can't they?" he began.

"They sure can, but they're right. I *am* a klutz. I can't even throw a ball straight."

"And all the other boys can?"

"Even some of the girls. What's the matter with me? Am I stupid or something?"

"Heavens, no. Look at all the things you do well. You get better grades than most of them; you're a great singer; and I know firsthand how good you are at Scrabble."

"So what?"

"So maybe you can learn to throw a ball too."

"Nah, I could never be as good as Warren. He can even throw lefty."

"You don't have to be that good, but you can learn to throw better than you do now."

"How can I do that?"

"Well, I can't teach you because I can't throw a ball either, but your brother's pretty good. I bet he'd teach you. Do you want to give it a try?"

"Well, okay. Maybe it'll work."

The boy agreed to let his older brother help him handle a ball and, after months of practice, won the admiration of a surprised classmate who asked, "What happened? You caught it."

"What if I disapprove of my child's friends?"

I was visiting a friend one day when her fifth-grade son Jody brought his friend Ray home from school. Jody was still saying his "hellos" and telling what happened in math class when Ray dashed to the refrigerator, calling out "Got anything good to eat?" My friend calmly rose and found the boys some milk and crackers. "Catch," Ray yelled at Jody, tossing a saltine at his nose. My friend remained calm as she led the boys to the dinette, where Ray proceeded to put his glass of milk on the floor for the dog to drink.

· 323 ·

In the course of the afternoon, Ray pulled flowers from the garden, cracked a window throwing stones over the rooftop, and tied a clothesline around Jody's neck to play bandit. When his mother took him home, I asked my friend in amazement, "why did you let him behave like that?"

"If he were mine, I wouldn't," she explained, "but he's Jody's friend, and I didn't want to embarrass Jody." I spent the next thirty minutes giving a lecture, to which, being a good friend, she listened. So did Jody.

What can parents do when they disapprove of their child's friends?

· Make it clear, both to your child and to his friends, that the guidelines that govern his behavior govern the behavior of his friends as well. Jody does not throw crackers, feed the dog from the table, throw stones, pick flowers, or tie ropes around his friend's neck; he knows he is not allowed to. If he cannot control his friend's actions, then you have to. You explain the rules to the child, and if he persists in breaking them, you either send him home or assume supervisory duty for the remainder of the afternoon.

· While you should avoid saying you do not like your child's friend, say that you do not approve of his friend's behavior. You can be more specific and add, "I would not feel good about your playing at his house, and I hope you will not ask him over here again." This works with a younger child. With an older child, however, who has more freedom to come and go as he pleases, you may run into an argument and ensuing resentment. Stand your ground.

· Point out that although your child is a wonderful boy, his friend affects the way he behaves as well. Be specific about the guidelines he has sidestepped when playing with this particular friend, guidelines he adheres to with other friends.

· Don't be alarmed if your child seeks out a wild playmate. He probably will not want him for a close friend, but rather as a personal stand-in who acts out all the outrageous fantasies he is far too well behaved to act out himself. Chances are, the association will be short-lived and will leave no lasting effects.

"How much supervision does a child need when with a friend?"

Although there is very little to say on this subject, what needs saying is important:

· Never let your child have a friend over when you are not at home. Although you may feel safe leaving your child alone for short periods of time, you cannot take the responsibility for someone else's child. Unsettling as it may be both for you and the children, take them with you if you have to go to market or to pick up another child somewhere.

· Never let your child go to another child's house unless an adult is going to be there. If you are uncertain, phone and find out before granting permission. Because many parents consider a sibling two or three years older able to stand in for an adult, you will have to evaluate the situation before making your decision.

· Even with an adult present, supervision is often lax, with children allowed to run wild while a parent or baby-sitter shuts herself off in the TV room. If you know the family your child is visiting, you know what kind of supervision to expect; if you do not, you will have to rely on what the parent promises and, later, what your child reports.

· Do not let your child meet a group of friends unless you know specifically where they are going—to a movie, bowling, to the ball field, and so on. In the case of elementary school children, know who is planning to supervise them, and do not allow them to go unsupervised. Junior high schoolers are mature enough to go to public places alone, but insist on knowing when they are leaving, when they will be finished, where they are going afterwards—to someone's home or the ice cream shop, for instance—and at what time they will be home.

Prejudice

As the song in *South Pacific* goes, "You've got to be taught to hate." The baritone is not singing about hating a single individual but hate as a group stereotype. Prejudice.

Preschool often provides a child's first experience with children of different races and nationalities. Unless they have already been "taught to hate," they comment on the different physical characteristics they observe in their classmates as unemotionally as they comment on the blue wall or the tiny teddy bear. Small children see what they see. Without reinforcement, they make no judgments. I recall with tenderness a preschool scene: a white girl runs her hand over a black girl's head in total concentration at discovering a new texture; a moment later, the black girl reaches for a long, straight strand of the white girl's hair, stroking it with her thumb. They smile at each other and change the subject that had required no articulation: "Wanna play house?"

· 325 ·

By elementary school, children are more aware of social connotations and easily begin to stereotype, often without understanding what they are doing. A child brings a question home from school: "Mom, is it true that black kids are dumber than white kids? Josh said it is." Or a child repeats a joke: "Why is a Chinese family worth less than our family? . . . Because it is full of chinks." Or a child shares his hurt: "Jimmy said I can't go to his birthday party because I'm black." The roots of prejudice are sending up shoots that overrun the acceptance that led to earlier friendships.

By junior high school, children are well versed in racial and national stereotypes, although they acknowledge positive characteristics in individuals—as in "Some of my best friends are Jews." By and large they readily comply with social expectations, having few interracial friendships, virtually none with members of the opposite sex. Knowing this, I was surprised and pleased when my eighth-grade granddaughter, rattling off a list of adjectives to describe her best friend, neglected one that became evident upon display of her photograph: She was black.

"She's pretty," I commented, hoping to elicit an explanation for her omission.

"Yup," she said, "and smart too."

"She's black?"

"Yup. And lots of fun. You'll meet her."

There was no explanation because there was no need for one.

It is difficult in American society for children to grow up without prejudice because the world around them sends continual signals of middle-class WASP superiority. Television, comic books, songs, and toys, despite a new awareness and halfway efforts to change, still have a majority of white He-Man and She-ra dolls, white talk-show hosts and fathers in sitcoms, white country singers, and white space heroes. Furthermore, age-old color symbolism, which permeates even a small child's subconscious, reinforces prejudice: Black is the dark side of life— the villain's hat, the scary dungeon, the witch's hair, the magic of evil; white is the chaste side—angel robes, wedding gowns, falling snow, Santa's beard, cameos and clouds. Black is dirty; white is clean.

I heard a preschool child crying in the hall one day because "Jennie said I was black."

"Black is beautiful," I insisted, echoing posters from the sixties.

The little girl continued to weep, finally sobbing through her tears, "But I'm brown."

Black is dirty. Studies report that, when given a choice of a black doll or a white doll, little black girls in far greater numbers select the white doll. Fortunately, the past thirty years have seen great strides if not in eliminating white prejudice, at least in enabling both races to acknowledge black contributions, capabilities, and indisputable value to history. At last black *is* beautiful.

Still, with society continuing to wall itself within a bastion of stereotypes, children are highly vulnerable to prejudice as it pushes in upon them from all sides. If parents can raise children without prejudice, despite societal pressures, they will lead the world one generation closer to peace. How can parents do it?

• At the most obvious level, avoid any show of prejudice yourself. Don't use negative epithets such as "nigger," "kike," "Jap," and so on. Don't tell or encourage the telling of racial jokes. Don't make generalizations about racial or national groups. Don't turn one person's fault into a racial characteristic: "Lazy," "greedy," "dumb," "criminal," and so on apply only to individuals.

• At a more subtle and far more difficult level, try to overcome the teaching of prejudice that is done not by direct word and deed but by implication. All-white and all-black neighborhoods, friends limited to similar socioeconomic groups, domestics who are inevitably minorities: These life patterns print themselves on a child's awareness. While you may be unable to alter the patterns into which your family's life falls, you can overcome them. Encourage interracial and intersocioeconomic friendships. Take a firm stand against efforts to prevent integration of your neighborhood. Expose your child to situations in which members of minority groups are in equal, not servile, positions. Finally, treat any people in your service with the same respect you accord your friends and insist that your child does the same.

· Keep in touch with the books your child reads and the TV shows and movies he watches. Ask him to be on the lookout for indications of prejudice as if he were a detective tracking down clues. Discuss his findings with him. He will soon be able to detect evidences of prejudice in the classroom and in the community.

When a child is aware of prejudice, it cannot sneak unnoticed into his subconscious; and when he sees his parents as role models of tolerance and acceptance, it will not insinuate itself into his consciousness. Your job, therefore, as parents is to help him recognize prejudice wherever it arises and to assess your own attitudes and actions to preclude its ever arising in you.

· Special Peer Concerns of Junior High Schoolers ·

· 327 ·

"Is it all right for a child to have a crush?"

Just before and even concurrent with the early stirrings of boy-girl interest comes a stage that puzzles and frightens many parents: Caroline develops a crush on an older girl; Adam idolizes an older boy. No longer do their children rush home from school for milk and cookies and an outpouring of the day's ups and downs. Instead Caroline calls as she runs out the door, "I'm going to help Molly baby-sit," and Adam shouts, "Joe said he'd let me clean the garage with him."

No wonder parents are puzzled: Carol put up an awful fuss the last time they asked her to baby-sit with her little sister, and Adam found ten excuses not to clean the garage. Similarly, no wonder they are concerned: Carol keeps a photograph of Molly in her notebook, and Adam carries around a clipping about Joe from the school newspaper. "Carol says . . ." and "You know what Adam does? . . ." have become the most frequently heard phrases in the house.

Often the preteen's crush is on an adult, a neighbor or teacher who, as one girl explained, "gives me goose bumps every time I see her." Surely she was describing that early rush of infatuation she will feel in a few years over a boyfriend.

Not understanding the developmental stage through which their children are passing, parents often find themselves in the middle of it with some concern: Their son or daughter has fallen in love with a person of the same sex—"Is my kid a homosexual?" In a society as homophobic as ours, few fears are so compelling. They are easily dispelled, however, when parents understand that for a child about thirteen to have a same-sex crush is as normal and healthy as for a toddler to clutch a blanket. Both are transitional objects. When a little child, Linus-like, carries his blanket wherever he goes, he is experimenting with independence while keeping contact with a touch of home. Soon, secure on his own without Mommy or Daddy, he will be able to leave the blanket behind.

In the same way, a preadolescent is striking out on his own into an unexplored world. Up till now, while he has known companionship and even intimacy with friends, love has been confined to his parent relationship, with Freudian undertones of sex buried deep in his unconscious. Before he is mature enough to handle sexual love in an adolescent male-female relationship, he too has to edge toward it cautiously, feeling his way before making a commitment. His security blanket is the infatuation of a crush, with which he extends his reach beyond parent love to test the water of sexual love before plunging in.

This stage is usually short-lived. Parents can best help their children through it by understanding its importance to their growth. Don't belittle it. Don't nag. Don't get angry. Hire a baby-sitter and let the garage stay messy for a while. If you feel that you have been replaced in your child's affection, remember that rejection comes with the job of parenting and that you earn your gold star only when your children are able to make their own way alone. Till then, let them hold on to their security blanket.

Boy-crazy, girl-crazy

When children reach junior high school age, they undergo a transformation as startling to their parents as the emergence of butterflies must be to their caterpillar memories. The girls who hated boys, the boys who hated girls in fourth and fifth grades begin to develop an interest a year later, although they dare not show it. By seventh grade there is no hiding: The secret interest has burst into a consuming passion, often driving more trivial matters such as homework and family into obscurity.

Parents, loath to see their babies enter the realm of adults, can no more hold back the stirrings of sex than Alexander could hold back the tides. Hormones are at work. So are expectations, as boys and girls who have watched their older siblings and schoolmates enter puberty, breathlessly await their turn. The time is ripe, riper actually than the children, who still need a year or two of experimenting with their fears and their strivings before they are comfortable in pairs.

A few guidelines may help parents through these tremulous years.

• Don't make fun of your junior high schooler's interest in the opposite sex, and try to prevent sibling teasing.

• Although you must insist that he fulfill his school and home responsibilities, do it with a gentle hand. Remember, he is as intensely preoccupied with his own thoughts and feelings as you probably were on your wedding day or your first job.

• Even though a junior high school boy or girl is not yet mature enough for the intimacy that comes with dating, many of your child's friends will date. Therefore, your child will put the pressure on you for permission to do the same. At twelve and thirteen, channel your preteenager's dating into boy-girl group activities, such as parties, picnics, movies, and so on. Don't push, but make arrangements if your child initiates them. At fourteen your child should be able to handle a real boy-girl date to a public place such as a movie, a school dance, or a sports event.

• Don't be shocked by some very overt "making out." At this age children are still innocent enough to think that anything as much fun as kissing can be done in public. I remember an eighth-grade party where a kissing couple, seeing me pass sandwiches, stopped long enough to ask without the slightest embarrassment whether I had any tuna on rye. The trick is for parents to make themselves visible at regular intervals and to keep the house lights on.

• Don't be overcautious about your child and sex. If the restraints you use are too binding or are kept on too long, she will break out in spite of you. If you don't let her ease into a boy-girl relationship with your guidance, she will burst into it with no guidance at all. Almost as many teenage pregnancies result from too much parental protection as from not enough.

Your children's school years are filled with academic learning, tested each year in blue books, evaluated from A to F, and registered on charts. University deans of admission and future employers will read their files, confident that the statistics record growth and learning. Surely math and reading, science and history leave their mark, but nowhere are there charts and graphs and cross-tabulated figures to evaluate the impact of peer relationships. Yet ever-greater growth and learning lie

· 329 ·

in the pleasure and pain of school friendships, in the security of be-longing and the desolation of exclusion as your children risk intimacy and experiment with love.

The author Charles Kingsley was once asked how he accounted for having had such a beautiful life. He did not attribute it to skills acquired or knowledge gleaned in school. He answered, "I had a friend."

I hope parents will recall his words—and find comfort in them—the next time they hear themselves scold, "No, you can't go to your friend's. You have more important things to do right here."

CHAPTER 23

Hazards: School Safety and Health

Drastic changes have taken place in the lives of children over the past fifty years. No place are they revealed more dramatically than in school, where the following scenarios might take place:

- 1940. A child runs into trouble at school: He comes home with a black eye from a fight with a classmate. Mother weeps at the incorrigibility of her child while Dad teaches a lesson with a hairbrush.
- 1973. A child runs into trouble at school: She sits in the office while the principal phones Mother or Dad that she was caught smoking pot in the lavatory. The school suspends her for a week, and her parents ground her for a month.
- 1989. A child runs into trouble at school: The police drive to his home and knock on the door. When his

mother answers, they announce, "You had better come with us. Your son was caught selling crack."

The old saying that although school is a waste of time, it keeps kids out of trouble for twelve years no longer holds true. On the contrary, school is the arena in which most of the trouble takes place, even when its origin lies elsewhere. As a result, a parent waving good-bye to her child on the schoolbus can no longer return home or to work with peace of mind because deep in the recesses of her mind lie fears that create cross-country headlines: AIDS, guns, cocaine, pregnancy, pollution, cancer, bombs, sex abuse, and fire.

Parents face a dilemma, afraid that if they warn their children of the hazards that surround them, they overfrighten them; and if they remain silent, they underprotect them. Fear or injury: Which is worse?

A child's world is fraught with dangers that he has sound reason to fear. Contrary to Franklin Roosevelt's warning "We have nothing to fear but fear itself," I believe that *not fearing* puts us in greater jeopardy. Fear, like pain, is one of nature's protective mechanisms, without which a child might never learn not to run in front of cars or play with fire or jump off buildings. Fear becomes a liability only when, based on imaginings instead of facts, it paralyzes. For instance, a fact-based fear of snakes teaches a child to keep his distance from rattlers and water moccasins, but an imagined fear keeps him out of the garden and the reptile house at the zoo as well.

While fear, therefore, protects a child from injury, information protects him from paralysis. Parents have the responsibility of providing both. This chapter aims to point out areas of potential danger surrounding your children in school and to suggest ways in which you may help your children avoid injury from them.

· Checking Safety Factors ·

Building maintenance

Because some states are more rigid than others in demanding careful maintenance of school buildings, it is impossible to list the general requirements to which your child's school should adhere. However, certain safety standards are universal.

Be sure the maintenance committee of the PTA makes at least two inspections of the building with the maintenance staff every year—one in the fall and one near the end of the school year—looking for any of the following evidences of need for repair.

Outside:
   Loose bricks or broken siding
   Potholes or broken walks
   Broken windows, loose frames on windows or doors
   Broken doors or windows or broken locks on either
   Roof deterioration
   Poor drainage

Inside:
   Cracked walls, ceilings, or floors
   Loose boards
   Lavatories—broken toilets and sinks, loose tiles, insecure doors
   Misplaced storage boxes
   Overcrowded classrooms
   Problems with plumbing and electrical systems
   Cafeteria and kitchen—dirty equipment, stoves and refrigerators
      needing repair

· 333 ·

As the maintenance staff will be far more alert to the areas that need checking than these few guidelines suggest, the PTA representatives should listen carefully to their comments and take detailed notes of areas in need of repairs. These should be reported to the full PTA membership and to the school board, which should make plans accordingly. Should the board delay, the PTA maintenance committee must prod them into action.

Fire safety

While fire regulations differ somewhat by state, the basic requirements for schools are fairly similar.

· There must be smoke alarms in specified places.
· There must be fire alarms. If possible, fire alarms should be connected to the city alarm system. In rural areas, where this is impossible, the fire alarms should be connected to the nearest fire department.
· Fire extinguishers are required in certain locations throughout the building.
· There must be fire exit doors. These must be unlocked from the

inside and clear of storage and debris. The New Jersey school made famous by "Lean on Me" principal Joe Clark was found to have fire doors chained closed for the purpose of keeping students from leaving school without authorization.

· The school must have a specified number of fire drills during the year, depending on the height of the building and the number of pupils.

· A fire safety course may be required at specified grade levels.

· The fire department must make a yearly inspection of the building, checking safety and alarm equipment, and report its findings. In some states regulations for public and private schools may differ. Secure through the PTA a copy of the fire regulations to which your school is subject. A fire and emergency committee should be appointed to ensure the school's compliance with the regulations and should receive a copy of the fire department's report following its yearly inspection. The committee should follow up necessary improvements with the school board.

School bus

States are currently undergoing debates on the issue of seat belts on school buses, with experts arguing on both sides. Many of those who argue against seat belts want to have the backs of bus seats raised as a safety alternative. While some states have already voted to require seat belts, they limit their use to buses of a specified size and age.

Drivers of school buses must be specially trained and certified in most states. Before being hired, their past history is checked for arrests and driving violations, and they must pass a physical examination and be fingerprinted. Despite these precautions, statistics on school bus accidents indicate that unqualified drivers manage to slip through the red tape and hold the lives of schoolchildren literally in their hands.

Although most school districts hold bus drivers responsible for order on the bus as well as for driving, some districts assign a parent or staff member to police student behavior. Under either system, controlled behavior on the bus is often difficult to achieve, as evidenced by the third grader who told me, "Our driver is better than theirs because he lets us stand on the seats, and their driver stops and makes them sit down."

School buses must be inspected regularly, usually every six months. In addition, in many states schools are required to hold emergency drills to advise driver and students what to do in case of accident.

Most schools assign a staff member to supervise children as they leave buses in the morning and board them at the close of school, assuring that all get safely on the right bus, with none left behind.

Parents should appoint a PTA committee to check school bus regulations in your state and district and to ascertain that your school abides by them. In addition, if you consider the regulations too lax, approach the school board with suggestions for expanding them. Some PTAs have insured greater safety by assigning volunteers to ride the buses each morning and afternoon.

Traffic regulation

Most states assign each school district the responsibility for regulating traffic and parking at its schools—that is, the direction and speed of traffic and the allocation of parking and no-parking areas. While the district usually has no authority to hire a crossing guard on a public highway, it can obtain permission to do so from the local municipal traffic bureau. Most states allow only adult guards, not children, to direct traffic; children, however, may serve as patrols to direct students.

Be aware of traffic conditions around your children's school. If you find potential danger areas, you should report them to the superintendent of schools for the district and have his office and the PTA draw up a safer traffic plan.

· 335 ·

Disaster and civil defense

Most states require contingency plans for evacuation in the case of emergencies, among which may be listed hurricane, earthquake, tornado, ice and snow storm, power failure, chemical and radiological accident, and recently, bomb and hostage threat. In time of war, enemy attack has been added as a possible emergency.

Check the state requirements that your school is obliged to meet; these can be obtained from the state education department, the local school district, or the school board. The PTA fire and emergency committee should meet with the principal or the staff member to whom she has delegated responsibility for handling emergencies in order to evaluate the existing plan. If it appears inadequate, parents and school personnel should develop a new emergency plan in conjunction with local fire and police authorities. Even with careful planning, however, evacuation plans can never ensure the safety of the entire school population: too many "ifs" hang in the balance. Still, despite its shortcomings, a carefully worked out emergency plan should be on hand, with specific instructions for handicapped children and personnel.

Protection against violence

In January 1989 a New York kindergarten boy entered his classroom with a loaded pistol. In that same year a Chicago woman opened fire in an elementary school, a California man gunned down five children in a school play yard, an Arkansas junior high boy shot a fourteen-year-old girl on a school bus, and a nine-year-old Virginia girl was raped at knifepoint in the school lavatory. Three million crimes are committed each year on school property, some as mild as theft, many involving injury and death. According to *U.S. News and World Report*, 135,000 students carry guns to schools in the United States every single day; although most of them are in grade 9 and above, a sizable number are found in lower grades too.

The thought of waving your child off to school at nine and cradling her dead body at noon is too shattering to picture as possible in any but the most crime-ridden cities. Yet because crime has redesigned even the picture-postcard suburbs and rural areas, the thought is too frightening to blot out. Parents and school personnel, who at first felt as helpless as the classroom full of children held hostage at gunpoint, are beginning to take control. Many schools in different parts of the country are taking the following precautions:

- Parents are patrolling halls, doorways, and school grounds.
- Schools have set up parent "receptionists" to screen entrants at the front door, which is the only door left open to the outside throughout the day. Fire exits can be opened only from the inside.
- Schools have hired school guards or, particularly in urban areas, police officers to patrol.
- Schools have developed code words to send over the loud speaker system in case of trouble.
- Students and school staff are required to wear visible identification tags.
- Metal detectors are set up at the entrance to detect knives and guns.
- Courses for grades as low as kindergarten have been developed with the aim of minimizing student violence: courses in values, in the danger of guns, in nonviolent conflict resolution, in law.
- Children are being taught how to react to violent situations: to remain quiet, calm, and obedient if held

hostage; to fall on the floor if there is shooting; and so on.

Like you, I find it difficult to acknowledge these measures which fit more plausibly into some unshakable nightmare. Yet they are real . . . for real reasons.

Maximize your child's safety by presenting the issue at a PTA meeting and appointing a committee to work with the school in developing an antiviolence program. This might include:

- Courses such as those just listed.
- A system of patrols.
- Guidelines to follow in case of school violence.
- Safety measures within the building—doors other than fire exits locked from the outside, lavatories patrolled regularly, little-used stairwells blocked off, and so on.

In addition, you can help your children protect themselves by teaching them to avoid fights, to report incidents of bullying to a school authority, and to alert their teacher if they see a stranger loitering in the playground or in the halls. While not unduly frightening your child, you should make her aware of danger signs and of action she can take to avoid dangerous situations.

· 337 ·

· Checking Health Factors ·

While the physical plants that house schools are probably as safe as or safer than they used to be, our raised consciousness has alerted us to dangers into which we used to send our children unaware.

Asbestos

When a correlation between certain types of cancer and exposure to asbestos was discovered, state and federal health departments expressed concern about school buildings. Inspections were undertaken, and finally in 1988, a federal law was passed requiring the inspection of all school buildings for evidences of asbestos. Those buildings in which asbestos was found were required to develop programs to eliminate it and implement those programs no later than July 1989. Because of the tremendous cost involved, the law has not been speedily implemented.

Get your PTA to ask for a school board report on the inspection of your school building, if it has not already done so. Ascertain the date of the inspection and demand a copy of the report. If asbestos was discovered, ask to see the plan that was drawn up to eliminate it and find out whether implementation of the plan is underway. If there is no plan or if implementation of a plan has not yet begun, have the PTA take the matter to the state Department of Education. If that gets you nowhere, take the matter up with your U.S. senator and/or congressman. There is no excuse for laxity on the part of the school board in this matter.

Lead

The use of lead paint on toys and in schools and residences in the United States has been prohibited for many years. However, lead poisoning has been detected in many children, particularly those from low-income urban areas, with the cause attributed to flaking paint from schools and apartments. Preschool children often pick off and eat peeling paint, while older children may simply breathe it in. Lead has also been discovered in some school drinking water, most recently in New York and New Jersey.

If there have been cases of lead poisoning reported among the children in your school, get your PTA to contact the school board. If your school building is old and you have any reason to suspect the possibility of lead paint, the building should be checked at once by the Department of Health; if lead is found, the situation should be corrected immediately. At the same time, the school board should have the Board of Health test the school drinking water for evidence of lead. If lead is present, the school must have a new or overhauled plumbing system.

Radon

The latest danger to home and school of which parents have been apprised is the presence of radon, an odorless, invisible gas that has been detected seeping into buildings through basements. Exposure to radon over a period of time has been linked to cancer.

Because the test for radon is easy and inexpensive, the PTA could ask the principal to authorize the head maintenance worker to conduct the test, or the PTA could work through the school board. Although not required, a radon test is advisable and should be made, not only in the basement, but on at least the first two floors of the school as well.

If radon is detected, the school board will have to employ an engineering firm to develop and implement plans to eliminate it.

Medical care

Although health is a major concern of parents, only thirteen states require school districts to provide registered nurses for their schools. Of the other thirty-seven states, twelve have legislation pending, while the remaining twenty-five let local school boards make the decision. As a result, many schools have no school nurses at all, and children who become ill during school hours are cared for by a staff member, usually a physical education teacher. On the other hand, some schools have not only a registered nurse but a medical doctor, psychiatrist, and dental hygienist as well.

· *339* ·

All schools require immunization for measles, polio, diphtheria, mumps, and rubella. Some schools may administer urine tests for drugs and sickle cell anemia tests to children at specified levels.

Children with contagious or infectious diseases are not allowed in school. As AIDS is not listed as either contagious or infectious, children with AIDS may not be excluded from school. Legal test cases, which have caused a great deal of heartache to both schools and families, have resulted in the admission of AIDS children to classrooms alongside their peers. However, fear and lack of information—or what parents and educators want, *proof of safety*—still bring on new lawsuits from time to time.

Parents should be aware of the medical facilities and services offered in the child's school. At the least it should have a school nurse, if not in residence because the school is too small, then shared by nearby schools. A medical doctor should be on call. At the other extreme, a large school may have a health clinic, either as part of the school program or leased to an outside agency. You should know exactly what procedure the nurse and/or doctor follows in case of illness or accident.

You should be equally aware of liability in the event of a child's accident in school, on the school grounds, or on a school trip. You can check through the school board: Is the school adequately insured? In case of accident, who is notified first—teacher or parent? What if a parent cannot be reached? Is parental consent required before treatment can be administered? Is a consent release from all parents kept on file in case of an accident emergency? A PTA committee should investigate all these areas of the school's medical program. If the PTA is not satisfied with the findings, they, in conjunction with the school board, should set about revising the program.

· Checking Food Safety ·

Every school food department must comply with the state sanitation code, which regulates the cleanliness of facilities in which food is stored, cooked, and eaten. Regular inspection is required. It must also comply with the National Child Nutrition Act of 1966, which regulates the nutritional value of menus and dispenses surplus food and funding for deprived children. In states that impose sales tax on meals eaten in restaurants, adults in the school population must pay a tax on the meals they purchase at school; children pay no tax.

While most states forbid the installation of commercial vending machines in public schools, many schools have their own vending machines for the convenience of students. The school administration, rather than the food service department, is often responsible for the selection available in this way.

Be aware of both sanitation and nutritional requirements for your children's school; they can be checked through the school board. The board should immediately correct any indications that the school is falling short of standards; if not, the PTA has the responsibility of reporting noncompliance to the state Department of Education and the Board of Health.

With the recent focus on health and nutrition, vending machines have become a source of debate in many schools. Food-conscious parents have fought and won battles to eliminate soda, candy, and junk foods from vending machines and, in many cases, to eliminate vending machines altogether. If the school has no food service, children bring their lunch. Some PTAs have even extended their fight to the cafeteria, demanding that potato chips and the like be banned.

Parents are rarely hesitant to complain about school lunches. In fact, they are quicker to find fault with a lunch menu that does not excite their child's taste buds than with an academic program that does not excite his mind. As a principal, I used to eat in the cafeteria every day, finding the meals nutritious and tasty enough; yet there were always complaints that "Jimmy doesn't like salads," and "Janie won't eat chicken." Finally, in desperation I pointed out to parents that I was running a school, not a restaurant, and therefore preferred to spend my energy on providing gourmet learning, not gourmet food. I wish all parents would be critics with similar priorities.

If parents find fault with the school food, let it be for reasons other than personal taste: Get rid of vending machines; forbid junk food in the cafeteria; demand broiled instead of fried foods; insist on salads and less salt and sugar; ban artificial sweeteners. As the findings of studies indicate more definitively than ever before a correlation between nutrition and learning, take a stand for food that will do your children good. And . . . be sure they eat breakfast!

CHAPTER 24

Hazards:
Parent Concerns

· Sex-related Concerns ·

Sex education

Thirty years ago I heard Dr. Mary Calderon say to a group of teachers, "Don't think the question is whether or not kids should get sex education. They're getting it, no matter what you say. The question for you to decide is *how* they will get it." Yet then and now teachers and parents have sat at endless meetings debating this issue so fraught with fear.

If anyone challenges Dr. Calderon's statement that children are being educated in sex without any help from their parents or teachers, all she has to do is look around. A sixth-grade girl sneaks a copy of *Playgirl* into school and passes a picture of a man with an erection among her classmates. A seventh-grade boy rapes a neighbor. In a guidance class, when the counselor asks, "Any questions?" an eleven-year-old stops her dead with this one: "Why do people like oral sex?" A six-year-old announces that he will never get married "because no one's going to put my penis inside her." A second grader brings a condom for Show and Tell. A million American teenagers become pregnant every year. Yes, children are getting sex education in distorted and often life-damaging ways.

Four-fifths of the states in the United States have faced this reality and instituted some form of sex education in their schools, although it is usually in high school—too little, too late. The remaining fifth consistently vote down sex education in school, usually on two grounds, both of which are unfounded.

The first argument is that sex education belongs in the home because parents have the right to tell their children about sex. No one disputes a parent's right to teach children about sex; in fact, professional sex educators urge it. The trouble is that many parents will not discuss sex with their children—either from embarrassment or from a belief that sex is dirty and should not be talked about. Many other parents who attempt sex education do an inadequate job of it, by not starting early enough or by surrounding it with harsh moral judgments that frighten rather than instruct.

The second argument is that sex education in schools "puts ideas into children's heads." Nonsense, sex education just tries to straighten out ideas that are already there. Only if a child were raised on a desert island with no TV, movies, popular songs, and newspapers, and with no animals or children of the opposite sex to glimpse could he grow up sex-free, like a teddy bear.

· 343 ·

A good sex education program not only does not put ideas into a child's head; it actually takes a lot of ideas *out*. Studies reveal that among children who have had sex education, promiscuity is far lower and the association of sex with love far higher. The greatest safeguard against parents' worst fears for their children—pregnancy and AIDS—comes in the form of sex education.

I advise parents to stop reacting emotionally to sex education and inform themselves with facts. A letter to the following agency will elicit some helpful material:

AASECT
(AMERICAN ASSOCIATION OF SEX EDUCATORS,
COUNSELORS AND THERAPISTS)
435 North Michigan Avenue
Suite 1717
Chicago, IL 60611-4067

Invite a speaker from AASECT to lead a discussion of sex education at a PTA meeting and point out different kinds of programs that are working. Then appoint a committee composed of parents, teachers, and school and district administrators to follow up by investigating the sex education programs of other schools. The committee should meet with individuals or groups opposed to sex education so that the PTA can address their objections and fears. The committee must plan a comprehensive sex education program carefully and appropriately and then support the school against objections in getting it underway. While 93 percent of schools across the country claim to have some kind of sex education, a great majority consider their programs inadequate, and only a handful have certified sex educators planning or teaching the programs.

Sexual promiscuity

The cry of the sexual revolution, which began in the sixties, was for freedom; today the cry is for rights. Children embark on sexually active lives, often in junior high school, no longer with the sense of moral wrong of prior times but in the belief that sex is their due. "Why shouldn't we?" young people ask me. "We're not hurting anyone."

Countering their argument is not easy because sex seems the same kind of harmless fun they used to have on bikes and roller coasters, and today's children are used to taking their fun when and where they find it. Instant gratification. Is it true, however, that they are not hurting anyone?

Primarily they are hurting themselves. They are undertaking a deeply emotional experience on the most superficial physical level—like reading *Hamlet* in fourth grade or getting drunk on fine old wine. What a waste! By the time they are mature enough to get the full impact of *Hamlet* or aged wine or sex, they will have irreparably diminished it.

They are also hurting their sex partner, using another person for their own gratification. As the ultimate bonding of two people, sex is a language of commitment, not a game to be played with partners as they become available. "Anyone for tennis?" is a fair call to fill one's need on the tennis court, but a similar call for sex leads to exploitation.

Millions of thirteen- and fourteen-year-olds report that they do not want to be sexually active but find themselves under too much peer pressure to resist. "How can I say no?" they ask. Or as an eighth-grade boy put it, "Do you think it's easy to be a virgin?" No, I don't think it is easy when classmates boast and brag about their exploits. I don't think it is easy when sex becomes the symbol of being grown-up. I don't think it is easy when happiness depends on being one of the crowd. No, I don't think it is easy when you are thirteen or fourteen . . . or younger.

Sexual promiscuity has been traced to two kinds of parenting. In one, parents do not discuss sex with their children other than to teach that it is a sin to be avoided on pain of damnation. In the other, parents are lax. They themselves may be sexually promiscuous or may allow their children limitless sexual stimulation from sources such as TV, magazines, and family conversation. A recent study found that a group of fourteen-year-olds averaged four and a half hours a day watching TV shows that exposed them to over seven depictions of sexual intercourse. In addition, four-fifths of the girls had seen the top six X-rated movies. (Sex abuse also leads to sexual promiscuity.)

Parents, follow neither extreme, but run a middle course. Discuss sex openly with your children and answer their questions, dealing with the subject as you would with any other subject that relates to their growth and learning. Do not turn sex into a moral issue or frighten your children with threats. However, supervise their magazine reading and TV and movie watching in order to avoid exposure to material that presents sex in distorted and overstimulating ways.

Some children say no to sex and shrink in shame; others say no and stand tall. You can arm your child with a positive self-image, strong enough to withstand shattering from peer pressure. Although the importance of establishing self-image has been mentioned in different connections throughout the book, Chapter 25 deals with it head-on.

· 345 ·

Pregnancy

Pregnancies among young girls have risen to such a degree that many schools have made accommodations unheard of till now: special classes in prenatal care; home study for girls who have given birth; the dispensing of birth control pills and condoms to avoid pregnancy; counseling on a pregnant girl's options.

If pregnancy is an issue in your child's school—and it is in many junior high schools—find out what provisions exist for both prevention and care. Furthermore, ask the school board or the superintendent's office whether there are regulations controlling a parent's right to information if her daughter is pregnant and requiring parental consent for counseling. If you are not satisfied, work through the PTA to effect changes.

When Dr. Alan Guttmacher headed Planned Parenthood, he often began speeches by saying "There is nothing more tragic than a baby having a baby." I challenge the imagination of all parents to place their little girl on a delivery-room table pushing down hard on an about-to-be new life, and then see whether those parents continue to shout against sex education. The only safeguard against your little girl's pregnancy that is stronger than a good sex education program in her school is your openness and honesty in dealing with sex at home.

AIDS

Although children with the AIDS virus are allowed to attend regular classes in schools, the issue remains before the courts in several states. C. Everett Koop, the surgeon general of the United States during eight years of the AIDS panic, estimated that by 1992 between ten and twenty thousand preteens would be infected with the AIDS virus. His prediction reinforces parent fears for their children, although Dr. Koop stated repeatedly that they cannot catch AIDS from a classmate through casual contact.

· 346 ·

Dr. Koop advocates sex and drug education as the strongest safeguards against AIDS because sexual activity and drug injections are the major sources of contagion. While he supports abstinence as the safest preventive measure, he feels more certain that education in the use of condoms will reach a larger percentage of school audiences and will—at least in the short run—provide surer protection.

Know how your child's school is handling the issue of AIDS. If you are in doubt about the validity of the actions the school is taking, invite a medical doctor to discuss the matter at a PTA meeting. In addition, you should fully inform yourself on the subject: The local library will have recent articles and books. A very helpful booklet entitled "Risk and Responsibility" concerning both AIDS and pregnancy is available from

THE ALAN GUTTMACHER INSTITUTE
111 Fifth Avenue
New York, NY 10003
(212) 254-5656

You can get additional information from your state Department of Education and

THE U.S. DEPARTMENT OF EDUCATION
Division of Health
Washington, DC 20208-5644

Sexual abuse

As much as awareness of sexual abuse has increased over the past decade, few people realize the diverse behaviors it includes. In an informal survey of parents and preteens that I conducted recently, over three-quarters of the parents and almost a 100 percent of the children questioned thought sexual abuse was limited to incidents of intercourse and sodomy. In fact, most cases of sex abuse are far more subtle.

Parents and children have little difficulty identifying violent sexual abuse, which includes rape and sadomasochistic practices, often resulting in murder. The gang rape of a woman in a Massachusetts bar two decades ago raised the awareness of television viewers and newspaper readers to this horror. I recall some years later a young girl raped with a broom handle by a gang of girls in the school lavatory; and as I write today, a New York jogger and a New Jersey teenager have become the victims of even more brutal incidents.

Physical sexual abuse is not always violent, however: French kisses and an adult's genitals in a child's hand or on her cheek cause no bodily pain. Even sodomy, masturbation, genital fondling, and child pornography draw no blood and leave no wounds on a child's body, although they may destroy her emotionally.

Even more difficult to detect is nonphysical sexual abuse, which draws children in through subtle maneuvering and keeps them there through guilt. A favorite teacher, a coach, or an older student takes a special interest in a child, plans times to be together alone with her and displays affection through hugs and kisses. Unsuspecting, the child is flattered and enjoys the extra attention and closeness. Rather than resisting, she falls into deeper and deeper sexual abuse: Under the guise of game-playing, she may have to undress the abuser or to strip herself naked; she may be asked to listen to and repeat sexual obscenities; she may be exposed to photographs of sexual acts or to other children engaged in performing them.

At this stage, the child no longer wants to play and feels what many children describe as "wrong." Although they long for extrication from the entanglement, as they believe themselves responsible, they are too guilt-ridden to ask for help. Even without the use of force or physical

· 347 ·

contact, the child has been seduced and soon finds herself a frightened partner in physical sex acts, perhaps even intercourse. As unthinkable as this scenario may sound to parents, as the statistics stand in 1989, one in three of their little girls will be abused sexually before they are eighteen, and one in seven of their little boys.

Short of pregnancy or a sexually transmitted disease, signs of sexual abuse are difficult to identify and even more difficult to prove. However, certain physical and behavioral changes in a child may be considered signs of possible abuse when seen, not singly, but in a cluster:

- Genital itching, infection, discharge, or injury or pain.
- A sudden interest in sex, sex games, and sexual words.
- Signs of stress—poor sleep and nightmares, fear of particular people and places and of being alone, regression to habits of babyhood.
- Trouble in school—withdrawal, poor work habits.

If you observe a cluster of these signs in your child, try to get her to talk to you about them. These questions might elicit the truth.

"You seem afraid to go to the playground recently. Is there anyone there who frightens you?" or "What do you think about when you can't go to sleep at night? Is it something that happened that bothers you?" or "You're awfully concerned about sex these days. Is it because the kids talk about it a lot in school, or what?"

In addition, take your child to the doctor for a checkup. He may relieve your worry by identifying physical symptoms as no more than the usual vaginitis or allergy. If, however, he sees signs of possible sexual abuse, get in touch with the Child Protective Agency in your area. The hot-line number will be listed in the phone book under "Sexual Abuse" or "Child Abuse." This agency will help you identify sexual abuse if it exists and will serve as your guide in taking action.

You can reduce the chances of your child's becoming a victim of sexual abuse in two main ways.

First, arm your child against sexual abuse.

- As soon as she is old enough to understand, teach her that her body is her own personal treasure and belongs to no one else. You can begin while you bathe and dress her and encourage her to bathe and dress herself. Tickling is an intrusion; avoid it. Stop patting and stroking the minute she tries to distance herself. Don't force yourself on her body in any way that can be avoided.
- As she gets older, talk with her about good touching, like hugs

and love pats, and bad touching, like slaps and touches in places that are private.

· From the very beginning, encourage your child to talk freely to you about anything, and don't silence her by expressing anger or shock.

· Develop mutual trust that promises that you will keep her secrets and she will keep yours. Let her know, however, that if other people tell her to keep secrets she considers "wrong," she should not keep them, but tell you instead.

· Teach your child that she is in control of her body, even with grown-ups, and that she can exert that control in two ways: by saying no and by telling you.

· As suggested in other sections of the book, set up role-play situations in which your child has a chance to try out her response to a "wrong" advance.

· Explain honestly to your child that some sick grown-ups try to play sexually with children, that it is illegal, and that the adult, never the child, is to blame.

You can find more detailed help from many books, such as the following: *Coping with Sexual Abuse* by Judith Cooney (Rosen Publishing Group, 1987) and *When Your Child Has Been Molested* by Kathryn B. Hagans and Joyce Case (Lexington Books, 1988). Other sources of help include:

· *349* ·

NATIONAL COMMITTEE FOR THE PREVENTION OF CHILD ABUSE
332 South Michigan Avenue
Chicago, IL 60604–4357
(312) 663-3520

SIECUS
(SEX INFORMATION AND EDUCATION COUNCIL OF THE U.S.)
130 W. 42nd Street
New York, NY 10036
(212) 819-9770

Second, urge your school to reinforce the efforts you are making at home.

· Ask the PTA to invite a speaker from AASECT or SIE-CUS to address parents and school personnel on the subject.
· Check with your district office and the state Depart-

ment of Education for existing programs and materials used in other schools.

· Ask the principal to appoint a teacher and several parents to outline a presentation on sexual abuse for every grade in the school. SIECUS will give you guidelines to follow, in addition to printed materials for use by children. Also, pamphlets for children and guides for adults are available from:

NETWORK PUBLICATIONS
PO Box 8506
Santa Cruz, CA 95061-8506

A coloring book is available from:

YWCA
310 East Third Street
Flint, MI 48502

A workbook is available from:

LUTHERAN SOCIAL SERVICES
North 1226 Howard Street
Spokane, WA 99201

· Drug Abuse ·

"What is a drug?"

A drug is a substance, other than food, that when ingested creates a body change: Nora's mother gives her two teaspoons of penicillin twice a day to kill the strep infection in her throat; Josh takes Tylenol to reduce his flu fever. Because the drugs both children take produce a change that helps the body, they are medicine. Drugs that produce changes harmful to the body are poisons, such as arsenic and the chemical wastes polluting our air and waters.

Drug abuse, simply stated, is the wrong use of drugs—the misuse of medicines such as morphine, amphetamines, and tranquilizers, or the deliberate use of poisons, such as nicotine and airplane glue. In both forms drug abuse destroys the minds and bodies of millions of

American children every year, through ill health, depression, suicide, and crime. Tragically, the drug abuse of James Wilson and Laurie Dann led beyond their own minds and bodies to elementary schools in Greenwood, South Carolina, and Winnetka, Illinois, where they killed seven children. It is little wonder that parents list drugs as the number-one school problem with discipline running a poor second and academics barely measurable.

While the drugs used by children fall into different categories, there is rarely one lone drug of choice; children tend either to use several drugs in combination or to graduate from a less potent drug to a more potent one. While the antidrug campaign has alerted parents to the dangers of drug abuse, it has provided very little information on the nature of it. "Everyone says that kids do drugs," a parent told me recently. "What I want to know is *how* they do them." He has a point.

Children use different drugs in different ways:

· They inhale glue and gasoline if they have no money and cocaine if they have.
· They pop pills and capsules. LSD, PCP, and mescaline are used far less than they were fifteen to twenty years ago. The easiest capsules and pills for children to obtain are those readily available in the pharmacy with a doctor's prescription (or a forged one) and in their parents' medicine chest—amphetamines, tranquilizers, barbiturates, and sedatives.
· They inject heroin and cocaine.
· They smoke crack, marijuana, and cocaine. Crack has become the number-one drug of children because it is cheap and obtainable almost everywhere.
· Sometimes they drink crack and PCP too.

There are two other drug categories that children use widely although parents tend to exclude them.

Alcohol

As drug use among children has declined, alcohol use has risen sharply and is dramatically noticeable in the soaring numbers of youthful members of Alcoholics Anonymous. Most children find liquor in their own homes or available for purchase at a store by older friend. Because liquor is legal and their own drug of choice, most parents express far less fear over a child's drinking than taking other drugs, despite the fact that more children abuse alcohol than any other drug.

Nicotine

Minors spend $3 billion a year on cigarettes, despite the heavy emphasis on antismoking campaigns and classes to which children are exposed from kindergarten through high school. Actually, children constitute the only segment of the American population not reflecting a decline in smoking over the past decade, and they often experiment with cigarettes in early elementary school. Children are former Surgeon General C. Everett Koop's target for a "Smoke-Free Class of 2000." "Drinking is different from smoking," the National Education Association publication *Today* quotes Dr. Koop as saying. "With smoking you can assume that everyone is at risk for developing disease, so no one should smoke."

"Who abuses drugs?"

The United States boasts the highest drug abuse among children of any industrialized nation in the world. Why? What exists in this country that drives us to the top of the list? Although scientists and social scientists have not been able to isolate an undisputed cause of drug abuse, they have correlated factors that have a significant bearing.

- Genetics. Some children seem to be born with a predisposition to addiction.
- Vitamin deficiency. It has been found that addictive children, especially alcoholics, are low in certain essential vitamins. They may turn to drugs subconsciously as a supplement.
- Broken homes. A higher percentage of children who use drugs come from broken homes.
- Imitation of parents. Children whose parents abuse drugs are more likely to become drug abusers themselves.
- Personality disorders. Drug-abusive children seem to be unable to cope with the stresses of childhood.

To date, because no studies have been conducted to determine a correlation between these factors and drug abuse in different parts of the world, the reason for America's lead in childhood drug abuse remains a moot point. Several facts are clear, however.

- Sixty percent of marijuana users began between sixth and ninth grades.
- The seventh grade is the starting level for most drug abuse.
- Over half of the children who are heavily into drugs contemplate suicide at some point; one-fifth of them actually attempt it.
- A child with low self-esteem is in danger of drug abuse as early as fourth grade if he feels it will win him acceptance in the peer group.
- Equally vulnerable is the spoiled child who, used to instant gratification of every wish, has developed no controls to say no.
- Drug abuse seems to draw a greater number of children who are into acid rock and heavy metal music.
- Children who smoke cigarettes have a greater tendency to become drug abusers than those who do not.
- A high percentage of alcoholic children, as well as those with addictions to other drugs, report starting to drink at home as early as nine years old, not only with their parents' consent but with their parents' offerings of drinks at parties.

Children get into drug abuse for three main reasons:

1. Escape from a painful situation to which they see no other solution—loneliness, failure at school, parental conflict, and so on.
2. Peer pressure to do what the group does or be rejected.
3. Parent role modeling. As in the acquisition of other habits, children follow the pattern set by their parents.

"What are signs of drug abuse?"

Drug abuse is a process that develops in a series of levels. Parents able to identify signs in their children at the bottom levels may be able to forestall progress toward addiction.

Phase one: predisposition

While the heavy use of any drug is likely to lead all children to addiction, only those children genetically predisposed to addiction are made vulnerable with even minimal use. Although you have no sure way of knowing into which group your child falls, you may pick up a few clues. For instance, if a parent, grandparent, or other close relative is an alcoholic, and especially if several of them are, your child may carry a genetic leaning in that direction as well. In addition, you may observe a strong food craving in your child that, while seemingly harmless, may prophesy more hazardous cravings to come, like the alcoholic in the old movie *Days of Wine and Roses* who as a child had an addiction to chocolate. This does not mean that every child who nags for a Hershey bar is destined for drug addiction, but rather that if a child's craving leads to lying and stealing change to buy and hide those Hershey bars, his parent should be aware.

Phase two: use of drugs

Drugs are available to the child determined to secure them—at home, in school, and on the street. Money to buy them is available too—at first in his piggy bank, then in his mother's purse, later in a pawn shop where he hocks his watch or a stolen radio, and finally in the income he receives from selling drugs. Although it has been reported that people can become dependent on crack after only one use, most drug addiction develops slowly.

· 354 ·

Drug abuse begins with *experimentation*. Children are born curious, staring as infants at strange objects to determine what they are, reaching out to touch them and try them as they grow older. In this way they learn about faces and rattles and kittens and fire. In this way too, as they grow older, they learn about drugs. Just as a child experiments with hairstyles and clothes and food and sex, so he experiments with drugs—a cigarette, a drink, a shared few puffs of marijuana, a sniff of glue.

Without contributing factors, a child may play around with a sample of drugs and say, "So that's what it's like." The end. He may even tell his mother and father. I know a seventh grader who, while relating the day's events in school, included, "Guess what I did in recess today?" When his parents failed to guess, he announced, "I drank vodka. Yuck."

Signs: At the early stages of experimentation, you can rarely detect visible signs. You might notice sudden drowsiness or hyperactivity in your child; you might smell alcohol on his breath or strong peppermint to hide it; you might notice the level in one of your liquor bottles is lower than it was or see a few capsules from a bottle of amphetamines or tranquilizers gone. But then again, you might notice nothing at all amiss.

Unfortunately, for many children drug experimentation does not end with "Yuck," but progresses to regular social and recreational use. They begin to drink or smoke or sniff or pop pills with their friends on weekends. Drug use becomes for them a pattern of behavior similar to the drink at a business lunch, the glass of wine at dinner, and the beer at a ball game.

Signs: As children get more and more deeply into drug use, parents will be aware of changing behavior. Your child may invent cover stories for where he has been and become irresponsible about his schoolwork; his marks may begin to drop. You may find money missing from your purse or wallet and evidence of drug paraphernalia tucked out of the way in his room.

From social-recreational use, drugs may develop into a major focus of a child's life, a real drug problem. No longer does he limit his use of drugs to weekend socializing, but finds he needs drugs to help him through stressful situations such as dates and exams. He begins to take drugs when he is alone and now perhaps not only by drinking, sniffing, and pill popping, but by mainlining as well through injection. The urgency of getting money to buy the drug and the fear of not getting it preoccupy him so completely that he maintains few, if any, of his previous interests and involvements.

Signs: Parents who have been unaware of their child's drug involvement previously cannot fail to see it at this stage because the signs are blatant: serious academic, personality, and/or truancy problems at school; hostility and outbursts of anger at home; wide mood swings; a different set of friends; bloodshot eyes and coughing; continual fatigue; possible criminal involvement.

The final stage of drug abuse is dependency or addiction. The child, unable to function without the use of drugs, has become his own captive. Where at first he was the controlling factor in his drug use, he is now its slave. His body demands the drug first thing in the morning, and he goes to school stoned, if he goes to school at all. His body demands the drug during the day and in the evening and again the next morning, and he has no choice but to meet its demands. In between times he panics for fear of not having the drug or the money to secure it and resents his dependency. He steals and lies and, riddled with guilt, seeks drugs for release from his pain. He loathes himself and seeks more drugs and loathes himself further.

Signs: A parent I know summarized the signs of a child's dependency on drugs when she said, "I have lost him." "Lost" is an appropriate word because the addicted child has slipped from the world of activity and interrelationships into his own private maelstrom, swirling around alone like a bit of flotsam, deeper and deeper into bottomless depths. He has left family, friends, and school; work, play, communication, and the future. While his body may sit at the dinner table and even at his classroom desk, it is empty; he is not inside.

Phase three: parents who allow it to happen

Every day in the United States as children are discovered in drug-related crimes, parents cry out in shock, "I can't believe it! I never knew!" Yet parents are, in many cases, partners in crime themselves for it is they who have enabled their child's drug abuse to develop at any stage.

· A large percentage of drug abuse begins at home with parents condoning cigarettes and marijuana and sharing sips of their drinks. I know parents who laugh as they watch their six-year-old drink the remains of their guests' drinks after a party and a father who rewards his ten-year-old with some of his beer when she brings him a can from the refrigerator. These parents are paving the way for their children to head into drug abuse with no awareness of the consequences of their actions.

· An even greater percentage of drug abuse—probably all, in fact—begins in a far less conscious way at home. The human mind protects itself against wounds with greater effectiveness than medieval knights in all their armor by using the impenetrable defense of denial. What is too painful to allow in, the human mind keeps out. Although signs of their child's drug abuse surround them—altered behavior and moods, new unsavory friends, trouble at school, the smell of marijuana and liquor, and so on—parents will not see them. To see them is to admit fear and failure; to remain blind is to live in the American dream family.

· 356 ·

While in denying reality parents secure their own peace of mind, they also hold back the help and guidance at all four stages that might prevent their child's addiction.

If they could acknowledge their child's *experimentation* with drugs, they could say, "Okay, I understand why you had to try them, but you've had your fling. Let's see why you should call a halt right now."

If they could admit an awareness of their child's *social use* of drugs, they could say, "I know a lot of your friends do this and that it's hard to say no. But do you know what you're getting into? Let's take a look down the road."

If they could face the fact of their child's *drug problem*, they could say, "You're out of control of your body, just as if you had a broken leg and couldn't walk. We love you and want to get help for you. We want you to be whole again. You can be if we all work at it."

And finally, if they confront the tragedy of their child's *dependency*, they could say, "Let's stop fooling ourselves—you're in deep trouble. You know it, and we know it, and we are all miserable because of it. But let's not give up. Let's determine to lick this thing together because we are a family, and we love you."

Words will not cure your child of a drug problem; only he can do that. They will, however, let him know you are there for him. Feelings of alienation are part of his problem; belonging is most of his cure. When you face drug abuse in its first stages, you have a far better chance of combating it than if you look the other way until your child develops a dependency problem.

"How do I help a child who is abusing drugs?"

When parents stop denying evidences of their child's drug abuse, they not only stop enabling it to continue but actually take the first step in helping their child to overcome it. While a child's degree of dependency determines her ability to kick the drug habit, there are other contributing factors over which parents have some control.

Once parents admit to themselves that their child is taking drugs, they have the obligation of confronting her. Do not do it in anger: not "How could you betray us this way? We are furious." Do it instead in loving concern: "We are worried about you and want to see you happy again."

· *357* ·

Confrontation is not easy. Your child may deny and argue and fight, accuse you of spying and not trusting her with a great display of injury. Don't let your fear or feelings of guilt silence you, however. You can help her only when you both acknowledge the problem. On the other hand, your child may have been longing for you to discover and help her end her drug problem. Her response may not be an argument, but tears of relief and newfound hope in the comfort of your caring.

The most common argument children use when parents confront them on the issue of drugs is "You drink. What's the difference?" Some convincing points you can use as counterarguments run like this:

- "It is legal for adults to drink; what you do is not legal."
- "I drink to be sociable; you use your drugs for other reasons—to escape problems or to keep up with the crowd."
- "I know how my body handles alcohol, and I limit my

drinking. You do not know, and you may do yourself harm."
- "Science shows that adults are less susceptible to the effects of alcohol than children are to alcohol and other drugs."
- "Many drug addictions begin with childhood drinking. Why take the chance?"

When you confront your child, if she acknowledges the drug problem, you can provide a great deal of support in helping her overcome it. At the early stages:

- Set limits on her hours.
- Check where she is going.
- Discourage friendships with other children who use drugs.
- Encourage friendships with her predrug friends.
- Keep lines of communication open; talk with her about her feelings, her friends, drugs, and so on.
- Reinforce her successes and areas of strength.
- Discuss alternative ways of coping with stress.

At the later stages get professional help: family or individual therapy, a self-help group, or peer counseling. Peer counseling and other self-help groups can be located through the following agency:

NATIONAL SELF-HELP CLEARINGHOUSE
25 West 43rd St.
Room 620
New York, NY 10036
(212) 642-2944

At the stage of dependency get your child into a full-time drug program (agencies are listed below). You will find the following books helpful in making a choice: *The 100 Best Treatment Centers for Alcoholism and Drug Abuse* by Linda Sunshine and John W. Wright (Avon, 1988) and *Rehab: A Comprehensive Guide to Recommended Drug-Alcohol Treatment Centers in the United States* (Perennial Library, 1988) by Stan Hart.

When you confront your child, however, she may not acknowledge the problem. She may lie to you or, worse, lie to herself. "I can quit any time I want" indicates the same kind of denial you may have used before admitting the truth. If your child does not acknowledge drug abuse, you may try several different approaches.

Much as you hate to, professionals advise you to search her room for evidence of drugs. When you find them, do not be manipulated into accepting phony explanations such as "I found them," or "Alice left them here." There is only one explanation: Your child uses drugs.

If your child persists in refusing to acknowledge her use of drugs, you have two avenues of action: (1) You can use a product called Drug Alert which, with a kind of litmus test, detects the presence of drug residue, or (2) You can have a blood or urine test run. While a last resort and one from which parents turn in dread, a test may turn out to be the action that saves your child. For further information on this, contact a local hospital or medical laboratory or:

AMERICAN DRUG SCREENS
Box 3068
Dallas, TX 75221

If you find that, despite her denials, your child is taking drugs, you must exert whatever influence you have to get her into a rehabilitation program—not through threats and coercion, but through caring concern. This may involve having a sibling or one of her close friends (or former close friend) talk to her, or a teacher or counselor of whom she is particularly fond. It may involve having an outside drug counselor or a former addict who has kicked the habit come and speak with her. It most certainly involves your continued support and faith in her and the knowledge that your love for her creates as much suffering in you as her drug abuse creates in her.

· 359 ·

Drug abuse among children has spread so widely that many groups have developed to help distraught parents. Your state Alcohol and Drug Abuse Agency has a great deal of information. In addition to your local chapter of Alcoholics Anonymous, the following provide information, speakers, videotapes, and advice to which parents should turn without hesitation when faced with a drug problem at any stage.

COCAINE HELPLINE
(800) COCAINE

DRUG HELPLINE
(800) 662-HELP

NATIONAL CLEARINGHOUSE FOR ALCOHOL INFORMATION
PO Box 2345
Rockville, MD 20852

NATIONAL CLEARINGHOUSE FOR DRUG ABUSE INFORMATION
PO Box 416
Kensington, MD 20795

NATIONAL CONGRESS OF PARENTS AND TEACHERS
ALCOHOL EDUCATION PROJECT
700 North Rush Street
Chicago, IL 60611

NATIONAL FEDERATION OF PARENTS FOR DRUG-FREE YOUTH
8730 Georgia Avenue, Suite 200
Silver Spring, MD 20910
(800) 554-KIDS

NATIONAL PARENTS' RESOURCE INSTITUTE FOR DRUG EDUCATION
100 Edgewood Avenue, Suite 1002
Atlanta, GA 30303
(800) 241-9746

MOTHERS AGAINST DRUNKEN DRIVING
669 Airport Freeway, Suite 310
Hurst, TX 76053

"Can I prevent drug abuse?"

Drug abuse prevention does not come with a guarantee. However, schools and parents can do a great deal to *almost* prevent it, especially if they work together.

What Schools Can Do

All states mandate drug education in schools. Some, such as New York, New Jersey, and Connecticut, mandate drug education in some form from kindergarten through high school, although, sad to say, enforcement is lax. Others select sixth grade or junior high or even high school as the focus for drug education programs.

Twenty years ago forward-looking schools had drug programs that did little more than supply children with basic information; I remember at a faculty workshop sitting around a table on which the principal was burning a sweet-smelling material. "This is synthetic marijuana," he explained. "I want you all to know what it smells like so you can explain it to your students."

Ten years later, aware that information alone was not stopping—and may even have been adding to—the drug problem among children, schools adopted a new approach: scare tactics. Former addicts came to school to show how drugs had ruined their lives, and students were taken to prisons for a firsthand lesson in this-could-happen-to-you-too.

That didn't work either, as the rising bar charts of teenage drug abuse demonstrated. Today successful drug programs don't want to scare children; they want to reach what psychologists feel is at the very core of drug abuse, low self-esteem. And they want to reach it early enough to turn it around. As a drug expert in the Connecticut schools was quoted by *The New York Times* as saying "If you can get children to feel good about themselves, to feel capable and important and necessary, then you're not going to lose them to drugs."

For the first time schools that use this kind of program are beginning to see it pay off in concrete results: less drug use among high school students who were in the program earlier. Like smallpox and polio vaccines, it may eventually eliminate an epidemic that has kept educators and parents in constant fear.

If your school is still using an archaic approach to drug education or if it does not introduce it at all until junior high or high school, put your parent power to work. Talk to the PTA. Talk to the principal. Talk to the district superintendent. The following suggestions may activate your school.

· A number of new programs are being used successfully, among them those designed by The Consultation Center of the Psychiatry Department of Yale School of Medicine (203) 785-5463; Here's Looking at You 2000, originating in Seattle but with information available from the Bronxville, New York, schools (914) 337-5600; Quest International in Granville, Ohio (614) 587-2800 or 522-6400. Take a look at what these programs do.

· Your school can secure federal funds to pay for a drug program through the Drug-Free Schools and Community Act of 1986.

· Many schools have developed programs in conjunction with their community, involving businesses, police, and drug treatment personnel. Among the more successful is the Governor's Alliance Against Drugs in Massachusetts, information on which is available from the Massachusetts Department of Education in Boston. Check it out.

What Parents Can Do

During one of my parent workshops, discussion focused on how to keep children from getting involved in drugs. Amid anxiety and expressions of grave concern from other parents, one father spoke up, supremely confident that he had the answer. "You all sound scared of your kids," he said. "Not me. I'm going to lay down the law when they reach junior high: no drugs. That's it."

"How can you be sure they'll obey you?" a mother asked timidly.

In the self-assured tone that the head of the KGB must use, he gave his answer: "They always do."

I never saw that father again. His children, who were in first and third grades then, must have reached high school by now. Did they obey their father? I wonder.

It is true, most little children obey their parents because obedience is the pathway to love. But I often think that for every yes forced from a small child, a repressed no lies waiting to burst forth when he becomes older. Parents cannot legislate drugs. If they could, the multibillion-dollar drug trade would not prosper among children, and drunken driving would not account for the highest youth accident rate. That father must have had a rude awakening.

Is there, then, no way for parents to prevent their children's involvement in drugs? Let me answer this way: While there is no way to *assure* noninvolvement, there are ways to help prevent it. Studies have found that certain parenting goals and the practices that enable families to reach them produce a far higher percentage of non-drug-involved children than their counterparts.

· The single greatest common denominator among children who abuse any kind of drugs is low self-esteem.

Your job as a parent is not to raise children who avoid drugs through fear of punishment, but to raise children who think too highly of themselves to abuse their minds and bodies.

· Authoritarian parents build rage within their children who, fearful of expressing it at home, release it like a charge of bullets in ways that will inflict the most painful wounds. Drugs are effective bullets.

Your job as a parent is to develop a family community in which children and parents both contribute to decision making and feel free to express their ideas and feelings so that repressed rage does not develop.

· Parents who themselves abuse drugs set up a model for their children to copy and produce a high percentage of drug abusive children.

Your job as a parent is to avoid the use of any kind of drug that is not medicinal and to use even medicines, with the exception of over-the-counter aspirin, cough syrup, and such, only according to a doctor's prescription. The single exception may be alcohol. Drink in moderation and only for social or recreational purposes—never as an escape route from problems.

· Children who remain dependent on their parents to determine the course of their lives lean heavily on the peer group for leadership. When peer pressure pushes them in the direction of sex or drug abuse, they weakly give way.

Your job as a parent is to help your children not need you, to let them grow and go little by little as they are able.

· Overindulged children expect instant gratification of every wish. When faced with problems that cause frustration and pain, they reach for the easiest way back to "happiness," which frequently is through the forgetfulness or highs of drugs.

Your job as a parent is to let your child work through his own problems and know the pain of not having everything he wants. The knowledge that he can survive will give him the confidence to say no.

· Children get involved in drug abuse by living for the moment, without looking at the consequences of their actions. They make decisions that sound like fun at the time with no sense of what may result in the future.

Your job as a parent is to give your children the freedom to make decisions and then to hold them accountable for the results of those decisions. This has been discussed in detail in Chapter 15.

· While it is true that children who abuse sex and drugs lack self-discipline, it is equally true that a lack of self-discipline gets them involved with sex and drugs in the first place. Children who are raised to depend on outside enforcers to assure proper behavior fail to develop inner enforcers to keep them on the straight and narrow when no one is watching; and no one is watching in school lavatories or dark corners.

Your job as a parent is to raise a child whose personal values preclude involvement in drug abuse, one who serves as his own disciplinarian. If you raise a child to behave "because I say so," you have blocked the development of his inner controls by superimposing yours. Chances are he will see no need to behave when he doesn't hear your voice. If, on the other hand, you raise a child who behaves because *he* says so, you have listened to him and accepted him and stood by when he erred. He will use the inner controls he developed from loving and being loved.

· *363* ·

When I speak with parents, they shake their head and sigh, "It's a different world today!" By "different," of course, they mean "harder" because they have to contend with drugs and sex and violence and the shattering sense of losing control. They are right. It is a different world today, but then, it always has been. My parents had to deal with polio epidemics and the depression; their parents had to deal with female subjugation and World War I and high infant mortality; as a parent I had to deal with youth revolutions in sex and schools and drugs. We have all had a rough time raising children. Parents are not promised a rose garden.

While the job of parenting may not be harder today, wide-open communications bring us into closer contact with new and horrifying hazards. We read of a kindergarten teacher confronting a drunken five-year-old; hear the sobs of a parent whose second grader has committed suicide; see a parent collapse upon learning that her ten-year-old lies dead of bullets in a school yard; and learn how a barely adolescent girl gave birth to a baby in the lavatory and then drowned him in the toilet.

As the song in the musical *Oliver* goes, it's a hard life—for both parents and children. Not what happens outside, but what they build between them determines the ways in which each of them will meet and cope with the stresses which that hard life hurls at them.

CHAPTER 25

Where Learning Begins

· Good Students—Good Parents ·

"What is a good student?"

Parent:	How can I make my child a good student?
MSM:	What do you mean by "good student"?
Parent:	You know. Getting high marks.
MSM:	Oh.

Rarely do I address a PTA group without engaging in this dialogue. Obviously, getting high marks is well up on the list of priorities that parents establish for their children. The dialogue continues.

MSM:	Why do you want your child to get high marks?
Parent:	So she can get into a top college. (I have heard even parents of first graders say this!)
MSM:	What do you mean by "top college"?
Parent:	You know. Yale, Vassar. People respect it because it's hard to get into.
MSM:	Oh.

Obviously, acceptance by a status college rates high on the list as well.

MSM: Why do you want her to go to a top college?
Parent: So she can get a good job when she graduates.
MSM: Oh.

I read from these conversations that the aim of school is a status college, and the aim of college is a status job, and I have an uneasy feeling that the aim of parenting is a status child. Hardly anyone thinks of wonderment as the goal of school and lifelong growth as the goal of college, regarding diplomas as badges of learning rather than of success. As a result, education in the United States seems to be veering onto a self-destruct course from which neither parents nor politicians have been able to redirect it. Statistics paint a dim picture today; and as the old Chinese proverb says, "If we do not change our direction, we are likely to end up where we are headed."

When you consider it from the viewpoint of parents, however, the emphasis placed on high marks makes good sense as a survival technique. After all, As on the report card are marks of distinction that separate winners from losers; and because winners provide parents with far more hassle-free child rearing, who can blame them for the push? They have their own failures to live down; so grant them success in offspring with a string of As instead of Cs or worse and with a degree from Yale instead of Podunk U.

As logical as this reasoning may appear on the surface, at a deeper level, parents—and all of us—are still left with the unanswered question: What is the goal of education? Is it to make parents feel like winners? Is it to help them achieve status? Not really. When I follow up the dialogue quoted above, probing beneath the quick and easy answers to touch on parents' inner hopes, they reveal far loftier educational dreams:

- "I want my children to love learning."
- "I hope school will turn them into lifelong learners."
- "Books aren't what learning is all about; I want my child to learn how to live."
- "If we had real education, it would teach kids to give back to the world as much as they got, maybe more."
- "Let's face it: Our children are the future, so school had better teach them to make peace."
- "Science and technology haven't gotten us very far. I

hope my kids will learn to find beauty and get some understanding of values."

Parents in the group talk with growing intensity, their cynicism and materialism fading into unselfconscious echoes of the dream of America's presidential parent, George Bush, for a "kinder, gentler nation." They do not emphasize the need for high marks any longer, not because they believe high marks preclude learning, but because they face the fact within themselves that high marks do not measure learning. There, confined in a school auditorium, they talk their way to a truth that could renew their children's lives and create a brave new world led by future thinkers such as Einstein and future artists such as Truman Capote, who themselves failed in school, and by future nurturers of humankind such as Eleanor Roosevelt, who never finished school at all.

As Chapter 13 argued, marks are arbitrary and have nothing to do with a child's being a "good" or "bad" student. Often the most intellectually curious children are so bored that they fail everything, while the dullest memorize well enough to pull down straight As. The only "good" or "bad" that marks indicate is measurable compliance . . . and I say this as a former teacher in a system that demanded marks and as a current teacher in a system that still does. The most shining comment on my granddaughter's final report card this spring, among a constellation of stars, was this: "She is an original thinker and learns for the fun of learning." The teacher who wrote that knows what a good student is.

Parents, when you ask how you can make your child a good student, forget As and B pluses, which mark the teacher's tests, not your child's mind, and look for excitement, originality, daring, commitment, and joy instead. When those qualities are applied to learning, every child is a good student, not just in school but throughout life, where he has to pass the real test.

The final scene of my dialogue with parents runs like this:

Parent: So how can I make my child a good student?

MSM: You can't.

Parent: You're saying I have no influence over how he does in school?

MSM: No, I'm not saying that. I'm saying that you can't make him a good student. You can do something far more important, though—you can help him make himself a good student.

Parent: How can I do that?

How indeed? The answer, I believe, lies in the wisdom of Ralph Waldo Emerson, who came up with the idea that heroism was not the accomplishment of great feats but the pure manifestation of self-trust. This being the case, what makes a child a good student? Heroism. The courage to learn.

Learning is change, change from not understanding something to understanding it: Rolling over, crawling, walking, running, jumping—they all represent change from one level of knowing to another. Status quo means security because it allows a child to keep a firm footing on what she already knows without stepping further; it keeps her safe. Change entails risk because it propels a child, like a diver on a diving board, into new depths, where she may find herself lacking and fail; there she is vulnerable to hurt and shame and impotence. Only a hero can take that plunge.

From his earliest moments of life, a child is forced to decide between accepting things as they are or daring to make a change: Should he lie afraid in his crib or scream for Mother's comforting arms? Should he wait till someone gives him the rattle or try to crawl to it himself? Should he stay with the easy book or try one with big words? Should he sit quietly in class or raise his hand with an answer? The result of his decision in each case determines not only the rate of his development, but his self-confidence in making the decision next time. If his cry brings Mother . . . if he reaches the rattle . . . if he struggles through the book with big words . . . if he ventures an answer in class—if, with fear and trembling, he dares the unknown, he will, like Peter Pan, crow, "What a very remarkable fellow I am!"

What is even more wonderful is that even if he does not quite make his way to the rattle . . . even if he stumbles over the big words . . . even if his answer is wrong, he will feel like crowing. Having the courage to dare is the stuff of heroes.

I weep for children whose parents thwart their efforts to risk a challenge and for those whose parents so berate them for their failures that they dare not muster courage to try again. I weep for the unsung heroes forced to abandon heroism—for the kindergarten child who will not try to make a friend for fear of being rejected . . . for the second grader who sits silent in class for fear of giving a wrong answer . . . for the fourth grader who bullies his classmates for fear they will see his weakness . . . for the sixth grader who enrages the teacher because he dares not displease his parents . . . for the junior high schooler who pops pills because he dares not face his pain.

I weep too for the parents of those children, angry and hurt and ashamed, and trying as hard as they know how to turn their children into good students. Only they don't know how. They have been setting up roadblocks to learning for a long, long time. They have made their children afraid to risk change.

"What *is* the relationship between parenting and learning?"

Midway in my first year of teaching, I got an uneasy feeling that no one had warned me about previously. Although some children in my class were learning with ease and enthusiasm, others, despite my attention and efforts, not only didn't learn, but didn't want to learn. I tried; they resisted. I said I was their friend; they grew hostile. I gave extra help; they forgot their homework. I got nowhere; neither did they.

Slowly it dawned on me that something must have turned those children off before I ever got them, and in search for the handle, I spoke to teachers they had had earlier. "Linda *never* did her work" was the common theme; "Bobby *always* created trouble." In fifth grade, third grade, kindergarten. And still in my seventh grade. At that moment I learned what my studies of child development and parenting have confirmed ever since: that the kind of parenting children receive at home has a large share in determining the kind of learning they are able to do at school. If a child has been raised in ways that destroy his self-esteem, he sees himself as a loser and will not risk attempts to succeed. If a child has been raised in ways that drive him to erect defenses in order to survive, he will not lower those defenses to risk change. If, however, a child has been raised in ways that create self-trust, he will dare leap ahead into darkness with confidence to turn it into learning's light.

· 369 ·

"How do I create self-trust?"

In Utopia there is probably a blueprint given to parents at the time of their baby's birth: A Program for Success in School—Ten Ways to Make Your Child Confident. Relaxed mothers and fathers, relieved of decision making and anxiety, raise relaxed children who all turn out to be A students and make their parents proud. We don't live in Utopia, though. We live in a world where blueprints work in the construction of buildings, but not of people; so parents have to design their own blueprints.

The first tool to use is your instinct. You can usually tell what's right for you and your child: Follow that feeling. An abusive parent feels wrong when he vents his rage on his child. "I need help," we hear him say. "I don't want to do it again." A twelve-year-old with her month-old infant in her arms admits, "I have to give him a bottle, but I'd rather be with my friends." They, on the brink of desperation, hear the voice of instinct.

You and the millions of parents like you hear the voice too, whispering when to say no and when to say yes, when to hold and comfort and when to discipline, when to insist and when to relent, when to let go and when to hold on, when to laugh and play and when to listen and weep. Sometimes the voice speaks so softly you can hardly hear it; and sometimes you drown it out in the roar of your own needs. Listen closely, though, and you will hear the parent you *want* to reach out to the child who *will* be.

"Aren't there any guidelines?"

Yes, there are some guidelines. You probably feel like the mother who told me, "I'm never sure about my instinct. Can't you give me some specific dos and don'ts?" I understand how you feel. You are faced with the job of sculpting a child as Michelangelo sculpted *David*— helping her emerge from the inner layers of marble in the unique and perfect shape she was intended to be. It's the biggest job of your life, and you want help that is tried and true.

The following guidelines have been tried as closely as millions of parents can try them and have been found as true as social science studies can research them. Testimony to their value can ultimately be seen only in the children who have emerged from the marble as adults.

"What are the don'ts?"

· Don't be an authoritarian parent who, whether by force or manipulation, controls her child like a puppet on a string. Authoritarian parents deny their children self-trust by making them feel unimportant. Don't be like Annabel, a mother I knew in Connecticut as my children were growing up: head of the Brownies and then the Girl Scouts, church youth group leader, class mother, and always a volunteer chaperone for school trips and dances. Whatever group her daughter Lucy joined, there was Annabel, planning it, directing it, showing the children how; and there was Lucy, shy, inept, friendless, managing a wan little smile when other children commented, "Is there anything your mom can't do?"

· Don't be an overprotective parent who wards off fear and guilt by preventing his child from taking even minimal risks. Overprotective parents deny their children self-trust by making them feel incapable of coping with life. Don't be like Daniel who forbade his daughter playmates outside the family, wouldn't let her ride the school bus, fought her battles with teachers, and even made her attend a local college so she could live at home. She is a grown woman now, dependent on her husband and ineffective as a mother.

· Don't be a permissive parent who avoids confrontation by always saying yes to her child's demands. Permissive parents deny their children self-trust by making them feel they live outside any ordered system except the one they create to suit themselves. Don't be like Marian who gave her son *carte blanche* from the time he was a toddler. She thought she was saying "You have the right to do whatever you want," but he heard "Nobody cares."

At a rap session I conducted a few years ago, a member of the group shared her distress over the fact that her parents set no guidelines for her. "I have the freedom to do whatever I want," she explained.

"Sounds good to me," another girl called out.

"Want to change places?" asked a boy.

"Hey, I'm up for adoption," a third said with a laugh.

"It's not funny," the original speaker replied. "I hate it. I'm scared. Right, I can do anything I want: I can stay up all night or eat nothing but ice cream." She paused. "Or throw myself in front of a train or jump from a window."

"You wouldn't do that," the first boy interjected to break the stunned silence of the group.

"Maybe not, but my parents wouldn't stop me," she finished, joining the group silence. After a while she turned to me and asked, "Dr. Miller, do you think it's fair for kids to have to make decisions like that all day?"

I could only answer with a shake of my head and a hoarse no.

· Don't be an overindulgent parent who, as a psychologist explained, buys his child gifts because he can't afford love. Overindulgent parents deny their children self-trust by making them feel unloved and unlovable. Don't be like Mark, a corporate executive father who leaves home before breakfast and returns after the children's bedtime. He works weekends at home or plays golf with clients,

· 371 ·

leaving his children's picnics and ball games and piano recitals for his wife to attend. They are strangers to him but the envy of their classmates with their private phones and TVs, their Atari, Nintendo, and Apple computer and with every new game and toy that hits the market. Once a year the children meet Mark in New York for lunch and a trip to F.A.O. Schwarz. They pretend the toys fill up the empty space left by their father, but there aren't enough toys in the whole store to do that.

· Don't be an abusive parent who maims her child's body or, more subtly, her spirit. Abusive parents deny their children self-trust by making them feel like objects for exploitation instead of like people worthy of love. Don't be like Tony, who demanded so much of his children that no matter how well they performed, it was never good enough . . . or like Wendy, so wrapped up in the problems and hurts of her divorce that she turned a deaf ear to her child's cries for attention.

All destructive parenting practices destroy a child's self-trust, drain him of the natural-born courage that risks the change of learning. Whatever form destructive parenting takes, it defeats the purpose of parents who want to turn their children into "good students." While some of them may go through school as good performers and others may even manage to extend their performance into adulthood, low self-esteem blocks their path to coping with the eventual lesson of learning, which is life. While they may abound in talent, they will lack self-worth; while they may find success, they will lose themselves.

Truman Capote, despite the extraordinary talent that brought him financial success and lasting fame, spent a tortured life in what his biographer Gerald Clarke calls "an endless search for love." A fruitless search it was: No matter how may others professed love for him, his lack of love for himself denied them all. "Something in life has done a terrible hurt to me, and it seems to be irrevocable," Clarke quotes him as saying: Capote—alcoholic, drug addicted, lonely, loveless.

Truman Capote is only one of many whose self-destruction we witness and ask, "How could they? They had everything!" Elvis Presley, Sylvia Plath, Marilyn Monroe, and a long line of people whose destructive parents made them feel they had nothing. Truman Capote spoke for them all—and for the millions of nameless others whose lives are wasted in feelings of worthlessness instilled by parents: "[My mother] locked me in, and I still can't get out."

"What are the do's?"

When you reverse all the don'ts, like a photographer developing negatives, you come up with a picture of what we all hope to be—a "good" parent whose child trusts herself and dares take the risk of learning. For that kind of parent, there is only one guideline.

Be a *nurturing* parent: Meet your child's needs. This does not mean give her everything she wants; often *not* giving her what she wants may be the way to fill her need. The Children's Defense Fund identifies a child's basic needs as follows:

· The need to feel wanted and accepted. In other words, love your child for what she is, not for what you try to make of her. Love her when she makes mistakes; love her when she fails; love her when she hates herself; and love her even if she is so full of herself she is obnoxious. Let her know that nothing she does can make you stop loving her.

· The need for continuity in relationships. Teach her that relationships are made of solid stuff, not of sexual whims or financial needs or opportunistic moments. Teach her the values and traditions passed, along with the seed of life itself, from parents to children, along the endless chain of generations. Keep the chain intact for her, despite death and divorce. Teach her that love carries responsibility and friendship mutuality, and that neither is lightly come by.

· The need for trust in the world in which they live. In infancy let her not cry in vain for comfort, but learn that warm milk and safe arms are nearby. As she gets older, walk the fine line between intrusion and support: Be there when she needs you. Let her grow knowing she can solve her own problems and knowing too that she can reach out in confidence for help.

· The need for thoughtful guidance in coping with the demands of growing up. Set up rules; explain them so she understands; hold her accountable. Address her concerns with the values upon which you address your own. Support her efforts at independence, but don't be afraid to offer a few words of advice gleaned from your own experience. Don't be hurt if she turns them down.

· 373 ·

When you set up a style of parenting that meets these four basic needs, you're being Michelangelo—chipping away marble so that your child will emerge whole. She won't have to build up defenses to shield her vulnerability or hide to protect herself from hurt. She will trust herself enough to risk the changes of life and learning. She will be what you hope for, a good student.

Nurturing parents serve their child in more ways than one. They meet her needs, as we have just seen, but they also set up role models for her to emulate. They become the stencil from which their child draws herself.

Two psychologists, Allison Davis and Robert Havighurst, wrote a book called *Father of the Man* (Houghton Mifflin, 1947), in which they stated the following: "Children have a trick—comforting or embarrassing as the case may be—of taking their parents' shapes. Sooner or later they will pull this trick on you—no matter how long they may keep it up their sleeve."

Children learn to take their parents' shapes for the same reason that they learn to talk or walk or drive a car: The effort pays off. Seeing constant evidence of greater parental status, competency, and control, children figure that what works for their parents will work for them. If parents handle conflict with physical aggression, their children hit; if parents show consideration to others, their children are caring. The cycle of abuse goes round and round, and so does the cycle of love. As a nurturing parent, therefore, you are bringing forth from the marble not only a good student but another nurturing parent, who may at last begin to change the shape of a nonnurturing world.

· 374 ·

· The Perfect Parent? ·

From time to time parents—usually mothers—ask me, "How would you describe the perfect parent?"

I answer, "Nonexistent."

There is no perfect parent. Furthermore, there is no need for mothers and fathers even to try to approach perfection. First of all, they will never make it, but will keep struggling like the frog that attempts to reach a rock by jumping halfway there each time.

However, even if there were a perfect parent, she could not do a perfect job of parenting and would probably die of frustration if she tried. It is true that the worst of children's lives can be made better by good parents, but it is equally true that the best of children's lives can never be made perfect. The stumbling block is the nature of childhood itself. Put yourself for a minute in the place of a child—not an abused or abandoned one, but a child in a good home, loved and understood:

· You are smaller than anyone else.
· You have less knowledge.
· You have little experience.

· You have no power.
· You are totally dependent.
· You are told what to do and when to do it, and you
  either have to obey or be punished.

Taken from any angle, a child's life is fraught with misery, and the poets of the past who wrote of "the perfect bliss of childhood" fed us a myth. Childhood hurts. Even that nonexistent perfect parent would be unable to create perfection from it.

Parents need not abandon all hope, however, as if bringing offspring into childhood were like shoving them through the gates of hell. There is no need for parents to be perfect, only to be what today's psychologists call "good enough." I interpret that to mean that all parents really have to do is help their children grow in the weedy garden of childhood—to till the soil, keep the crabgrass to a minimum, sprinkle fertilizer, and rejoice in the violets as well as in the floribunda roses.

The twenty-five chapters of this book offer guidelines to help you cultivate your child's educational garden. You are the first and the chief gardener throughout your child's life. You always have been, but for the first time since educators invented schools, you have the title of Teacher as well as the job.

Shortly before President Bush's education summit in 1989, National Public Radio asked teachers around the country what they thought would most help American education. Teachers replied that schools would do a better job if parents sent their children to school in physical and mental condition to learn. They didn't say what we hear debated far and wide—vouchers or a longer school year or a stronger war on drugs. They didn't say more money; they didn't say smaller classes; they didn't say stricter discipline. They said parents. You.

There's a lesson in what those teachers said: Help your child grow. Become a part of her learning. Get involved at home. Get involved at school. Be part of the teaching team. You don't have to be a perfect parent; the teacher doesn't have to be a perfect teacher; and your child doesn't have to be a perfect student. Just be "good enough"—let all three of you be good enough—to make the teaching team a winner.

As a member of the teaching team, you have a voice in calling the plays. As a member of a winning teaching team, you have the power to change the shape of the game. I hope you will use that voice and that power to demand the best education for your child and for every child so that all children will be more than good students. They will be fulfilled people in a fulfilling world.

Index